Philosophy of History

Philosophy of History

Twenty-First-Century Perspectives

Edited by

Jouni-Matti Kuukkanen

BLOOMSBURY ACADEMIC
LONDON • NEW YORK • OXFORD • NEW DELHI • SYDNEY

BLOOMSBURY ACADEMIC
Bloomsbury Publishing Plc
50 Bedford Square, London, WC1B 3DP, UK
1385 Broadway, New York, NY 10018, USA
29 Earlsfort Terrace, Dublin 2, Ireland

BLOOMSBURY, BLOOMSBURY ACADEMIC and the Diana logo are trademarks of
Bloomsbury Publishing Plc

First published in Great Britain 2021
This paperback edition published in 2022

Copyright © Jouni-Matti Kuukkanen, 2021

Jouni-Matti Kuukkanen has asserted his right under the Copyright, Designs and Patents Act, 1988, to be identified as Author of this work.

Cover design: Terry Woodley
Cover image: Iceland River Delta (© Justinreznick / Getty Images)

All rights reserved. No part of this publication may be reproduced or transmitted in any form or by any means, electronic or mechanical, including photocopying, recording, or any information storage or retrieval system, without prior permission in writing from the publishers.

Bloomsbury Publishing Plc does not have any control over, or responsibility for, any third-party websites referred to or in this book. All internet addresses given in this book were correct at the time of going to press. The author and publisher regret any inconvenience caused if addresses have changed or sites have ceased to exist, but can accept no responsibility for any such changes.

A catalogue record for this book is available from the British Library.

Library of Congress Cataloging-in-Publication Data
Names: Kuukkanen, Jouni-Matti, editor.
Title: Philosophy of history: twenty-first-century perspectives /
[edited by] Jouni-Matti Kuukkanen.
Description: London; New York: Bloomsbury Academic, 2020. | Includes bibliographical references and index.
Identifiers: LCCN 2020027557 (print) | LCCN 2020027558 (ebook) | ISBN 9781350111844 (hardback) | ISBN 9781350227972 (paperback) | ISBN 9781350111851 (ebook) | ISBN 9781350111868 (epub)
Subjects: LCSH: History–Philosophy–History–21st century. |
Historiography–History–21st century.
Classification: LCC D16.8 .P458 2020 (print) | LCC D16.8 (ebook) | DDC 901–dc23
LC record available at https://lccn.loc.gov/2020027557
LC ebook record available at https://lccn.loc.gov/2020027558

ISBN: HB: 978-1-3501-1184-4
PB: 978-1-3502-2797-2
ePDF: 978-1-3501-1185-1
eBook: 978-1-3501-1186-8

Typeset by Deanta Global Publishing Services, Chennai, India

To find out more about our authors and books visit www.bloomsbury.com and sign up for our newsletters.

Contents

List of Figures   vii
List of Contributors   viii

1. A Conceptual Map for Twenty-First-Century Philosophy of History *Jouni-Matti Kuukkanen*   1

Part I Debating Key Concepts in Philosophy of History

2. Encompassing the Future *Jonathan Gorman*   23
3. Historiographical Knowledge as Claiming Correctly *Jouni-Matti Kuukkanen*   44
4. Where the Extremes Meet *Frank Ankersmit*   66
5. Postmodern Theory with Historical Intent: A Deconstructive Approach to the Past *Ethan Kleinberg*   85

Part II Popular History, Populism and Politics

6. The Affective Dimension: What Theory of History Can Learn from Popular History *Allan Megill*   101
7. Tales of Im/mobility: Unhistorying Migration *Claire Norton and Mark Donnelly*   126
8. Historical Evitability: The Return of the Philosophy of History *Aviezer Tucker*   143

Part III (Re)drawing the Boundaries of Philosophy of History

9. History and Philosophy of History (HPH): A Call for Cooperation *Herman Paul*   165
10. The Paradigm Shift in the Contemporary Humanities and Social Sciences *Ewa Domańska*   180
11. More-Than-Human History: Philosophy of History at the Time of the Anthropocene *Marek Tamm and Zoltán Boldizsár Simon*   198

12 In Defence of a Humanistically Oriented Historiography:
    The Nature/Culture Distinction at the Time of the
    Anthropocene *Giuseppina D'Oro*   216

Notes   237
Works Cited   257
Index   285

Figures

1	Beth Israel Synagogue, 'Edenbridge'	107
2	Holy Ascension Ukrainian Greek Orthodox Church, 'Maryville'	107
3	Saint Nicholas Ukrainian Catholic Church, 'Maryville'	108
4	Saint Helen's Roman Catholic Church, Brooksby	108
5	Ethnic map of the RM: A later perception	120
6	Maryville School: All that remains	121
7	*Our Courageous Pioneers*	121
8	Robert and Lil (Vickar) Gitlin: Two of many	122

Table

8.1	Four Ideologies as Philosophies of History	145

Contributors

Frank Ankersmit is Emeritus Professor of Philosophy of History and Intellectual History at Groningen University. He has written some fifteen books on philosophy of history, political philosophy and aesthetics – most of them focusing on the theme of representation. He is presently working on a book on Leibniz and historical representation. He is the founding editor-in-chief of *Journal of the Philosophy of History*.

Mark Donnelly is Associate Professor at St Mary's University, Twickenham, London. He has published articles and essays in the fields of history theory, public history, memory and contemporary cultural politics. He co-edited *Mad Dogs and Englishness: Popular Music and English Identities* (2017). He also co-wrote *Doing History* (2011) and *Liberating Histories* (2018) with Claire Norton.

Giuseppina D'Oro is Reader in Philosophy at Keele University. She is the author of *Collingwood and the Metaphysics of Experience* (2002), and of numerous papers on Collingwood's philosophy of history, action and metaphilosophy. In 2016–17 she was principal investigator (with Paul Giladi and Alexis Papazoglou) on a Templeton funded project 'Idealism and the Philosophy of Mind'. She is the editor of Collingwood's *An Essay on Philosophical Method* (with James Connelly, OUP, 2005), of *Reasons and Causes: Causalism and Anti-Causalism in the Philosophy of Action* (with Constantine Sandis, 2013) and of *The Cambridge Companion to Philosophical Methodology* (with Søren Overgaard, 2017). She is also editor of *Journal of the Philosophy of History*.

Ewa Domańska is Professor of Human Sciences and holds her permanent position at the Department of History, Adam Mickiewicz University in Poznan, Poland. She is a corresponding member of the Polish Academy of Sciences. Since 2002 Domańska has been a recurring visiting professor in the Anthropology Department of Stanford University. Her teaching and research interests include history and theory of historiography, comparative theory of the humanities and social sciences, and genocide and ecocide studies. Her most recent publications include *Necros. An Ontology of Human Remains* (2017, in Polish); 'Animal

History', *History and Theory*, vol. 56, no. 2, 2017: 265–85; 'Posthumanist History', in *Debating New Approaches to History*, ed. by Peter Burke and Marek Tamm. Bloomsbury Academic 2018: 327–52 and 'Theory as the Practice of Freedom: Hayden White in East-Central Europe', *Rethinking History*, vol. 23, no. 4, 2019: 558–64.

Jonathan Gorman is Emeritus Professor of Moral Philosophy at Queen's University Belfast and a Member of the Royal Irish Academy. He is on the editorial committees of the *Journal of the Philosophy of History*, *History and Theory* and *Rethinking History*. He has held academic positions at the universities of Birmingham, Queen's Canada, Princeton and Maynooth, and as a young analytical philosopher worked on the epistemology of narrative for his Cambridge PhD, the first results of which were published as 'Objectivity and Truth in History' in 1974. Publishing also in the philosophy of law, he is the author of *The Expression of Historical Knowledge* (1982), *Understanding History* (1992) and *Historical Judgement* (2007), in addition to many articles and reviews in the philosophy/theory/ethics of history/historiography.

Ethan Kleinberg is the Class of 1958 Distinguished Professor of History and Letters at Wesleyan University and editor-in-chief of *History and Theory*. He is the author of *Haunting History: For a Deconstructive Approach to the Past* (2017) and *Generation Existential: Martin Heidegger's Philosophy in France, 1927-61* (2005). He is the co-editor of *Presence: Philosophy, History and Cultural Theory for the Twenty-First Century* (2013) and as a member of the Wild on Collective (with Joan Wallach Scott and Gary Wilder) he is a co-author of the *Theses on Theory and History* (theoryrevolt.com).

Jouni-Matti Kuukkanen is Professor of Philosophy at the University of Oulu in Finland. He received a PhD from the University of Edinburgh and has held academic positions in the Universities of Durham and Hull in the UK and Leiden in the Netherlands. He has written and published on philosophy of science, and specifically the historical philosophers of science and Thomas Kuhn, philosophy of the historiography of science and philosophy of history and historiography. Kuukkanen has been awarded Fulbright and EURIAS fellowships. His book *Postnarrativist Philosophy of Historiography* (2015) was chosen as the best monograph in philosophy of historiography in 2016 by the International Commission for the History and Theory of Historiography. He is also editor-in-chief of *Journal of the Philosophy of History* and a director of the Centre for Philosophical Studies of History at the University of Oulu.

Allan Megill is Professor of History at the University of Virginia, working in the history of ideas and theory of history. He has been appointed to a Foreign Expert Professorship in the Department of World History of Shanghai Normal University for the period from 1 September 2020 to 31 August 2023. He is the author of *Karl Marx: The Burden of Reason* (2002) and *Historical Knowledge, Historical Error: A Contemporary Guide to Practice* (2007), and of numerous articles, as well as editor of *Rethinking Objectivity* (1994) and co-editor of *The Rhetoric of the Human Sciences* (1987). He is on the editorial boards of *Journal of the Philosophy of History*, *History and Theory*, *Rethinking History* and *Journal of the History of Ideas*. He has been a Fudan fellow at Fudan University and a Guangqi fellow at Shanghai Normal University.

Claire Norton is Associate Professor at St Mary's University, Twickenham. She is interested in how forms of past-talk (particularly art) can be deployed to contest the otherization of marginalized communities, and the limits and ethical implications of historical representation. She is the co-author, with Mark Donnelly, of the books *Doing History* (2011) and *Liberating Histories* (2018) and several articles on the use of histories as an articulation of power. She has also written books and articles on identity formation, the imagination of political space and the manipulation of the 'religious other' from an Ottoman perspective in the early modern Mediterranean world including *Plural Pasts: Power, identity, and the Ottoman sieges of Nagykanizsa* (2017), *Conversion and Islam in the Early Modern Mediterranean: The Lure of the Other* (2017) and *The Renaissance and the Ottoman World* (2013).

Herman Paul is Professor of the History of the Humanities at Leiden University, where he is currently directing a project on 'Scholarly Vices: A Longue Durée History'. He is the author of *Key Issues in Historical Theory* (2015) and *Hayden White: The Historical Imagination* (2011) and (co-)editor, most recently, of *Epistemic Virtues in the Sciences and the Humanities* (2017), *How to Be a Historian: Scholarly Personae in Historical Studies, 1800-2000* (2019) and *Scholarly Personae in the History of Orientalism, 1870-1930* (2019). Following up on recent articles in *History and Theory* and *Modern Intellectual History*, he is currently writing a book on virtues and vices in nineteenth-century German historical studies. He is editor of *Journal of the Philosophy of History*.

Zoltán Boldizsár Simon is Assistant Professor at Leiden University and a board member of the Center for Theories in Historical Research at Bielefeld University. Zoltán has written on the philosophy of history and on the challenges posed by current prospects of the Anthropocene and technology to our understanding of history and the human condition for journals ranging from *History and Theory* and *History of the Human Sciences* to *The Anthropocene Review* and *European Journal of Social Theory*. He is the author of *History in Times of Unprecedented Change: A Theory for the 21st Century* (2019) and *The Epochal Event: Transformations in the Entangled Human, Technological, and Natural Worlds* (2020).

Marek Tamm is Professor of Cultural History at the School of Humanities in Tallinn University. He is also Head of Tallinn University Centre of Excellence in Intercultural Studies. His primary research fields are cultural history of medieval Europe, theory and history of historiography, and cultural memory studies. He has recently published *Rethinking Historical Time: New Approaches to Presentism* (ed. with Laurent Olivier; 2019), *Juri Lotman – Culture, Memory and History: Essays in Cultural Semiotics* (ed., 2019), *Debating New Approaches to History* (ed. with Peter Burke; 2018) and *Afterlife of Events: Perspectives on Mnemohistory* (ed., 2015). He is editor of *Journal of the Philosophy of History*.

Aviezer Tucker is a philosopher of historiography and history and a political theorist, currently a Gvirtzman Memorial Fellow at the Davis Center at Harvard, and previously taught and held research positions at the Australian National University, New York University, and Columbia University. He is the author of *Our Knowledge of the Past: A Philosophy of Historiography* (2004) and editor of the Blackwell *Companion to the Philosophy of History and Historiography* (2008). Further information is available at www.harvard.academia.edu/AviezerTucker.

1

A Conceptual Map for Twenty-First-Century Philosophy of History

Jouni-Matti Kuukkanen

Philosophy of history is something that is needed now more than ever. Why is this the case? Because we are struggling to understand extremely worrying political upheavals and environmental and health crises like populism, human-induced climate change and the coronavirus pandemic. It is evident that not only human but also non-human actors shape history profoundly. Philosophy of history makes it easier to understand these phenomena and our time more generally; what is more, it helps us to understand how they could be comprehended in the first place.[1]

Philosophy of history is a reflective discipline; it provides a meta-level perspective on history, no matter whether 'history' is understood as an effort to understand events and processes, as historiography, or as the events and processes themselves. Attempts to apprehend history are typically holistic and synthetic initiatives that look for links between various historiographical objects such as events, processes and actions, rather than atomistic and analytical measures that would break larger compounds into their constituents. How is it that we can make sense of and understand these things and arrange them in specific relations? Do events, processes and actions have any sense or meaning, as and by themselves?

Perhaps, philosophy of history could be defined as a discipline whose subject is the *condition of the historical*. That is, it is concerned with the question under what circumstances and what premises something is, can and should be considered to be part of history, either as a historiographical object of history writing and interpretation or as an entity in the object world itself. The difference between philosophy of history and the writing of history may be a line drawn in sand, but it is still the difference between a reflective meta-discipline and an operative object discipline. The focus of the former is on the concepts, organizing principles and presuppositions that are used and required in the latter. Naturally, nothing prevents a philosopher of history from saying something about the meaning and significance of events themselves and vice versa, a historian from saying something about what comprehending history consists in.

Given that philosophy of history is a reflective discipline, it is ironical that the history of philosophy of history itself is fairly conservative and moderately unreflective. Typically, it is first a story of the speculative or substantive philosophy of history, and then, the emergence of the critical or analytical philosophy of history and, finally, the march of narrativism or the narrativist philosophy of historiography. Although it is not my intention here to reinforce the traditional narrative about the history of philosophy of history, it is worth outlining it briefly for the benefit of the reader.

The speculative or substantive philosophy of history refers to those philosophers who focus on questions dealing with the nature of history: its direction, laws, moving force, meaning and so on. This covers many great names from the history of philosophy like Kant, Hegel and Marx and others like Herder and Vico. Spengler and Toynbee are usually regarded as early twentieth-century speculative philosophers despite the fact that their works analyse the development of cultures and rely more on empirical studies than on philosophical systems. In addition, Fukuyama's *the end of history* thesis is typically subsumed under this category of philosophy of history.

Prior to the emergence of the critical or analytical philosophy of history, whose birth can de dated to the 1940s, there was only speculative philosophy of history. However, it is worth noting that the terms 'substantial philosophy of history' or 'speculative philosophy of history' were coined by 'critical or analytical philosophers of history' in an apparent attempt to demarcate themselves from their predecessors (see Walsh 1951: 14–15). Tucker has remarked that '*speculative* philosophy is essentially a term of abuse' (Tucker 2009: 4). Indeed, 'speculative philosophers of history' were accused of overriding or disregarding facts that conflicted with 'the tenets of cherished doctrine', of conceptual imprecision, and of formulating 'hopelessly' vague or tautological hypotheses. Perhaps worst of all, speculative philosophers were seen to rely on unexamined *a priori* assumptions (Gardiner 1981: 2).

It is fair to say that the foundational paper of the analytical philosophy of history is Carl Gustaf Hempel's 'The Function of General Laws in History' published in 1942. And it is no exaggeration to say that the discussion that follows is to a large extent an offshoot of this paper. In general, the analytical philosophy of history had close ties with logical empiricism. The central concern was whether historiography is a science or entails a scientific model of explanation. Some other notable names of the analytical tradition are Arthur Danto, W. B. Gallie, Maurice Mandelbaum, Louis Mink, William Walsh and Morton White. For a detailed account of the history of the analytical philosophy of history, see Jonathan Gorman's chapter in this book.

The third component of the conventional narrative of the history of philosophy of history, narrativism, emerged in the early 1970s with the publication of Hayden White's (1973) *Metahistory: The Historical Imagination of the 19th Century Europe*. Another landmark publication is Frank Ankersmit's (1983) *Narrative Logic: A Semantic Analysis of the Historian's Language* published ten years later in 1983. 'Narrativism' is generally understood as a shift regarding the scientific status of historiography with a realization that history writing is conditioned by and contains various literary tropes and features. Narrativists typically emphasize that, like in literature, historians produce texts and that texts contains narratives which are not evaluable by empirical or even by any epistemological means.

I have provided this traditional account of the history of philosophy of history so that the reader gets a basic understanding of the intellectual landscape in which the philosophical debates on history have taken place and which still influences what is written. One will quickly realize that this conventional account does not easily accommodate all scholarly traditions. One concrete example exemplifying how it streamlines a more complicated history is the way it disregards the Dutch tradition in theory and philosophy of history, which took root in the 1970s largely independently, it seems, from either narrativism or analytical philosophy of history. Analogies and interest with and concern over the social sciences rather over literature seem to have been formative for this tradition (Bos 2018). Gadamer and Collingwood are not easy to situate in this account either, even bearing in mind that there was something like analytical hermeneutics. The clear lesson is that history is richer than the views of history: numerous warranted accounts of the history of philosophy of history can be composed, depending on what concepts are taken as organizing notions of this past.

One should always remain intellectually curious and attentive to alternative modelling. The chapters of this book are perhaps most fruitfully understood through the set of concepts and conceptual pairs laid out below, which have various genealogical links to numerous traditions in the history of this field. If philosophy of history can be organized around the rich set of concepts and organizing principles found in the chapters of this book, so arguably can its history or histories.

*   *   *

There are good reasons to say that we are now in a novel situation without any clear paradigms, looking for new ways to go forward, or perhaps, any way to go forward. Philosophers and theoreticians of history, and perhaps historians and other scholars interested in the historical, are eagerly looking for new organizing principles. The catalyst for the project that led to this book was the conference *The Role of Philosophy of History*, held at the University of Oulu, 5–7 October 2017. Most of the writers of this book gave a keynote address at the conference, and subsequently, more scholars were invited to address remaining gaps in the intellectual terrain. The aim of this book is to provide an overview of cutting-edge philosophy of history now and looking forward in the twenty-first-century.

The purpose of this introduction, in turn, is to provide the reader a map for navigating the wide field of philosophy of history. Considering how different, and sometimes contrasting, the chapters of this book are, I believe that this kind of map is needed. Some have called for the end of dichotomies and binaries, for example Domańska, Tamm and Simon in this book. While I fully understand this sentiment, when one considers the broad scope and contrasting ambitions of the chapters in this book, it seems that the time of binaries is not yet over. Or perhaps it will be the case that some binaries will prove useless, while others or new ones will prove their mettle. In any case, the contributions of this book can be fruitfully placed in relation to each other by way of conceptual tuples. This discovery was enlightening for me, and I hope that it will be so for the reader too. The map that emerges is like a metro map in which numerous nodes are linked with numerous stations, or conceptual positions, but not one of them is linked to all.

The nodes that structure the conceptual map of this book could be divided into general philosophical concerns as well as more specific issues within the philosophy of history, although it is difficult to make clear-cut distinctions as to what is what in this regard; often, concepts are relevant both in philosophy generally and in philosophy of history specifically. The conceptual set includes such binaries as postmodernism/post-postmodernism; humanism or anthropocentrism/posthumanism or post-anthropocentrism; liberalism/the crisis of liberalism or post-liberalism; the era of truth/the era of post-truth; naturalism/anti-naturalism; pragmatism/anti-pragmatism; affectivism/

rationalism; narrativism/postnarrativism; empiricism/post-empiricism; realism/anti-realism; popular history or history from below/professional or sanctioned history; and a critical or deconstructive/conservative or preservative approach to history. Conceptual links go from one chapter to another through several lines.

This conceptual map indicates that contemporary debate in philosophy of history revolves around these poles. There is also something else that is found in various degrees of explicitness in all these chapters: a future-oriented perspective that tries to redefine the contours of philosophy of history by taking inspiration from tradition, by introducing new key concepts, by redefining old concepts or by redrawing the boundaries of philosophy of history.

Further, all the chapters in one way or another consider the relation between philosophy and history, or between philosophers of history/historiography and historians. The million-dollar question concerns the form of their cooperation: What form should this cooperation take? Is one field or the other or its practitioners more dominant? Should historians provide empirical substance to prevent philosophers of history from talking about straw men or fictional presuppositions? Should philosophers offer concepts that provide shape, order and insight for the object field, which would be an unorganized mess without this conceptual clarity? Imre Lakatos's Kantian epigram of history and philosophy of science springs to mind: 'Philosophy of science without history of science is empty; history of science without philosophy of science is blind' (Lakatos 1971: 91). Is the situation the same regarding philosophy of history and history? Or do these fields mesh more intimately with one another?

Someone might point out that Lakatos talked about 'history of science' and not about 'science', and therefore the proper relation is between philosophy of history and history of history. This is true (read Herman Paul's contribution in this book on this idea). Nevertheless, (contemporary) science and (contemporary) history cannot be excluded from the history of science and the history of history, respectively. The question of cooperation deals with the relation of a philosophical approach and a historical approach – the former being a reflective endeavour which tries to make sense of the latter, more practical venture.

* * *

Some readers may find the plurality of the contents of this book perplexing. The chapters not only focus on different concepts and topics but also vary in style and degree of philosophical abstraction. Some are more explicitly philosophical, while others are concerned with the issues closer to the heart of practising historians. One worry is that this state of affairs widens the existing gulf between theory (or philosophy) and practice. It has been argued that many historians, who are mainly interested in the tangible problems of history writing and research, are doubtful about the value of philosophical and abstract theoretical reasoning.[2] This concern is understandable, but I think that the scenario of a deepening rift can be avoided.

First, philosophy of historiography is in a better situation than many other subjects engaged in meta-level reflection of an object discipline. The distance between history writing and practice and their philosophical and theoretical analyses is relatively narrow. Understanding the practice and the practical problems of history research and writing is well within the reach of those who identify primarily as philosophers. Through her education any philosopher is familiar with multiple books, interpretations and disagreements of history. As members of their community, they are automatically consumers of history. To consider the matter the other way around, philosophical argumentation and concepts can be grasped without any superhuman efforts by practising historians, although philosophical problems are perhaps less well known as historiographical disputes. In this sense, I believe that the proximity of the object and meta-discipline is greater than in many other similar philosophical areas. For example, it may be challenging for a philosopher of science to follow and understand contemporary cutting-edge science even if she has a relevant science degree.

Secondly, philosophically, it is not clear that there is a *principled difference* between theoretical and philosophical problems and practice. That there is such a difference in kind cannot be merely assumed, but it needs to be argued. Indeed, one significant philosophical approach, pragmatism, wishes to establish exactly that there is no such a distinction but at most a difference in degree between theory or philosophy and practice of history. This is to say that on the basis of surface differences one should not jump to the conclusion that there is a fundamental cleavage between the approaches.

Naturally, the ultimate challenge is to show that familiarity with 'practical problems' is useful for a philosopher and that understanding philosophical and theoretical questions benefits the historian. I suggest to the reader that it is not possible to write history that is free of theoretical or philosophical load and presuppositions. Choices regarding epistemological, methodological, ethical concerns and so on must be made implicitly or explicitly in practice. Similarly, doing philosophy of historiography without familiarity or concern for the 'real' questions of historiography would very likely amount to building straw men. It is instructive to conceive of the chapters in this book as constituting their theoretical or philosophical content like a sliding scale. Variations between them are differences in degree rather than in kind. This plurality and smorgasbord of theory and practice should be celebrated, not deplored. Of course, not everything is for everyone, but I appeal to the reader to read chapters that appear more philosophical and those that appear inspired by practical concerns – and only then judge if and in what way they might be useful.

It is nevertheless worth asking, can one detect any emerging tendency or pattern on the basis of this collection of chapters beyond the set of organizing concept and guiding concerns? Any judgement of that kind should naturally always be taken with extreme caution. Although this sample of writers contains many influential players in contemporary theory and philosophy of history and historiography, one is not warranted to treat this group as representative of the entire field. Having said this, some preliminary musings can be outlined. It may be that the zenith of narrativism is now behind us. The influence of narrativist philosophy, and specifically Hayden White, is probably most clearly seen in the contributions by Claire Norton and Mark Donnelly (Chapter 7) and by Ethan Kleinberg (Chapter 5), but even they are now exploring new ways to write history and ground philosophy of history.[3] It is also notable that interest in a more substantive type of philosophy of history appears to be gaining in strength. The analysis of language in different ways assumed a central role in both narrativism and the analytic philosophy of history. However, language plays a far smaller role in posthumanist adaptations (Domańska, Tamm and Simon) as well as in applications of large-scale models to history in a more traditional form (Tucker), if in any notable role at all. This trend could perhaps be summed as follows: 'We seem to be moving from the literary approach to a new substantive philosophy of history, decentring the human from the perspective of the Anthropocene. Well, quite a revolution.'[4]

Good examples of this trend can be found in the Anthropocene and other post- and non-humanistic concepts that have recently emerged on the horizon of philosophy of history. Further, it is also notable that interest in histories from below or popular histories is gaining in strength (Megill, Donnelly and Norton). But are there still other rising stars that can be discerned in the pages of this book and that will prove to be enduring? This is something that I cannot answer here; only time will tell. It is more common that new approaches using old concepts and drawing on existing intellectual traditions acquire new formulations and applications than that entirely new organizing concepts appear. Maybe pragmatism in philosophy of historiography will grow in importance and improve in precision. This would at least represent a principled effort to bridge the perceived gap between theory and practice, and between philosophy and historiography. Indeed, perhaps pragmatism is the practising historian's philosophy. And if it is not, perhaps some other new 'paradigm' will emerge in philosophy of history and historiography at some stage. But then it should also be observed that the need for a paradigm is itself a question of great philosophical controversy. Would an improved systematicity be a good or a bad thing? Should philosophy of history remain eclectic and accept that it means scoring less in rigour?

* * *

I found it helpful to divide the chapters of this book into three sections, reflecting those aspects that are most central to the set of chapters: The first section is called 'Debating key concepts in philosophy of history' and consists of chapters by Jonathan Gorman, Jouni-Matti Kuukkanen, Frank Ankersmit and Ethan Kleinberg. These chapters reflect on the tradition of philosophy and philosophy of historiography, focusing on some foundational concepts such as representation, explanation, understanding, inference, narrative, *a priori*, naturalism, realism, empiricism, deconstruction and pragmatism. Through analysing the meaning and significance of these concepts, these chapters stake out a position regarding what concepts and approaches should guide contemporary philosophy of history now: philosophy of temporal understanding (Gorman), inferentialism (Kuukkanen), Leibnizian representationalism (Ankersmit), and postmodernism and deconstruction (Kleinberg). The second set of chapters is in the section called 'Popular histories, populism and politics' and includes Allan Megill's, Claire Norton and Mark Donnelly's and Aviezer Tucker's contributions. The first two chapters argue for the significance of histories from below, in the form of popular histories (Megill), and of the histories of marginalized groups like migrants and refugees (Norton and Donnelly). Populism with its denigrations of disenfranchised groups poses a special challenge for professional historiography and its canons. The third chapter of this set seeks to establish why philosophy of history and historiography have unique perspectives and tools to make sense of populism and avoid past mistakes (Tucker). The final set of chapters is in the section entitled '(Re)drawing the boundaries of philosophy of history' and includes chapters by Herman Paul, Ewa Domańska, Marek Tamm and Zoltán Boldizsár Simon, and Giuseppina D'Oro. They all advocate, or resist, a paradigm change for philosophy of history. The suggestions emerge specifically from redrawing boundaries of some ingrained distinctions, such as human/nature. The current ecological crisis of climate change looms large in the background of the discussion. The proposed new, or old, orientations include history and philosophy of history (HPH), post-humanistic paradigm shift (Domańska), more-than-human history (Tamm and Simon) and humanistically oriented historiography (D'Oro). As a philosophical nominalist, I firmly believe that other reasonable categorizations of the chapters of this book and of their concepts are possible.

Debating Key Concepts in Philosophy of History

Philosophy of history had its 'heyday' some decades ago. It was both intellectually and institutionally in a much stronger position in academia than currently. How did it reach this state, and could it achieve it again, asks Jonathan Gorman in his 'Encompassing the future'. Gorman's chapter tells a story of the development of analytical philosophy, with its emphasis on explanation, understanding, causality and narrativity. The heyday of philosophy of history emerged because those philosophers who had not taken historians' explanations of human action seriously started to pay attention. To a large extent, this blossoming was constituted by the writings of such philosophers as Bryce Gallie, Arthur Danto and Morton White in the 1960s.

It seems that there were two particularly important topics: What should philosophers' relation be with historiography? And is historiography a science, or not? The latter question is taken up in Ankersmit's chapter too. As J. H. Hexter (1967) indicated in his review of Morton White's *Foundations of Historical Knowledge* (1965), analytical philosophers' accounts run the risk of being intellectually imperialistic and/or incorrect about historiographical practice. It is notable that these philosophers' conceptions of knowledge and explanation typically stem from debates in the philosophy of science, which are modelled upon the sciences. One wonders whether these accounts are relevant for historiography.

Gorman argues that Danto, M. White and Gallie's approach was not only analytical but also pragmatical in the same wide sense as Kuhn's was. Gorman attempts to understand this intellectual setting through empathizing with White (and others) by 'ascribing thoughts and attitudes to them, by doing our best to put ourselves in their position and attempting ... to see things from their point of view' (30).[5] Approached from this perspective, White, Danto and others were not imperialistic, but they put forward a responsible account of meaning, knowledge and truth, having received their training in the atomistic version of empiricism, which cannot accommodate holism. Rejecting Cartesian scepticism of whether we can really get into the mind of another, Gorman suggests that there is a shared human world and a contingently specifiable human nature in that our fellow human beings are alive, have memories, beliefs, hopes, expectations and so on. This is sufficient justification for taking practical steps towards empathizing with others.

His idea of a shared human nature through which one can understand people of the past is similar to D'Oro's postulation of the *human* past as the unique research object of historiography. By contrast, Domańska, Tamm and Simon wish to extend the scope to *non-human* phenomena and objects in the study of history. But is there any hope for a new heyday of analytical philosophy of history? If so, Gorman argues that it must be organized around something that historians also find genuinely interesting and suggests that analytical philosophers should study 'the notion of temporally extended imagination as being foundational to the construction of that shared reality of which we are conscious' (42). In actuality, this might result in moving from a philosophy of historiography to a more comprehensive philosophy of temporal understanding.

Gorman's view of philosophy of history is pragmatist in the sense that it requires that philosophers' notions and explanations also have practical significance, for historians and beyond. Jouni-Matti Kuukkanen's chapter argues for one specific pragmatist approach called 'inferentialism'. His chapter tackles a classical question: In what sense is historiography an empirical discipline? It is a common idea of empiricism that knowledge is tied to evidence received from the external world. Kuukkanen notes that there is a specific problem with this empiricist idea: despite the fact that 'evidence' entails that something is evident, no claim in historiography can ever be evident in the literal sense of the word. Using this as an intermediate judgement, he draws another conclusion: knowledge is never immediate but always mediate and inferential. For this reason, 'understanding historiographical knowledge and its justification requires a new kind of approach which penetrates into the inferential structures of claiming in historiography' (49).

The discussion in his chapter is organized around various fundamental concepts in philosophy: empiricism, evidence, representation and inference.

Kuukkanen's approach builds on an observation that even if 'history is typically presented through writing, writing is derivative of doing' (44). It is therefore necessary to ask when claims, as linguistic acts, are warranted, and more specifically, when a claim about the past should be accepted and when rejected. This entails that not all claiming amounts to knowledge, which means that only that which is correctly claimed counts as historiographic knowledge. Thus, the name of the chapter: 'Historiographical knowledge as claiming correctly'.

Kuukkanen suggests that the focus must be on the criteria that determine this acceptance or rejection of individual claims. Drawing on the pragmatist tradition of inferentialism, as developed by Wildrid Sellars, Robert Brandom and Jaroslav Peregrin, Kuukkanen studies the warrants for claiming by way of analysing claims, in the spirit of 'practice revolt', in a book on Finland's civil war in 1918. His suggestion is that there are various kinds of resources for warranting linguistic acts and inferences: archival material, scholarly literature, shared historiographical and moral beliefs, textual context and coherence, and the authority of the historian. Finally, one can distinguish the critical historian from the conservative on the basis of how actively and deeply one penetrates into defeasible inferential structures of historiographical claiming, including hypothesized facts and events. The more actively and deeply, the more critical the historian is. This emphasis on reflectivity and deconstruction resembles Kleinberg's criticism of petrifying ontological realism in history.

Frank Ankersmit's chapter 'Where the extremes meet' is critical of the value of naturalism and pragmatism, and to an extent, of empiricism too. Arguing from a rationalist point of view, Ankersmit rejects the popular naturalistic approach of contemporary philosophy. 'My argument will be unreservedly *a priorist* and thus sidesteps what has become known since Kuhn, Quine and Rorty as "naturalized epistemology"' (66). He writes that it is necessary to possess an Archimedean point of view in philosophy of history and to use *a priori* argumentation in order to fruitfully discuss and compare the variable accounts of historical knowledge and the semantics of the writing of history suggested by the 'causalists', 'hermeneuticists' and 'narrativists'. This Archimedean point for Ankersmit is historical representation.

Ankersmit asks a classical question: What is the relation between historiography and the sciences? While they have traditionally been conceived of as going in different directions, Ankersmit finds that their paths cross. It is Leibniz's philosophy that establishes the common ground between historiography and the sciences. A key observation is that the representation and the represented are identical and that they emerge only through the writing of history. Or more radically, *'historical reality only comes into being when the past no longer exists'*, because from the moment that 'past reality exists no longer; it has then died like a tree's branch from which life withdrew [and] as long as the past still existed it was not yet *historical*, but *actual reality*' (76). A shared feature between mathematics and historical representation is that the sign as a mere written, and by itself meaningless, symbol stands for itself. No changes in the sign, like a text in historiography, are allowed. Ankersmit defends the rationality of historiography by reference to Leibniz's philosophy. This Leibnizian idea for rationality is that 'the historian will always have to steer a careful middle-of-the road between several principles' and maxims like variety, order, diversity, the number of subjects and volume (82). The Leibnizian 'economy principle', which can also take the form of mathematical calculus, is where 'the sciences and the historical representation meet each other again' (66).

While Tucker criticizes postmodernists for espousing the same epistemology as contemporary populists do, 'emotivist politics with truth', which makes it impossible to separate fact from fiction, Ethan Kleinberg suggests that it is exactly the postmodern theory and deconstructive approach that is now needed to neutralize the problem of post-truth of our times. Kleinberg argues that the fault lies with the conventional historian's unreflective and untheoretical mindset, which spends little time and effort reflecting on how historical narratives are constructed and on the theoretical assumptions that underpin these constructions. Kleinberg argues that the dominant position of 'ontological realism' is 'a commitment to history as an endeavour concerned with events assigned to a specific location in space and time that are in principle observable and as such are regarded as fixed and immutable' (86). In order to make our thinking more deeply historicist, it is necessary to understand the *hauntological* nature of the past in that it haunts us by being simultaneously absent and present. The past is like a ghost in Charles Dicken's *A Christmas Carol*, not 'fixed and immutable object but a fluctuating bundle of physical and temporal contradictions' (91).

Kleinberg asks us to consider how the haunting of working-class history in previous historiographical accounts paved the way for E. P. Thomson's *The Making of the English Working Class*. The problem was that labour history was not considered a possible past for the historians that preceded Thompson; but then, it must be remembered that Thompson and his contemporaries had their blind spots, too, as they could not conceive of the possible past of women, for example. Indeed, the deconstructive approach emphasizes the irreducibly 'polysemous nature of the past'. The past cannot be mastered; the past is always chaotic and heterogeneous. The capability 'to imagine a narrative of multiple and seemingly conflicting pasts' (88) is a professional virtue and not an epistemological problem, argues Kleinberg.

Popular History, Populism and Politics

History is not only a matter of reasoning but also a matter of feeling, Allan Megill reminds us in 'The affective dimension: What theory of history can learn from popular history'. We saw earlier that Ankersmit underlines the rational nature of historiography. It would be wrong to say that Megill argues against rational, or reasoned, professional historiography. Instead, he emphasizes the significance of histories from below. He is interested in popular histories that represent people's own pasts, histories produced by people themselves and that preserve, for them and others, history's affective dimension. Megill recounts the story of immigrants to the Canadian prairies who in the early decades of the twentieth century settled in the harsh environment of the Rural Municipality (county) of Willow Creek, no. 458, in east-central Saskatchewan. The area he focuses on, which is near the centre of the 'RM', is of particular interest because it attracted many 'ethnic' settlers who, in a relatively limited space, built four houses of worship: a synagogue, a Ukrainian Catholic Church, a Ukrainian Greek Orthodox Church and a Polish Roman Catholic Church. Further, in the RM as a whole the settlers built thirteen houses of worship, a large number for a relatively small population. Why were there so many, Megill asks.

Starting from a personal connection to the area, Megill reconstructs the situation that the settlers faced. They built houses of worship partly because they wished to remember their roots and carry forward their traditions in a country distant in more than one sense from their places of origin. In the harsh conditions in this new and strange land, the houses of worship 'preserved, for a generation or two, customs and rituals. … It maintained a space for sociability and entertainment, functioned as a source of useful information, and to a limited extent could offer help to individual families in distress' (115). Over time, however, much of the history of the rural municipality turned out to be a history of loss: of population, of institutions, of a way of life. Out of this situation of loss came two popular histories of the area, which Megill has examined closely. These histories, chronicles of past community and familial life, are 'rooted in feeling', a fact to which, Megill suggests, the theory and philosophy of history should pay close attention. Megill notes, in addition, that these popular histories give space to and honour not only the particular (the different ethnicities and religions inhabiting the RM) but also the general (the politics and the schools of the RM). In this regard, he suggests a distinction between *popular* history, which includes the general in its purview, and *populist* history, which 'cleaves to one people, in whose name it claims to speak' (124).

Claire Norton and Mark Donnelly highlight another group from below and its affective dimension in history: migrants. What is the responsibility of historians in context of recent demonization of migrants, ask Norton and Donnelly. They do not blame historians but emphasize that our present era of populist politics their practice, nevertheless, legitimizes 'national-political communities as singularities whose cultural autonomy and territorial sovereignty need "defending" from outsiders who want to make a claim on them' (127). They argue that 'doing' history cannot be disconnected from its effects and consequences and that, in the case of migrants, ethically responsible 'doing' requires rethinking historiographical practice and foundational conceptual categories.

Norton and Donnelly's chapter is an attempt to ponder 'meta-history questions from the starting point of migrant experiences' (128). A key problem is that historians rarely give a voice to refugees themselves, 'write about refugees *as* refugees' (128–129), but tell their stories through various institutions such as aid and relief agencies. Donnelly and Norton's chapter is a plea for a specific kind of intervention on the behalf of migrants and for giving voice to this disenfranchised group and to the suppressed more generally. On the other hand, they doubt whether historiography, as it has been practised up until recent days, is capable of accounting for the perspectives of those who struggle. 'The figure of the contemporary migrant ... cannot be brought within the boundaries of conventional (western) historiographical practices without bringing those practices into disrepute' (126). For example, they question 'methodological nationalism', according to which history and the social sciences normalize the idea of nation state.

There is a lack of proper historization of migrants and refuges (also) in Europe and specifically regarding how the borders of the 'Fortress of Europe' are controlled. This absence applies to both historiography and refugee studies. Norton and Donnelly try to remedy this failure to listen to the voices of those who have lost their place on earth by using the UN's Universal Declaration of Human Rights as a setting and soundboard for understanding migrants' experiences of im/mobility and inequality. Norton and Donnelly are sceptical about whether historiography can be of much '*practical* value to groups of migrants today' (130), and put their faith more in art than history in telling authentic migrant stories: 'Artists have far more successfully mobilized the image of the migrant in their past-talk as an oppositional force against, and critique of, the unequal political and economic implications of globalization' (141–142).

In his chapter 'Historical evitability: The return of the philosophy of history', Aviezer Tucker analyses the situation we are witnessing currently in which passions override rationality in politics. His chapter is a call for a rehabilitation of the philosophy of history, arguing that the discipline offers an unparalleled historical perspective and tools for making sense of the current crisis of liberalism. Tucker argues that the four great ideologies of the twentieth century – totalitarianism, liberalism, progressivism and populism – have their own unique philosophies of history.

Tucker uses the notions of 'contingency' and 'inevitability' to analyse some key moments in the current crisis of liberal democracy: the election of Trump, Brexit, the EU's subsidies for the authoritarian Hungarian regime. He writes that 'historical inevitability and economic determinism are back in vogue for the first time since the 1930s' (148). The educated class deem themselves powerless when faced with forces that undermine, weaken and deconstruct the post-war liberal world order. The lesson seems to be that passions trump rationality: 'Modern democracy commenced with Robespierre and now resulted and concludes with Trump. History repeats itself first as a tragedy, then as a comedy, and finally as a reality show' (151). Still, in actuality, it is extremely challenging to judge what processes are contingent and what inevitable in history, as there is simply so much evidence available. Tucker urges us to listen to history in light of the danger of repeating it: 'Today's populism advocates an amalgam of policies that failed in the past two centuries, leading to two world wars and the deepening of the economic depression of the 1930s' (158).

(Re)drawing the Boundaries of Philosophy of History

Herman Paul's chapter is a call for cooperation between historians and philosophers of history. He envisions that this cooperation could take place under the label 'HPH', quite like there have been, and still are, energetic cooperative efforts under the label of 'HPS' (history and philosophy of science). Paul's call appears to be made from an empirically minded historian's perspective. HPH advocates direct empirical accountability of philosophical ideas, the theme of which is also discussed in the chapters by Ankersmit and Kuukkanen. However, he is not looking for a 'marriage' between historians and philosophers, as the relation in HPS has sometimes been conceived of, albeit typically as a failed marriage. Paul rather suggests that historians and philosophers of science should find a 'hermeneutic space' between them: 'The purpose of this exchange is not to reach common ground or to institutionalize learning processes that hopefully yield new ideas and fresh approaches, but to facilitate learning processes that hopefully yield new ideas and fresh approaches' (168).

There are four main motivations for HPH, argues Paul. Perhaps the main reason is the 'need to naturalize philosophy of history'. History 'should not primarily be studied *conceptually* … but *empirically*' (169). The desire to test philosophical claims empirically is the second and a closely related motivation. The third is that HPH enables historians to reflect on the applicability of the tools they employ, such as 'causality' and 'intention'. In addition, within the hermeneutic space of HPH, philosophers may acquire a wider view of the history of historical studies in general and not only for testing purposes. One challenge for HPH is the diversification of topics studied in history. Quite like historians of science in HPS, historians in general have in past decades extended their interests and the themes far removed from philosophers' more traditional concerns with explanation, representation, narratives and inferences. Historians have recently studied historians' working manners, social codes, commemorative practices and gendered self-images, for example. Despite this diversification of interest, Paul thinks that the historians' topics still provide fruitful material for philosophical ruminations and weighing of their fit with the theories of historical studies. It is worth adding that the invitation to participate in discussions under HPH is extended, for example, to sociologists and anthropologists and beyond the practices of disciplinary history.

It is fair to say that Domańska, Tamm and Simon envision a future of a much deeper naturalization, at least if naturalization is understood as decentring both the human and philosophy as uniquely humanistic enterprises that apply their own approach distinct from the sciences. Perhaps the coronavirus pandemic as a historical phenomenon with a non-human origin adds strength to their appeal. Domańska attempts to situate the study of the past within current trends in the humanities and social sciences in her chapter 'The paradigm shift in the contemporary humanities and social sciences'. Exploiting extensive empirical studies, she suggests that we are already moving towards a new paradigm, or towards a new research programme in Lakatosian language, which has variously been called 'new materialism', 'posthumanism' and 'non- or anti-anthropocentrism'. This paradigm change is conditioned by particular crises of our time like the problems of capitalism and migration, the crisis of liberal democracy and even 9/11, but perhaps even more significantly by the ecological crisis.

While the old 'degenerative' 'interpretivist-constructivist paradigm' has not yet been overthrown, Domańska argues that the change required cannot be sought within the traditional framework of humanism, postmodernism and narrativism (including postnarrativism). While the older paradigm has covered such disciplinary trends as gender and queer studies, postcolonial studies, ethnic studies and disability studies, transforming humanistic scholarship into a form of political activism, the new paradigm constructs a knowledge that critiques and/or rejects humans' central position in the world in the context of the ecological crisis and climate change. The challenge has to do with situating humans in the non-human world and our 'understanding of scholarship as adjusting to the changing reality and a resumption of the debates about whether scholarship (the human and social sciences) has any survival value for the human species and for life in general' (190). What does this new posthumanist paradigm mean for the study of history? This is a situation in which fields like environmental history (in its contemporary form), animal history, biohistory, neurohistory and so on challenge the Blochian idea of history as 'the study of people in time'. As a result, knowledge about the past must also become 'a future-oriented knowledge that facilitates adaptation and is relevant insofar as it supports the continuation of life of various species (in both social and biological contexts)' (193).

The profound technological, ecological and also societal changes that point towards 'unforeseen changes ... beyond the human condition' form the background of Marek Tamm and Zoltán Boldizsár Simon's chapter 'More-than-human history: Philosophy of history at the time of the Anthropocene', too (198). They lament the failure of philosophy of history to apprehend these experiences historically. The transformation of philosophy of history into a philosophy of historiography in the post-war period is regrettable for Tamm and Simon. In this turn, philosophy of history and historiography lost their common topic: historical change. Tamm and Simon make the plea that the concept of history ought to widen to be multispecies, multiscalar and non-continuous, and that the resulting new philosophy of history would address the concerns of a 'more-than-human world'.

Like Domańska, Tamm and Simon also argue that the Blochican conception of history in which the object of history is man is now arcane. The human must be decentred, and dualities, such as natural history versus human history, written history versus deep history, national/global history versus planetary history, overcome. The new notion of history means studying 'the animals' experience of being with humans' (206) and realizing that historians' 'curiously short time period' (209) is only two seconds in the twenty-four-hour clock of the history of organic life, for example. The non-continuity of history can be described as 'discontinuous, abrupt, disconnective, disruptive transformations' (212) as a result of the entanglement of the human and the natural world and of unforeseen technological advancements. These historical changes challenge philosophers of history to analyse epistemological questions anew, consider whether historical knowledge can be grounded in human experience, and to ponder whether anthropocentrism really is inescapable.

But do Anthropocene narratives confuse an important distinction between the natural and the historical past, asks Giuseppina D'Oro. Against the recent Anthropocene-inspired questioning of the possibility of a humanistically oriented historiography, D'Oro defends the view that the concept of the historical past is *sui generis* and distinct from that of the geological past. She argues that the historical past is not a short segment of geological time, the time of the human species on earth, but the past investigated from the perspective of a distinctive kind of interest that emphasizes uncovering the norms which governed historical agents in different periods of time. The past for the Egyptologist or the Roman historian is not the same past studied by the palaeontologist or the geologist, not because it is infinitesimally short in comparison to geological time but because the questions asked by historians concerned with Egyptian or Roman civilization are not the same kind of questions as those asked by empirically minded scientists.

D'Oro argues that the accusation that the distinction between the historical and the natural/geological past rests on an unacceptable form of human exceptionalism is based on the conflation of the concept of the historical past with that of the human past, and that maintaining the nature/culture distinction has important implications for praxis. If the distinction between nature and culture is collapsed, and the corollary that historical agents are not distinct in kind from natural agents (such as yeast and microbes) is accepted, then 'the anticipation of the future would become a mere spectator's sport analogous to the activity of predicting the weather' (218): collapsing the nature/culture distinction, D'Oro argues, undermines the possibility of political action against the very threat (climate change) that motivates Anthropocene narratives in the first instance.

* * *

The debate on the meaning of the Anthropocene, posthumanism and the dichotomy between the human and natural past is bound to continue, as is the critical conversation on all the other key concepts of this book. This book offers more food, and perhaps ammunition, for argumentation. My intention has been to provide not only a brief and informative but also an even-handed description of the field as viewed through these chapters for the benefit of the reader. *However, if the reader wishes to understand what each author genuinely argues for, the only option is to go to the original work and judge the content herself first-hand.* The reader is encouraged to read these articles and consider how they are linked with other chapters and in what other unmentioned ways they could be connected. To this end, let me propose a small number of questions that the reader may find instructive to consider and keep in mind while reading the chapters published in this book:

1. What are the intellectual resources that the history of the philosophy of history provides for understanding contemporary research and writing of history? What forms of cooperation can we forge between scholars of different persuasion, and further, as human beings in our societies? Can we ever get access to individuals' experiences and literally understand them?
2. What are the best ways to comprehend our place in the world? How do history and philosophy of history define and redefine our place in it? By what means can we influence the course of history?
3. How can philosophy of history help us to understand social, political and environmental phenomena like the refugee crisis, the rise of populism and the virus pandemic? Does this understanding commit or entitle us to some specific conceptions of history? What are the forces that shape our history?

In the end, then, the reader who has studied all the texts of this book may have formed a judgement of the preferred conceptual line or lines in philosophy of history and of the practical value of this scholarly enterprise. I hope this journey results in many discoveries and positive surprises. May this book help in orienteering towards the future of both philosophy of history and history in the twenty-first-century.

Part One

Debating Key Concepts in Philosophy of History

2

Encompassing the Future

Jonathan Gorman

The Heyday: Hempel versus Dray

The heyday of analytical philosophy of history was not the heyday of so-called speculative philosophy of history, which, after medieval religious conceptions, arguably began with Kant or Herder. The speculative approach had been squashed by Karl Popper and Isaiah Berlin, so far as analytical philosophers were concerned; Patrick Gardiner was able to write an introductory book (1952) in analytical philosophy of history without referring to the speculative version at all, although W. H. Walsh, who had published his *Introduction* one year earlier than Gardiner, had felt it necessary to apologize in case it was thought to be speculative (1951: 11ff.).

There were also non-analytical and non-speculative reflections in historical theory: Ranke, for example, had made claims about history telling how it 'actually was' and that encouraged in particular American historians so much that in 1885 they made him the first honorary member of the American Historical Association (Ranke 2011: xi). Yet, despite Ranke's strong influence (Novick 1988), American historians worried about the historical relativism described by Carl Becker in 1910 (Meyerhoff 1959: 120–39) and its implications for the nature of historical facts. Other historians may recall that Bury asserted that history was a science in 1902 and that Trevelyan denied it in 1903 (Stern 1956: 209, 227; Evans 1997: chapter 1). Some theorists took their cue from Hegel's idealism: F. H. Bradley wrote *The Presuppositions of Critical History* in 1874, Michael Oakeshott wrote on historical causation in (inter alia) 1933, and R. G. Collingwood's 1936 lectures became particularly influential among historians through *The Idea of History* (1946). Yet none of these did much to influence *analytical* philosophy of history. William Dray's collection *Philosophical Analysis and History* (1966) did not include anything by Collingwood, despite the obvious debt to him in his

Laws and Explanation in History, which itself explicitly (1957: Preface) owed so much to his teacher Walsh, who himself explicitly owed so much to Collingwood (1951: Preface to the First Edition, 10).

The heyday of analytical philosophy of history began with Hempel's work 'The function of general laws in history' (1942), which had 'attained the status of a kind of classic in the field', as Patrick Gardiner observed (1959: 269). Hempel had confidently applied to historical explanation the theory of causation from the very fruitful, successful and influential analytical programme of mainstream Hume-based (1739: Book 1, Section XIV) empiricist philosophy of science. As such Hempel's work might have remained no more than a minor extension of an existing successful philosophy to (for analytical philosophers) the extramural discipline of history in which few analytical philosophers *qua* philosophers were interested.

However, the heyday of the analytical philosophy of history developed with the responses to Hempel from the wider intellectual world of social theorists, for his article provided a focal point for those wondering about the possibility of a genuinely scientific social 'science'. That issue, reinvigorating the traditional question of how far history was itself a science, began to attract the attention of a few analytical philosophers. The heyday arguably reached its highest point when William Dray responded to Hempel in 1957 with his book *Laws and Explanation in History*, and the Hempel-Dray philosophical debate stimulated many analytical contributions. Both Hempel and Dray allowed 'science' to set the agenda, whether with the explicit positivism of Hempel's logical empiricism or with Dray's 'ordinary language' view that 'tested' philosophical analyses against actual historiographical practice. As Hempel's assertions about causal explanation in history gained this wider traction, analytical reflection about the usual mainstream philosophical issues required that attention be given to historians' modes of thought: historical method, how historians behaved or how they wrote.

Analytical philosophy of history thus had its heyday in virtue of being valued, not by historians (who took little notice until philosophers started saying things about narrative) but by those analytical philosophers who had not previously taken seriously historians' explanations of human action. Causes versus reasons in the explanation of human action was an ancient philosophical debate that was advanced by that discussion and continues today, but as the debate progressed it crystallized into what is now called the philosophy of action, with Donald Davidson's 'Actions, reasons and causes' a notable contribution (1963). Over the years the debate left behind any new input from historical examples. Once the main points of the Hempel-Dray debate had been absorbed, later analytical philosophy of human action made no further significant reference to historians' explanations, causal or otherwise. When philosophical outsiders were admitted to later discussions in the philosophy of action, they were from psychology or economic theory or anthropology or robotics, but not from history.

The Heyday Ebbing: Analysis of Narratives

However, by the 1960s those few remaining analytical philosophers still interested in historical understanding had also moved on to the analysis of narratives. Analytical philosophers' attention to narratives was mainly a brief continuation of their interest in causation. Three main works in analytical philosophy of history addressed some of the issues involved in making sense of narratives: Bryce Gallie's *Philosophy and the Historical Understanding* (1964), Arthur Danto's *Analytical Philosophy of History* (1965) and Morton White's *Foundations of Historical Knowledge* (1965). Each of these philosophers made some important contributions to the theory of history: Gallie, for example, described the need for a historical story to be 'followable' and introduced the idea of 'essentially contested concepts'; Danto introduced the notion of 'narrative sentences' and with that made a contribution to making sense of temporal language; White described and analysed historical discourse in terms of fact, law and value and used Hempel and the then current standard philosophy of science more explicitly than the others.

From the point of view of mainstream analytical philosophy, all three were contributing in some small way to the analytical discussion of the nature of causation, a continuing and central analytical issue as the advance of twentieth-century physics forced a reconsideration of some fundamental concepts of science, in particular space, time and causation. Gallie, who had followed closely the debates in the philosophy of science, argued for an interpretation of historical causation in terms of necessary conditions rather than in terms of the then standard Hempelian model accepted by Danto and Morton White. However, neither Danto nor White had been mainstream contributors to the philosophy of science, and rather than producers of the 'standard' model they were consumers of it. They took for granted Hempel's philosophy of causal explanation and tried to develop it as a way of structuring narrative explanation in history.

Very few analytical philosophers, centred on the sciences as they mostly were, thought that it was worth pursuing Gallie's view that causes might be necessary conditions, and the debates about causation became flooded instead with more complex arguments relating time, space, logic and probability. If historians actually explained in terms of necessary conditions, that in itself was of very little philosophical interest and merely showed that historians were missing most of the subtleties that physics or even the developing social sciences embraced. Again, very few analytical philosophers, centred on the sciences as they mostly were, thought any continuing philosophical interest arose from the detail of how causal explanation might structure historical understanding presented in narrative form. Causal explanation was best understood through the sciences, and the philosophy of science was developing well in regard to that. That the analytical philosophy of causation might be shown to be applicable to historical narrative understanding was to be expected. How exactly it was to be done was a minor interest.

By the late 1960s those few analytical philosophers who had taken a special interest in historical understanding seemed to have drawn all they could from their brief excursion into thinking about historiography. Gallie moved on to political science; Danto concentrated instead on art and aesthetics; Morton White moved on in intellectual history. That ended the 'heyday' of the analytical philosophy of history. Moreover, significant objections to the heyday of philosophy of science itself were already looming after Thomas Kuhn's *The Structure of Scientific Revolutions* (1962). Yet discussion of Kuhn's problematic relations between the analytical philosophy of science and the history of science involved very little connection with any remaining discussion in the analytical philosophy of history.

Historians' Objections

Historians have mostly ignored philosophers of any stripe. They have long made and continue to make their own contributions to theorizing about history. 'Some historians', says Richard J. Evans, thinking particularly of Geoffrey Elton's *Return to Essentials* (1991), 'have even disputed the right of non-historians to write about the nature of historical knowledge at all' (1997: 11). Those few historians who gave Hempel any attention mostly thought that analytical philosophy was not to be taken seriously as a player in mainstream historical debates, and that Bill Dray, who had begun his academic life studying history, had as a philosopher in later life done little more than refine Collingwood's position on empathetic understanding, a position most historians were happy to live with if they thought about it at all. Unlike Dray, they took little interest in Hempel's theory of causation. But when Morton White and Arthur Danto extended what Dray had called 'covering law theory' as a way of analysing historical narratives, for a short period around those works' publication in 1965 some historians found the approach less easy to ignore.

White's and Danto's science-sourced causal structures were in general not accepted by historians or by non-analytical theorists of history, and historians' responses were in the main loud and, to begin with, simple. J. H. Hexter spoke for many historians in characterizing the Hempelian solution to the nature of historical understanding as one which mistakenly assimilated history to science. Hexter saw the analytical philosophers' model as being imposed on history, so that Hempel, White and Danto should be seen as making a prescriptive power grab where the foundations of knowledge were concerned. The philosophers imposing the model, White and Danto particularly, had unpleasant traits of character: reviewing Morton White's *Foundations of Historical Knowledge*, Hexter ascribed to White 'an intellectual imperialism generated by the sin of intellectual pride' (1967a: 28). White, he said, was 'peremptory, pre-emptive, and prescriptive about "meaning", "knowing", "understanding", "explanation", and "truth"' (1967b: 31).

This objection looked for a moment like simple name-calling, and philosophers had long taught each other not to engage in arguments ad hominem. However, what I have quoted is only part of Hexter's point, which was in its way more philosophical. In effect he attacked the status of Hempel-based so-called models of historical explanation by posing a philosophical dilemma: these models from analytical philosophy were either prescriptive or descriptive. If prescriptive, then they were indeed a power grab by a disciplinary rival that failed to take history seriously as a knowledge producing discipline. Aware that the fact/value distinction (to which philosophers like Hempel were committed) applied as much to philosophy itself as to anything else, Hexter knew that prescriptive claims – all matters of valuation – were not seen as rationally supportable within that empiricist philosophy and ultimately depended on taste and temper. So such empiricist philosophers of science had no business setting standards for what ought to be done in history and were contradicting their own position in attempting it.

On the other hand, Hexter's argument continued, if an empiricist model of explanation such as Hempel's was descriptive of history rather than prescriptive for history, it was flatly false. Historians knew better than philosophers did what was going on in history. History was a major epistemic discipline that involved successful methodological practices in which they were experts. It was clear to all that analytical philosophers' reading of historical works was at best cursory and their experience of historical practice largely non-existent. When it came to describing what historians did, historians used evidence grounded in their experience, while the philosophers were offering abstract intellectual speculative constructs that failed to fit the facts of the epistemic practices of historians.

Arthur Danto complained about this review by Jack Hexter of his and Morton White's books, describing it as 'vagrant and irrelevant' (1967: 42); 'What Hexter evidently wants … is some sort of exact composite portrait of the working historian' (1967: 41). Responding to Hexter in *The New York Review of Books*, Danto knew he would have historian readers and presumably thought that this supposedly authoritative rhetorical riposte would be effective for them. It wasn't. If anything was wrong with Hexter's demand, it wasn't obvious. Analytical philosophers were aware of objections like Hexter's even though they didn't get the problem from him, for it arose in relation to their work in analytical philosophy of science. Some of those philosophers brazenly accepted one choice posed by the dilemma and thought that, power grab or not, philosophers did indeed know better than historians what counted as knowledge. They imposed on history models derived from science just because science rather than history really was an epistemically licit discipline for reasons that they thought obvious.

Others accepted the other horn of Hexter's dilemma: as late as 1976 Leon J. Goldstein affirmed as an assumption for his own philosophy of history, in *Historical Knowing*, that 'history is an epistemically licit discipline which deserves to be taken seriously on its own terms' (1976: xi), which meant that philosophers should not impose on historians alien criteria of knowledge. However, agreeing that history was epistemically licit left wholly unclear what kind of 'description' rather than 'prescription' Goldstein and others similarly placed were themselves engaged in. Should analytical philosophers provide an 'exact portrait'? Should they be writing the history of historiography? Few thought that (theorists had to wait until Peter Novick in 1988 for that to be done well), but they nevertheless felt that in some way they had to do better, although, whether merely describing or rationally redescribing either historical methods or writings, the philosophical nature of what they were doing was not wholly clear to them.

But in the 1960s it wasn't wholly clear in philosophy of science either. What had driven the problem was the nature of philosophy itself and the common characterization of it as finding fundamental, and so universal or exhaustive, categorizations or truths which – being universal or exhaustive – necessarily applied to philosophy itself. Just as medieval theology had held the immanence/transcendence distinction to be categorically foundational and exhaustive, just as Descartes had held the mind–body distinction to be categorically foundational and exhaustive and just as Kant had held the *a priori/a posteriori* distinction to be categorically foundational and exhaustive, so the Humean empiricism that underlay the so-called standard analytical philosophy of science expressed by Hempel and used by White and Danto carried on that ancient tradition and involved its own supposedly fundamental categorizations: fact/value, analytic/synthetic, prescriptive/descriptive, for example.

Such distinctions were and are problematic. It is easy to invent categorical and exhaustive distinctions for, given elementary laws of logic, one can sort the world in terms of either asserting or denying any arbitrarily selected assertion whatsoever: either that assertion or its denial are bound to be true, which makes the distinction empty in its application. To make such distinctions work one needs to provide separate contentful criteria for each side of the distinction, and then at least semi-metaphysical (rather than merely logical) grounds that support the claims to the absoluteness of the distinction and the exhaustiveness of its application. On the whole such grounds have not been found. Maybe the elementary laws of logic are themselves at risk.

Analytical philosophers had long worried about their own methods, and the journal *Metaphilosophy* was founded by 1970. Categorical distinctions could not be taken for granted at a metatheoretical level, so Hexter's descriptive/prescriptive dilemma, while a proper one to pose in objection to philosophers committed to that very distinction, was ad hominem in its effect and not in general sound. Analytical philosophy was itself supposed to be in some way 'scientific', but what counted as 'scientific' would be the upshot of philosophy of science, and the way to construe it would depend on the development of that subject.

By 1962 Kuhn had begun to revolutionize philosophy of science by historicizing it, using a broadly pragmatic approach. Falsification by 'facts' was not involved except superficially. Hexter's presupposition, that philosophers of history being 'scientific' about history required that their models be falsifiable by the facts of historical practice, involved an understanding of the philosophy of science and its application in metaphilosophy that was already being overturned. After Kuhn's 1962 book, and apart from Goldstein, a dilemma like Hexter's found little traction among analytical philosophers of science and hence little traction among analytical philosophers of history either.

Hexter's Empathy with Morton White

While there were in the context of analysing narratives significant differences between them – mainly between Danto and Morton White, on the one hand, and Gallie, on the other – all three analytical philosophers of narrative were nevertheless in some central sense, like Thomas Kuhn, philosophical pragmatists. By 1965, and somewhat out of touch with the latest developments in philosophy of science, they probably thought themselves committed to the epistemic priority of science. They were well informed in the American tradition of pragmatism, particularly its then outcome in Quine's work, which dated in relevant aspects from his 'Two dogmas of empiricism' of 1951. Quine had argued by then for the continuity between science and philosophy without any principled distinction between those subjects. It was no doubt their pragmatism that led Danto and White to an interest in history anyway; pragmatism's interest in history had gone back to Peirce, on whom Gallie had written a book (1952). Like Quine, they did not distinguish 'analytical' from 'pragmatic' philosophical approaches, as some others wished to do, and they saw their pragmatism as being part of the analytical tradition.

Those analytical philosophers who did read Hexter's review of Danto and White would have seen it as intemperate, and Hexter – like many historians – was a master of invective. Analytical philosophers, while familiarly bullying each other in seminars, nevertheless saw and continue to see themselves as operating according to standards of logic rather than rhetoric and as going wherever the arguments lead. Hexter's describing Morton White as assuming 'an intellectual imperialism generated by the sin of intellectual pride' (1967a: 28) addressed the person and not the issue. Nevertheless, respecting the place of invective in discussion between historians, let us take Hexter's point seriously as a historical assertion about Morton White's character or thought processes. Is it true that White was a proud intellectual imperialist? It is appropriate to use 'empathy' to assess this, being a method widely viewed by historians, not least Hexter himself, as at least one acceptable and characteristically historiographical way of making sense of individual actions. We may then attempt to empathize, at least in summary, with White's intellectual attitudes at the time he was writing *Foundations of Historical Knowledge*.

Empathizing with individuals involves ascribing thoughts and attitudes to them, by doing our best to put ourselves in their position and attempting (at least in a metaphorical sense) to see things from their point of view. When we do this we are imagining being in their situation, but we are imagining what we hold to be real and not merely imaginary, although we must allow that it takes evidence to support a claim that our empathizing is successful rather than merely the construction of something fictional. In so far as we succeed in empathizing with others, we are sharing with those others a world of 'thoughts' or 'ideas', and this may well drive the sense that some idealist philosophy is required here, but a commitment to that is not required and we do not need to share with those others any particular philosophical position about the status of those ideas.

There are various characteristics to be picked out from within their point of view so understood. We are trying to get into their world not only as they are aware of it but also as they are unaware of it. Collingwood famously analysed this historiographical method as the 're-enactment of past thought' (1946: 215 and *passim*) and it is common to understand him as referring to another individual's conscious thought. However, as I have argued elsewhere (2008: 97 and *passim*), it is plausible to hold that that interpretation would make impossible the recovery of another of Collingwood's notions, 'absolute presuppositions' (1940: *passim*), just because they are understood as assumptions which are so firmly taken for granted that they are not a part of the past individual's conscious deliberation. In the history of philosophy we often have to recover unconscious assumptions by the analysis of explicit thoughts, an analysis that might rely on predicate logic, conversational implicatures or other time-extended notions of dialogue or argumentation.

It may be that few of us recognize ourselves well, as the Scots poet Robert Burns remarked: 'O wad some Pow'r the giftie gie us to see oursels as ithers see us!' (1786). Morton White's conscious thought surely did not include some explicit recognition on his part that his intellectual attitudes were proudly imperialist. But they may possibly have been so anyway, consciously unexamined as we might take them to have been. Yet any historian would need some evidence for this, and it is difficult to see what logical analysis of his writings would yield such a result. However, there is some important evidence against this ascription as a particular feature of White's character, namely that White shared his attitudes with other analytical philosophers. As I remarked earlier, he was himself, like Danto, a consumer of covering-law theory rather than a producer of it, intent on applying this idea in the apparently alien intellectual land of history. That does, indeed, have an imperialist look.

However, neither White nor Danto questioned the empiricist foundations of covering-law theory with its commitment to certain positions on knowledge and truth. Pragmatically, these were for them the best answer. I stress 'for them', for pragmatism is wary of universalizing. Those foundations operated just as Collingwood described in introducing his idea of an 'absolute presupposition': the empiricist assumptions were for White and Danto psychological rather than Cartesian certainties, unexamined presuppositions underlying the beliefs and attitudes involved in their ordinary analytical philosophical ways of life, contingently uncriticized and uncriticizable by them at the time (Walsh 1963:

160ff.; Collingwood 1939: chapter 8; Collingwood 1940). While they probably gave the matter no conscious attention whatever, a Kuhnian revolution in their analytical philosophy was not in their view required by their pragmatism, and as pragmatists they were engaged in what Kuhn would have called 'normal' rather than 'revolutionary' analytical philosophy (2012: *passim*).

The empiricist foundations of covering-law theory were uncriticized and uncriticizable by White and Danto at the time because they were not entertained as conscious thoughts for examination, they were at no point doubted and neither White nor Danto perceived any serious alternatives to them with which they might be actively contrasted. Problems not frameable in the empiricist terms familiar to them were not recognized. Hexter complained that it was explicit in White's approach that he did not allow the elements of historical writing outside the causal skeleton of explanatory and descriptive statements to be expressive of knowledge of the historical past. White responded that he had made plain the literary or evaluative elements in historical writing. But it was not the claim that the literary or evaluative elements were there which offended Hexter, but rather the implication that such elements had nothing to do with knowledge, the implication that any feature of historical writing outside the 'scientific' skeleton had no explanatory or truth-telling use.

Hexter did, it may seem to us today given our familiarity with Hayden White's position (1973), offer Morton White and Danto what we might now judge to be, and to have been at the time, a serious alternative to their approach: he thought that certain literary elements, which he called the 'rhetoric' of history (1968), were themselves an essential way of expressing historical knowledge. The rhetorical side of historical writing, which may be seen as the ordering or 'emplotment' of sentences in a narrative, has an explanatory and truth-telling use. This is sure to remind us of Hayden White's position ('emplotment' is his word, 1973). But Hayden White in 1973 fared no better than Hexter in 1967. Neither White nor Danto nor analytical philosophers generally recognized any possible alternative here. They ignored later theories of narrative with their frequent use of or references to literary approaches. They found these literary approaches, with their implicit denial of 'compositionality' – that Hume-based assumption that meaningful expressions should be sorted into 'simple' and 'complex', with the 'complex' exhaustively to be grasped in terms of 'simples' – unacceptable, holding as these analytical philosophers characteristically did to atomistic, empiricist and Fregean theories of meaning, reference and truth, theories (as they thought) appropriate to science. Only a 'fancy view of historical truth', Morton White claimed in due course without argument (1967: 28), would permit such an approach. Yet this was not imperialist stonewalling but simple blindness born of normal philosophy, well described by Kuhn albeit in different contexts.

Holistic Meaning Pragmatically Understood

I have argued elsewhere that the main characteristic of narratives, which I prefer to call 'accounts as-a-whole' because there are various ways of structuring them, is their time-extended nature: both in the time it takes to read, write or understand them and in the temporal extension of the period covered and to which they give meaning. Such accounts, I have said, are to be understood as shareable with others in a shared historical consciousness in both reading and writing. To be shared, communicable thought – and therefore language – is essential.

As a whole, each account sorts the shared world it describes in an analogous manner to that in which atomistically understood concepts may be, in a neo-Kantian way, thought of as sorting the world in their less, or non-, temporally extended ways. Pragmatic choices of reference and description are in principle available to us (argued for in Gorman 2008: *passim*). On pragmatic grounds, it is often the case that modes of reference and description are established and there is no practical room for revising them. Nevertheless there are continuing opportunities for choice in many situations, particularly when it comes to sorting our understanding of the world and making our future. The role of 'narrative theories' in any meaningful structure is contingent. We do not face a binary choice between Frege and narrative theory. It is appropriate here to illustrate possibilities by presenting examples of different ways in which the meaning of a time-extended experience can be given by quoting from the classical Latin author Plutarch:

> They sent a dispatch scroll to Lysander to recall him.
> These scrolls are made up in the following way. When the ephors send out a general or admiral, they prepare two cylindrical pieces of wood of exactly the same length and thickness, each corresponding to the other in its dimensions. One of these they keep themselves, the other being given to the departing officer, and these pieces of wood are known as *scytalae*. Then whenever they want to send some important message secretly, they make a long narrow strip of parchment, like a leather strap, and wind it round the cylinder with the edges touching, so that there is no space between the folds and the entire surface of the *scytale* is covered. Having done this, they write their message on the parchment in the

> position in which it was wrapped round the cylinder, and then they unwind the parchment and send it without the cylinder to the commander. When it reaches him, he has no means of deciphering it, as the letters have no connexion and appear to be all broken up, and he has to take his own cylinder and [306] wind the strip of parchment round it. The spiral is then arranged in the correct sequence, the letters fall into their proper order, and he can read round the cylinder and understand the message as a continuous whole. The parchment, like the cylinder, is called a *scytale*, just as the thing that is measured often has the same name as the measure. (1960a: 305–6)

Notice that it is an accident of language, a mere contingency of symbolic presentation, whether the 'letters' that have no connection when not in correct spiral form are rather whole words or even whole sentences. The message has to be understood as a continuous whole regardless. Logically, the 'whole' in this case is not a narrative, but probably has the pragmatic status of a command.

A second example from Plutarch:

> The King of Persia gave Themistocles leave to speak with complete frankness about the affairs of Greece.
> Themistocles replied that human speech may be compared to an embroidered tapestry, which shows its various patterns when it is spread out, but conceals and distorts them when it is rolled up, and for this reason he needed time. The king was pleased with this simile and told him to take as much time as he chose. Themistocles asked for a year, and in that time he mastered the Persian tongue sufficiently well to converse with the king without an interpreter. (1960b: 104)

But even a carpet entirely in the Persian tongue still needs to be unrolled, of course.

Classically trained as they undoubtedly were, Morton White and Danto were nevertheless not open to conceptions of meaning beyond the atomistic approach of their version of empiricism. That version was an absolute presupposition for them. Absolute presuppositions are recognizable with historical hindsight when it might be found that alternatives had been in principle available, but which were not in fact noticed or practicably noticeable at the time. Only later philosophers – perhaps even White and Danto themselves – might be able to bring these to mind in an examinable manner because, with hindsight, they could perhaps then recognize that there had been alternatives to them that lay beyond the limitations of the presuppositions they had once unthinkingly had. More likely, they would have tried to avoid what C. E. M. Joad called the 'acute mental discomfort' involved in the required 're-arrangement of mental furniture'.

'This last', Joad continued, 'is a task from which we increasingly shrink as we grow older and after middle-age are usually unable to perform at all' (1944: 13).

However, Hexter's response did not amount to presenting a recognizable alternative. For White and Danto, looking forward along what they thought of as the path of further analytical philosophical development, there was no way forward in the future without the science-appropriate empiricist and Fregean assumptions they were taking for granted. There was no self-doubt. There was no ground for examining the presuppositions. It was not that White and Danto were imperialistic in their attitudes, but rather they were responsible, middle-of-the-road in their unexamined acceptance of what was for them established theory. Hexter's denial of their attitude was intellectually irresponsible, indeed, revolutionary from their point of view. Normal philosophy would collapse if Hexter's unFregean claims about truth, knowledge and explanation were followed through. That Danto and White thought in such terms was understandable in terms of proper historiographical empathizing with them.

Shared Imagining

When we empathize with some past individual such as we are imagining doing now, we should recognize that this is in principle no different from empathizing with somebody in our present world. Can we 'really' get into the mind of another? It is a familiar problem in philosophy, derived from Descartes's position, whether we can get into the mind of another person and indeed we cannot, according to him, be certain that that other person has a mind at all. It is a philosophical advance on Descartes, in the world of analytical philosophy most explicitly derived from Wittgenstein, to recognize that much if not all of 'mind' and the correct application of mental predicates lies in the public realm. We share much with other people, and we are in fact able to understand them, often to the point of being able to ascribe a range of beliefs and past experiences to them and also to trust them to act appropriately in a wide range of circumstances. We also know that some people are untrustworthy, or have mental problems we are not familiar with, or experiences we have never had, or speak in languages difficult to interpret, or are secretive and unwilling to share.

When I moved from Edinburgh University to Cambridge to work with Bryce Gallie, I was warned by one of my tutors, George Davie (the expert on the Scottish Enlightenment), that, in his experience of Gallie, I would not be able to find out what he thought philosophically by talking to him but would have to read his publications. That turned out to be and still is true, and it makes no difference to my understanding of him that Gallie died in 1998. Facial cues or turns of phrase are indeed no longer available, he is not able to confirm or disconfirm an attempt to grasp his thinking, but since he would not have done that anyway such face-to-face evidence would not have been of much help if he were here now.

Such as these are familiar practical hurdles that we all have to jump in understanding other people. We need not import the alleged Cartesian impossibility of entering another's mind as a ground for holding it impossible to empathize with a past individual, as if it were yet a further ground for scepticism with respect to knowledge of the past. There is no difference in principle from empathizing with a present individual, merely the absence of some cues we might otherwise have. On the other hand, in such practical terms, once a person is dead, we often have evidence about what they thought which was not available to us when they were alive. I do not need, in my use of empathy in what I am saying here, to carry some extra burden of proof with regard to understanding others in the past beyond what is required in the present. In summary, if you can empathize with me, then I can empathize with Morton White (who, now irrelevantly to the present issues, died in 2016).

Imagining empathizing with the more general case, I imagine that I, like them, am trying to give some meaning to the imagined space and time they are in, some meaning to the world that they are conscious of being in and some meaning to the time-extended experience they are living through. 'Meaning' here is not some merely metaphorical expression. Rather, that 'whole' of spatially and temporally local experience which empathy gives us expresses the world so experienced in a full-blooded way, so that I can draw on a non-Fregean conception of empirical meaning and hold that whole to be what Quine called a 'unit of empirical significance' (1951: 42). Helpfully, Quine's view in 'Two dogmas' was that the term and the individual statement are not 'units of empirical significance', and that the 'whole of science' is, although we should not accept his view that these are incompatible alternatives. Taking pragmatism seriously – indeed, more seriously than Quine did – I hold that it is a pragmatic or contingent matter what a 'unit of empirical significance' can be, depending on the different purposes we may have. It is not just Quine's 'whole of science', 'terms' and 'individual sentences' that can be 'units of empirical significance' but, centrally for historical understanding, a typical historical account, sorting and expressing as it does that whole time-extended world with which we seek to empathize.

Nevertheless, we need some of the atomistic empiricist elements and pragmatism enables us to keep them. As Frege said, 'It must be laid down that a letter retains in a given context the meaning once given to it' (Geach and Black 1966: 1), and it is a characteristic feature of language that it be reliable in shared contexts. This does not, however, require that symbolic units be universally applicable in the sense of having eternal reidentifiable meanings regardless of context. We do not need to think of our temporally extended worlds as quasi-mathematical and requiring to be sorted in terms of fixed and simple meaningful terms, although there are areas of discourse where that is indeed our aim. In the small areas of life – operating with 'moderate-sized specimens of dry goods', in J. L. Austin's words (1962: 8), it is helpful in all manner of ways to have established meanings. For example, it seems to us that objects persist through time and persistence of word meaning can reflect such contingencies. Establishing each word or symbol or other signifier to mean 'the same' is similar to making, in monetary systems, each relevant coin worth the same. Yet currencies can collapse; trust is essential. Mutual trust and our faculty of memory enable us to hold the meaning of certain words constant in localized situations. But such as these are not the only units of empirical significance. It is also characteristic of a shared world that its temporal extension means that it can be structured in terms of concepts and modes of presentation that can cover change and can themselves change and that includes the stories we write about others or tell ourselves. Here evolutionary change is better than revolutionary change, since trust is better preserved thereby.

When empathizing, I imagine that I am engaging with a being that is alive, that has memories, beliefs, hopes, expectations, although I accept that their memories may be excellent or poor, their beliefs well-grounded or perhaps self-contradictory or weakly held, their situation hopeless. Others are hopeful, with plans that they propose to carry out and with sufficient confidence to succeed, seeing themselves as engaged in ongoing actions in states of affairs in which they play, or seek to play, a part. The world in which they see themselves as living may be perceived by them as fixed or as changeable. I imagine that they have inherited, learnt or developed a complex range of attitudes. I imagine they are rational much of the time, but I would be very careful what sense to give to that and do not need to commit myself to a particular position on the matter. Any of these characteristics might be consciously or unconsciously held, if our theory of mind permits such a contrast.

I imagine that I share a 'human nature' with them, but I am very wary of all the philosophical models that have been offered for that. For example, Plato's Socrates thought, in simple summary, that some people were motivated by reason, others by so-called spirit and others again by desire. This threefold suggestion has over the millennia morphed into some assumptions widely used today in some contexts of social theorizing, in particular that humans are motivated by desires and means-ends beliefs. There are theories which make desire-maximization essential to understanding human choices. Some have attempted to model such reasons as causes of actions, in ways that might allow covering-law theory to get a grip on understanding human action. Kant gave morality a central place in our supposedly universal rational essence. Dray rightly brought to our attention the calculations under constraints of appropriateness that individuals might make. Yet all these philosophical models are flatly false if they make any claim to being exhaustive as characterizations of that human nature which we empathize with in the general case. Where they are true, they are contingently so, applying to some and not others, and varying in their applicability with cultural situations and over historical time.

Supposedly universal models of human nature such as these outdated offerings miss out on the most obvious feature of the general case of empathetic imagination, which is that we are attempting – I will not say, how successfully – to put ourselves in the position of another and looking all around their world for ourselves, spying out the spatial and social surroundings and looking forwards and backwards in time, as far back and as far forward as we can, reconstructing relevant memories and imagining their future as they imagined it. In so far as such looking requires conceptualization rather than what might once have been called raw experience, we have to conceptualize that world in which we find ourselves when empathizing with another.

It is an abstract Descartes-led scepticism that our conceptualization of another's world may be radically different from theirs, but we should hesitate before thinking that to be a practical problem. It is structurally similar to that problem on which first year philosophy students cut their teeth, whether you 'really' see as green what I 'really' see as red, but where our use of those words has been such that we always agree on what colour something is. Rather, the evidence by which we are able to empathize with another person, either past or present, drives the conceptualization to be used in making sense of their world. There may not be any choices to be made here, either for us or for those we empathize with. It is a factual question, determinable by evidence, whether or how far any difference in fundamental modes of conceptualization exists between us and those we empathize with. It remains the case that they knew things we don't, and we know things they didn't. It is contingent what those things are.

Making the World

There is a sense in which we share consciousness with those with whom we successfully empathize just in so far as we share with them the meaning they make of their world. It might be thought that merely sharing language with them would ensure this, but, apart from possible differences in language, there are various ways in which the meaning we make of their worlds will not necessarily be the meaning they make. We have hindsight, and can use what Danto called 'narrative sentences' to redescribe their world in ways that they might not have available to them (1965: chapter VIII). Even in our present we may well be rivals with other people alive now as to how to give meaning to the world in which we currently live. 'Sharing' that world with them will have its contingent limitations. Nevertheless, we may instead agree with them, and may also agree with those already dead as to what meaning is to be made. We may, for example, share a vision that they once articulated and be carrying on with its implementation. We can give meaning to our world by making it through our actions. On the other hand, in the case of individuals sufficiently distant from us in the past or the present we will not have been, or be, for them a part of their imagined future, not a part of the world they were or are trying to make. Their ability or inability to grasp and control their future is essential to our understanding of them, the more so the more they differ from us.

The world sorted in the holistic temporal way that I have described thus includes (among other things) the past, present and pragmatically foreseeable future in which a person actually lives. Despite Morton White's confidence, he was not able to make his future academic philosophical world beyond the very immediate. Framing the future of philosophy, in particular the philosophy of history, in terms of the Hume-derived atomistic empiricist assumptions he brought to it was a failure. As a matter of historical fact, the future of philosophy of history in our intellectual inheritance was made by Hayden White, not Morton White. Similarly, it was Kuhn, not Hempel, who framed the one-time future of philosophy of science; I heard Hempel admit defeat in Cambridge in 1971. It is a contingency whether and how far anyone gets to make or control their future, but in general I share the view of Vico that we make the world in which we live.

We can see this more clearly using one of Danto's examples of a narrative sentence: 'The Thirty Years War began in 1618' (1965: 152). Nobody in 1618 could have known that the Thirty Years War was beginning, because they would have had to wait thirty years to find out how long it had been. But that is not a point of principle, as if it was impossible to know things thirty years ahead; it depends on how much power someone had in 1618. Imagine some Roman emperor in charge. It is easy to imagine that, with overwhelming power for hundreds of years on the European stage, the imperial machine the emperor controlled might well have continued to wage a planned war for thirty years and then called it off. But we do not need speculative examples. Historians are very aware of facts such as these. How politicians in power can make the future world is exemplified by historian Maurice Cowling describing high politics in his 1971 book *The Impact of Labour 1920-1924: The Beginning of Modern British Politics* (1971: Introduction, 3–10, *passim*):

> The first context in which high politics was played was the context in which politicians reacted to one another. The political system consisted of fifty or sixty politicians in conscious tension with one another whose accepted authority constituted political leadership. In this context significance arose from mutual recognition; not from office, but from a distinction between politicians, inside parliament and outside, whose actions were thought reciprocally important and those whose actions were not. It was from these politicians that almost all initiative came. The language they used, the images they formed, the myths they left had a profound effect on the objectives other politicians assumed could be achieved through the political system.
>
> … High politics was primarily a matter of rhetoric and manoeuvre.
>
> … Political rhetoric was an attempt to provide new landmarks for the electorate. Political manoeuvre was designed to ensure that the right people provided them.
>
> … Rhetoric … was an attempt at constructive teaching, an effort to persuade the new electorate to enter the thought-world inhabited by existing politicians.
>
> … Party politics issued in … a rhetorical persuasion to adopt the language and expectations of the politician who used it, a succession of affirmations designed to sound resonantly in the ears of whatever audience was being addressed.
>
> … The central political achievement was not representation but rhetoric.

It was that rhetoric, once successfully taken up and acted upon by the relevant audience adopting the thought-world in question, that made the future world: *verum factum*, to use Vico's epistemological principle (Pompa 1975: 78–83). Generalizing from this and with an eye to theorizing the reality of history, it is not representation but rhetoric which makes our world. This is not the world that science describes, but the actual world in which we live, a world that, in contingent fact, does support the scientific endeavour (at least for a while, with its frequent denigration of so-called experts).

Philosophically foundational here is empathizing with others, with seeing things from their points of view, which is now to be understood in terms of sharing with them a thought-world that is temporally extended. It is contingent what that temporal extension is or where power may lie in controlling it. Making that world meaningful cannot be done with theories of meaning that, like Frege's and drawing on atomistic empiricism, allow as conceptions of time only the point-present or the quasi-mathematically eternal. Similarly, the time-extended advantage, that narratives and similar structures have in giving meaning to our world, only on occasion, in favourable circumstances, permits a reduction to either causal analysis or rational analysis as those were understood in the logical empiricist heyday of analytical philosophy of history.

The theoretical principle that 'we can choose' how to sort the world needs to be understood as directing theoretical attention to the myriad contingencies of when choices of conceptualization are available, what those choices are and who the 'we' might be that has a realistic opportunity to choose in such contexts and the power and ability to carry through any decision. That is, in effect, the power and ability to create a future, whether that involves an advance in theorizing or a political programme.

Identifying the 'we' here takes us into value-laden political territory. Richard Rorty (1989) was right to seek 'solidarity', rather than dogmatic universal certainty, as the ground for knowledge and so, given sufficient confidence, for political action. Yet, if 'we' is to be identified by an identity of 'interests', arguably his Marxist father, James Rorty, was also right in thinking 'Americans would do well to rid themselves of 'the democratic dogma expressed in the phrase "We, the people". We have never had in this country any such identity of interest as is implied in that first person plural' (Novick 1988: 572). There are non-Marxist interpretations of 'interest', of course. Yet one interpretation of 'interest' is surely all but universal: the future of the human race, where our recognition of 'the Anthropocene' – so far, by doing little more than merely naming it – bodes well for our also recognizing the possibility of meaningful solidarity in dealing with, for example, climate change, in the imagined future. Yet this, too, is disputed, and perhaps 'we' all are fighting in the dark. There is, in any event, no 'essence' of history; there are a number of ways of giving meaning to time-extended experience.

If we are to have a heyday for analytical philosophy of history again then we will need to find something in the work of historians that analytical philosophers will find new and valuable with respect to their mainstream interests, preferably something that preserves the traditional analytical philosophical respect for science. The arguments so far presented here suggest that analytical philosophers should attend closely to the notion of temporally extended imagination as being foundational to the construction of that shared reality of which we are conscious. The empathy required for that enables understanding of the world in which we live now. In principle this need not be a philosophy of *historiography* at all. It is a philosophy of temporal understanding, but historical methods may well be essential to that.

Temporal understanding, historical consciousness, is a matter of imagining (at least) the past. We imagine the present, too, for this enables us to share it. These imaginings, however, are not fictional, not 'mere imagination', for it is a matter of imagining the past or present 'reliably'. In the case of the present, mutual engagement with others provides the required confirmation of reliability. We may wish to contrast imagining the past with imagining the future, and perhaps suppose that a clear contrast is available between the 'reliability' of the imagination in each situation, in particular that imagining the past can be supported by evidence and memory while imagining the future cannot. However 'evidence' can involve in many cases 'scientific' results that, in principle, can be extrapolated – as with universal and statistical generalizations – to both past and future. Moreover, 'memory' in the sense of historians relying on people with 'direct causal connections' to events, as Hempel might have supposed, is of very limited use. Even when historians try to get 'as close as possible' to any 'direct causal connections' by using testimony, for example, or by recording oral history, both of which require trust and testing on the historian's part, they are still engaged in the primary task of trying to empathize with, or to share, the world imagined by their subjects. Our remembered world remains an imagined world. This may seem to be a broadly idealist assertion, but it does have support from neuroscientific research, which an analytical philosopher's respect for science requires us to notice.

Thus Kourken Michaelian remarks (2017),

> A multitude of findings demonstrate that remembering the past and imagining the future have similar phenomenologies, involve similar cognitive processes, and rely on similar brain regions. ... For obvious reasons, imagining the future does not presuppose the existence of a causal connection between the subject's current representation and his experience of the represented event. If episodic remembering is a process of the same kind as episodic future thinking, then we may have to admit that remembering the past likewise does not presuppose the existence of a causal connection between the subject's current representation and his experience of the represented event.

The construction of both imagined past and imagined future thus have in principle the same foundation, and a substantive philosophy of history can spread in either direction of time, as we imagine that.

Historians empathize particularly well with the temporally extended shared structures that I have referred to and that they so characteristically describe in narrative terms, and as a matter of contingent fact both analytical philosophers and neuroscientists have much to learn from historians in this regard. We analytical philosophers need to recognize and value such historical understanding, and if we do it may well yield another heyday for the analytical philosophy of history. We now can decide to do this; thereby we will encompass the future of the analytical philosophy of history.

3

Historiographical Knowledge as Claiming Correctly

Jouni-Matti Kuukkanen

This chapter considers in what sense historiography is an empirical discipline and what historiographical knowledge is. Through brief conceptual examinations of empiricism, evidence, representation and inference, it suggests that understanding historiographical knowledge and its justification requires a new kind of approach, which penetrates into the inferential structures of claiming in historiography. In brief, historiographical knowledge is claiming correctly. The chapter argues also for a practice revolt, demonstrating by way of a case study on a historiography of the Finnish civil war, how philosophy and historiography mesh with each other. The key task is to examine how a historian's claims are practically warranted within his text. There are at least six different kinds of linguistic acts with variable textual and non-textual grounding.

In the Beginning There Was the Deed

'In the beginning was the Word', writes John in the Bible. But this gets it wrong. The word did not come first but second. In the beginning, there was the deed, and the word comes after the deed. Saying the word is already doing something. This idea was crystallized by Wittgenstein (1972) in his quotation of Goethe in *On Certainty*, which reverses the order of John's claim: 'In the beginning was the Deed' (§402).

The latter statement captures the view of this chapter and of my research project more generally. It is that the correct *philosophical* approach to historiography is the one that understands historiography as a practice; even if history is typically presented through writing, writing is derivative of doing.

My primary interest is in knowledge and only secondarily in language. And I won't be analysing Wittgenstein (or Goethe or Faust) in this chapter, but attempting to apply the above idea in the context of historiography. This chapter begins with a wonder: that there is something like *historiographical knowledge,* even though historiography deals with the matters long gone, and typically presents its conclusions in a literary form. Even if one were a sceptic regarding the existence of knowledge proper in historiography, like some postmodernists are, it is still possible to think that historiography produces claims, beliefs and interpretations that purport to increase our understanding of the past. It has to be asked, whether these products of historiography really constitute knowledge, and if they do, what kind of knowledge.

Because knowledge, or alleged knowledge, of history is expressed in words, words are significant epistemically. And because the production of words, and claims, is doing something, the focus regarding this knowledge must be on the kinds of acts that make this doing. Although the focus is still on language, claims *in* language, they are understood as tokens of acts, as linguistic *acts.*

It sounds natural to assume that not all imaginable linguistic acts constitute knowledge, and further, that not all linguistic acts are appropriate, and yet further, that not all acts expressed in words are linguistic acts. (And then there are, of course, many acts that are not linguistic at all.) For these reasons, the most important philosophical question is concerned with the kinds of acts that are appropriate *and* with the conditions of these appropriate acts. When is a claim dealing with the past knowledge? What does it mean that it is knowledge? When is a claim appropriate in the first place? And how to judge it? What makes a linguistic act linguistic? Is it that it must be meaningful, as opposed to those acts that, although expressed in words, are meaningless, for example?

These are some of the questions, philosophically the most fundamental ones, of my new pragmatist research project. However, this chapter is not an essay in philosophy of language. This is not an essay in epistemology although knowledge is a central theme; but is a paper in philosophy of historiography in which both philosophy of language and epistemology are extremely relevant. It would also be wrong to assume that philosophy of historiography has a sharply carved object of research, historiography, as if its investigation, armed with all philosophical theories of language and epistemology, would approach this object, historiography, from an external point of view and test those philosophical theories against this object. If this was the case, then it would seem that the task ahead is straightforwardly descriptive. It is better to say that my project operates *philosophically within historiography.* That is, my aim is to deal with the 'real' issues of history and historiography, trying to make sense and give them some specific meaning. It might be said that, while I am not writing history, I am *writing historiography philosophically*, because this writing intends to make the practice of historical research and writing meaningful and structured, engaging with the issues of what historians write about history, for philosophical purposes. This is what I imagine that writing does in any case. It navigates around various particulars of the world, giving names and providing senses to them, and linking them together. Without this kind of practice the world would remain inert, and through writing it becomes operative and meaningful for us.

Let us begin, then, with an assumption that historiographical knowledge takes the form of claims about the past. There are different kinds of claims, and even whole books amount to claims in some argumentative context. For example, a historian may claim that the Finnish civil war began on 27 January 1918 or that the red guard in the war was democratic or that the war was a war of liberation, and an infinite number of other claims. If any of these is accepted, one acquires a new belief about the past. The starting point in a philosophical reflection on historiographical knowledge is the question, whether claims like these should be accepted or rejected. This is clearly a *pragmatic* matter: it is a question, whether one incorporates a new belief into his belief system, or not. The central question is, how and why this is done? Or, if a new belief is rejected, what is the reason for rejection?

It should be noted that this conception of knowledge is perhaps 'knowledge lite', as by invoking the concept of knowledge, I do not mean to say that knowledge is or must be necessarily a 'true justified belief' or some adjusted variant of this tripartite definition. This classic definition still seems to provide the framework in which analytic epistemology discusses knowledge, although of course a great number of modifications have appeared since Gettier's celebrity article (Gettier 1963). In any case, I do not wish to begin the discussion on knowledge from the premises of this framework. 'Knowledge' in historiography denotes here *a sentence that deals with actions and events of the past, that is accepted and considered to be belief-worthy*. Naturally, the inquiry into the acceptance (and a judgement of belief-worthiness) and rejection (and a judgement of belief-unworthiness) of claims is intimately linked with the grounds for a respective reaction. Trivially and not very informatively we can say that a rational believer accepts correct claims and rejects incorrect claims. This may not be very enlightening, but even then it brings attention to *criteria used to determine* whether a claim is correct and should be accepted, or whether it is incorrect and should be rejected. Further, something pivotal comes to the fore regarding historiographical knowledge through this perspective: it is that no claim is evident in historiography, as I will argue next. To put the matter differently, the criteria for acceptance and rejection cannot be that something is intuited clearly or that it is immediate to the mind that it should be accepted because of this. This may sound like a platitude, but it in fact has interesting consequences with regard to the empirical status of historiography and to the nature of evidence and of historiographical judgement. I deal with each of them in turn next.

A Paradox of Empiricism in Historiography

It sounds uncontroversial to state that historiography is an empirical discipline. Does it not have a research object, the past, which is separate from the historian, the nature of which cannot simply be logically deduced or reached through a conceptual analysis? What would be a more natural starting point than that historians attempt to formulate descriptions of that research object on the basis of empirical evidence? Further, it is equally intuitive to think that historians' claims stand or fall depending on how well corroborated their empirical evidence of this past is. To put the matter yet alternatively, the yardstick of historians' claims is their empirical tenability rather than their success in explicating meanings or logical truths, for example. If one claims that Nazi Germany attacked Poland in 1939, this claim is justified if evidence points to the conclusion that this was indeed the case (viz. that Nazi Germany in fact attacked Poland).

So far so good, but there is a serious problem with this image of historiography as an empirical discipline: in practice, historians writing about history, say about the Second World War, are presently able to receive no *direct evidence* from their research object. There is simply nothing to observe, because everything under description happened in the past (like tanks rolling over the eastern border of Germany), and therefore, it is not possible to acquire any direct output from this research object, which could then be tested against it. Empiricism is typically understood to entail that it is experience that is the source of knowing, and experience is often taken to refer to phenomena that are sensed or observed. Empirical evidence has been understood as sense data or sensory experience, for example, by the British empiricists, Russell, Quine and the logical positivists. It can be safely said that in historiography its objects of research, objects in the past, cannot be sensed or observed, and therefore its knowledge cannot be knowledge derived from the senses.[1]

The paradox is that historiography is presumptively an empirical discipline in that it is focused on acquiring knowledge of the past on the basis of evidence from this past, but it simply cannot be one in the *traditional sense* of empiricism, because no perceivable output emanates from its research object. The point now is not that historians would not have any observable objects in their purview but that there is no immediate link to the research object in the way there is in the laboratory sciences, for example, between observable output and its origin. The matter is no different even if a field of history mainly studies material artefacts, as archaeology does, because they also are *relicts*, quite like archival documents, from the past. Does this mean that historiography is not epistemologically accountable? No, it does not, because direct empirical support is not the only way to ground one's claims and be epistemologically accountable. But this means that knowledge in historiography is *never immediate but always mediate*. The significance of this conclusion cannot be overemphasized. The focus is on the character of historiographical knowledge, and specifically, on the character of the reasoning that leads to that knowledge.

An etymological insight into the origins of the word 'evidence' makes the problem even more explicit. 'Evidence' has several roots and connotations, but one of them stands out and exposes problems with regard to historiography. 'Evidence' stems from Medieval Latin *evidentia* meaning obvious, evident or clear, and 'evident' means obvious to the eye or the mind. Now the problem is that there is very little, if anything, that is evident regarding historiographical knowledge. Nor is there any method that could be used to test whether a belief is obvious. If historians were intuiting something that is immediate to the eye or the mind, like the colour sensation, perhaps some beliefs would be evident.[2] But there is very little scope for immediacy or explicitness in historiography (and, in fact, little in the sciences either). And again, the situation is the same with historical material artefacts, as it is arguably not obvious what a specific stone or a piece of pottery (assuming that that it's a piece of pottery has been determined) is historically. That *something is or was the case* in history cannot normally be intuited immediately, but is inferred from something else. If one claims that the Russian Revolution took place in October in 1917, the judgement that this is the case cannot possibly be evident or present to the mind in the sense of immediacy. A simple reason is that the Russian Revolution took place a long time ago, as the claim itself makes explicit, and is no longer available to be observed, sensed or intuited. Another reason is that a typical judgement that something is the case deals with the kinds of phenomena that cannot even in principle be conceived of as being present to the mind in the way that the sensations of colour can be.³ No one could have witnessed the historical phenomenon Second World War although millions of people naturally witnessed countless acts that are subsumed under the colligatory concept of the 'Second World War'. Naturally, one may be *led to* think that something is evident in historiography, but this is a cognitive error characterizing a specific conservative attitude towards historiographical knowledge, as is argued in the epilogue. The point now is that there are no grounds to think that something is explicit, immediate or evident in historiography.

The etymological link between evidence and evident is introduced here in order to shed light on the specific nature of justification in historiography. What should be concluded here is that *all* knowledge in historiography is mediate or inferential, as no historiographical belief can be verified or intuited directly.⁴ One could not verify directly even those witness statements that could be, in principle, verified if one were situated temporally differently, because the present and the moment of witnessing are separated by temporal distance, which makes the introduction of an intergenerational causal chain necessary.⁵ This does not mean that there is no empirical knowledge component in historiography, but it means that the empirical component is mediated, and thus a judgement on what the case is is inferred from other statements and beliefs. This link between one claim that something is so and so and another claim is essential. Understanding historiographical knowledge and its justification requires a new kind of approach which penetrates into the inferential structures of claiming in historiography.

What Is Inference?

A key concept of this project is 'inference' and a corresponding principled philosophical position is inferentialism, with some caveats however. It might even be claimed that the concept of 'inference' so well characterizes historiographical knowledge that it is strange that it has not been proposed previously.⁶ How so? 'Inference' means that something is not explicit, immediate or evident, and for this reason, 'what is the case' must be deduced, derived or concluded from something else.⁷ As remarked earlier, a typical case assumed to be immediate, for example, is a sense impression of a colour.

What is inference then? According to dictionaries, 'inference' has many meanings but one of them appears to be the most prominent. It is often used as synonymous with derivation, deduction or conclusion from evidence or even from facts. However, more generally, inference can be understood as a move between two linguistic items. Sometimes, based on the original meaning in the sixteenth-century Latin, 'inference' is said to mean to 'bring in' and 'bring about'. The key issue is that there are two poles, points or positions and by way of an inference one moves from one to another. Naturally, this is not enough, since this move should not be any random step between two points but the *move* taken should be somehow *legitimate*.

Merriam-Webster's Dictionary provides a particularly interesting definition of 'inference': 'the act of passing from one proposition, statement, or judgment considered as true to another whose truth is believed to follow from that of the former'.[8] Traditionally several kinds of inferences have been distinguished, such as induction, deduction and abduction, but it should be noted that these inferences are not all necessarily truth-preserving. And while inference is sometimes meant to suggest or hint, its strongest sense is involvement by logical necessity or entailment. Let us then understand inference as a *legitimate* or permissible move between two points, which are two sentences, propositions or statements.

In recent decades, inferentialism has been developed into a comprehensive pragmatist philosophy of meaning as an alternative to representationalism. More precisely, inferentialism is developed by Robert Brandom, whose philosophy builds extensively on Wilfrid Sellars's thinking. Jaroslav Peregrin defines it as a view that meanings are constituted by inferential rules. The most natural home of inferentialism as a meaning theory is logic and the idea that the meaning of logical constants is their inferential rules, that is, the set of inferences that are allowed. For example, the meaning of 'conjunction' is constituted by the following rules:

$$\frac{A \& B}{A} \quad \frac{A \& B}{B} \quad \frac{A \quad B}{A \& B}$$

This would be the complete inferential definition of its meaning, as these are the only steps allowed with conjunction. This definition tells us that from two conjoined propositions A and B, it is possible to derive either A or B, and if there are two independent propositions A and B, in our assumptions, it is legitimate to combine them to a conjunction A and B. The situation is different with the symbols of natural language, as they do not have a fully determined set of rules, and even if they did, the specification of these rules would probably be impossible.

Following the example of 'conjunction', we can think of the 'inference' of inferentialism as a two-place relation. 'Representation' of representationalism is typically also a two-place relation. The crucial difference between the two is that while the relation in the latter is a static state of reflection or mirroring between a subject and an object, getting it right with regard to the object, in the former it is a dynamic movement (of inferring) from one to the other. The rules of inferences are guides for action, and they naturally subsequently extend beyond any two units. Representation entails that the object stays always distinct and even distant from the subject, and this basic constellation is the root cause for various kinds of epistemological problems in their relationship, which boils down to whether the object can be described, re-presented, and if it can, how well (accurately, inaccurately, not at all) can it be?

Richard Rorty is arguably one of the most important and significant critics of representationalism, who made his fame to a large extent by his book *Philosophy and the Mirror of Nature*. Rorty's reprensentationalism signifies a certain ideology that has bewitched Western philosophy ever since the seventeenth century. He writes that representationalism as a view of 'knowledge as an assemblage of representations' was a 'product of the seventeenth century' (Rorty 1980: 136). The title of the book and the book's central metaphors capture well the idea of representationalism. He says that 'the picture which holds traditional philosophy captive is that of the mind as a great mirror, containing various representations – some accurate, some not – and capable of being studied by pure, nonempirical methods. Without the notion of the mind as mirror, the notion of knowledge as accuracy of representation would not have suggested itself' (Rorty 1980: 12). The idea of the mind as a mirror, and as mirroring the world, is forceful, and furthermore, it suggests a standard of correctness. The ideal view is the one which is indistinguishable from the object it mirrors. Rorty writes that 'the notion of an unclouded Mirror of Nature is the notion of a mirror which would be indistinguishable' (Rorty 1980: 376). Through the metaphor of mirror the meaning of representation is sensible. If the object is mirrored so successfully that it is indistinguishable from the object, although it is still distinguishable as a numeric entity, it is indeed a perfect re-presentation of the object.

Brandom's reading of the history of philosophy agrees with that of Rorty. The main representationalist villain for Brandom is Descartes, who defined humans as representers, that is, as the 'producers and consumers of representings'. Brandom writes that 'the states and acts characteristic of us are in a special sense *of*, *about* or *directed* at things. They are representings, which is to say that they have representative content. To have such a content is to be liable to assessments of *correctness* of representations, which is a special way of being *answerable* or *responsible* to what is represented' (Brandom 1998: 6) We might imagine two extreme positions of representationalism which stem from its internal logic. At one extreme, there is direct representational realism according to which our mind and language are transparent mediums of description. At another extreme, there is idealism, which says with the voice of Bishop Berkeley, as one of its best representatives, that we are always locked inside our minds and out of the world that our mind intends to represent.

While it would be very interesting to continue analysing representationalism, it is necessary to return to the notion of inference. To repeat, my primary interest is in knowledge and more specifically in historiographical knowledge, rather than language and meanings and the philosophy of language. Therefore, instead of trying to define meaning by way of inferential roles, my intention is to define knowledge in historiography through the roles that inferences and inferentiality play in historiographical reasoning. The starting point is that inferentialism is a dynamic approach to stating and to knowledge, taking the notion of inference as the most fundamental notion. Inference refers here to the relation and then to the dynamic action of inferring between two non-logical items.

Inferentiality in Historiography

Now the bare bones of my metaphilosophical view have been outlined through a brief discussion of four concepts: empiricism, evidence, representation and inference. Historiography as practice entails that historiographical knowledge is doing, that is, claiming about the past. Naturally, not all types of claiming and not all kinds of claims count as knowledge; there must be restrictions as to what can be inferred from a claim, and there must be inappropriate conclusions. Since only those inferences that are legitimate count as knowledge, the view entailed could be expressed concisely with the following slogan: historiographical knowledge is claiming correctly.

It should be emphasized that 'inference' does not refer to logical or formal inference, but rather to any form of permissible derivation between two linguistic or propositional items. In this sense, inference can be a customary or a socially sanctioned way to move from one statement to another. This is close to what Sellars dubbed 'material inference', which is, for example, an inference from a statement that 'x is red' to 'x is coloured'. Another example is an inference from 'it's raining' to 'streets will be wet', which is not genus-species or determined-determinable (DeVries 2005: 32). Each permissible material inference reflects the place of an object or characteristic in an entire linguistic framework or an outline for a complete world-story. It is important to notice that material inference, although formally invalid, should not be considered as a formally incomplete inference but as a complete good inference. Sellars says that the rules of material inferences are the rules of *conditional assertion*, whose validity depends on evidence and grounds or on the authority of other sentences. In other words, derivability means 'that it is permissible to assert B, given that one has asserted A, whereas it is not permissible to assert not-B, given that one has asserted A' (Sellars 2007: 19).

The biblical quotation in the beginning about the primacy of the word refers obviously not to a mythical moment of creation as in the Bible but to the logical priority between saying and doing. It also refers to the relation in which saying and doing stand with the world. An important element of Brandom's inferentialism is that one should look beyond the syntactic of language and behind linguistic appearance. Together with Wittgenstein, Brandom argues that not every expression that seems representational is really representational. In other words, even if an expression appears to be referring on syntactic grounds, it does not mean that it necessarily really refers. According to Brandom, Wittgenstein argues that we should not assume merely on syntactic grounds that claims necessarily have representational content: 'That terms are used to refer (or fail to refer), predicates are used to describe or characterize (or misdescribe), and sentences are used to claim (truly or falsely)' (Brandom 1998: 75). The key question is not what object is being referred to by the term, what property is being ascribed by the predicate and what fact would make the sentence true, but what is *the use of these expressions* (Brandom 1998: 75; my emphasis). Practice is at the base of his philosophical project. In his words, inferring just is 'a certain kind of move in the game of giving and asking for reasons' (Brandom 1998: 158), pragmatics taking priority over semantics. Inferring is part and parcel or the '*social* practice of communication' (Brandom 1998: 158).

I will not go any deeper into Brandom's rich philosophy here. The ingredients mentioned earlier can be used to detail, not the metaphilosophical approach in philosophy of historiography on this occasion, but the outlines of the respective philosophical approach to historiography. Now it is time, not only to preach pragmatism but also to turn towards practice. Kleinberg et al. have called for a 'theory revolt' and appeal for the relevance of theoretical reflections for historiography.⁹ While I fully support the spirit of this initiative, it is worth making an appeal the other way round too: theoreticians and philosophers should engage with the practice of historians and show the relevance of theorizing and philosophizing *in* this practice. Let me be clear. I do not call for this only because theory and philosophy can consequently be shown to be useful for historiography. The main reason for this 'practice revolt' is that only through practice can the meaning of theoretical and philosophical views be satisfactorily determined.

There are three specific questions to answer:

(1) What kinds of inferences and claiming are there in historiography?
(2) How are they justified?
(3) What defines the difference between legitimate and illegitimate inferences in historiography?

It is not possible here to answer these questions at any length. However, I sketch a preliminary typology of claiming in historiography (question 1) by reference to an actual book of history: an award-winning Finnish book *Revolt at Factories. Kuusankoski 1918* (in translation) by Seppo Aalto.[10] This book provides an account of the Finnish civil war in 1918 at the Kuusankoski factories, which were the biggest factories in the pulp industry in Europe at the time, employing more than 3,000 workers at their zenith. I could, of course, have chosen to analyze a different book. The point is that Aalto's book represents good quality scholarship in historiography. In this chapter, it is possible only briefly to signpost how answers could be found to the two other questions (2 and 3).

Let us now return to the idea of claiming. Claiming in historiography can take place on more than one level. The key idea in my *Postnarrativist Philosophy of Historiography* (2015) was that historiography is a performative practice. The outcomes of historians' practice, books, are performative and argumentative acts in the argumentative context on a certain topic. For example, this topic could be the Great War or the origins of the Great War. There are a large number of alternative views on it. The outbreak of the war has been understood as a result of Germany's premediated struggle for power, of Russia's imperial ambitions, as an automatic process which could not be stopped once it was triggered, as a process of sleepwalking and so on.[11] Any new historian must situate his work in this field by making a credible argumentative intervention for his view in relation to the existing discursive state.

It might then be said that *books are book-length claims* of how the past should be seen and that the entire text is an embodiment of this claim. However, books and the claims they constitute operate on the disciplinary level. The book itself consists of a high number of claims. In other words, it is equally possible to investigate the nature and warrant of singular claims as it is to investigate the nature and warrant of an entire book as a claim. While Quentin Skinner is an appropriate intellectual inspiration for entire texts (e.g. 1988), J. L. Austin is fitting for the sub-book-level investigation, because he focuses on sentences. His idea in *How to Do Things with Words* (1975) is that our utterances have various uses and functions in our language, descriptive use being only one of them. For example, he famously said that the exclamation 'I name this ship the "Queen Elizabeth"' does not in essence describe something but does something: baptizes a ship at a launching ceremony.

Austin focused mainly on spoken language and his intended scope of analysis was language in general. I am here interested in written language and claiming in written language, and in a specific field, historiography, exemplified by one book. And it should be made clear that for the purposes of my analysis, I have not consulted Austin at length. Instead, I see some analogy and some inspiration in what Austin did. My approach focuses on the kinds of claims that a historian makes in his study. Now before proceeding any further, it is in order to mention another possible aspect of investigation, which is, however, not attempted here. Ankersmit has correctly noted that philosophy of history in the mode of studying the language of historiography should focus on the level of the text: how a set of sentences when organized together as a text produces something qualitatively different than the same set when its components, sentences, are taken in isolation (e.g. Ankersmit 1995: 155; 2001: 245). However, it can still be said that an even more comprehensive understanding of historiography can be achieved, if we *also* study the functions of singular claims and of the parts of the text itself. It is a central hypothesis of this chapter that claims in historiography have more than one function, and if all statements are erroneously assumed to be one of a kind, a view of how individual claims are integrated as a text will be skewed.

Claiming in Historiography: A Case Study of *Revolt at Factories*

Semantical questions take often priority when language is studied. That is, it is the questions of reference and truth-functionality, or in general the relation between language and the world, that are in focus.[12] Viewed from a semantical point of view, the following sentences from the book *Revolt at Factories* express factual statements about the world or the past:

(i) 'The revolt broke out only at the end of January' (Aalto 2018: 95).
(ii) 'The general strike, the great citizens' assembly in the struggle for suffrage and demonstrations sensitized workers to their societal influence' (Aalto 2018: 41).
(iii) 'The red guard was in its essence a democratic army' (Aalto 2018: 281).
(iv) 'The militia has proved very tangibly that it was a ruling authority over the state officials regarding administrative matters in factory districts' (Aalto 2018: 74).
(v) 'Viljo Talvela did not necessarily shoot the masters' (Aalto 2018: 286).

Only statements that express clear valuations, pose questions and show empathizing on the side of the historian stand out as non-factual, like the following:

(vi) 'Johansson was indeed a *bad* man' (Aalto 2018: 161).
(vii) '*Why* did factory workers unanimously support the reds?' (Aalto 2018: 98).
(viii) 'This is *understandable*, since every factory worker could himself observe that the gentry did not suffer from the shortages as the workers did' (Aalto 2018: 67).[13]

The first sentence (vi) in the last set regarding Johansson is naturally clearly value-laden. The second sentence (vii) is a clear question. Neither (vi) nor (vii) is not normally to be understood as referring and truth-functional. The third sentence (viii) in this set exemplifies an attitude of empathizing regarding the feelings of the workers. Naturally, it presupposes some factual description of the workers' reactions and mentality. By contrast, the whole set of previous sentences ((i)–(v)) are at least in principle both referring and descriptive of the various states of the world.

As Austin and the later Wittgenstein have remarked, the factual and descriptive use of language is only one way or one possible 'language game'. If all the statements are forced into the box of factual-descriptive language, the view of how language works will become lopsided. In any case, if it assumed that all claims are similar descriptive claims, we will miss quite a lot of the depth of the linguistic functions of many sentences. There are two issues to understand: (a) What are the roles that different parts of the text play? (b) How is each part, and its role, justified *in the text*?

(a) The first general observation is that the set of factual statements can be broken into a few functional roles, some of which are more familiar than others in the history of historiography. Now it might be possible to say that the sentence (i) and others of its kind are straight factual statements. Normally, a claim like this does not need further qualifications or assurances. The sentence (i) is also true, since the civil war begun on 27 January 1918.[14] Further, perhaps it might be said that types of (ii) and (iii) sentences exemplify, and require, historians' judgement and assessment, which is traditionally called 'interpretation'. Although (ii) is, in effect, a claim about the causal effect of certain societal matters on the mentality of workers, reaching the conclusion is clearly a matter of the judgement in the way that (i) is not. The statement (iii) could be understood either as a valuation, or simply as a factual statement reached through a historian's assessment of the situation. That is, it could be a statement regarding the assumed inherent nature of the red guard or it could be based on an assessment of certain practices of this army (respect for democratic principles in choosing the leaders of the guard, for example). Even in the latter case, the conclusion could not be determined through a straight descriptive approach. The colligation of various kinds of particulars regarding and the assessment of their meaning is required. The statement (iv) is a similar statement in that regard: it requires gathering information of various deeds at the time and reaching a conclusion on that basis. The statement (v) is a modal statement expressing doubt or qualification regarding the state of affairs. This makes it different in terms of its functional role from a straight factual statement. The functional roles of the statements (vi) and (vii) are clear from above. The former is a value-laden assessment of Johansson's nature, and the latter is a question. Finally, the functional role of sentence (viii) is that it both explicitly exemplifies the historian's reasoning, bringing forward his assessment of how this state of affairs should be understood and this historian's empathizing.

There are also some parts of the text that are clearly modelled after the question–answer model, in which an answer is given to a query. One of them in the book by Aalto is the question: Why did the workers support so unanimously the reds? After roughly five pages of consideration, the answer is given: it was the socialist ideology, which drove workers to fight for their rights and eventually against their masters (Aalto 2018: 98–105). And amidst more narrative parts, there are several similar sections in the book. In this particular book, an entire chapter is devoted to answering the question: Who was responsible for the executions in the Winter and Spring of 1918 in Kouvola? The question is raised (Aalto 2018: 250), and then the answer is given forty-four pages later almost in the end of the chapter (Aalto 2018: 294).

(b) We get a much more nuanced and varied understanding of historiographical claiming when the focus is shifted to what *entitles* these expressions. The key question here is: What must be presupposed in order to claim legitimately that something is so and so? Viewed from this perspective, significant differences between the previously mentioned sentences start to emerge. Further, the supporting network and the inferentiality of historiography become visible.

The first category is the type (i) sentences. Semantically, they can be regarded as true sentences. Sometimes it is said that these kinds of sentences state facts, or that propositions that these sentences express (language neutrally), if true, are facts. But how can a historian justify and reach the claim that 'the revolt broke out only at the end of January'? One thing is that determining that the starting date is exactly 27 January is a convention, as explained in note 14 of this chapter. The date could be earlier in January too. And here is the answer to the question. In a case like this, the historian typically adopts the convention without any problematization. An indication of a convention is that there is no reference to archival material or literature; it can be omitted because this particular date is generally accepted in *historiographical discourse*. It is very easy to imagine other similar simple factual statements, like the birth date of a well-known historical agent. Naturally, if he is not generally known, the establishment of the date requires additional grounding. Perhaps it could stem from the discovery of a birth document saying, 'N.N. was born at dd.mm.yyyy.' In this case, the justification for a sentence giving this birth date can be reduced to this one document. One document or one mention in a document is enough, in so far as normal methodological procedures are followed to ensure the reliability of this document.

Now let us move on to the type (ii) sentence, which says that 'the general strike, the great citizens' assembly in the struggle for suffrage and demonstrations sensitized workers to their societal influence'. What kind of warrant is required to state this?

Statements like these have been traditionally called 'interpretations', suggesting that a set of facts is seen in a particular light and that they are given some kind of specific gloss in this way. The idea thus seems to be that, first, there are these more or less unproblematic propositions of the state of affairs, and when they are known, these facts are coloured in some subjective way by the historian. While 'interpretation' may fit the bill here, it is not very informative either. What is important here is to study the inferential grounding of these sentences. These sentences, even if labelled as 'facts', do not emerge by itself and are not self-justifying. They clearly derive from other claims and beliefs.

Now it would be easier if the sentences (or the paragraph) like this one were footnoted, because that would give a clue for a next step in the chain of reasoning that establishes its warrant. It would require the reader to follow this chain, typically, either to an archival document or to a scholarly literature. Statements. or at least some of them, would be grounded in archival material or in other scholars' work. However, as noted earlier, there are also beliefs that are so widely accepted that they do not need footnoting. This is the case here, but there is also a crucial difference from the type (i) sentence. The type (ii) sentence is more interpretative, which means that its justification relies on a wider web of beliefs of the historian or the system of beliefs shared in a historiographical community. Let us take another similar statement for a closer inspection: 'Faced with the power of the masses, the Russian Tsar trembled' (Aalto 2018: 41).

There are three key questions here. What does this statement stem from? Is this statement justified? If it is, in what does its justification consist? In order to render this statement justified, the defender of it must be able to bring a number of other statements to its defence, which themselves are justified. Justification means that a statement defended can be inferred from another justified statement.[15] What kinds of inferences from what kinds of statements would make the statement 'Faced with the power of the masses, the Russian Tsar trembled' justified?

This statement refers to the events in 1905 and specifically to the General Strike of 1905 in the Russian empire. In order to stay in power Tsar Nikolai II was forced to allow the establishment of democratic institutions like the Duma in Russia and a national parliament in Finland (which was part of the Russian empire). In the latter, this process led also to universal suffrage. Further, the Tsar's responses involved granting many other democratic rights in the whole Russian empire. In its essence, the warrant-conferring statements would be something like the following: due to serious civil unrest and the general strike in 1905 in Russia, the Tsar Nikolai II was *forced* to agree to the establishment of a Duma with legislative powers and various kinds of civil rights for the Russian people. In a way, the sentence 'Faced with the power of the masses, the Russian Tsar trembled' can be understood to entail this set of sentences describing the situation in more detail. However, this does not mean anything like an analytic entailment but something like a contingent entailment. In other words, this entailment is not necessary by virtue of the meaning of this sentence, but the inference to the Tsar's trembling becomes warranted through these kinds of statements, once they are stated. Like Sellars and Brandom, we should speak of material inferences here, like an inference from 'faced with the power of the masses' to 'the establishment of democratic institutions' in *this historiographic discourse*. The historiographic discourse defines the whole historical world and way to talk about the past, much like Sellars stated that each permissible inference reflects an outline for an entire linguistic framework or a complete world-story. The description could be yet much more nuanced while still enabling this same inference. It could describe in more detail what happened at that time, like Russia losing a war against Japan, the February Revolution and unrest in the army and of the public, the establishment of the Duma initially with consultative powers only and the fear of the Tsar that a massacre might occur in the empire as a result of tensions.

This provides some idea of inferential relations. However, the question whether this sentence is warranted has not yet been answered. Its warrant depends on whether the inference for supporting sentences can be regarded as legitimate, and my suggestion is that the inference is legitimate here, that is, it follows from the kinds of previously mentioned statements. Yet, justification also depends on the status of the statements it is inferred from. It is fair to say that historians in general believe that there was a general strike in 1905 and that the Tsar was forced (thus non-voluntarily) to agree to the establishment of the Duma and that it eventually became a legislative body eroding his power. Naturally, we could go on investigating the justification of these statements in more detail, that is, investigating from what statements they are inferred. But I shall not do it here.

How can the historian then claim that 'the red guard was in its essence a democratic army', that is the sentence (iii)? This sentence appears in the context of the description of the execution of the 'whites' by the red guard. One of the leaders of the red army, Aret Sundström, did not have enough voluntary executioners and went on a mission to find and persuade foot soldiers to help him in executions. The claim about the democratic nature of the red guard refers to the fact that only very few foot soldiers agreed to execute their 'white masters'. Mere antipathy and the hatred of the ruling classes was not a sufficient reason to kill unarmed civilians. We see that 'democratic' is used here as an honorific term to denote something like humane behaviour (and not, for example, to refer to the principles of organization of the army). It would be possible to criticize its use and say that 'democratic' does not mean being respectful for human life but that its meaning is more precise. However, if this idiosyncratic use is accepted, then its justification depends on whether it is correct to claim that the foot soldiers were not prepared to execute willingly their masters. Here the grounding is an incident, which is thus used as an exemplification, in which Sundström tempted the man called Kauppila with the help of Cognac to join him on a killing 'excursion'. This testimony is footnoted in the text, and thus based on archival material in the National Archives of Finland. Further questions are naturally possible, like how reliable this testimony is and how generalizable this incident is.

The sentence (iv) that 'the militia has proved very tangibly that it was a ruling authority over the state officials regarding administrative matters in factory districts' differs from the type (iii) sentence with regard to its justification. This statement is not a straight factual statement either. It is clearly an assessment of the situation at the factories of Kymi in Autumn 1917. But this assessment cannot be safely made by reference to general historiographical discourse and there are no specific literature references either. This is what I call a *textual conclusion,* as the inference stems from a description that precedes this inference. In other words, this inference is a conclusion of that description. Aalto describes here the struggle for control between the workers' security guard on one side and the official factory police and the municipal police force on the other, which nominally focused on the shutdown of beer sales in the factory community. Quite amusingly for a contemporary reader, the workers had demanded that selling beer be forbidden due to all kinds of social problems that it had caused, while both the municipal and official factory police required that shops and bars stay open and keep selling beer.[16] According to Aalto, the outcome of this standoff was that the municipal police force had to back off and retreat from the work premises and the village of Voikkaa in a tense atmosphere, while the workers decided to ban beer sales in the presence of the head of the local constabulary.

In fact, Aalto provides not a single reference to the literature or to archival material to ground this claim (iv) (Aalto 2018: 72–7). There are then two sources for justification: the authority of the historian and the coherence of the account. In other words, it is necessary to trust that the historian attempts to tell this account and all information as sincerely and as accurately as possible. Further, the readers must trust that the author is also professional in the sense that he is able to study and interpret archival material, for example. There is no reason to doubt these. The account is also meaningful and coherent, which entitles a conclusion that the highest authority was in the hands of the red militia. For these reasons, the sentence (iv) can be seen as warranted.

Then the sentence (v) 'Viljo Talvela did not necessarily shoot the masters' hides quite a lot of background material. The starting point is that two influential men were executed in 26 April 1918 (commercial counsellor Gösta Björkenheim and Dr Kaarlo Hjelt). The key evidence for suspicions that Talvela was the murderer is the fact that he committed suicide (presumably guilt-ridden) and that he was seen wearing clothes that belonged to the victims. The qualification 'not necessarily' stems from the fact that Talvela was also known as a 'wheeler dealer', who could have gathered the garments once the victims had been executed. He had allegedly done so in another incident. The text on respective pages (284–7) exemplifies historiographical reasoning very well, as both supporting and undermining evidence is introduced and many potential suspects are considered, with the final message that it is inconclusive who was behind this heinous act. Here the justification is mainly textual reasoning added with some literature and some archival material.

Further, it is entirely reasonable to inquire after the justification of the sentence (vi) 'Johansson was indeed a bad man'. In this case, this sentence is inferred from both a certain and, in this case, a widely shared value-system and some factual statements regarding Johansson's behaviour. The whole name of this man is Moses Johansson, who was a pulp industry worker and a radical revolutionary. Why was he then 'bad'? Because he was merciless towards the 'whites' and was always prepared to act according to 'Moses's laws'. In other words, he was always prepared to execute enemies. It is naturally a widely shared belief that it is morally wrong to kill other human beings at will, although the 'common morality' admits many exceptions, like the war situation. Yet even in war, overt willingness and preparedness to kill captured enemies and civilians is typically understood to be morally indefensible. Now assuming that the description of Johansson's behaviour is correct, and here again we must rely on trust, this sentence is warranted.[17]

Finally, questions can be understood textually reasonable on the premise that they are generally interesting or emerge through the text somehow. Typically, they go beyond the text and raise issues that are of concern more widely in the historiographical discourse. Why is it reasonable to wonder and explain why the workers in the Kymi areas supported the red power so unanimously as in sentence (vi)? The reason is that the degree of support was unusually high in this area: it is estimated that 2,000 out of 12,000 adults worked actively in favour of red Finland, and the latter figure includes elderly people. Because Aalto provides an appropriate historical description underlining these unique characteristics of the region, the question is reasonable in this textual context and the exploration that follows is justified (Aalto 2018: 98).

Empirical Discipline After All

It is time to return to the dilemma mentioned in the beginning: historiography aspires to be an empirical discipline but does not have access to any observable phenomenon of its research object. The past action is behind us and cannot be simulated again for the purposes of observations and testing. But there is another paradox in the offing. This chapter is philosophical in nature, but I have provided empirical evidence, from a text, for the chapter's conclusions. Philosophy has not typically been thought to possess a clear research object and verifiable knowledge, but instead has been characterized as being conceptual, analytical, speculative, literary and by other similar non-empirical predicates. Should we then conclude that historiography cannot be a properly empirical discipline, but philosophy of historiography can?

Naturally, there are grounds to state that historiography is indirectly an empirical discipline. Its source materials are traces of the people and acts, like a footprint is a trace indicating that someone has walked in sand. However, I think that we should not get fixated on traditional constellations regarding the nature of knowledge but instead focus squarely on how historians' claims are justified in practice and then attempt to evaluate the tenability of their warrants. Therefore, the key question is whether inferences to historians' claims are appropriately warranted. And the key output of this chapter is that there is no strict distinction between empirical and non-empirical here, but some inferences may stem from material, some from conceptual, some from moral, some from textual grounds. In general, we have seen that there are at least the following kinds of linguistic acts and grounds for linguistic acts in historiography:

- inference from archival material,
- inference from literature,
- inference from shared beliefs (historiographical and moral),
- textual inference,
- textual coherence and
- the authority of the historian.[18]

Evidence in historiography can then in general be understood as anything that makes something reasonable to be believed. And this is exactly what calls for a 'practice revolt' and a pragmatical (and not only pragmatic) approach. In order to study the inferential structure, it is necessary to study the nitty-gritty and follow inferential chains and networks wherever they lead in order to see from where the reasonableness of historians' claiming stem. Some preliminary steps were taken above but the real practice revolt requires much more extensive and tangible investigations. Before anything general can be said about the warrants in historiographical claiming, the inferential structures must be understood in more detail. Nevertheless, something can be said already now. Warrant is to be found in the practice, in the kinds of inferences and in the kinds of grounds and assumptions of those inferences. Further, this talk of inferential structure is indicative of a familiar position in epistemology, after all: coherentism. It says roughly that statements and beliefs are justified to the degree of support they acquire in the web of beliefs through inferences from other statements and beliefs. This means that inferential grounding should be extensive enough; that the supporting circles are wide, dense and deep enough.

Another conclusion signposting future research is the issue of what inferential moves are legitimate and why. This may be a hopelessly general answer, but at least it will indicate what some key areas of investigation are in the future. Inferences in historiography are legitimate when they are inferred from the kinds of sources above following the correct rules specific to this discipline. Rather than viewing historiographical knowledge as the matching of statements with their object, knowledge in historiography should be seen as permissible linguistic acts. Historians should be understood to form a specific kind of language community, or perhaps communities, considering the various types of historians that there are, with their own kinds of rules governing legitimate and illegitimate inferential moves. The future research must focus on specifying what these rules are: What exactly is claiming correctly in historiography?

Epilogue: The Conservative and Critical Historian

It is my suggestion that we should distinguish two archetypical historians: the conservative and the critical. The difference between the two refers both to the attitude regarding how the past should be studied and to the reflection of this attitude on the level of writing. The conservative historian believes that history is composed of self-evident phenomena, like events and facts, which are to be temporally ordered as *non-inferential facts* in a historian's narrative. The governing mode is descriptive, and the historian's text is a re-presentation of the past. It is natural to him to choose a straight narrative account of 'what happened' as a mode of presentation. By contrast, the critical historian does not think that anything is (self-)evident in history. There may be facts, but facts are defeasible. That is, 'fact' presupposes certain assumptions, and any 'fact' is inferred from those. A good example of how even the simplest 'facts' or events are not given is Orlando Figes's (2014: Ch. 1) view that there are no less than eight different ways to date the Russian Revolution. In addition to the customary view that it took place in the Autumn months of 1917, it is not unreasonable to think that the revolution lasted until the end of civil war in 1921. The revolutionary period can also be seen to have endured until the death of Lenin in 1924, and even until the defeat of Trotsky and the left in 1927. Other options include that only the onset of new revolutionary period in 1929 or the retreat from Utopian ideals in the mid-1930s ended the revolutionary period. Yet one more alternative is 1937–8, when the great terror begun. Figes's own proposal is striking, because he thinks, as the name of his book *Revolutionary Russia 1891-1991* suggests, that the revolutionary period begun in 1891, when the Russian public's moderate revolutionary reaction set it against the autocratic ruler and endured, not only through the time between the world wars but also throughout the Cold War, bringing the revolution to a close only in 1991, when the Cold War ended and the Soviet Union collapsed. It thus looks that there is no fact of the matter regarding the Russian Revolution. Instead, there are different ways to construct it reflecting different underlying assumptions and suggestions.

More generally, the critical historian assumes that all historiographical knowledge is defeasible and therefore hidden assumptions should be made explicit. The focus must be put on those assumptions and their mutual inferential relations. It is natural for the critical historian to begin with a 'deconstructive' approach criticizing and trying to change some view of history. Further, the critical historian typically shows reasoning that leads to deconstruction. In effect, he digs into the inferential structure that enables claiming in historiography. Naturally, the critical historian cannot dispute everything. The Cartesian systematic method of doubting everything is not feasible, but scepticism always presupposes commitment to numerous states of affairs. Anything but not everything can be questioned. Scepticism works piecemeal. Still the degree of criticism and the explication of reasoning in writing distinguishes the conservative and the critical historian. At its best, the historian is a critical reasoner making the inferential structures explicit, deconstructing some of them and constituting some other to replace the deconstructed parts.

4

Where the Extremes Meet

Frank Ankersmit

Introduction

In this chapter, I take up again the old issue of the relationship between history and the sciences. I approach the issue in this chapter from a new perspective, namely from that of Leibniz's philosophical system. My argument will be unreservedly a priorist and thus sidestep what has become known since Kuhn, Quine and Rorty as 'naturalized epistemology', 'post-positivism' or 'pragmatism'. I shall therefore begin by saying why I don't hesitate to take up that challenge. Secondly, having thus cleared the way for my own approach, I shall briefly justify my choice for Leibniz. Thirdly, I will argue that for Leibniz the representation and the represented are identical and, next, why we nevertheless must hold on to these two terms. In the first place because Leibniz's monadological metaphysics compels us to do so and, next, since this is how we must conceive of his notion of the sign. Fourthly, in the notion of the sign we may find here a common ground between mathematics and historical representation. But from there the sciences and historical representation move into different directions. Algorithms play no role in historical representation, whereas scientists don't attribute meanings to signs as historians do. Fifthly, in the end the sciences and historical representation meet each other again when it comes to argumentation. I'll explain this in terms of what has been called Leibniz's 'economy principle' having its roots in the calculus he had discovered at roughly the same time as Sir Isaac Newton.

Why Philosophy of History Needs a Priorist Argument

Two phases can be discerned in twentieth-century philosophy of science: an a priorist phase represented by logical-positivism and Popper's falsificationism and an anti-apriorist phase to be associated with Kuhn's historicism, Quine's naturalized epistemology and contemporary pragmatists. Regardless of one's final opinion about the protagonists of the a priorist approach one cannot fail to be impressed by the boldness of their account of science and of scientific rationality. Anti-apriorist philosophy of science cannot boast of such spectacular results. Think of the relativism often associated with Kuhn's picture of scientific knowledge, or of the all-pervasive scepticism of Quine's account of science. For how else could one characterize his thesis of the underdeterminacy of theory and/or the Quine-Duhem thesis, of what he referred to as the inscrutability of reference and as the indeterminacy of translation? Whatever one's opinion on the credibility of the logical positivist and the falsificationist account of science, one could not possibly deny to its adherents having seriously tried to explain how and why the effort to explain the greatest miracle in modern history has been possible, namely the amazing success story of modern science in the last three centuries. Kuhn's relativist and Quine's scepticist account of science had, on the contrary, the peculiar side effect of transforming that miracle into an unfathomable mystery. If we are amazed by that success story – as we have ever better reasons to be – we will be even more amazed by it after having read Kuhn or Quine. For if there are such excellent reasons to be sceptical about the scientist's knowledge claims, how could science succeed in getting where it presently is? Did Quine, perhaps, forget about certain mechanisms in the practice of science which amply compensate for its innate shortcomings? And if so, what are these mechanisms and how could they be triumphant over these shortcomings? I shall be the last to question the achievements of anti-apriorist philosophy (of science) or of the history and sociology of science. Nevertheless, I think it is only fair to say that one will look in vain here for a thesis as spectacular and thought-provoking as the logical positivist's account of science or as Popper's falsificationism. Undoubtedly, the anti-apriorist philosopher will now respond that it is unwise to hope for more than what *they* have on offer. Well, perhaps, but who would not feel disappointed?

Quine's main argument against a priorist philosophy was, first, that it made room for itself by distinguishing between analytic and synthetic truth, while appropriating the former for itself and assigning the latter to science. And, secondly, that we shall have to abandon the analytic–synthetic distinction. There is no need to recite here Quine's sophisticated argument against the traditional view of analytical truth. For a simple example may suffice. Take the statement 'if X is the son of Y, X cannot be the daughter of Y'. The apriorist would claim this to be an analytical truth, since the meaning of the words 'son' and 'daughter' logically excludes the possibility that X could be both Y's son and Y's daughter. However, now that transgender operations have become possible, this allegedly analytical and eternal truth has been falsified empirically. Hence, whereas apriorism claims some statements to be analytically true – and irrefutable – by virtue of the meanings of the words used for stating them, Quine does not hesitate to say, 'No statement is immune to revision. Revision even of the logical law of the excluded middle has been proposed as a means of simplifying quantum mechanics'. (Quine 1971: 43) In this way Quine pulled the rug out under the apriorist philosopher's feet – and with this from under most of traditional philosophy.

Since Quine's argument is nowadays accepted by many as κτημα εισ αει in philosophy, it is worthwhile to recall that since Strawson and Grice in the 1950s down to the present it has been criticized by many philosophers and logicians. But instead of elaborating on this I'll state now my own position about apriorism. It is, basically, that I don't see in Quine's argument against the analytic–synthetic distinction an obstacle to an apriorist approach to the issue of the writing of history – which will be my topic in the remainder of this chapter (Ankersmit 2020, forthcoming, section 6). Obviously, this must come as a bit of a surprise; so I'll explain myself. Quine's target was the philosophers pretending to found scientific knowledge on *a priori* philosophical considerations.

But this is not what I'm going to do here. It's not my intention to 'found' historical knowledge. Instead, I shall focus on the preliminary question of whether there exists such a thing as historical knowledge and above all, if so, how it is expressed. This is not the kind of question that interested Quine and his followers a lot, for the simple reason that they all agreed about what was at stake in the discussion on scientific knowledge. For them knowledge is typically expressed in terms of scientific theories, either simple ones, such as the gas-law of Boyle-Gay Lussac, or complex ones, such as quantum-mechanics. Easy. Now, the big problem with historical writing is that you have no easy answers there. There are no theories in historical writing as there are in the sciences; worse still, it is not in the least obvious what should count as their equivalent in historical writing. Quine himself agrees,

> In softer sciences, from psychology and economics, through sociology to history (I use 'science' broadly), checkpoints are sparser and sparser, to the point that their absence become the rule rather than the exception. Observation categoricals are implicit still in the predicting of archeological finds and the deciphering of inscriptions, but the glories of history would be lost if we stopped and stayed at the checkpoints.[1]

This is a remarkably frank and candid statement, opening up again the old abyss between the sciences and the humanities. And, indeed, if we agree, with Quine, that scientific knowledge is expressed in terms of scientific theories and that these always need these 'checkpoints' or 'facts of the matter', than history is not a science. With the implication that applying Quine to history will be like trying to translate French into English with the help of a Russian/Chinese dictionary.

This thrusts the philosopher of history back to a very elementary and primordial stage. If historical knowledge is not expressed in terms of theories, what is then its logical form? As far as I'm familiar with contemporary philosophy of history, answers to that question are a matter of assumption rather than the conclusion of well-considered argument. Indeed, there's no lack of such answers. To begin with, there is Ranke's well-known 'zeigen wie es eigentlich gewesen' (to show how it has actually been). Next, the suggestion that historians offer causal explanations of the past. This suggestion has a number of variants; think of Mackie's INUS-conditions, of counterfactual analysis, of explaining the past in terms of Baysean probability, as was so brilliantly proposed by Avi Tucker in his *Our Knowledge of the Past* (2004) and so on. Thirdly, since Schleiermacher there has been an immense variety of hermeneutic interpretations of historical writing, all of them to be located between the extremes of Collingwood, on the one hand, and Gadamer, on the other. Fourthly, one can think of the narrativists, claiming that the historical text as a whole is the vehicle of historical knowledge. Again, there are a number of variants. Some, like Ricoeur and Carr, propose a phenomenological reading of the historical text, while others again, such as Mink and White, prefer a rhetorical or literary approach. Finally, there are the crossovers between these major positions.

Now, in contemporary philosophy of history the causalists talk to causalists, the hermeuticists to hermeneuticists and the narrativists to narrativists. The preliminary question of who is right about historical knowledge is thus abandoned for the subsidiary question of who stands strongest in each individual paradigm. But the protagonists of all paradigms all agree that there exists such a thing as the discipline of historical writing, that there are books and articles written by historians and that these are debated in scientific journals. But each of them projects his own paradigm on that reality and will then see only what he had projected on it already. The practice of history then functions like a mirror making the protagonists of each option recognize themselves as if they were looking in a mirror.

This gets me to the crux of my argument. Suppose we wish to initiate a debate between these paradigms and to ensure it is conducted fruitfully, how can we achieve this? My answer is, basically, that under these circumstances a return to *a priori* argument is inevitable. For we then need, above all, an exposition, as detailed and elaborate as possible of how one of the paradigms (or its sub-paradigms) conceives of historical knowledge and of the essentially semantic question of where we must locate the vehicle of historical knowledge. Now, drawing up such an exposition is, basically, an a priorist deduction of what follows from the choice for the option one prefers. The next stage is to compare all these aprioristically generated accounts of what historical knowledge is with the empirical reality of historical writing and to try to discover which of them presents us with the best fit.

Admittedly, there is no guarantee that in this way the handicap of the mirror-image will be overcome. For a truly unbiased comparison of the different paradigms is unlikely. The only remedy is to continue the a priorist deduction of what is entailed by some paradigm down to the very end. It may even be that such a deduction will finally produce a common ground between some or perhaps all different paradigms, and from where one may work one's way backwards, or upwards again. In this way the sources of disagreement might be identified; and these would then be the obvious point of departure for further discussion. But, again, without a priorist argument one will get nowhere. Next, a priorist argument is used here only to establish what logically follows from the adoption of anyone paradigm in philosophy of history and, hence, definitely not as an attempt to offer a foundation of historical knowledge. Its role is merely auxiliary here – in this way my argument sidesteps Quine's anti-foundationalism. Decisive is not a priorist argument *as such*, but the question which paradigm best fits the actual practice of historical writing, after the most central insight of each of the paradigms has been elaborated – by means of a priorist argument – down to its very last consequences.

As far as I know, philosophers of history have not yet even begun to address this issue. Hence, if one extrapolates Quine's criticism of the analytic–synthetic distinction – with which I feel no need to quarrel in this context – into a total ban on all a priorist argument, one will be clueless when addressing the very elementary issues in philosophy of history I have in mind here. The philosopher of history will then be much like the sea captain hoping to get his ship from point A on the globe to point B without maps, without a compass, without a chronometer and without all the other instruments needed for navigation.

In sum, we will need an Archimedean point in philosophy of history, so that one can draw up from that point, by means of a priorist argument, a conception of historical knowledge and of the semantics of the writing of history. In my previous writings I chose this Archimedean point in the notion of historical representation. But, clearly, this is too vague: for what is meant with the term 'historical representation'? That term will have to be exchanged for something leaving no room for misunderstanding. Think of the geometrician wishing to discuss the circle. Then the mere word 'circle' will not suffice, nor definitions such as 'a curved line' or 'a line dividing all the points in a flat plane in such a way that no point within that line is also without it'. Only a definition such as 'all the points of a flat plane being at the same distance from a certain point P' will do the trick. On the basis of this definition of the circle the geometrician can proceed and discover properties of the circle – by means of a priorist argument – that were not mentioned in the definition. So that's what we would need for historical representation. Taking this into account I propose the following definition: 'A historical representation is the ordered set of all true statements to be found in historical texts as could have been written in the West since the beginning of the nineteenth century.' I add two comments: First, since the days of Plato and Aristotle many theories have been developed on what a true statement is. These theories have no bearing on the problem of historical representation; so let anyone adhere to whatever (well-considered) theory he or she prefers. This is easy to see. There is a logical distinction between a set of statements and these statements, since the latter has the subject/predicate form, whereas the latter has not. The latter is the precinct of *a priori* reflection on historical representation, whereas I am happy to leave the former to the discussion of what has been said in two thousand years of Western philosophy on sentential truth. It follows that we must strictly distinguish between historical research (what is expressed in terms of statements) and historical representation (what is expressed in terms of sets of statements). Whoever fails to respect this distinction sins against Frege's requirement not to confuse matters of logic with matters of psychology.

Why Leibniz?

Self-evidently, the next question is whether this definition of historical representation invites us to adopt a specific variant of a priorist argument and if so, which one this is. This question is not difficult to answer. Leibniz's name immediately comes to mind. First, since Leibniz scholars such as Dillmann, Köhler and Mahnke[2] already pointed out that for no prominent philosopher in the history of Western thought the notion of representation has been of so central importance as for Leibniz. Next, as I argued elsewhere, Leibniz's so-called praedicatum inest subjecto principle is ideally suited for establishing what is entailed by the definition of historical representation presented here. As the principle's name suggests, the idea is that all of a subject's properties can analytically be derived from the notion of the subject. The claim is the logical counterpart of Leibniz's metaphysics stating that the world consists of what I elsewhere referred to as 'strong individuals'.[3] These differ from the kind of (weak) individuals that are not individuated by all and only all of their properties. Obviously, common sense demands us to prefer the weak to the strong individuals. Moreover, the idea of they strong individual also conflicts with the nowadays almost universally accepted thesis of the theory-ladenness of empirical facts, assuming that no individual resists being subsumed under some general law.

However, if historical representation is defined as I did a moment ago, the choice for the strong individual is inevitable. For according to that definition the statements of a historical text do two things. First, what is expressed by them is *ex hypothesi* assumed to be true of the past they are about. This firmly ties a representation to a specific part of the past and prevents it from starting to float freely through the centuries. Second, the nature of a representation is self-referentially or recursively determined by the statements it contains. As a result, the relationship between the representation and its statements repeats Leibniz's 'praedicatum inest subjecto' principle – and in both cases all of a thing's properties can logically be derived from the very notion of that thing. Since Leibniz's account of the individual – called by him a substance or a monad – deviates so widely from modern conceptions of it, whereas it gets to the heart of historical representation, Leibniz's logic and metaphysics seems to be the most suitable instrument available for a further elaboration of a representationalist account of historical writing.

The Metaphysics of Leibnizian and Historical Representation

The two presently dominant theories of representation are the resemblance and the substitution theory of representation. According to the former, a representation resembles what it represents; think of the drawing of a tree and the tree itself. Now, think of a red spot on a map of France representing Paris. This spot does not *resemble* Paris, nevertheless in the practice of mapping and map-reading the red spot is made to function as a cartographic *substitute* of the actual city of Paris. This is why theorists such as Gombrich, Goodman and

Danto prefer to substitution theory to the resemblance theory of representation. It may be that there is more truth in the resemblance theory than the adherents of the substitution theory are willing to allow, so that one had best look for some prudent mix of the two. But both theories agree that the representation (drawing of a tree, red spot on the map) and what it represents (a tree, the city of Paris) are different things. However, in Leibniz's theory of representation, the represented and its representation are identical. Obviously, it is an at first-sight counter-intuitive theory of representation: For why still speak of a represented and its representation if both are identical?

In order to see what Leibniz had in mind here we'd best focus first on his metaphysics. Leibniz's metaphysics is based on two seemingly conflicting assumption. The first one is that the monads are 'windowless': they can only perceive what is within themselves. This is the source of his radical individualism. The second one is that what a monad perceives is the totality of all other monads (constituting together all of the universe), if seen from the perspective of *that* monad. The tension between these two assumptions is taken away by Leibniz by the further assumption that what each windowless monad perceives in its inner self agrees with how all the others perceive their inner selves. The perceptions all monads have of the monadological universe are all in complete agreement with each other. This is what Leibniz calls his principle of pre-established harmony. Thanks to it there is a reality of which all monads have the same perceptions. Leibniz calls this reality the 'phaenomena bene fundata'. It is a merely 'phaenomenal' reality, not to be confused with the actual metaphysical reality of the totality of all the monads. But it is 'bene fundata' – well-founded – since it has its foundation in the monadological universe. Phaenomenal reality is the world *we* perceive while being unaware of metaphysical origin. Leibniz's system is, basically, an attempt to derive from his monadological metaphysics the nature of both the monads and of the world of the 'phaenomena bene fundata' by means of a few logical principles, such as the 'praedicatum inest subjecto' principle we encountered already, the contradiction principle, that of sufficient reason, of the indivisibility of monads, of the identity of indiscernibles and of proportionality. In all of the history of philosophy never a system has been constructed in which metaphysics was so logical and logic so metaphysical.

Leibniz attempt to solve the tension between these two assumptions with an appeal to God's intervention will convince few people. I would not hesitate to see here the main weakness in his system. But the problem mercifully disappears if it is applied to historical writing. The decisive datum here is that that *ex hypothesi* historical representations consist of true statements. Let's assume the validity of the following two principles: (1) true statements[4] are never incompatible with each other and (2) all statements about the world are either true or untrue – *tertium non datur* (*pace* the dialecticians and *n*–valued logic). It follows that whereas Leibniz needed an appeal to God in order to uphold his principle of pre-established harmony, that principle is unproblematically thrown into our lap as soon as we translate his system to historical writing and see his monads as historical representations. It is as if past reality has been so kind and obliging to do for the historian all the infinitely complex computations Leibniz had assigned to God.

But there is one more problem with the system. Leibniz requires us to conceive of the monadological universe as an infinity of monads mirroring themselves in each other, without there being anything outside or beyond this basic metaphysical fact. This almost inevitably invites the complaint that this cannot be since it would reduce the Leibniz's universe to the nonsensical status of a house of mirrors where everything mirrors everything else – but with the all-important qualification that there is nothing to begin or to trigger this endless mirroring process. So if we are prepared to go along with Leibniz's metaphysics we must postulate, in addition to his metaphysics, something existing *outside* and *independently* of this endless mirroring process and that is actually mirrored by the mirrors, just as in a house of mirrors nothing will happen as long as nobody had entered it. A metaphysically upgraded version of the 'phaenomena been fundata' being the obvious candidate; and then 'representational order' has been restored again. For then the world of the 'phaenomena bene fundata' are the 'representeds' and that of the monads that of their representations. However, as we will immediately recognize, this is at odds with Leibniz's claim that (1) there is no reality outside the monads and how they represent the world and (2) that the 'phaenomena bene fundata' must be located in that reality and not outside it. As Cassirer perceptively put it,

> The universe, as represented by the monads, is the sum and the totality of all spatial- temporal phenomona: but precisely these phenomena themselves present to the mind in their order and with their intimate lawlike connections a content and a fundament more certain and solid than could possibly be demanded. Here thought finds its final halt and objective destination. [...] So it is mere self-deception if some metaphysics would pretend to be able to go beyond this phenomena. Hence, Leibnizian philosophy has no answer to offer to the question of why there is this ever-changing manyfold of representations (my translation).[5]

If Leibniz's critics continue to protest and reiterate that there simply *must* be something that is mirrored, discussion will copy that between realists and idealists. Realists always snap at the idealist: 'Don't you see that chair and table over there, so how could you possibly deny that there is a reality outside ourselves?' To which the idealist will reply: 'Of course I see that chair and that table. But you have still not grasped my point when I said "esse est percipi". So it is with Leibniz, though he would probably prefer to say that being is both perceiving and being perceived.

This identity of being and of being perceived is the metaphysical justification of Leibniz's identification of the representation and the represented. As Leibniz sees it, (1) the representation *is* the represented as represented by the representation and (2) the represented is the representation that is represented by that represented. Admittedly, a difficult and mind-boggling conception. Perhaps the following comparison may be helpful. Think of a landscape and a painting of that landscape. It then seems natural to say that the painting is the representation and the landscape the represented. But is it? Or think of two painters painting the same landscape – and when doing so producing two different paintings of the same landscape. Then there must also be two different representeds: each of the two painters projects his own represented on that landscape.[6] But our common thinking about what goes on here fail to do justice to this: we will unproblematically say that the landscape *itself* is the represented and not what the two painters projected on it.

But this could not possibly be correct. For representeds always correspond to representation, and if representations differ, their representeds must do so as well. So our commonsensical belief that the represented and the represented thing are identical is mistaken. This, then, is where Leibniz is, as always, more precise and radical than we ordinarily are ourselves: (1) he differentiates between the landscape and what the painters project on it and (2) subsumes the former in his metaphysics as the 'phaenomena bene fundata'. The traditional picture of a represented reality and its representations that effectively resists an identification of the represented and its representation is then turned upside down, resulting in the Leibnizian picture compelling us to identifying both with each other. And identifying both cannot be rephrased into saying that we then have only representations, or only representeds – for that is not what Leibniz says. Whereas the advocates of the resemblance and the substitution theory of representation argue that the representation and the represented are different, they are identical in the theory of representation proposed by Leibniz. And so it is with historical representation.

Next, Leibniz has a theory of the sign which is the semantic counterpart of the metaphysical argument recounted. But before turning to this, I'll explain why Leibniz's metaphysics agrees so remarkably well with historical representation and why the former can thus be said to give a metaphysical account of the latter. Most revealing here is a passage written by Arthur Danto I quoted already at other occasions in my own writings since it marvellously summarizes in a few most suggestive sentences the gist of Hegel's philosophy while avoiding its pitfalls (by the way, I welcome the implication that this gets me closer to Hegel):

> And something of the same sort is true for the historical period considered as an entity. It is a period solely from the perspective of the historian, who sees it from without; for those who lived in the period it would be just the way life was lived. And asked, afterwards, what is was like to have lived then, they may answer from the outside, from the historian's perspective. From the inside there is no answer to be given; it was simply the way things were. So when the members of a period can give an answer in terms satisfactory to the historian, the period will have exposed its outward surface and in a sense be over, as a period. (Danto 1983: 207)

The idea is that a historical period is a historical period only 'from the outside'; if seen or experienced 'from the inside' it is not. Then it simply is how things are. So something is a historical period only from a perspective or point of view later than it – an at first-sight trivial insight, but which has an unexpected implication for how we must conceive of historical reality. In order to see this, we must start with the recognition that events as such are neither past, present or future; it's only the speaker's temporal position with regard to them that makes so. Hence, events are part of past reality only when we have discovered, decided or concluded – and only absolutely compelling considerations obtain can make us do so! – that we *now* live in a basically later time. But right from that moment past reality exists no longer; it has then died back like a tree's branch from which life withdrew. As long as the past still existed it was not yet *historical* but *actual* reality. Whereas common sense demands us to situate historical reality in the past itself – this is the historical ontology almost universally accepted in contemporary philosophy of history. But with Danto we must recognize, this is not how it is. To put it with a dash of paradox: *historical reality only comes into being when the past no longer exists*. Historical reality exists in its representations only – and we should avoid looking for something behind, or beyond it. This, then, is where Danto and Leibniz agree with each other.

From Metaphysics to Logic and Semantics

I expect that the idea of this identity of the representation and the represented must still sound a bit puzzling. Fortunately, Leibniz translated his metaphysics into a theory of semantics that may dispel the doubts one perhaps still has.

In an absolutely crucial essay in his writings Leibniz comes to discuss a chiliogon, hence a polygon with a thousand equal sides. His argument is that we then have the *word* 'chiliogon' – what he refers to its *notion* – but not its *idea*. He intends to express with this qualification that we have no imagination of a chiliogon, such as you may have of 'a thousand', 'equal' and 'side', or, for that matter, of a triangle, a pentagon or an octagon. You can have an 'idea' of those. Next, the geometrician may make use of these 'ideas' in order to discover the properties of the chiliogon as a *thing* (as an intensional object). This is how the three concepts 'notion', 'idea' and 'things' are related in Leibniz's semantics. Nevertheless, even though we have no 'idea' (or grasp of the meaning) of the word 'chiliogon', we shall go on to use that word when appealing to the 'ideas' of 'thousand', 'equal', 'side' and of 'words' mentioned in already accepted geometrical truth in order to deepen our knowledge of the 'thing' chiliogon. As Leibniz puts it,

> Yet for the most part, especially in a longer analysis, we do not intuit the entire nature of the subject matter at once but make use of signs instead of things, though we usually omit the explanation of these signs in any actually present thought for the sake of brevity, knowing or believing that we have the power to do it. Thus when I think of a chiliogon, or a polygon of a thousand equal sides, I not always consider the nature of a side and of equality and of a thousand (or the cube of ten), but I use these words, whose meaning appears obscurely and imperfectly to the mind, in place of the ideas which I have of them, because I remember that I know the meaning of such words but that their interpretation is not necessary for the present judgment. Such thinking I usually call blind or symbolic; we use it in algebra and in arithmetic, and indeed almost everywhere. (Leibniz 1976: 292)

If we use words like chiliogon for 'blind' or symbolical geometrical argument ('calculatio caeca'), they do not stand for something *else* (e.g. their 'meaning') but for *themselves*. They have then become empty *signs*, where I define the word 'sign' as the symbol that stands for itself. Just as the letters 's', 'm', 'q' or 'r' stand for themselves. These letters do no stand for certain sounds as someone might wish to object. Think of the different ways in which the letter 'a' is pronounced in the English words 'bad', 'all' or in the French 'beau'. If we see the letter 'a' on a piece of paper, it merely says: '*This* is the letter a.'

When discussing the resemblance and substitution theory of representation we found that symbols ordinarily stand for something else than themselves. Hence, we should see sign as symbols whose content had evaporated ever more and more until it was finally reduced to zero. Think of a red spot on a map standing for Paris, representing or symbolizing that city. The distance between the representation and the represented still is huge here. Think next of a ship and a model of that ship: it then is much smaller already. In the case of a painting and the most exact copy that modern science can produce of it the representation and its represented will be almost identical. And then, ultimately, in the sign the representation and its represented have then become identical. However, that does certainly not mean that at that stage these two notions should have lost their meaning; it is true that their extension now is the same, but not their intension. And we need that difference in intension, in order to define the sign – namely, as the symbol that stands for itself. If we had to abandon the notions of the representation and the represented it was impossible to define the sign. Furthermore, the necessity to go on using the two words also locates the notion of the sign within a more encompassing account of representation. So here we find the link between the metaphysics of representation discussed before and Leibniz's semantics of the sign.

But having signs only is not sufficient. Signs should also be part of a sign-system, of an 'alphabet', as it is called nowadays. That sign-system can be as simple as the numbers from 0, 1 to 9, or comprise the letters of the alphabet itself as is the case in letter-algebra as introduced by Vieta in the fifteenth century. Moreover, the alphabet should be such that it allows for 'blind reasoning' with the help of some appropriate algorithm. For example, one can divide and multiply numbers with the decimal system, but not with Roman numbers. This theory of the sign and algorithms was one of Leibniz's greatest discoveries and earned him the honour of often being called the father of mathematical and symbolic logic. Sybille Krämer summarized it as follows:

> Operative writings fulfil a double task: they serve as a medium and, at the same time, as an instrument for mental operations. Put metaphorically, with them languages are employed as a technique. It is this double function, to represent and, at the same time, to calculate with what is being represented, in which the intellectual power of calculation has its roots. What makes them into a 'symbolic machinery', into a mechanical 'amplifier of the intellect' is that the rules of the symbolic operation are not guided by what the symbols mean.[7]

When referring to signs as 'operative writing' Krämer wishes to emphasize that the sign always is something we can write down, something having a distinct physical form on paper that cannot be exchanged a confused with other such signs. Leibniz's blind calculation always requires something *with which* we can calculate. In the absence of signs the algorithms of arithmetic, and of other variants of mathematics, there is simply nothing to go on if one wanted to perform a certain calculation; calculation would then be impossible. But as soon as we have signs and an appropriate algorithm we can calculate with the signs regardless of what the signs *mean* – where 'meaning' is understood to be something that necessarily differs from what it is the meaning of. Or, to put it more poignantly and in any case more correctly: in that case the signs are meaningless. Indeed, their meaninglessness is not a handicap but the very guarantee of the correct results of blind calculation.

Now, my claim is that Leibniz's argument recounted just now enables us to establish what the *Naturwissenschaften* and the *Geisteswissenschaften* – that is historical representation – have in common and from where they move into different directions. If we conceive of the sign as a written symbol standing for, or representing itself, there's no difference between mathematics and historical representation. In order to see this, I propose to discern between two functions of texts expressing historical representations. In other words, between the text *as such* and, next, as the vehicle of historical knowledge. We have to do with the text *as text* when saying, for example, that it has a certain title, consists of ten chapters, that sentence number x in the text is sentence s and so on. *As such* the text is a symbol, albeit an unusually complex one – and, moreover, a symbol standing for itself and, hence, a sign. The second function of the sign manifests itself when we say things such as that for certain reasons this text does or does not contribute to our knowledge of historical reality. Neither in mathematics nor in historical representation are any changes allowed once the form of the sign has been fixed by means of a self-referentially defined description. The objection that in history, as opposed to arithmetic and mathematics, omitting from or adding some sentences to a historical text will make little or no difference because this will leave the text's *meaning* unaffected (Ankersmit 2018: 778, 479) fails straightaway since historical texts, *as signs*, *have* no meaning. Surely, signs have properties – the sign for zero looks like a circle (unless different conventions have been agreed upon) and a historical has the property of consisting of a specific set of sentences (which is not a matter of convention, by the way) – but having a meaning is not one of them.

Making up for this will also compel a more accurate interpretation of the phrase 'the meaning of the text'. Since the text as text is a sign and, hence, cannot be said to have a meaning, that phrase can only stand for the meanings we project on, or associate with, the historical text *as sign*. I deliberately say meaning(s) in the plural in order to highlight one more misleading aspect of the phrase 'the meaning of the text': apart from mistakenly suggesting the text to have a meaning it is also misleading when implying that there should be only one such meaning. But as I argued elsewhere a text's meaning is intertextual and always co-determined by the meanings attributed to other historical texts in the way suggested by Saussure (Ankersmit 2012: 201, 142–53). Consequently, we could only attribute to a historical text *as text* a fixed and unchanging meaning after all possible texts about the past have been written. The sign then *has* a meaning as the words in a dictionary have a meaning.

This, then, is the common ground of mathematics, the sciences and historical writing. But from here both move into different directions. The notion of 'meaning' is our clue here: mathematics can thrive thanks to the absence of meaning as signs and algorithms are sufficient for the mathematician and discussions of meaning could only lead one astray. Whereas such discussions about meaning are the historian's guide to historical knowledge. Nevertheless, even here a certain parallelism can still be observed. Mathematics knows signs such as the number π, the natural logarithm e, the infinite, imaginary numbers, complex numbers and so on; all of them are tied to logarithms for their proper use. Their introduction was conditional for the development of mathematics. Though, admittedly, the differences outweigh the similarities by far, the same could yet be said about the historian's signs. For their evolution can also be interpreted as the development of ever better signs – better in the sense that representational meanings can be grafted on them furthering an ever successful conception of historical reality. However, whereas the use of signs is ruled by logarithms, signs are the vehicle of meaning in historical representation. This gap is unbridgeable.

Historical Rationality

Let's now turn to the question whether Leibniz's philosophy may shed some new insight on the issue of historical rationality. Several answers to that question can be given, as it seems to me – all of them having in common being non-epistemological. I restrict myself here to what is, in this context, the most important one. Leibniz has a fascination for maxima and minima making him unique among the august group of the ten to fifteen great philosophers in the history of Western thought to which he undoubtedly belongs. This fascination announces itself already in his well-known claim that God decided to create 'the best possible world'. See it this way: God disposed of certain means to create the universe, but an unrestrained appeal to one of those means would be detrimental of what could be achieved by one or more other means – and vice versa. Put differently, the use of these means did not always and necessarily mutually reinforce that of others; on the contrary, an ill-considered use of one of them might undo what could be achieved with the help of others. Perfection thus goes overboard with Leibniz and is exchanged for a (merely) optimal us of the means one has at one's disposal. This is what has been called Leibniz's 'economy principle' (Vogl 2016: 40 ff.).

Leibniz had this fascination for maxima and minima for both a metaphysical reason – the principle of continuity – and a mathematical one – his calculus. I leave aside the question how these two hang together and focus on the latter. Now, the reader will recall from secondary school that differential calculus allows one to calculate the local maxima and minima of a function by establishing where the derivative of that function has the value zero. And we move away from maxima and minima where the value of the derivate function approaches the infinite (either plus or minus). The next crucial step in Leibniz argument is his move from monad of substance to function – a development recorded already in Ernst Cassirer's book *Substanzbegriff und Funktionsbegriff* of 1910. The move need not surprise since the monad is the series of representations it has of the universe from the day of its creation down to the end of the world. So there always is a relation between each phase of its 'life' and the representation it will then have of the universe – in this way the latter is a function of the former. Leibniz speaks here of the 'lex series', that is the law of the succession of the states in which the monad finds itself. By the way, Leibniz's move from substance to function is the most important one, since it clears the road for an overcoming of the limitations of Aristotelian logic by making room for the logic of relations needed for an account of modern science. It seems that Leibniz was not aware of this himself.

Instead of addressing this admittedly most crucial issue, we'd better turn to the question what the foregoing implies for historical representation. But before getting to this, one obstacle has to be removed. It could be objected that the move from Leibniz to historical representation could never be made since Leibniz's system is a metaphysical and logical account of God's creation as it is given to us, while the historian faces the difficult task of what form he should give to his monads, that is, to his representations of historical reality. The objection is correct. But, in fact, this is a matter of having 'to bite the bullet': the position of the historian is not unlike that of God in Leibniz's system. Indeed, the historian 'creates' historical reality (though not the past!) by means of the representations he offers of it. I recall to mind here the observation that historical reality comes into being in the form of its representations. Three answers can be given to the question what Leibniz's calculus and his notion of the differential quotient may tell us about historical rationality – one answer concerns historical writing and the other historical reality. With regard to the former issue two quotes are instructive:

> It follows from the supreme perfection of God that he has chosen the best possible plan in producing the universe, a plan which combines the greatest variety together with the greatest order; with situation, place, and time arranged in the best way possible; with the greatest effect produced by the simplest means; with the most power, the most knowledge, the greatest happiness and goodness in created things which the universe would allow. For as all possible things have a claim to existence in God's understanding in proportion to their perfection, the result of all these claims must be the most perfect actual world which is possible. Without this it would be impossible to give a reason why things have gone as they have rather than otherwise.[8]

And elsewhere Leibniz writes:

> Some general remarks can be made, however, about the ways of providence in the government of affairs. It can be said, then, that he who acts perfectly is like an excellent geometrician who knows how to find the best construction of a problem; or as good architect who makes the most advantageous use of the space and the capital intended for a building, leaving nothing which offends or which lacks the beauty of which it is capable; or a good family head who makes such use of his holdings that there is nothing uncultivated and barren; or a skilled machinist who produces his work by the easiest process that can be chosen; or a learned author who includes the greatest number of subjects in the smallest possible volume. (Leibniz 1976: 305, 306)

When isolating those elements from these quotes that are applicable to historical writing and representation Leibniz's criteria for historical rationality can be summed as follows: the best representation is the one which succeeds in combining a maximum of variety with a maximum of order, a maximum of effect with a minimum of means, a maximum of unity within a maximum of diversity or the greatest number of subjects in the smallest possible volume. When trying to satisfy this principle of historical rationality the historian will always have to steer a careful middle-of-the road between two or more mutually opposing principles. The historian may drown his readers in a mass of historical facts. He can also restrict himself to the formulation of some historical claim or major thesis. Both are unsatisfactory. In the former case the historian's readers will ask themselves what message the historian actually wanted to convey with his text. In the latter, the reader will wish to know why he should allow himself to be convinced by some such major thesis and, hence, wish for more detail. In this way the pendulum between thesis and content will always swing back and forth.

In continuation with this, Leibniz also has a suggestion for what the historian should focus on in his representations of historical reality. When discussing meaning in the previous section, we found that the contours of historical meaning and, hence, of historical reality are the products of the interactions of historical representations. Hence, no historian addressing a certain historical topic can afford to disregard where these maxima and minima can be found in these previous representations. This will be, for him, where in historical reality 'things really happen' and what, therefore, must be the focus of his attention, at least for the time being. For the historian will in all likelihood hope to show that 'things really happened' at a place at least slightly different from what was, until now, common wisdom. If not, why write a new book on a certain topic? And then the differential quotient is, again, decisive. Where it is zero – hence, where we can find the maxima and minima – is where 'things really happen'. On the contrary, where the differential quotient approaches to the infinite (either plus or minus), the curve whose gradient the differential quotient describes, will come ever closes to a straight line. Here is no change anymore; here 'history' has come to a standstill. As Leibniz puts it:

> For as a lesser evil is a kind of good, even so a lesser good a kind of evil if it stands in the way of a greater good; and there would be something to correct in the actions of God if it were possible to do better. *And as in mathematics, when there is no maximum nor minimum, in short nothing distinguished, everything is done equally, or when that is not possible nothing at all is done*: so it may be said likewise in respect of perfect wisdom, which is no less orderly than mathematics, that if there were not the best (optimum) among all possible worlds, God would not have produced any.[9]

So, Leibniz explicitly links here himself maxima and minima to decisive change.

I add, finally, three comments: My argument is not that differential calculus itself is somewhere at the basis of historical representation, but that differential calculus has its counterpart both in the writing of history and in our conception of historical change. Next, I do not claim anything particularly deep or revealing with these criteria for historical rationality. On the contrary, anyone only superficially familiar with the writing of history will immediately recognize what I have in mind with these criteria. Even more so, the less obvious and self-evident these criteria would be, the more reservations I would have about them. Claims about the nature of a discipline regarded with amazement and disbelief by that discipline's practitioners tend to be short-lived.

On the other hand, the fact that this account will in all likelihood immediately appeal to both practising historians and philosophers of history – insofar as the latter are willing to look at history without unhelpful philosophical prejudices – does not in the least diminish the importance of the criteria of historical rationality expounded here. On the contrary, one need only imagine what would be left of historical writing and representation without them! Both historical reality and historical writing would disintegrate into an incoherent and incomprehensible chaos. Thirdly, in this chapter, I derived by a priorist argument from an a priorist definition of historical knowledge an account as complete and detailed as possible of historical debate and of the criteria of historical rationality. Again, these criteria are not very surprising – nevertheless, abandoning them would mean not only the end of historical rationality but also the end of history as discipline. So much, then, for the pragmatist's dogma of anti-apriorism.

Conclusion: Where the Extremes Meet

This chapter has been an attempt to clarify the nature of historical knowledge and of historical rationality. My claim was that the notion of 'historical representation' gives us the best grasp on that problem. No philosopher from both the past and the present is of more interest when addressing the issue of representation than Leibniz. Representation is the heart of Leibniz's philosophical system. Moreover, I've tried to show that Leibniz's conception of the monad's representation of the world and of the 'phaenomena bene fundata' agrees in all relevant aspects with historical representation and with how we must conceive of historical reality, as different from the past. Historical reality emerges when the past no longer exists.

Our conclusion must be that in spite of their immense differences historical writing, on the one hand, and mathematics and the sciences, on the other, share a common ground. We could never find out about this common ground by restricting one's focus on the practice of science only. Such a narrow focus blinds one to the semantic and logical aspects of science that are decisive for an adequate understanding of both science and history.

5

Postmodern Theory with Historical Intent

A Deconstructive Approach to the Past

Ethan Kleinberg

We are living in a moment of thin historicization. What I mean by this is the tendency to use historical narrative structure or context as an explanatory scaffold with little or no reflection on the way that the historical narrative or context in question was constructed or the theoretical assumptions that underpin such a construction. As such our moment is decidedly untheoretical. What's more, and perhaps counter-intuitive, is that the academic world and disciplines have become so thoroughly historicized in this way that the general public and students in our universities no longer see a reason to turn to history as a discipline or a tool of critique. One could look to trends of declining enrollments in departments of history throughout the United States, but I think this point is also obvious in the new historicism of literary studies or the inclusion of history as one means of approach to area or interdisciplinary studies. One could also point to a relatively recent 'historical account' of the famous 1914 Christmas truce that appeared in the *Wall Street Journal*, authored by Stanford professor of biology, neurology and neurosurgery Robert M. Sapolsky (Sapolsky 2014). In Sapolsky's account, the key to understanding the truce lies in an understanding of evolutionary rituals of cooperation. The issue here is not to address the substance of Sapolsky's contribution. Instead, I use this example to point out the way that Sapolsky's 'historical' intervention renders the disciplinary historian redundant and unnecessary.

As other areas of academia have widened their zone of engagement by historicizing their fields, disciplinary historians have narrowed theirs. The current emphasis on mimetic representation of past events, that is on making the objective accurate representation of past events the *raison d'être* of the discipline, has led history into what appears to be a self-imposed obsolescence – the increasingly narrow zone of experts speaking to and writing for other experts. What's more, this quasi-theological notion of realistic representation requires that the historian take up a 'de-historicized' position as it were from which to neutrally observe and represent past events 'as they really happened' from a God's eye view as it were. In 1969, Reinhart Koselleck emphasized the irony that 'history pure and simple' (*Geschichte Schlechtin*) or 'history itself' (*Geschichte Selber*) did not originally refer to the quasi-theological notion of realistic representation but instead signalled the need for theory in history precisely to address the historicized entanglement of the historian with their object of study (Koselleck 2002: 4). But today, the quasi-theological notion of realistic representation is the dominant theoretical position of most conventional historians and most history departments. I call this position 'ontological realism' which I define as a commitment to history as an endeavour concerned with events assigned to a specific location in space and time that are in principle observable and as such are regarded as fixed and immutable.[1] Here the historian accepts that there is a possibility for epistemological uncertainty as to our understanding of a past event, but this is mitigated by the ontological certainty that the event happened in a certain way at a certain time. Central to this position is a commitment to empirical data that serves as something of a false floor to hold it. In the end, getting the past 'right' is a question of historical method. This is where we see how the rapprochement between our historical condition and historical methods is predicated on the de-historicized characterization of our current practices as contained within a permanently enduring present that fosters a similarly misconceived representation of a permanently enduring past.

So one question we need to ask is what holds the ontological certainty of the past event given the possibility of epistemological uncertainty in recounting that event? Most conventional historians either avoid or defer this question working purely on the assumption that method is sufficient to bring the past into the present. It is this emphasis on the de-historicized presence of the past in the present that allows 'history' to function as a contextual explanatory scaffold but only so long as one does not question it. Thus, in effect, the current strategy of de-historicization avoids the problem of historicism only by ignoring it. The irony is that it is precisely the de-historicized variant of disciplinary history that is the basis for the thin historicism which other disciplines and academic units have appropriated rendering the discipline of history increasingly redundant and obsolete.

In this thin version, it appears that 'historical thinking' is pervasive as a master key deployed to unlock the treasures of other academic analyses. In actuality, we no longer think historically at all because these endeavours lack the critical understanding of how historical narratives are constructed or inquiry into the underlying assumptions that hold them up. This undertaking should be the job of historians and philosophers of history, but the desire to pursue such issues is lacking. This has opened the door to pundits and politicians who have taken advantage of the lack of critical reflection to their own ends. In this way the academic emphasis on mimetic representations of past events as they 'really happened' has had cultural and political ramifications as well. The very positive expansion of subjects and areas deemed worthy of historical investigation is undercut by the way these challenges to prior historical narratives rely on the same thinly historicized conceits as those they seek to engage or replace. Innovations in, and expansion of, subjects and types of evidence have led to a 'crisis for orthodox history by multiplying not only stories but subjects, and by insisting that histories are written from fundamentally different – indeed irreconcilable – perspectives or standpoints, none of which is complete or completely "true"' because they rely on the view that each of these accounts is a correction that presents the event as it happened (Scott 2005: 201). This then leads to the increased specialization of fields which reduces the audience and impact of these accounts as well. Here, keep in mind that I am not taking issue with the increasingly heterogeneous subjects of historical analysis but the strikingly homogenous understanding and methods by which the histories of these subjects are recounted. If the criteria is mimetic representation of the past as it really happened, either only one account can be true or somehow all must be true. In the hands of pundits and politicians, this perspectivalism has provided cover for the pick-your-own-truth culture, exemplified by Donald Trump's 'very fine people on both sides'. These 'post-truthers' operate in decidedly bad faith and do their scholarship poorly in regard to the rules of the guild, but the one-to-one correlation they assert between the evidence they present and the facts or truths they claim is the same as that of many conventional scholars: alternative but equivalent. The confederate statue is the past event, not a representation, and to tear it down is to destroy the past itself.

Here again we see the emphasis on ontological realism and the presence of the past in the present. But the past event cannot be made present and thus any reappearance is the untimely visitation of a ghost. This leads to a more troubling question about the category of ontology itself and specifically the ontology or hauntology of the past. I use the term 'hauntology' to expose the ways that historians take the spectral haunting absent past and silently replace it with a representation of it that appears to have the properties and essence of a present object (in French 'ontologie' and 'hantologie' carry the same pronunciation). The hauntological approach is one that is attuned to the way the past, like a ghost, is both present and absent. But it also allows one to imagine a narrative of multiple or seemingly conflicting pasts that stand at odds with the current trend of thin historicization and its obsession with mimetic reproduction.

But if we are to consider the past as akin to the ghost and history as a hauntological endeavour (or as holding a latent ontology for those of you who are squeamish), then it is worth asking what it is that troubles us about the ghost? In *Specters of Marx*, Derrida asks '*What* is the ghost? What is the *effectivity* or the *presence* of the specter, that is, of what seems to remain as ineffective, virtual, insubstantial as a simulacrum?' (Derrida 2006: 10). The ghost or spectre is troubling precisely because it is the past come again but emptied of its physical properties and disobedient to the rules of time and space. 'One cannot control its comings and goings because it *begins by coming back*.' What is troubling and powerful about the ghost is not that it is present (which it is) but the ways that its presence disturbs all the spatio-temporal categories by which we have come to make sense of the world around us. The ghost troubles both time and space and thus one cannot make sense of it.

For Derrida, the porous and disturbing nature of the past that haunts us provokes us to question the historical ground on which we stand and the borders by which we divide past, present and future. We cannot actually say what the ghost means. Like the past it has no ontological properties but nonetheless it *is*.[2]

Most conventional historians are in this sense *ontological realists* in their research, writing and teaching, even if they also claim to be epistemic sceptics, epistemic relativists, or even if they feel that there's a great deal of hermeneutic entanglement between the historian and the past. But, as Louis Mink observed in 'On the Writing and Rewriting of History' from 1972, such a belief 'in the actuality and immutability of the past is based on a cluster of unconscious and invalid analogies' (Mink 1987: 93). For Mink these included such analogies as between temporal distance and spatial difference, between memory and perception, or between a past present and a present past. To these I would add the faulty analogy between the formal narrative presentation of a past 'as it happened' and the 'ontological reality' of that past. According to Mink, the ability to hold these analogies is indicative of the incompatible views we hold about the reality of the past: about the relation of historical knowledge to its object whatever that be and about the relevance of historical knowledge to the possibilities of action which lie before us.

Mink sums up this paradox by articulating the way historians hold the simultaneous views that 'everything which belonged to the action when it was taking place in its own present belongs to it now that it is past' alongside the conflicting realization 'that the past isn't there at all' (Mink 1987: 93). Mink sees this paradox as the motivating force behind all serious philosophy of history. I see it as proximate to what I refer to as the latent ontology of a past that is and isn't and one of the most salient values of a deconstructive approach to history is that it draws attention to the ways historians often maintain the teleological power of a principle whose possibility they refuse. But it bears asking as to the motivation that allows one to hold such incompatible views?

In 'History and Fiction as Modes of Comprehension', Mink reflects on why some stories bear repeating and I think his response to this question will help us gain purchase on the previous one. Mink tells us that some stories bear repeating

> because they aim at producing and strengthening the act of understanding in which actions and events, although represented as occurring in the order of time, can be surveyed as it were in a single glance as bound together in an order of significance, a representation of the *totum simul* (that Boethius regarded as God's knowledge of the world) which we can never more than partially achieve. (Mink 1987: 56)

Latency is removed from the equation as is the surprise of the unexpected possible. One can of course imagine or read a history as if one did not know the outcome, one might not know the outcome, and thus one follows the story from beginning to end. But in the 'configurational comprehension of a story which one *has followed*, the end is connected with the promise of the beginning as well as the beginning with the promise of the end, and the necessity of the backwards reference cancels out, so to speak, the contingency of the forward references' (italics in original). The indeterminacy of the future is cancelled out by the given-ness of the past that is grasped in the present. Here, 'to comprehend temporal succession means to think of it in both directions at once, and then time is no longer the river which bears us along but the river in an aerial view, upstream and downstream in a single survey' (Mink 1987: 57). This aerial view can be considered as a God's eye view or that of La Place's omniscient scientist in his *Philosophical Essay on Probabilities*. Each of these points to the issue of temporality and the desire for a static snapshot that arrests the temporal flow. On such a reading, and I would argue that by and large this is the reading of most conventional historians, time is never out of joint and assuming one has the right methodological tools, one can master the past and recount it in the form of a realist narrative. This is the quasi-theological notion of realistic representation that underpins thin historicization.

If I may modify a passage from Derrida's 'Freud and the Scene of Writing', this ontological realist position is dangerous, 'not because it refers to writing, but because it presupposes [that the past exists as] a text which would be already there, immobile: the serene presence of a statue, of a written stone or archive whose significant content might be harmlessly transported into the milieu of a different language [or time]' (Derrida 1978: 211). The danger lies in the assumption that there is an unerasable and indelible trace left in the past by which the ontological reality of the past can be determined. But 'an unerasable trace is not a trace, it is a full presence, an immobile and incorruptible substance, a son of God, a sign of parousia and not a seed, that is, a mortal germ' (Derrida 1978: 230). The stability afforded to identity is not the property of a mortal being who exists in and through the indeterminacy of time, such a fixed, immutable quality belongs to a God, or to the dead, and here I think we gain purchase on the force and seduction of ontological realism and thin historicization. The fiction of a stable past is the fiction of a stable present. Indeed, I would say that it is the meaning we don't or can't find in the present that thin historicization claims to find in the past.

But such a narrative cannot account for the latent ontology of the past or the ways that past possibles condition our possible pasts. What I mean by this is that our knowledge of the past is conditioned by what presents itself to us both in terms of its remains and in terms of our reception. The limits of what we are willing to accept as 'past possibles' conditions what we are willing to accept as possible pasts. That which lies beyond this realm appears to us as simply impossible, like a ghost. But the ghost is only impossible insofar as it is a remainder of a different time and place and its untimely presence disturbs us. The latent past is not the impossible, but it was possible and it did happen though perhaps it has been rendered inconceivable or unimaginable and thus exiled beyond the realm of what now appears as possible. It is when what lies latent appears, returns, that history is haunted and we are confronted with the possibility that our understanding of the past is only partial. This partial past is one possible past to be sure but one that does not account or budget for a host of past possibles that have been suppressed, effaced, lost or forgotten, and these are the ghosts and spectres that haunt us in the present. The history of Sleepy Hollow is not only that of charming rustic settlers prone to tales of the supernatural but also and importantly that of a violent dispossession of Native Americans. When what is latent of the past becomes manifest it opens new historical possibilities. Of course, these remnants of the past are only 'new' in the sense that they can now appear within the realm of the possible as a possible past thus altering history itself.

This is all to say there is no 'past' to be recovered in the form of the realist narrative or as a determinate object of history because that is not the structure of the past. This is neither the ontology nor the reality of the past and thus I think there is light to be gleaned in thinking of the past itself as blinking in and out of our existence like a Christmas light. It certainly gives me occasion for a visit from the Ghost of Christmas Past in Charles Dickens's *A Christmas Carol*.

Dickens describes the Ghost of Christmas Past as

> a strange figure – like a child: yet not so like a child as an old man, viewed through some supernatural medium, which gave him the appearance of having receded from view, and being diminished to a child's proportions. Its hair ... was white with age; and yet the face had not a wrinkle in it, and the tenderest bloom was on the skin.

Here one can imagine this spirit as the object of history: an aged object from the past transported to the present by the historical author who imbues it with youth and the 'tenderest bloom of the skin' even while signalling its age: the whiteness of its hair. It is in this way that the historian presents the 'old man' of the past event as a 'child' as though through some supernatural medium.

'But the strangest thing about [the Ghost] was, that from the crown of its head there sprung a bright clear jet of light' though it also possessed a 'great extinguisher for a cap'.

> Even this though ... was *not* its strangest quality. For as its belt sparkled and glittered now in one part and now in another, and what was light one instant, at another time was dark, so the figure itself fluctuated in its distinctness: being now a thing with one arm, now with one leg, now with twenty legs, now a pair of legs without a head, now a head without a body: of which dissolving parts, no outline would be visible in the dense gloom wherein they melted away. And in the very wonder of this, it would be itself again; distinct and clear as ever. (Dickens 1843: 39)

The past here is no fixed and immutable object but a fluctuating bundle of physical and temporal contradictions. Young and old, near and far, light and dark – a figure that is at one moment indecipherable and in the next 'distinct and clear as ever'. Its strangest quality is never strange enough and here one must wonder what if anything is gleaned by the tautological assertion 'it would be itself again' that prefaces the statement 'distinct and clear as ever', the ontological realist's dream.

But I want to go back to the quality of the Ghost that is and is not the strangest thing about it. This is the bright clear jet of light that sprung from the Ghost's head though I also note the 'great extinguisher for a cap, which it now held under its arm'. The strangeness of this light evokes images of Freud's category of the 'uncanny' or 'unheimlich' as 'the name of everything that ought to have remained hidden and secret ... and has become visible'. The past is there, all of it, every possibility lying latent though vying to burst forth. Upon encountering the Ghost, Scrooge had a special desire 'to see the Spirit in his cap; and begged him to be covered', to keep hidden and secret that which ought to remain so but the Ghost would not comply. Nevertheless, after a long evening of strange encounters Scrooge could no longer bear to be haunted by the past and began to wrestle with it:

> In the struggle, if that can be called a struggle in which the Ghost with no visible resistance on its own part was undisturbed by any effort of its adversary, Scrooge observed that its light was burning high and bright; and dimly connected that with its influence over him, he seized the extinguisher cap and by a sudden action pressed it down upon its head. (Dickens 1843: 62)

On my reading, ontological realism bears an uncanny resemblance to the extinguisher cap and the historian who wields it to Scrooge. For like Scrooge, the historian who wrestles with the past does so with an adversary that offers no visible resistance on its own part and is undisturbed by any effort on the part of the historian. The disturbed remains haunt us and not vice versa. But more important is Scrooge's 'sudden action' in response to his observation that the light of the past exerted influence over him. The conjuring trick of ontological realism is that it allows the historian to exert his or her own influence over the past, by restricting its light and all that its light reveals, pressing down and concealing the past possibles that expose other possible pasts in the same way that Scrooge pressed the extinguisher cap down upon the Ghost of Christmas Past. 'But though Scrooge pressed it down with all his force, he could not hide the light: which streamed from under it, in an unbroken flood upon the ground' (Dickens 1843: 63). You cannot kill a ghost. The past continues to haunt history.

Derrida links the ghost to the trace and to *différance* thus challenging notions of absolute priority or absolute foundations. I want to link *différance* to the project of history. Derrida writes: 'If the word "history" did not in and of itself convey the motif of a final repression of difference, one could say that only differences can be "historical" from the outset and in each of their aspects' (Derrida 1972a: 12; 1982: 11). History, as conventionally conceived, is precisely the repression of differences in an attempt to generate a singular intelligible narrative that necessarily overwrites those aspects that confuse, confound or contradict that narrative. Derrida presents *différance* as the counter to this repression offering instead the 'playing moment that "produces" these differences, these effects of difference' (Derrida 1972a: 12; 1982: 11). Thus what I am suggesting is that we imagine doing history with *différance* in mind, crafting the playing moment that produces these effects of difference.

To be sure, the purpose of history is to make the past legible and intelligible, and to offer a *poros* or pathway through the chaotic aporia of the past. And insofar as history serves to make the past legible in the present it should be seen as a writing whose function is to make present what is absent, to render legible that which would otherwise be illegible.[3] But as such it is 'a mark that subsists, one which does not exhaust itself in the moment of its inscription and which can give rise to an iteration in the absence and beyond the presence of the empirically determined subject who, in a given context, has emitted or produced it' (Derrida 1972c: 377; also in 1988: 9). Thus even the most methodologically sound and precise historical investigation is not only a necessarily partial investigation bound by the epistemological horizon of the historian's own time and place but also 'carries within it a force that breaks with its context, that is with the collectivity of presences organizing the moment of its inscription' (Derrida 1972c: 377; also in 1988: 9). This is not only because the historical work is itself haunted by the past it cannot contain but also because future historians can 'perhaps come to recognize other possibilities in [the historical work] by inscribing or grafting it onto other chains' (Derrida 1972c: 377; also in 1988: 9). The force of this rupture means that history can never rest in peace. But the rupture can also be seen as an incision that is the emergence of a mark that serves to make visible the various directions of space, providing orientation in an expanse previously devoid of any landmarks. This follows one sense that Derrida ascribes to the verb *différer* as 'temporalization and spacing, the becoming-time of space and the becoming-space of time, the "originary" constitution of time and space' (Derrida 1972a: 8; 1982: 8). This is a key aspect of the historical endeavour that seeks to situate past events in a specific time and place as best as one can based on the sources and evidence. In doing so the historian posits the coordinates of time and space through periodization or geographical demarcation. But lest the *poros* become the aporia we must recognize that the emergence of this mark 'derives from no category of being, whether present or absent ... for what is put into question is precisely the quest for a rightful beginning, an absolute point of departure, a principal responsibility' (Derrida 1972a: 6; 1982: 6).

For Sarah Kofman, 'one speaks of a *poros* (path) when it is a matter of blazing a trail where no trail exists or could exist properly speaking, of crossing what is impassable ... an *apeiron* which it is impossible to cross from end to end' (Kofman 1983: 18). The *poros* and aporia are necessarily linked, and this is the nature of the trail that the historian seeks to forge from a position in the present to the event in the past. But Kofman also reminds us that the term

> *poros* should not be confused with *odos* which is a general term that designates any sort of road or path. *Poros* refers solely to a sea or river route, to a passage that is opened across a chaotic expanse and which transforms it into an ordered and qualified space by introducing differentiated routes, making visible the various directions of space, providing orientation in an expanse previously devoid of any landmarks. (Kofman 1983: 18)

I see this as a particularly apt metaphor both for the past and for the endeavour of the historian who aspires to chart a route or passage over an unruly and at times indistinguishable expanse that churns beneath his or her endeavours. Indeed, most of the past recedes into the ocean leaving no discernible trace like the wake of a passing ship or an item lost overboard. If one comes along in a short enough amount of time one could follow the wake of the first passing ship or one that came soon after retracing their route even as evidence of the prior ships dissipate. Then again, at any given moment a sudden surge could bring evidence of past remains to the surface even as it disturbs or destroys the wakes that previously served as marks for orientation. More often, the historian works from a greater temporal distance relying partly on materials 'still immediately present, hailing from times which we are seeking to understand (*Überreste*/Remains), partly whatever ideas human beings have obtained and transmitted to be remembered (*Quellen*/Sources), partly things wherein both these forms of materials are combined (*Denkmäler*/Monuments)' (Droysen 1957: 332–3, §21; 1893: 18, §21). We could think of these as sea charts, buoys, shipwrecks or reefs that serve as the basis for navigation though the sources themselves may very well be the wakes of past ships: 'Has anyone ever thought that we have been tracking something other than tracks themselves to be tracked down?' (Derrida 1972a: 26; 1892: 25)

And as we saw with Dickens's Ghost of Christmas Past, the past itself is the most 'mobile, changeable and polymorphous of all spaces, a space where any path that has been traced can be 'obliterated' and as such is analogous to Hesiod's Tartarus (with the image of chaos itself). … In this infernal, chaotic confusion, the *poros* is the way out, the last resort of sailors and navigators, the stratagem which allows them to escape the impasse, the aporia, and the anxiety that accompanies it' (Kofman 1983: 19–20). The chaotic and polymorphous nature of the past provokes anxiety and in response to such chaos we seek an ordered way out. But here we must pay close attention to the way that the paths historians construct to bring order and intelligibility to the chaotic expanse; that is the past can themselves become impasses when a historical narrative precludes other possible voices, vantages or viewpoints. The pathway forged as an escape itself becomes a trap restricting one from straying off the straight and narrow ordained route from one point to another. The *poros* becomes an aporia restricting us from accessing other possible pasts and limiting what we can imagine just as Scrooge wielded the extinguisher cap in an attempt to restrict the light emanating from the Ghost of Christmas Past. Again we see the conjuring trick of ontological realism as the conventional historian exerts his or her influence over the past, by restricting not only our path but also the realm of past possibles that expose other possible pasts.

When E. P. Thompson wrote *The Making of the English Working Class* in 1963 it was not as though the working class had no past prior to this work. Indeed, Thompson states his intention to make explicit 'the agency of the working people' and 'the degree to which they contributed, by conscious efforts, to the making of history' (Thompson 1966: 12). What's more Thompson's work took issue with an understanding of history wherein 'only the successful (in the sense of those whose aspirations anticipated subsequent evolution) are remembered' and 'the blind alleys, the lost causes, and the losers themselves are forgotten' (Thompson 1966). Thompson sought to activate the latent ontology of this forgotten past by actualizing it through the project and writing of history. Thompson cautions that 'the working class did not rise like the sun at an appointed time', but nevertheless the working class had not appeared before as a topic of systematic historical investigation (Thompson 1966: 9). This itself is indicative of the restricted possible pasts available at that time. But the previous historical accounts had been haunted by the making of the English working class all along as had works of literature and art.

In one way for Thompson, it was precisely the presence of the 'owning class' that made the absence of the working one so glaringly visible. The absence of the working class in prior historical accounts haunted those histories. This imaginative reconceptualization of past possible actors and events rendered visible evidence in the official records of the ruling class that became a key source for Thompson's own historical account of the working class. Here again, it was not that this evidence did not exist previously, but it lay beyond the realm of what was imagined as a possible past. Once Thompson opened the possibility of a systematic history from the bottom up, a host of past possibles was made available as historical evidence through stories, folk art or song.

But we must also be aware that that while Thompson's achievement represented an imaginative leap that opened up a whole new realm of historical investigation it was not a theoretical reconsideration of history and thus resembles prior historical accounts in terms of method and narrative if not content. The limitations of Thompson's creative imagining are readily apparent when one considers his inability to imagine the possible past of women as historical actors in his account. To be sure, the limits of Thompson's creative imagination were bound by the possibilities open to him in his own time and space, but the theoretical limits of how he conceptualized 'history' and the 'past' are what allowed the *poros* he divined that led to a systematic history of the working class to itself became an aporia restricting access to other possible pasts. As this new pathway to the past became increasingly well travelled, other pathways were neglected, while still other possible pathways were left unexplored. One could argue for similar results in other fields such as women's history, history of gender and subaltern or postcolonial studies. Pioneering historians in each of these fields wrestled free the hidden or repressed and thus latent past to make possible the histories of groups and events that had previously resided as ghosts haunting the dominant historical narrative. Each of these histories presented a new opening, but because they were offered as conventional ontological realist histories, each opening was also a closure. And here we arrive at the increased specialization which reduces the field of exploration and leads to the perspectivalism of competing truth claims and ultimately 'post-truth'.

The simple inversion of the hierarchy arrests the possibility of a full deconstruction at the moment when what was absent is made present and in doing so locks the historical narrative in a closed system. This is what leads to the plurality of narratives, each considered singularly true, which results in the 'post-truth' conundrum. By contrast the full or completed strategy of deconstruction 'avoids both simply *neutralizing* the binary opposition of metaphysics and simply *residing* within the closed field of these operations, thereby confirming them' (Derrida 1972b: 56; 2002b: 41). It dissolves the 'post-truth' problem because the conflict and strife between competing historical narratives points not to the intractable problem of subject position but to the heterogeneous and chaotic nature of the past that ultimately cannot be mastered. Wrestle as we may we cannot make it do what we want.

Here is where I wish to modify a passage by Derrida to make the link between *différance* and history explicit. In the project of history, one can expose only that of the past which at a certain moment can become present, manifest, that which can be shown, presented as something present, a being-present in its truth, in the truth of a present or the presence of the present. Now if the past i̶s̶ (and I place a bar across the 'i̶s̶' both striking it out and indicating an obstruction that restricts all access) what makes possible the presentation of the being-present of history, it is never presented as such. The past itself is never offered to the present.[4] With acknowledgement to the way this modifies Derrida's argument but following this move, I see history as linked to *différance* because of the latent ontology of the past. The past as history i̶s̶, crossed out, present and absent. I replace the X/

strike through offered by Derrida with the bar/strike through to demonstrate the present/absent nature of the past event but also the ways that we are 'barred' (barré) from actually having that past event as such in the present. In this way the bar indicates and makes explicit the ontological-epistemological entanglement of history and the historian with the past. A deconstructive approach to the past addresses the historicized entanglement of the historian with their object of study and unhinges history from the quasi-theological notion of realistic representation, the 'de-historicized' position from which the historian claims to neutrally observe and represent past events 'as they really happened'.

The emphasis on *différance* as the crafting of the playing moment that produces effects of difference is in tension with a conventional approach to history that emphasizes presence because 'play is always play of absence and presence, but if it is to be thought radically, play must be conceived of before the alternative of presence and absence' (Derrida 1978: 292; 1967a: 426). This is an approach that recognizes and embraces both the latent ontology of the past that i̶s̶, and the importance of the imagination required to think radically. This 'concept', the past that i̶s̶, 'marks an irreducible and *generative* multiplicity. The supplement and the turbulence of a certain lack fracture the limit of the text, forbidding an exhaustive reading of it' (Derrida 1972b: 62; 2002: 45). Far from implying the death or abdication of the author, deconstruction for the writing of history requires a strong and careful historian whose rhetorical style guides the reader along the *poros* that simultaneously introduces and acknowledges the aporia.

What I propose is a mode of writing history that provides a *poros* or pathway to the past that activates the latent ontology making it present but without privileging that presence in the way that the ontological realist narrative does. In doing so this approach inhabits and appropriates the methodological and evidentiary commitments of traditional historical work but in a way that makes evident and legible the limits and barriers of conventional historical method. Thus fears that a deconstructive approach will inevitably lead to relativism are unwarranted because the very methods of the historical discipline are conserved.

> The movements of deconstruction do not shake up [*solliciter*] structures from the outside. They are not possible and effective, they do not focus their strikes, except by inhabiting these structures. Inhabiting them 'in a particular way', because one always inhabits and all the more so when one does not suspect it. Operating necessarily from the inside, borrowing from the old structure the strategic and economic resources of subversion, borrowing them structurally, that is to say without being able to isolate their elements and atoms, the enterprise of deconstruction is always in a certain way swept away by its own work. (Derrida 1967b: 39; 1997: 24)

Thus I advocate working from the inside to expose the limitations and restrictions of the historical practice but also to extend its scope and reach. Such an approach deploys postmodern theory working within the historical tradition to destabilize it and as such a deconstructive approach is always cognizant of the past as aporia and actively works to shake the ground it has laid. This is to be done by what Derrida has called a double gesture (*un double geste*) or double session (*la double séance*) wherein 'we must first overturn the traditional concept of history, but at the same time mark the interval, take care by virtue of the overturning, and by the simple act of conceptualization, the interval not be reappropriated' (Derrida 1972b: 81; 2002b: 59). Here, the possible past that one recounts cannot preclude other past possibles and thus necessarily remains open to other and alternative possible pasts. 'Therefore we must proceed using a double gesture, according to a unity that is both systematic and in and of itself divided, a double writing, that is, a writing that is in and of itself multiple' (Derrida 1972b: 56; 2002b: 41).

In contrast to the search for origins or the material past made present, which characterizes the de-historicized thin historicism of our current moment, a deconstructive approach to the past embraces the perturbations that the past returned convokes. In *Archive Fever*, Derrida discusses our relation with a tradition or legacy, one could even call it Wilhelm Dilthey's objective world, as a 'performative repetition' in which 'the interpretation of the archive can only illuminate, read, interpret, establish its object, namely a given inheritance, by inscribing itself into it, that is to say by opening it and by enriching it enough to have a rightful place in it' Derrida (1995: 108; 1998: 67).[5] Thus Derrida sees the relation with the past as a process of self-inscription wherein one reads and interprets the archive of the past in order to create a space for oneself in it in the present. Far from the fetish of mimetic representation or the master cipher of contextual explanation, such a move makes the past both available and relevant for us in the present while also illuminating the space for imaginative critique. Here, historical context is not a magical cipher but is itself seen as an argument about social relations and arrangements that cannot be presumed and should instead be interrogated (Kleinberg, Wallach and Wilder 2018).

If we are to start thinking historically again, thinking deeply and critically, we must discard the counterfeit 'historical thinking' of thin historicism and strive to enact a theoretical deconstructive approach that is commensurate, if never adequate, to the past that *is*.

Part Two

Popular History, Populism and Politics

6

The Affective Dimension

What Theory of History Can Learn from Popular History

Allan Megill

For some years now theorists and philosophers of history have shown great interest in history's affective dimension: a concern that is at the centre of Frank Ankersmit's *Sublime Historical Experience* (Ankersmit 2005) and has been taken up by Eelco Runia (Runia 2014), Ethan Kleinberg (Kleinberg 2017) and many other theorists of history. Historians themselves have long known that history is not only a rational, scientific enterprise but also a matter of feeling. Among classic historians, Leopold von Ranke declared that the historian must be capable of 'participation and joy in the particular', Jules Michelet contended that 'the first point' in the writing of history is 'to have enough passionate flame to reheat ashes long cold' and Jacob Burckhardt saw his *Civilization of the Renaissance in Italy* as requiring a sensibility akin to that of a lover of art (Ranke 1981 [1830]: 103; Michelet 1869: 144; Burckhardt 1890 [1860]). Along a similar line, Johan Huizinga wrote of a 'historical sensation', analogous to but different from aesthetic enjoyment, which offers

> the feeling of an immediate direct contact with the past, a sensation as deep as the purest enjoyment of art, a (laugh not) almost ecstatic sensation of not being oneself any more, of overflowing into the world outside me, contact with the essence of things, the experience of Truth through history. (Huizinga 1920: 259–60 [author's trans.])

Present-day historians also understand that history is a matter of feeling, although few are as forthright as Jackson Lears, who began one of his books by declaring that 'all history is the history of longing' (Lears 2010: 1). But while historians often turn their attention to the longings of those about whom they write, the role of affect in the production of historical works is usually not on their agenda. All history is indeed 'the history of longing', in the sense that all history deals, directly or indirectly, with people's desires, aspirations, attachments and hopes, as well as with their insecurities and animosities. The question I raise here, however, is reflexive, directed less at history's objects than at historical representation itself: How does 'longing' – however we might define it – feed into the making of histories? This question is of both theoretical and practical significance. Today, people in many countries debate whether deference ought to be accorded to historical sites and monuments, when the sites are places where horrible things were done and when the monuments celebrate causes that many people today consider to be in conflict with their values. Monuments to the US Confederacy (some of them constructed as late as the 1950s) remain prominent in the civic landscapes of many parts of the Southern United States. How legitimate, one might ask, is the continuing existence of such monuments?

This question cannot be answered solely on a theoretical level, because answering it requires research into whatever monuments one has in mind. A simple cemetery in which the bodies of Confederate soldiers were interred during the US Civil War or soon afterwards sends a different message than does a statue erected fifty or sixty years later that impressed its weight upon a public square, proclaiming it a space reserved for white people. Obviously, we ought to judge each site and monument in context, on its own merits. But we also cannot properly answer the question, 'What, if anything, ought we to do with this historical site or monument?', only on an empirical level. (By a historical site or monument, I mean any place or artefact that people come to see *as* historical.) Rather, answering the question requires some notion of what it *means* for a historical site or monument to have or to lack 'legitimacy'. 'Legitimacy', taken as grounding a general claim to continued existence, needs to be distinguished from mere 'authenticity'. We can imagine a historical site or commemorative monument that would be an authentic expression of National Socialist longing, without it being legitimate. But authenticity and legitimacy are surely also related to each other.

In the hope of opening a way towards insight on these matters, I examine in this chapter a specific and rather striking situation from which 'popular history' emerged. By 'popular history' I mean historical representations that arise from the longings and hopes of a 'people', ordinary people acting primarily on their own initiative with minimal (perhaps no) expert input or top-down direction. Further, by a 'people' I mean an assemblage of human beings brought together by their mutual experience of living, over a period of time, in a particular space or place. In the situation considered here, the social and natural environment fostered a generality that dampened but did not erase the particularities of origin that these people brought with them.

There are other senses of the phrase 'popular history' that are not at issue in this chapter. I am not concerned here with works written by historians in the hope of entertaining and perhaps educating a wide audience. Nor am I concerned with works produced by museum professionals, who plan exhibits, entire museums and historical recreations of various kinds that seek to teach people about the past, as well as to evoke, in Stephen Greenblatt's helpful terms, 'resonance' and 'wonder' on the part of the viewing and experiencing public (Greenblatt 1991: 42). I also do not touch upon the vast range of entertainments that now exist, such as films and TV series set in the historical past and interactive games that purport to put players into actual historical situations. (Originally the latter were board games, but they have now evolved into multiplayer sound-and-video games of considerable technical sophistication.) Finally, I do not mean works written with an explicitly propagandizing aim. (I use the term 'propagandizing' in a neutral sense, for, as we learn from Benedict Anderson [Anderson 1983: 40], every community of any substantial size requires propaganda for its maintenance.) These four overlapping genres are all worthy of study, but to the degree that they are created by experts (in history, museology, media and propaganda) they are not my concern here. In fact, we might better call them not 'popular history' but *popularizing* history, *curated* history, *interactive* history and *propagandizing* history.[1] In any case, these genres are less promising than popular history as a zone for gaining insight into the affective dimension of history.

I draw illustrative material for my argument from the situation and experiences of some settlers who came to Canada's Great Plains (also known as the 'Canadian Prairies' or the 'Canadian Interior Plains') early in the twentieth century and built for themselves a social and economic order in what previously had been rough unsettled bush. Fifty years after the initial settlers came to the particular place on which I focus, some of the people who grew up there began to produce works of popular history. These works recounted the experiences of their grandparents and parents as they turned wilderness into working farms, as well as their own experiences of what, by their time of writing, had become a thing of the past. Since this chapter discusses the genre of popular history *in concreto*, I must describe the place and time in some detail. My aim, however, is to cast light on the roots of popular history, and by extension on the roots of history more generally.

A Place and a Time

Between 1897 and 1929, some five million people immigrated to Canada (Swyripa 2004). The immigrants and their descendants had a huge impact on a country that, although territorially the second largest in the world, had counted only 4,838,239 residents in the 1891 census (Canada 1902: 2).[2] The immigrants settled in various parts of Canada, but about 500,000 of them took up a plot of land on the Canadian Prairies. It has been estimated that during the most intense phase of agricultural settlement, from 1897 to 1910, 714,260 people became homesteaders (an estimate arrived at by assuming 2.5 persons per homestead entry), of whom about 460,000 were immigrants (Widdis 1992: 259).

The Canadian Great Plains cover 1,900,000 square kilometres (733,600 sq mi), in the provinces of Alberta, Saskatchewan and Manitoba, between the Rocky Mountains in the west and the Precambrian Shield in the east ('Geography of Canada' 2019). I focus on one part of this vast region: a square of territory known as the Rural Municipality of Willow Creek, No. 458, which measures 18 miles × 18 miles and is located in east-central Saskatchewan.[3] (A Rural Municipality is equivalent to what in many jurisdictions is called a 'county'.) The southern boundary of the RM (at 52°50'N Lat) is 440 kilometres north of Canada's border (49°N Lat) with the United States.[4] In spite of its distance from the United States, the RM of Willow Creek, No. 458 is well within the southern half of the province, since Saskatchewan stretches 1,220 kilometres from the US border northward to the Northwest Territories. Fifty or sixty miles north of the RM's northern boundary agriculture yields to the unsuitable soil and the lakes and forests of the Precambrian Shield.

The RM itself was (and is) reasonably well suited for agriculture. Bush and trees had to be removed, and in many places better drainage was needed, but the surveyors, while noting these facts, ranked much of the land in the RM as 'class 2', the second-best grade of agricultural land (Fox 1979: 55–6). Moreover, unlike a large part of southern Saskatchewan, the region in which the RM is located receives ample precipitation (snow, rain). Finally, the short growing season at this high latitude is offset not only by the fertility of the soil but also by the long hours of unbroken sunshine in summer. These advantages came at a price, however. For decades after the first agricultural settlers arrived, the harsh physical conditions in the RM and in the larger region remained a matter of mortal concern. The settlers encountered intense cold and heavy snowfall in winter; a spring melt that made the 'grid roads', which at first were simply tracks marked out by the surveyors, difficult to travel on for weeks at a time; hordes of mosquitoes in late spring and summer; and early or late frosts, summer hailstorms and other conditions liable to ruin planting, growing or harvesting. Even as late as the 1960s it was possible for an unwary motorist driving on a winter's night on a provincial highway to die of exposure or of carbon monoxide poisoning after encountering an engine problem or inadvertently going into the ditch. However, my concern here is less the physical environment than the people who, in the early twentieth century, carved out farms and made this place their home.

Those who came to the Canadian Great Plains in this period were the fourth set of immigrants to appear on the scene. The first were the ancestors of the present-day Canadian First Nations. It appears that they arrived in the Americas, from Asia, about 13,000 years ago, coming via the Beringian land bridge, but evidence concerning their arrival on the Canadian Plains is lacking. Still, we know with certainty that First Nations people were living in what is now the 'Prairie Provinces' when European and Canadian explorers and fur traders arrived. This second set of arrivals came into the region between 1640 and 1840. The third group consisted mostly of people of British heritage who arrived from the 1840s to the 1890s and who mainly settled in southern Manitoba. The fourth and by far the largest set of arrivals, our concern here, came from eastern Canada, the United States, the United Kingdom and Continental Europe in the years 1897–1929 (Friesen 2019 [2006]).

Canada's 1901 census counted a mere eighteen residents in the territory that in 1913 began to function as the RM of Willow Creek, No. 458 (Canada 1953: Table 6–69, p. 189 of PDF format). There is no evidence that any member of Canada's First Nations was among the eighteen people counted by the census-takers, and I have found no evidence that First Nations people lived in the RM after it was founded. A series of treaties initiated in the 1870s had led to the granting of 'Indian Reserves' (and some other rights) to First Nations people in return for their ceding all the rest of the land to the British Crown (and thence to the Government of Canada). The 'Indian Reserve' closest to the RM of Willow Creek, No. 458 is 35 miles west of the RM's western boundary. The reserve system kept First Nations people segregated residentially and in many other ways from the rest of Canadian society for the next century.[5] The treaties were interpreted as providing a legal basis for excluding First Nations people from the homestead system, since 'treaty Indians' had already been granted land; in addition, 'Indians' were regarded as a primitive people. A second excluded group were the small number of Chinese people living in Canada (initially brought to Canada to work as railway-construction labourers): until well into the twentieth century, many (probably most) white Canadians viewed Chinese people as culturally alien.

I do not focus on the RM of Willow Creek, No. 458 because it was typical of rural areas in the Canadian Great Plains, although in many ways it was (most notably in its long-term loss of population). Rather, I was initially drawn to the RM by the presence within it of something distinctive – indeed, unique – in Western Canada, a rural synagogue surviving in situ (almost all Jewish immigrants to Canada gravitated to its cities). My first glimpse of the synagogue (and of three other quite distinctive houses of worship close to it) came when I noticed that several people had uploaded photographs of these structures to Google Earth™. I was primed to notice the photos because I spent most of my childhood in a small town of 2,700 people (let us call it, as in a Russian novel, the town of X) that lies a mere 7 miles southeast of the RM, and 19 miles from the synagogue. By the time I was a teenager, I was aware that there was, or had once been, a Jewish community somewhere north of the town of X, but I knew no details, and I had no idea that there was an extant synagogue (or rather, a synagogue building).

Several Jewish families lived in the town of X. My father bought two or three second-hand cars from a close neighbour, 'Ike' Vickar, who was the most trustworthy nearby car dealer (later, he would take his talents to the nearest metropolis, five hundred miles to the southeast, Winnipeg). My mother would sometimes send me to the local butcher, Bob Gitlin, to fetch a cut of meat after she phoned in the order. I knew vaguely that although almost all my classmates were either Catholic or Protestant, a few were Jewish. I learned from my parents that the minister of our family church had had a conversation with several Jewish people about the possibility of joining the United Church of Canada. I was once at a meeting for young people, at which someone who was an enthusiast for Esperanto spoke about the virtues of learning that language, which I had not heard of before: only much later did I learn that Esperanto had been invented in the late nineteenth century by a Jewish ophthalmologist from Białystok who was interested in the cause of world peace. Finally, once, when I was eight years old, I heard what I now know to have been a Ukrainian-Canadian speak in a highly disparaging way about 'the Jews', at a time when I did not know what a 'Jew' (or a 'Ukrainian') was.

Figure 1 Beth Israel Synagogue, 'Edenbridge', SK. Photo by Janette I. Stuart. All rights reserved.

Figure 2 Holy Ascension Ukrainian Greek Orthodox Church, 'Maryville', SK. Photo by Janette I. Stuart. All rights reserved.

Figure 3 Saint Nicholas Ukrainian Catholic Church, 'Maryville', SK. Photo by Rae McLeod. All rights reserved.

Figure 4 Saint Helen's Roman Catholic Church, Brooksby, SK. Photo by Janette I. Stuart. All rights reserved.

However, I was unaware of any *history* behind these experiences. Around 2016, I went to Google Earth in search of the rumoured Jewish settlement. I found more than I had expected. My first discovery was that someone had posted to Google Earth a photograph of the synagogue (Figure 1). The synagogue was located 560 metres north of the Carrot River on a heavily wooded forty-acre plot of land. It lay a few metres south and west of what at first glance appeared to be a crossroads, which was marked by the word 'Edenbridge'.[6] In addition, three miles west and a mile south of the synagogue, close to the south side of the Carrot River, I found posted a set of photographs of a strikingly decrepit Orthodox church. The church lay just south of a crossroads marked 'Maryville' (Figure 2). One of the photos showed graves in the foreground and a stormy sky above. These photos led me to notice another church, a bit more than 300 metres to the north, on the north side of the Carrot River, also evidently neglected, with broken but patched windows and door (Figure 3). Finally, my eyes were led to yet another church along the same stretch of road, 600 metres south of the decrepit Orthodox church (Figure 4).

Why did four houses of worship exist within such a limited space? Further, why the names 'Maryville' and 'Edenbridge', even though there was no visible indication of a once-existing village or hamlet? Although I had lived for fourteen years a mere 20 miles southeast of these structures, I had never seen them. Only because several people uploaded photographs of them to Google Earth did I begin to see the elements of a possible history – 'data' for a history, but not yet history itself. My interest in the RM grew when I learned, after locating a relative of one of the people who had uploaded a photograph, that there exists a large work of popular history – 960 pages long – entitled *Our Courageous Pioneers*, that chronicles the history of roughly half of the RM of Willow Creek, No. 458.[7] This informant sent me photocopies of a few intriguing pages of the book. I searched for the book online and bought the one copy that I found. The book informed me that 'Edenbridge' and 'Maryville' were the names not of hamlets or villages but of school districts. Edenbridge and Maryville were two out of a total of twenty-three school districts that had previously existed in the RM. Together, they took up 32 square miles – almost exactly one-tenth of the three hundred twenty-four square miles of the whole RM. Maryville School District (S.D. No. 2790) was established in 1911, with a schoolhouse coming into use in 1913 (before that, classes were held in private dwellings [Gronlid 1991: 525–36]).[8] Edenbridge School District (S.D. No. 2930), which was petitioned for in 1911 and established in 1913, lay directly east of Maryville School District (Gronlid 1991: 219–22; Rosenberg, N., ed. 1980: 23–38). The synagogue and the three other houses of worship are all located within the boundaries the two school districts.

The Process of Settlement: Local and Global Considerations

In 1904, the Canadian Northern Railway – competitor to Canada's first transcontinental rail company, the Canadian Pacific – came near to the future RM with an east–west railway line running parallel to and 4.5 miles south of what would be its southern boundary. A railway siding was established 13.5 miles due south of where the synagogue would be built; the stop, and the small settlement that grew up around it, was given the optimistic-sounding name 'Star City'. Another stop was established 12 miles west of Star City, 1.5 miles south of a settlement called 'Stoney Creek', which promptly moved itself to the railway and was renamed 'Melfort' (EncSK 2005: 594). Melfort was a bit less than 5 miles south of the southwest corner of the RM. Beginning in 1899, a few people had already settled south of the future RM, attracted by what was proclaimed to be the excellent soil there. Once the railway came, the stage was set for settlement on a much larger scale.

The settling of the RM of Willow Creek, No. 458 was linked not only to the coming of the Canadian Northern but also to national, continental and global developments. In the wake of the US Civil War, some Canadians regarded the United States as a potentially threatening power that might be inclined to seize land north of 49° N. latitude, even though the London Convention of 1818 (and other, later agreements) had established the forty-ninth parallel as the border between British territory and the United States from Lake of the Woods westward to the Pacific coast. From such a perspective it was worrisome that agricultural settlers were few in number in the territory of the present-day provinces of Alberta and Saskatchewan, and that the most easterly of the Prairie Provinces, Manitoba, was farmed in only a few localities.

To the disappointment of the boosters of the new Canada (founded only in 1867), the Canadian Pacific Railway, completed to the Pacific Ocean in 1885, had not brought in a flood of settlers. In fact, from 1881 to 1891 Canada had a record net *emigration* of 205,000 people, and even between 1891 and 1901 Canada still saw a net emigration of 185,000 people (Friesen 1984: 248). In those years, many job-hungry Canadians went to the north-eastern United States for factory work, lumbering and other occupations, and better-off people with farming experience went to the American Midwest, where an expanding railway network was opening up good homesteading land. In the 1890s, however, the situation began to change. In 1890 the US Census reported that there was no longer a distinct line between settled and unsettled land in the American West, thus signalling, according to the young American historian Frederick Jackson

Turner, the 'closing' of 'a great historic movement' (Turner 1920 [1893]: 1, 39, 296). Less portentously, almost all the good homesteading land in the United States had been settled by 1890. The 'closing' of the American frontier alone would have inclined people to look more seriously to the vast reaches of uncultivated arable land above the forty-ninth parallel, but other conditions were also militating in favour of northern settlement: there now existed much improved passenger steamships; there was an upswing in world commerce after 1896; and new farming techniques and wheat strains better suited to northern conditions were being developed (Friesen 1984: 249–54).

Without suitable policy, opportunity can easily go to waste. In 1896 an immigration-friendly Liberal government was elected in Ottawa, and an energetic and ambitious lawyer with business interests in Manitoba, Clifford Sifton, became minister of the interior. Sifton entered office with one great goal in mind: to bring about the settling of the Canadian West. In 1891, the four territories that would later be divided between Saskatchewan and, to its west, Alberta had a population of only 81,328 persons. Between 1891 and 1901 the population in these territories almost doubled, to 158,930, and from 1901 to 1911 it increased more than fivefold, to 867,095 in the two provinces (which came into being on 1 September 1905) (Canada 1912: 2, 5). During the First World War immigration almost stopped, but a strong increase through births swelled the 1921 census figures to 1,345,964 persons in the two provinces. Subsequently, the rate of increase slowed. Indeed, in 1931 Saskatchewan's population peaked at 921,785 persons (Canada 1936: 6), a level that it would not reach again until the late 1950s.[9]

Until 1896, the Canadian government had viewed the British Isles, followed by the United States, as the most appropriate sources of immigrants. Almost all migrants from these places spoke English and had a cultural affinity with English Canada. In a daring move for the time, Sifton and his colleagues decided to widen their recruiting efforts. Because the British Isles were not producing the desired quantity of immigrants with farming experience, and because internal migration within Canada did little to increase the country's overall population, they decided to pour resources into recruiting settlers from the land-poor peasantry of East-Central Europe. To be sure, Ukrainian, Polish, Hungarian, Romanian and Russian peasants spoke no English, and some followed 'strange' religions. But they were experienced farmers whose current situations often gave them little hope for improvement in their native lands. Sifton's recruiters also developed a fondness for Norwegian peasants, who were fewer in number than the East-Central Europeans but had the advantage of being Protestants of the familiar Lutheran sort.[10]

The Department of the Interior launched a multilingual publicity campaign that emphasized the availability of 160 acres of fertile land for each homesteader, at no cost save for a 10-dollar filing fee. The allegedly high fertility of the land was much touted, as was the close involvement of the Canadian government, which could be taken as ensuring that the offer was not a scam.[11] In addition to appointing new civil servants assigned the task of finding prospective immigrants with farming experience, the department made new arrangements and renewed old ones with scouting agents, international shipping companies and the Canadian railways, all aimed at encouraging promising immigrants to pull up stakes and come to Canada. The department also appointed people whose job it was to ensure that immigrants made their way without a hitch from landfall in eastern Canada to Winnipeg, Manitoba, where short-term housing was offered, as well as advice concerning where in the vast Plains region homesteads were currently available. The upshot was that in the period from 1897 to 1912, deliberate policy and contingent circumstance worked together to flood the Prairie West with agricultural settlers.

The Settling of the RM: The Particular and the General

In Spring 1905 a Lithuanian Jew named Louis Vickar came across a pamphlet in the Cape Town Post Office. Issued by the Canadian Department of the Interior, it offered 160 acres of virgin land in a place that was then still known as the North-West Territories of Canada (Rosenberg, N., ed. 1980: 49, 61 [as reported by a fellow immigrant, Harry Broudy]). Several years earlier, Vickar and a group of other Lithuanian Jews, including two of his brothers, David and Sam, had fled to the Cape Colony, driven out of the Russian Empire by its increasingly nationalistic and anti-Semitic policies. They set themselves up as retail merchants and small tradesmen near Cape Town and were doing reasonably well. They learned English, and by 1905, some of them were already British subjects, or close to being so. According to the story, Louis Vickar had an epiphany in the Cape Town Post Office – a vision of Jews as landowners and farmers, leading a new way of life in a new promised land (Rosenberg, N., ed. 1980: 59–62).

After much discussion, some members of the Lithuanian-Jewish community in the Cape Colony decided to uproot themselves once more and move to Canada.[12] An initial group of twenty-two people left Cape Town in spring 1906, sailing to England, then from England to Canada. Transferring to rail, the group got off the train at Winnipeg and sent two of their number to investigate areas in

Saskatchewan where homesteads were available. After first looking to southern Saskatchewan, where the climate was dry and the land unwooded, the two scouts arrived at Star City in May 1906. Although it was not the city that they had expected, they approved of the well-watered land (a bit *too* well-watered, many of the homesteaders would discover) that they found thirteen miles north, near the Carrot River. In the words of the surveyor, the land in this area, Township 47, Ranges 16 and 17 West of the Second Meridian, was either 'level' or 'rolling', and was covered variously with brush, poplar, 'balm of Gilead', willow trees and elder trees (report in Fox 1979, after p. 57). The survey had been carried out between September 1904 and January 1905 (Fox 1979, after p. 57, and p. 79), and now the land was available for settlement.

The two scouts constructed a log house with a sod roof that was large enough to give temporary shelter to the remaining members of the party, who arrived at Star City in August 1906 (Rosenberg, N., ed. 1980: 12–3, with photo). After slogging through wooded land interspersed with water hazards, accompanied by a wagon pulled by a team of sometimes recalcitrant oxen that carried their possessions, the settlers arrived at a one square-mile block of land technically known as Section 24, Township 47, Range 17 west of the Second Meridian, on which the log house was located. It is reported that the women expressed horror at the primitive conditions, and that the men said less (Rosenberg, N., ed. 1980: 11, 13, 61–2). But the settlers had no choice but to begin the work of carving farmsteads out of what was mostly dense brush and trees. Other Jewish immigrants followed. These included, in addition to the core group of Lithuanian Jews, other Eastern European Jews who had earlier moved to England and were working in the garment trades in London, as well as some others who came from the United States (Usiskin 1983 [1945]: 1–14; Fox 1979: 28–35, 36–7).

The 'Edenbridge Hebrew Colony' faced many challenges, from its inception in 1906 to its dissolution in the 1960s. In 1931, there were 45 families on the land, amounting to 185 people (Fox 1979: 166; Rosenberg, L. 1993 [1939]: 27). During the Great Depression there was a modest decline, by 1937, to forty-one families (Fox 1979: 166), but by that year at least half the adult sons of the Edenbridge farmers were living elsewhere, in larger communities (Fox 1979: 173). During or soon after the Second World War at least thirteen families left the land, and by 1949 only twenty-seven families were still farming – and the losses continued. Many of the Jewish settlers had combined farming with a trade or with commerce, making it easier for them to think of moving elsewhere. In more heavily populated places, they could be part of a more active and lively Jewish community, where their children *would* be able to obtain a better education and find suitable spouses more easily. Moreover, the business and professional opportunities available in such cities as Saskatoon, Winnipeg, Vancouver, Toronto, Montreal, Chicago and Los Angeles went far beyond what one could find in the RM of Willow Creek, No. 458 or in the small towns nearby.

The Jewish newcomers were the first non-Anglo settlers in the area that would become the Maryville and Edenbridge school districts. Almost immediately they were followed by Ukrainian and Polish settlers, and somewhat later by Norwegians. (British, Canadian and American settlers also homesteaded in the RM, but there were fewer of them than of 'ethnic' settlers.[13]) Each of the 'ethnic' groups built its own houses of worship. In Maryville/Edenbridge the first of these was Beth Israel Synagogue, built in 1908–9 on the northeast corner of Section 13-47-17-W2, on Grid Road 681, 600 yards north of the Carrot River. Western Ukrainian immigrants (who at that time were usually identified by the region they came from, thus as Galicians, Ruthenians or Bukovinians, rather than as Ukrainians) began arriving as early as 1906 in what would soon become the Maryville School District (Gronlid 1991: 538). The first visit by a Ukrainian Catholic priest came in 1908, and Saint Nicholas Ukrainian Catholic Church (Figure 3) was initially constructed in 1912. At its height it was a beautiful church, boasting an iconostasis imported from Galicia in 1925 that the congregation arranged to have painted by an expert icon painter. The church also had an outside bell tower and a baptistry (Gronlid 1991: 22–3; Kovch-Baran 1977: 132–3).

The congregation of Holy Ascension Ukrainian Greek Orthodox Church (Figure 2) was founded in 1925 by a dissident group in the St Nicholas congregation that longed for a church more Ukrainian and more Orthodox (Ukrainian Catholic churches follow Orthodox rites but owe allegiance to the pope in Rome). At first the dissidents held services in what had been St Nicholas's church hall, and then they looked to another Ukrainian Greek Orthodox Church, newly built in 1926, located 5 miles to the southwest. However, travel was difficult (few farmers owned cars before the second half of the 1940s, and the roads remained bad), and so in 1935 the congregation built their own sanctuary, Holy Ascension, just south of St Nicholas (Gronlid 1991: 17, 19). Finally, St Helen's [Polish] Roman Catholic Church dates back to 1912, when twenty-five Polish families arrived in the area (Figure 4). The church building, constructed in 1958, replaced two earlier buildings destroyed by fire (Gronlid 1991: 19–21). In addition, each of the four congregations built a separate hall for social events, giving it a place for fundraising and for secular singing, dancing and socializing. The halls also made it possible to invite as guests neighbours who were not of the same religion. Finally, every rural congregation in this period typically had its own cemetery. The four houses of worship located in the Maryville and Edenbridge school districts were no exception.

Thirteen houses of worship were built in the RM from 1906 to the late 1930s ('Homestead Map' 1980). Why so many? The Jewish, Polish and Ukrainian (and, not much later, the Norwegian) immigrants to the RM were 'strangers in a strange land'. They found themselves in a harsh climate in what, when they arrived, was an almost trackless wilderness. During much of the year travel and communication were difficult. Lighting, much needed in the dark of winter, was by coal-oil lamp. Radio was not a presence until the 1940s and was typically pulled in using a battery-powered set. Power lines came through around 1950. Home telephone service started to become common among rural people only in the 1950s (Gordon 2018; Gronlid 1991: 35–6). Although the land was fertile and the summer weather generally favourable to agriculture, disasters – such as hailstorms or unseasonable frosts or wheat rust or sow thistle or drought or a collapse in the selling price of wheat – could easily turn a season's work to nothing.

Under these circumstances the impulse of many of the adults among the new settlers – especially those who came from afar – was to adhere firmly to their respective customs and traditions. This meant adherence to their religion more than to their ancestral language, which among the children rapidly gave way to English. A religious congregation provided a link among people who had come to Canada from 'the old country'. It preserved, for a generation or two, customs and rituals from that distant place. It maintained a space for sociability and entertainment, functioned as a source of useful information, and to a limited extent could offer help to individual families in distress. It is perhaps significant that only two of the RM's thirteen houses of worship were established by 'Anglo' people (both, indeed, were Anglican churches). Ukrainians, on the other hand, built churches with remarkable enthusiasm: five of the RM's churches were Ukrainian.

The schematic map shown in Figure 5, which was first created in 1962 for the fiftieth anniversary of the RM (Willow Creek 1962), gives an accurate outline of the RM but an inaccurate outline of settlement patterns. Contrary to what the map suggests, immigrants did not settle in compact ethnic enclaves. Because homesteads were claimed by individuals, not by groups, and because normally only some quarter-sections in an area were made available for homesteading at any given time, it was usually impossible for all the families in an arriving immigrant group to settle on a single bloc of land. Instead, members of different ethnic groups tended to be interspersed with each other. This was certainly the case in the RM of Willow Creek, No. 458. This mixing of groups may well have intensified each group's awareness of its own particularity, but the mixing also compelled different groups to cooperate with each other on matters of common interest.[14]

The school names – Maryville and Edenbridge – have an 'Anglo' sound to them, but this is misleading. While we do not know what line of reasoning led to the choice of the name 'Maryville', the Virgin Mary is an important figure in both Orthodox and Roman Catholic Christianity. As for the name 'Edenbridge', it was chosen in 1910 when the Jewish community applied to have a post office set up in one of their homes. From one point of view, the name 'Edenbridge' evokes the Garden of Eden, a choice that one could regard as either darkly ironic or profoundly hopeful. In fact, the name was an anglicization of the Yiddish word 'Yidnbrik', which means 'Jewish Bridge'. The name was appropriate. The synagogue was on Grid Road 681 just north of where a steel bridge spanning the Carrot River had been constructed in fall and winter 1906–7. Some Jewish immigrants were hired to help build it, at 20 cents an hour. The bridge was essential for getting access to the nearest railway delivery and loading point, Star City, 13 miles to the south (Rosenberg, N., ed. 1980: 23).

While the religious institutions located in the RM sought to maintain the 'particularity' of the immigrants, its public elementary schools 'generalized' them, by bringing them and their children together in the common project of education.[15] Each school was administered by its own elected school board and not by appointed bureaucrats. As a result, the adult inhabitants, whatever their religion and native language, had to collaborate with each other in running the nearby school. As for the children, interacting with their fellow students and with the teacher turned them quickly into Canadians. In addition, there was an RM council, consisting of a reeve and six councillors, each of the latter representing one of the six districts into which the RM was divided. The council served as a mechanism for democratic self-governance, so that local decisions could be made locally rather than in the province's capital, Regina, 175 miles to the south. The council faced many practical problems, such as how to maintain the RM's roads and bridges and keep them passable, how to obtain the services of a medical doctor, management of the gopher problem and the weed problem and so on. Here too collaboration occurred that went beyond the particularity of each group.

Loss: The Wound of Human Time Passing

The history of the RM of Willow Creek, No. 458 after the 1930s has been largely a history of loss: loss of population, loss of institutions, loss of a way of life. As noted, only eighteen people were found to be living in the area in 1901. However, after the coming of the Canadian Northern, settlers flooded in, resulting in a count of 1,231 residents in the 1911 census (Canada 1953, Table 6–69, p. 189 of PDF format). Population continued to increase as the 'grid roads' were extended and improved. Each extension made more quarter-sections accessible for farming. The 1921 census counted 2,785 persons in the RM; the 1926 census, 3,293; the 1931 census, 3,745; and the 1936 census, 4,185 persons (Canada 1953, Table 6-69, PDF p. 189, for 1901, 1911 and 1921 figures; Canada 1949, at Table 6, PDF p. 229, for 1926, 1931 and 1936).

The 1936 count of 4,185 residents marked the apogee of the RM's population. Sometimes people who live in the RM today are surprised to learn how many more people lived there eighty years ago. Beginning even before Canada's entry into the Second World War in 1939, most of the RM's young people went elsewhere, for war, for work, for education. People born in the RM made their lives in Alberta, British Columbia, Manitoba and Ontario, as well as in Saskatchewan's towns and cities, or in the United States. The 1941 census already indicated a decline in population, to 3,918 residents (Canada 1949: Table 6, PDF p. 229). It would be tedious to chronicle the almost unrelenting decline of population that occurred subsequently. Suffice it to say that by 1991 the RM's recorded population had dropped to 1,002 people, and by 1996 to 918.[16] The census of 2016 counted only 630 people (Canada 2016), a decline of more than 80 per cent from the 1936 peak. The main reason for the decline was the continuing advance of agricultural technology, which gradually eliminated almost all the heavy physical labour that farming had previously required and made it possible for one person, with minimal help, to farm two or more square miles of land. A further factor was that during most of the period from September 1939 onwards, young people could easily find better-paying jobs in other places. Also, if a family placed a high value on education, this meant, sooner or later, leaving the RM, and such departures were almost always permanent.

The RM's Jewish residents were the most inclined to leave. They tended to be highly committed to their children's educations, and future within the Jewish community. In many cases they also combined farming with another business, such as running a dairy, operating a country store, being a butcher or a baker or selling or renting out farm equipment. Business and craft skills were more portable than quarter-sections. Moreover, farmers who were willing to stop raising animals could confine almost all their farm work to the May–September sowing, growing and harvesting season. Country-school education generally ended at Grade 8. Some families came to spend a large part of the year living as far away as Saskatoon, 140 miles distant, where there were excellent schools and a university. Other families stayed closer, some moving to the town of Melfort,

25 miles away from Maryville/Edenbridge, where there was electrical power, sewer and water, good telephone service and better schooling.

Loss of population led to the hollowing out of institutions. Little wonder that Beth Israel ceased to function as a house of worship in 1964. By 1968 the building was in such a state of dilapidation that everyone thought it doomed to demolition. Indeed, in front of the synagogue, in October 1968, a cairn was erected, on which was affixed a plaque that declared, contrary to all visual evidence, that the synagogue had already been removed ('On this site stood .... In 1964 the original synagogue was removed,' quoted in Rosenberg, N., ed. 1980: 51). Only in 1975 were the wheels set in motion for renovating the synagogue and preserving it as a historical landmark (Rosenberg, N., ed. 1980: 17, 41–2, 47, 49–55, 68).[17] By 1980, only five descendants of the Edenbridge families were still living on the land (Rosenberg, N., ed. 1980: 40). In November 1987 the 40 acres on which the synagogue was located became a protected wildlife habitat entrusted to the Saskatchewan Wildlife Federation. Finally, in 2003 the synagogue and its surroundings were declared a provincial heritage site. A friend who photographed the synagogue in July 2017 was prevented from photographing its cemetery when a large moose, standing athwart the narrow woodland track leading to the cemetery, insisted on blocking her car.

The members of other ethnic groups were more inclined to continue farming, but the loss of institutions affected them also. By 1963, Holy Ascension had only three members left, down from eighteen or more in 1948–9 (Gronlid 1991: 17, 18). On an unremembered day its last service was held. A peculiarity of Holy Ascension is that since it was 'autocephalous', having no formal connection to any higher church organization, no one knows who has responsibility for the church, let alone an ownership claim, as it slowly crumbles.[18] St Helen's Roman Catholic Church continued to flourish in the 1960s, but by 1980 it was down to eight families, and on 25 August 1985 there was a closing mass and a formal closing ceremony (Gronlid 1991: 21). Finally, St Nicholas Ukrainian Catholic, which registered 120 souls in 1961, was down to 21 families in 1967 and to 5 in 1990, the year of its closing.

From the point of view of RM residents who were still alive in the 1980s, the most striking break in the RM's history was the closing of its schools in the early 1960s. It was above all this event that inclined people to produce a popular history of the RM. Country schools, which during the period of their flourishing could be found within 5 miles of each other throughout the settled parts of the Prairie West, were the region's most important public institution. But by the late 1950s roads had been dramatically improved; a family car was becoming almost universal and the vehicles themselves more comfortable and reliable;

country stores were giving way to stores in nearby towns; family size had shrunk markedly; and farm units had become larger. Because of the declining number of rural pupils and because education beyond the elementary grades was increasingly seen as a necessity, in the 1950s the government of Saskatchewan decided to close as many of the province's one- and two-room schools as possible and to bus pupils to larger, consolidated schools. At its peak in the 1930s, Maryville School had had as many as 180 pupils; Edenbridge School, located 4 miles almost directly east of Maryville School, always had fewer.[19] Both closed in 1960. All that remains of them is one roadside sign, obscured by vegetation, commemorating Maryville School (Figure 6). All the other rural schools in the RM closed at about the same time (Gronlid 1991: 113ff.).

Recollection and Reflection: On Popular History

In the 1980s a collective of RM residents who as children had been pupils in eleven of the RM's twenty-three schools came together and produced a chronicle (more accurately, a *set* of chronicles) of these school districts, and to a lesser extent of the RM as a whole. (The eleven school districts covered about half the RM's total area.) As already noted, the work in question is a 960-page book (Figure 7). It has double-columned pages 8.5× 11 inches in size, and its full title is *Our Courageous Pioneers: History of Gronlid and Surrounding Districts of Argus, Athol, Edenbridge, Freedom, Maryville, Murphy Creek, Sandhill Creek, Taelman, Taras, Teddington*. It was produced by the Gronlid and District Historical Society, and was printed by Phillips Publishers, in Melfort, in 1991 (Gronlid 1991).

In two senses, *Our Courageous Pioneers* is not unique. First, local and regional history has been an enormously thriving genre in the Prairie West, and perhaps especially in Saskatchewan. There is hardly a town or village that has not been 'covered' by one or more local histories.[20] For example, in 1992 the people of Ridgedale, a village lying just outside the RM's eastern boundary, which in that year had a population of slightly more than 100 people, managed to produce a 696-page popular history dealing with the village and its surrounding school districts (Ridgedale 1992). Secondly, in the RM itself there were various works that preceded *Our Courageous Pioneers*. The most notable of these was *Edenbridge, The memory lives on ... . A History*, which in its 125 pages chronicles and illustrates many events and experiences in the lives of the Edenbridge community, from the initial idea of abandoning South Africa for Saskatchewan to (and beyond) the dissolution of the 'Edenbridge Hebrew Colony' in the 1960s (Rosenberg, N., ed. 1980).[21]

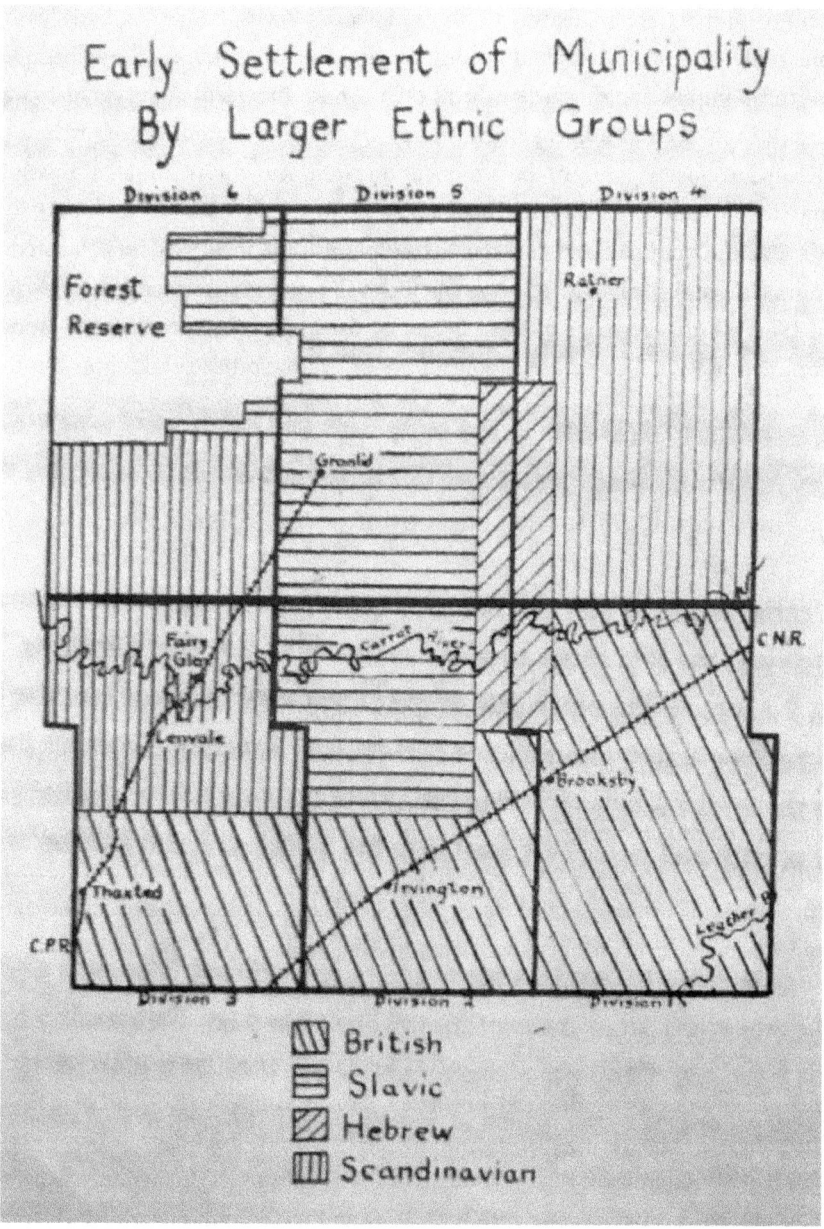

Figure 5 Ethnic map of the RM: A later perception.
Source: RM of Willow Creek, No. 458 [Willow Creek 2013], *Celebrating Our 100 Year Anniversary*, 8.

Figure 6 Maryville School: All that remains. Photo by Janette I. Stuart. All rights reserved.

Figure 7 *Our Courageous Pioneers*. Photo Credit: The Author.

Robert and Lil Gitlin

Figure 8 Robert and Lil (Vickar) Gitlin: Two of many.
Source: *Our Courageous Pioneers*, 272 (Gronlid 1991). By permission of Ron Gitlin. All rights reserved

Edenbridge, The memory lives on … . A History offers a mélange of photos, documents, memoirs, newspaper articles, poems, messages of congratulation and – perhaps above all – family histories. As the book's title clearly indicates, the ensemble was intended both to offer 'a history' and to preserve 'the memory' of something that by 1980 existed only in fragments. *Edenbridge* is based on two premises. One is that there existed something in the past that no longer exists. The other premise is that, although the past is gone, it also continues in the present and has the prospect of continuing into the future. The family histories tell us of descendants who now live in Flin Flon, Winnipeg, Moncton, New York, Toronto, Vancouver, Calgary, Chicago, Edmonton and London – to list only a few of the places that the family-history writers mention (Rosenberg, N., ed. 1980: 77ff.).

Our Courageous Pioneers both emulates and, in its conception and contents, exceeds *Edenbridge, The Memory Lives On … . A History* (indeed, the two works shared the same printer [Gronlid 1991: 2; Rosenberg, N., ed. 1980: 9]). Like its forerunner, *Our Courageous Pioneers* was born of a sense of loss – here, most notably, the sense of loss that arose in people's hearts as they thought about the long-gone country schools that they had attended (Gronlid 1991: 3). However, the 'effect of loss' (as we might call it) is greater in *Our Courageous Pioneers* than in its forerunner because of the greater magnitude of the loss. Edenbridge was a 'failed' Jewish colony whose slack was taken up by the existence of Jewish communities in other places, beginning with Melfort, Saskatoon and Winnipeg but not ending in those places. The disappearance of all the RM's country schools marked a break between past and present deeper than the break occasioned by the disappearance of a single synagogue or church, for others remained. There was an immense difference between a world wherein children walked to a nearby school or were conveyed there by horse power, and a world wherein they were bussed to a much larger school 10 or 20 miles away. Also like its forerunner, *Our Courageous Pioneers* highlights a continuity linking the lost past with the present and with a prospective future. In fact, the runner-up in the competition for the book's title was *We Have Come a Long Way*, which implies that there has been great improvement since 1913, and that 'we' will go even further in the future (Gronlid 1991: 4).

****

In *The Idea of History*, the philosopher (and also, on the side, a historian) R. G. Collingwood contended that 'history is neither αἴσθησῖς [aesthesis] nor νόμος [nomos], [nor is it] a combination of the two ... It is a wholly reasoned knowledge of what is transient and concrete' (Collingwood 1993 [1946]: 234). Collingwood was a great philosopher of history, but on this point he was wrong. Firstly, while history is concerned with what is 'transient', it is also concerned with entities that persist (Braudel 1972 [1949]). Further, history is undoubtedly reasoned knowledge – but it is not 'wholly' reasoned, for not everything in the field of history can be reasoned out. Finally, while I would agree that *for the most part* history is not *aesthesis* and not *nomos*, it does contain a *nomos*-oriented dimension as when the social science-oriented historian deploys theory in the interests of historical understanding, and it also contains a dimension of *aesthesis*, that is, feeling. What is missing from Collingwood's philosophy of history here – although not, I think, from his personal experience as an archaeologist and historian of Roman Britain – are the elements of sensibility and attachment (and of difference) that feed into history – if not directly, then into a domain of experience that makes history possible.

How do 'objects' (such as the four houses of worship noted earlier) become objects *of history*? In part it is a matter of people's attitudes towards these and similar objects, and in part it is a matter of what the objects themselves instantiated. The three churches and the synagogue all speak to us of death and transience, as seen by several facts: that they no longer function as houses of worship; that they are adjacent to places for the interment and commemoration of the dead; and that two of them are falling into ruin, exemplifying in their own architectural being the graveyards adjacent to them. These objects serve as stand-ins for the particular communities, now gone, that they brought together and, for a time, sustained – communities of people who in most cases have scattered to places far distant from the RM of Willow Creek, No. 458. By contingent circumstance much more than by design, these communities were situated within a social order where, amid particularity, generality (manifested as a commitment, albeit often disputed in its details, to the general good of the society) could also take shape. This latter commitment could take shape in part because the harsh necessities of this often cold and demanding place imposed a greater than normal level of social cooperation and in part because there existed institutions and practices that tended to cut across ethnic divides.

People came to Canada carrying an attachment to their own traditions and customs, but already in the first native-born generation the more general consciousness of being 'Canadian' – whatever that might mean – took root. Time and again in *Our Courageous Pioneers* the 'particularities of origin', as I would call them, are acknowledged and even celebrated, most notably in the book's 'church' histories and family histories. But the book also honours what I would call the 'generalities of existence', that is, the experiences and institutions that were common to all who lived in that place, especially in its time (now long past) of deep hardship. Indeed, the primary structuring element in *Our Courageous Pioneers* is the co-presence of and tension between generality and particularity. The generalities are to be found in religion, in the schools and, less obviously, in the local politics and formal and informal administration that enabled the running of the schools, the maintaining of roads and bridges and the carrying out of countless other tasks needed to keep the RM on an even keel. The particularities are to be found in the different religions, customs, traditions and languages that people brought to this place. We can distinguish, here, between 'popular history' and 'populist history'. Both are rooted in feeling, but the character of the rootedness is different. *Popular* history as exemplified here attempts to honour both the particular and the general. *Populist* history, in contrast, cleaves to one people, in whose name it claims to speak.

For theoretical purposes, the two most important lessons that arise from the history examined here are as follows. The first is that we theorists and philosophers of history – and not *only* theorists and philosophers – ought to attend to the affective, 'feeling' dimension of people's orientation to their pasts, not to reduce history to feeling but rather to take account of both history's affective and its thoughtful, reflective aspects. The second lesson is that we ought also to attend to how the popular historians of the RM of Willow Creek, No. 458 managed to preserve both the particularities of their beginnings and current situations (which they refused to turn into fixed identities) and a hard-to-define 'something' in which they all could potentially share. A merely 'authentic' history is one that would take one tribe, one particularity, as having an essential and self-contained identity. A 'legitimate' history is one that, while attending to particularity, does so in relation to something else, difficult to describe, that goes beyond what any particularity can offer. I do not mean to suggest that the popular historians of the RM of Willow Creek, No. 458 were endowed with a superior moral consciousness. It is better to say that the situation within which they found themselves inclined them to avoid both a reduction of the general to the particular and a dissolving of the particular into the general.[22]

Acknowledgements

This chapter owes its existence to an invitation I received to give the Robert D. Cross Memorial Lecture in the Corcoran Department of History, University of Virginia, in April 2017. My thinking has benefited from comments that people offered on that occasion, as well as at other presentations of this material, at the University of Oulu, Chinese Academy of Social Sciences, Fudan University, Shanghai Normal University, Capital Normal University and Xiamen University. I thank the many colleagues who have read and reacted to this material. (I defer specific acknowledgements until publication of the larger project of which this chapter is a part.) Corey Runkel and Derrick Wang contributed to the researching, text-editing and formatting of this chapter.

7

Tales of Im/mobility

Unhistorying Migration

Claire Norton and Mark Donnelly

Writing towards the end of the twentieth century, Giorgio Agamben argued in 'Beyond Human Rights' that 'the refugee is perhaps the only thinkable figure for the people of our time and the only category in which one may see today ... the forms and limits of a coming political community' (1996: 158–9). Reasoning that the concept of human rights was tied to the political-juridical order of state-nation territory, and diagnosing that the decline of the integrity of the nation state was unstoppable, Agamben believed that the time had come to build 'our political philosophy anew starting from the one and only figure of the refugee' (1996: 159).[1] Agamben's point here was not simply that the presence of the refugee contradicted the implied universalism of human rights discourses, when these rights were primarily awarded or withheld at the discretion of nation states.[2] It was that the refugee could not be incorporated within existing categories of political philosophy without disrupting to breaking point fundamental concepts at work in that system of thought.[3]

The purpose of this chapter is to borrow the shape of Agamben's idea and apply it to a consideration of metahistorical issues in the twenty-first century. Working in this way, we look to articulate our position that the figure of the contemporary migrant[4] cannot be brought within the boundaries of conventional (Western) historiographical practices without bringing those practices into disrepute – on the grounds that they are shown to be politically redundant from the point of view of those whose struggle is, in Arendt's phrase, 'the right to have rights' (2017: 388). In developing this position, we start from the same ground as Pihlainen when he states that 'claims for the *intrinsic* value of studying the past make no sense. There is no "in itself" to historical knowledge' (2017: xv). Rather, he maintains, the purpose of 'doing' history can only be conceived of in relation to effects and consequences. If historiography cannot produce effects that work in the interests of migrants now, then a long-established critique about it being a discourse that is largely disconnected from contemporary ethico-political challenges is relevant still. This is not to make the mistake of assuming that historicizing practices are irrelevant to the experience of migration or 'refugeeness'.[5] Quite the reverse: in the main they function negatively to authorize ideas about the legitimacy of national-political communities as singularities whose cultural autonomy and territorial sovereignty need 'defending' from outsiders who want to make a claim on them. The recent rise of anti-migrant rhetoric and violence in populist political campaigns illustrates the nature of the problem. No one seriously argues that historians are responsible for this backlash against vulnerable minorities. But the identity positions that are responsible for anti-migrant hostility seek to derive legitimacy from ideas about a historically constituted 'same' that is different from 'others'. As Hayden White argued,

> It is a troubling fact that 'history' or 'historical consciousness' or 'historical knowledge' has functioned more or less effectively over time as one of the instruments deployed by dominant social groups in the effort to 'control the imagination' of the multitude or at least of elites destined to control the multitude. (2011: 170–1)[6]

All this raises the question of whether historicization can bring anything creative to the migrants' self-management of their situation separate from other forms of 'context-work'. We will argue here that historians *qua* historians can make only the weakest of claims about the practical value of their knowledge work for migrants. Instead, we believe, other forms of past-talk should be seen as more productive resources for supporting their struggles for hospitality, dignity, rights and access to provisions and medical care.

There is a clear ideological motivation behind the approach that we take in this chapter. We seek to make a case about the political value of forms of past-focused work that engage with migrants as central subjects of the twenty-first century: a multitude whose numbers are likely to increase as movement of people is shaped by the effects of climate change, economic crises, war and border enforcement policies. Migrants experience the limits of what it is to be human when human rights are territorialized. They are a diaspora whose subjectivity is often produced by being exposed to the force of the 'state of exception' (Nyers 2006: xii). They include people whose situation when they are forced to migrate from one place to another was described by Bauman in the following terms:

> They do not *change* places; they lose a place on earth, they are catapulted into a nowhere, into [Marc] Augé's 'non-lieux' or [Joel] Garreau's 'nowherevilles', into Michel Foucault's 'Narrenschiffe', into a drifting 'place without a place, that exists by itself, that is closed in on itself and at the same time is given over to the infinity of the sea'. (2002: 112)

Those migrants who are subject to the classification regime of 'refugeeness' also experience the fact that, as Derrida remarked, every rich, capitalist country puts into practice a policy of border closings, a 'putting-into-hibernation of the principles of asylum' when it suits their needs to do so (2002a: 140).[7] In choosing to think about meta-history questions from the starting point of migrant experiences, our intention is to align our work with the fairly recent ethical turn in history theory, or with what has been called a concern with 'history in the world'.[8] This is not to claim a particular timeliness for our theoretical approach: far from it. To the extent that one might identify trends in history theory, the most recent movements in the field have been away from a focus on how language and representation function to mediate a sense of the historical, signalling that the paradigm of the linguistic turn in history theory is now most likely to be regarded as a tired orthodoxy that restricts creative thinking in the field. Against this state of affairs, we have to concede that our position remains grounded on what has become an unfashionably retro preference for the type of post-foundational or anti-representationalist critiques of the discipline that set much of the agenda in history theory since the 1970s.[9] We do not intend to use these critiques to probe the ontological status of history (in either of its guises as 'course of events' or 'textual category'). Instead, we are more interested in issues around rhetorical practices and the *consequences* of producing certain types of knowledge about the past for various circuits of consumption. For us, history theory represents a space in which to engage with the often-problematic ways that people experience or consume different types of mediated versions of 'pastness' in the present. In particular, we seek to draw attention to the fact that proposals to view the past in given ways – and in given forms – have ideological and political consequences which are rarely examined within the community of working historians.[10]

Some historians have written in detail about refugee issues, but viewed in proportional terms the subject is in the outer margins of the discipline's main areas of interest. Commenting on the strikingly small amount of work in the field, Peter Gatrell wrote that historians have shown 'actual resistance rather than simple apathy' in their engagement with the subject (2007: 43–5). This general point contains a more particular one, which is that historians rarely write about refugees *as* refugees. To the extent that they write about refugee issues at all, historians usually focus on aid agencies and relief organizations as the objects of their research (Gatrell 2013: 283). This disciplinary sense of priorities led Philip Marfleet to observe in a review of the historiography in 2007 that refugees are 'people whose absence from most historical writing is so marked that it constitutes a systematic exclusion' (2007: 136). Gatrell and Marfleet shared a hope that more historians would take up writing about refugees, primarily as a way of compensating for other disciplines' largely ahistorical approaches to the field of enquiry. Such a lack of interest in historicity was most visible in the cross-disciplinary field of refugee studies. Marfleet, for example, referred to a review by the editor of the *Journal of Refugee Studies* that surveyed the disciplinary basis of all articles submitted to the publication between 1988 and 2000. Only 4 per cent of these articles addressed 'historical issues', leaving Marfleet to conclude that 'in effect, contributors to the journal had declined to engage with history' (2007: 136). This was a matter of regret for him, because in his view refugee crises that were current at that time in Iraq, Darfur, Zimbabwe, Sri Lanka and Somalia could not be understood without history – 'yet we invariably approach them on an ahistorical basis' (2007: 137).[11]

In mitigation we do acknowledge that there are historians who write about refugee and forced migration issues without identifying their work as something that should be situated within the field of refugee studies.[12] Moreover, despite its marginal status within the academic discipline of history, there does exist a corpus of both synoptic and more narrowly specialized historical accounts of refugees.[13] Nonetheless, the real issue here is less about quantity than it is about the disciplinary self-identity that explains why historians collectively marginalize the subject. One of the most important of these assumptions is the 'methodological nationalism' by which, according to Wimmer and Glick Schiller, history and the social sciences naturalize the idea of the nation state. Notwithstanding the development of transnational, cosmopolitan, diasporic and regionally centred historical research projects, historians, they argue, 'reflect the methodological assumption that it is a particular nation that provides the constant unit of observation through all historical transformations, the 'thing' whose change history was supposed to describe' (2003: 580). Because refugees are stateless, they are predominantly excluded from historical accounts that refer to an otherwise 'uncluttered national past'.[14] This is not merely problematic at the level at which representational choices are judged to be ethically justified or not. The more critical issue is that the same discursive strategies by which refugees are excluded from narratives about imaginary 'historical communities' can also be summoned as rhetorical allies for processes by which they are excluded from the 'political communities' who have the 'right to have rights'. In this way, methodological nationalism creates the spaces in which contemporary discourses that work against the interests of refugees and migrants can be legitimized in relation to a sense of historical time – the time of the 'nation'.

Ultimately, political questions about migration involve negotiating between sets of imperatives: unconditional/conditional, absolute/relative, universal/particular (Critchley and Kearney 2001: xi). History's attachment to methodological nationalism – indeed the discipline's prime role in its development – makes it complicit with conditional and exclusionary ideas about 'belonging' to national communities that derive their sense of coherence from shared ideas about the past. This idea of 'belonging' can of course work at a supranational level, where states distribute citizens' rights across borders in mutual agreement with other states. At the cultural level the correlate of these extended legal frameworks are the 'affective geographies' at work in the production of new kinds of political imaginaries (Wacquant 2007). Such productions often seek to invoke their own type of historical legitimacy, referencing what they choose to claim as common traditions and experiences of the past. The 'Declaration on European Identity' issued at Copenhagen in 1973 is an example of the form, beginning as it does with members of the newly enlarged European Community defining their claim to a shared identity in relation to a 'common heritage'. But claims to belonging that are based on imagined communities which seemingly endure across historical time contradict unconditional ideas about 'hospitality' to others as fully Other. In this way, historically constituted notions of belonging function as an obstacle to the securing of residency and cultural or social rights by what Balibar called 'foreign foreigners' across the European Union, the ones who are excluded by a system of 'European apartheid' (2004: 44–5).

History as a discipline is therefore caught up in the politics of contemporary migration issues. However, we see no strong argument that academic history writing, judged as a discourse that *always produces political effects*, offers much of *practical* value to groups of migrants today. One can always consult historical accounts about forced migration in centuries past: the eviction of Jews and Muslims from Spain in 1492 and 1609 respectively, the expulsion of Huguenots from France in the seventeenth century and so forth. But such accounts do not themselves come with convincing explanations about how or why such work should be read now, nor who these histories are primarily for. This lack of direct engagement with contemporary political challenges is one of the main reasons behind the estrangement of history from refugee studies that was noted by Marfleet. Refugee studies, which largely formed in the 1980s as a nexus of law, political science, global development studies, anthropology and sociology, aims to be 'policy-relevant'. Its founding mission was to inform NGOs and states and international organizations about policy responses to urgent problems in the present. As a result, its practitioners have not been persuaded of the value of adopting the historical perspective, because they are unconvinced that studying older precedents helps them to understand contemporary iterations when the specificities of each are so different from one another. Equally, given well-rehearsed problematics concerning the ontological status of the past, and similar uncertainty about the epistemological status of claims to know the past-as-history, there are good reasons to reject any claim that historical accounts provide sufficiently stable grounds for acting within present situations.

This helps to explain why among the sixty chapters in *The Oxford Handbook of Refugee and Forced Migration Studies* (2014) only one is contributed by a historian. This single essay by Jérôme Elie, who is described in the volume as an 'independent historian and consultant on international migration and refugee issues', was framed as a plea for greater reciprocity between history and refugee studies. But, in fact, the essay is better understood as a symptom of their non-reciprocity. After acknowledging that historians could themselves do more to contribute to writing about refugees, it stressed that 'the wider refugee and forced migration studies community must start taking history seriously' (Elie 2014: 32). But in making this call Elie saw no reasons why historians should be expected to alter their practices in order to bring it about. He simply asserted that other scholars needed to recognize that 'more often than not, historians will aim to produce history of forced displacements for its own sake and not just with a "utilitarian" perspective. … Historians will (hopefully) not necessarily select a research topic or an approach solely for the benefit of other disciplines, a specific field of study, or to feed into policy' (2014: 32).

Gatrell not only shares Elie's essential point about reciprocity but also rejects the own-sakeism that accompanies it, preferring instead to offer a more nuanced explanation of how a 'historical perspective' might bring the situation of contemporary refugees into sharper focus. His main point here is that writing refugees themselves into historical accounts strongly reduces the risk of essentializing notions of 'the refugee'. By examining the different ways in which refugees have named and articulated their own experiences, he writes, we can better understand how refugees locate their self-description in extensive and intricate webs of meaning. In many cases, such webs of meaning include a sense of what Gatrell names as historical consciousness, which might function, for example, as a source of collective identity in exile or as a factor that helped to determine a given route of flight by specific migrants, literally following the tracks of earlier migrants with whom they believed they shared 'historic ties' (2013: 287–8). In other instances, it could mean invoking a historical allusion for instrumental purposes, such as emphasizing the seriousness of a predicament or supporting a claim for recognition and rights within a territory (2013: 293–4). These points are well made, however none of them really refers to the kind of historicism that continues to underpin most academic history research and writing. Instead they fit better with non-disciplinary concepts such as constructing genealogies, past-presencing, memory management and the use of the past in the production of certain kinds of subjectivities. The prime consideration here, therefore, is not one of identifying which 'historical' precedent is the most appropriate analogue for a given contemporary migration crisis. Nor is it one of historicizing the constellation of factors that produce situations of forced migration. More important than either of these is listening to the voices of those who experience what it is to 'lose a place on earth'.

One clear disciplinary similarity between history and refugee studies is the problem of silencing migrants themselves. Within the field of policy-relevant research this issue has at least been confronted directly, if not necessarily overcome. A key text here was Barbara Harrell-Bond's *Imposing Aid* (1986), which attempted to scrutinize the emergency assistance programme in the Yei River District area of southern Sudan in the early 1980s.[15] Harrell-Bond and her team of researchers from Oxford set out to counter the 'colonial mindset' by which migrants were excluded from all attempts to critically evaluate the workings of assistance programmes that were directed towards them. Their alternative approach emphasized the importance of listening to migrants' own understandings of their experiences and situation. The ambition here was to evaluate aid programmes against a background of understanding people's own efforts to organize and develop their communities (Harrell-Bond 1986: xiv). A critical dimension of Harrell-Bond's work was its argument that migrants were not *a priori* dependent and passive; rather, it was the practices and assumptions of humanitarian institutions and political structures that created (even demanded) the dependency of migrants on donors and providers of assistance (Fiddian-Qasmiyeh et al. 2014: 6).

In our view similar processes can be seen to operate in historical research and writing. Historiography reproduces the very same sense of migrant dependency and passivity that Harrell-Bond sought to contest in *Imposing Aid*. Again, the problems at issue are those of representation, silencing and exclusions. Because of a professional attachment to a certain conception of archive-based empirical investigation, those few historians who do write about migration usually do so through the optics of aid agencies and relief organizations. In particular there has been an over-emphasis on the role of the UNHCR since it established its central archive in Geneva in 1996 – with its now 10 kilometres of shelving space and 10 million digitized documents.[16] This is why Gatrell complained that 'refugees have been allowed only a walk-on part in most histories of the twentieth century, and even then as subjects of external intervention rather than as actors in their own right' (2013: 283). Of course there are occasional exceptions to this general rule – for example, Urvashi Butalia's use of oral testimonies and personal writings produced by refugees in the wake of Indian Partition (1998 and 2001), or Tony Kushner and Katharine Knox's social history of refugees in the 'age of genocide' (1999). In the main, however, Marfleet's point that refugee testimonies are 'discouraged and *actively* forgotten' in historiographical accounts continues to hold weight (2007: 145–6). Historicization happens *to* migrants, without their involvement, and lacking an explicitly articulated explanation of how or why it might help them now.

Inspired by Barthélémy Toguo's work *Purification*, a vast frieze combining handwritten articles from the United Nation's *Universal Declaration of Human Rights* with watercolour images of abused and tortured human beings, the second half of this article will use sections of the *Declaration* as a rhetorical strategy for exploring how forms of past-talk and practices of historicization, particularly by artists, foreground dichotomies of im/mobility and the inequities and inequalities inherent in the necropolitics that underpins a casual acceptance, by Fortress Europe, of the deaths and dislocation of hundreds of thousands of migrants in and around the Mediterranean (Mbembe 2003: 11–40; Toguo 2012).[17]

> *Article 13. (1) Everyone has the right to freedom of movement and residence within the borders of each state. (2) Everyone has the right to leave any country, including his own, and to return to his country.*[18]

The globalized, post–Cold War, neoliberal, capitalist world promised democratization, freedom of movement and egalitarian economic participation in free markets, but instead *crisis globalization* has ushered in a period of increased economic and travel inequality: a dichotomy of im/mobility (Demos 2013: xiii). The expectation of complete freedom of movement in a borderless world for those in the global north is accompanied by a securitization of their own borders and a restriction on the freedom of movement of those in the global south. The 'strong passports' of the neoliberal economic colonizers provide fast-track security clearance as they travel nomadically through a borderless 'smooth' space.[19] Yet, those subjected to the legacies of colonialism and the machinations of totalitarian capitalism are, by contrast, the sedentary – subjected to the institutionalization of the linear, metric, optic state space; those whose movements are criminalized; and for whom militarized borders, scopic regimes, visas and detention camps populate a fractured, 'striated' geography of borders that simultaneously facilitates the flow of goods and capital while restricting the movement of people.[20] Fazal Sheikh's *Desert Bloom* (2015) provides an artistic witnessing and intervention in the subjugation of nomadic peoples to the striated institutionalized, disciplined space of the colonial occupier. Sheikh documents the forced displacement and marginalization of the Bedouin of the Negev through the repeated destruction of their villages by Israel in the interests of resource exploitation and the imposition of settlements.[21] Similar tensions arising from the colonial imposition of immobility in their subjection of the nomadic is evident in the work of Anders Sunna (2014, 2017) and his depiction of the forced enclosure of the reindeer herds of the indigenous Sámi by the Swedish authorities, as well as the colonization and appropriation of the Sápmi region and compulsory transfers of entire Sámi communities.[22] His work, drawing on the experience of his family whose reindeer herds were forcibly removed from their pastures speaks back to the colonizing culture.[23] It tells a story of the pain and anger, of extensive institutional racism; of the subjugation of the Sámi to authoritarian architectures, assimilationist practices and policies enforcing immobility; as well as of the colonization of their space in the interests of the Swedish state's exploitation of their natural resources (Heith 2015: 69–83).[24]

> *Article 3: Everyone has the right to life, liberty and security of person. Article 14. (1) Everyone has the right to seek and to enjoy in other countries asylum from persecution.*

But this inequality in movement elides a far greater inequality. The denial of free movement to those fleeing from violence, oppression and economic or climatic catastrophe reveals the asymmetries inherent in the allocation of the basic human rights to 'life, liberty and security of person'. The closure of borders, the internment in camps, indeed the contortions surrounding linguistic definitions of who constitutes a legitimate migrant or refugee all actively violate article 3 and 14 of the *Declaration*. Moreover, the disassociatively negative response to migration among colonialism's heirs in the global north, and the implicit denial of human rights that this entails, arises, we argue, from the use such narratives play in defining and legitimizing the neoliberal capitalist system as a civilized ideology and masking the violence necessary to maintain its hegemony. It is through a contrast with an uncivilized, threatening, barbaric other that a self-image of Western democracy is created that emphasizes the values of freedom, human rights, equality and inclusive tolerance, but, perhaps more importantly, it is through this contrast that attention is distracted from the 'differential exchange value' with regard to the lives of the 'civilized' and the 'uncivilized' (Asad 2007: 94). That is, the narrative of migrants posing an existential threat provides a means by which populations in the global north can ignore the blatant unequal valuation of human life dictated by the market; they can ignore the dislocation and death of people arising from pollution, climate change and conflict; they can ignore the sale of weapons and torture equipment and the rendition of prisoners to regimes with dubious human rights' records; and they can ignore the fact that workers in the global south are exploited in order to protect capitalism and its beneficiaries. The narrative also effectively legitimizes the suppression of any resistance to this neo-economic colonialism by parsing such actions as a pre-emptive defence of borders and Western values, or the export of democracy and freedom. Yet embedded in the very concept of liberty that is at the heart of liberalism is a violence: not only the right to directly kill those perceived to be a threat to civilized order and liberal democracy but also a passive acquiescence in the incarceration, exploitation, disappearance and death of those fleeing violence, insecurity, starvation.[25]

Article 15. (1) Everyone has the right to a nationality. (2) No one shall be arbitrarily deprived of his nationality nor denied the right to change his nationality.

A stark example of the implicit violence, discrimination and colonial echoes within Western liberalism is the state revocation or denial of nationality or citizenship from the politically and socially marginalized in the interests of 'the public good'.[26] In *Where We Come From* (2001–3) Emily Jacir confronts the effective denial of nationality to Palestinians living under Israeli military curfew in the Occupied Palestinian Territories; Palestinians living in Israel, but classified as present absentees or internally displaced people; and exiled Palestinians denied the right of return to the land they were forced to leave, many of whom have not been granted citizenship of the countries in which they now live.[27] Jacir asks these Palestinians what she can do for them in Palestine/Israel: a place that she can travel freely within because of her 'strong' US passport, but they can't. She then undertakes these simple tasks, recording the act in a photo-text juxtaposition of wish and wish fulfilment. For example, she travels to Gaza to eat *sayadiyeh* as the person making the request is a Palestinian-Arab citizen of Israel and is thus prevented from travelling to Gaza; she walks in Nazareth because the person asking has a West Bank identity card and isn't permitted to travel there; she visits a mother and gives her a hug and a kiss because her son, despite having Gazan identity papers, left Gaza for Ramallah in 1995 and has not been allowed to return; for Hana, whose family were exiled to Lebanon in 1948, she travels to Haifa to play football with the first Palestinian boy she meets; and for Iyad, who lives in the Dheisheh Refugee Camp in the West Bank, she waters a tree in the village in the district of Jerusalem where his parents once lived before they were forced to leave.[28] None of the Palestinians who made the requests are shown in the photographs, and it is through their absence that Jacir 'allegorizes their deprived political status' while also demanding the universal application of the right to citizenship, family life and particularly the rights to a nationality, to equality, to freedom of movement and residency, and the right to return to one's country (Demos 2013: 104).

In addition to the denial of citizenship and nationality to exiled Palestinians or those who live in the Occupied Territories is the threat to Palestinian-Arab Israeli citizens of the revocation of their Israeli citizenship if they are deemed to engage in activities disloyal to the state. In 2017, Israel revoked the Israeli citizenship of Palestinian-Arab Israeli Alaa Raed Ahmad Zayoud after he attacked and injured four people. The court's deputy president argued that in the attack he had violated his commitment to maintain loyalty to the state (Wilford 2017).[29] That such a move is indicative of an entrenched and institutionalized inequality between different categories of Israeli citizen based on ethno-cultural or religious background and state colonial ambitions is evident from the fact that Jewish-Israelis who attack other Israeli citizens are not subject to such a revocation of citizenship. This existence of a de facto two-tier system of citizenship between 'real' citizens and 'deprive-able' citizens is not limited, however, to Israel (Mantu 2018: 39).[30] Increasingly, over the past few years UK citizens have been subjected to the forced removal of citizenship (and therefore either denial of re-entry to the country or deportation from the country). Ostensibly in a UK context such a denial of citizenship can only occur when the person either holds, or has the potential to hold, dual citizenship: a stipulation which limits the forced removal of citizenship to UK citizens who themselves migrated from elsewhere or whose parents or grandparents migrated to the UK. While not exclusively the case, many of the UK citizens who might find themselves subject to this revocation have ancestors from former British colonies, and thus the practice demonstrates an inconsistency in the rights accorded to UK citizens that is rooted in the legacy of British colonial inequality and racism. The case of Shamima Begum illustrates how the 'public good' defence can often be used to deny entry to those who have not been convicted of any crime, but have simply expressed opinions deemed to pose a threat to civilized order and liberal democracy. Begum, a UK citizen born in the UK, left when she was a child aged fifteen to travel to Syria in support of ISIS and married an ISIS fighter. Following the reporting in the British press of her comments made to a reporter from a Syrian refugee camp in February 2019, in which she expressed no regret for her initial decision to go to Syria, the Home Secretary chose to revoke her British citizenship.[31] This decision was based on the fact that her mother had originally been a Bangladeshi national, although Shamima herself had never been to Bangladesh, did not possess Bangladeshi citizenship, and Bangladesh had said that they would not grant her citizenship. In revoking her UK citizenship, the Home Secretary effectively left her stateless, without a nationality and immobile in a Syrian refugee camp despite the fact that she was a UK citizen.

Article 9. No one shall be subjected to arbitrary arrest, detention or exile.

Migration and the flight of refugees is often thought about in terms of mobility, but it may be more useful to think about it in terms of immobility: migrants are subject to diverse varieties of spatial control: incarceration, detention, periods of enforced waiting or exile. Much of the art of Emily Jacir makes a clear demand for the universality of all human rights while visualizing 'the inequality between those with rights and those without' in the context of Palestine/Israel (Demos 2013: 123). *Crossing Surda (a record of going to and from work)* provides a visual testimony to the ways in which the spatialities and architectures of Israeli military occupation in the West Bank produce uneven geographies, minimize Palestinian mobility and thus fragment society in socio-economic, political and cultural terms (Jacir 2003a). For eight days Jacir filmed her daily commute to Birzeit University through the Surda military checkpoint which blocks the road between the town of Ramallah and thirty nearby Palestinian villages, illustrating the difficulties and uncertainty Palestinians face in their basic daily travels.[32] Jacir notes that when 'Israeli soldiers decide that there should be no movement on the road, they shoot live ammunition, tear gas, and sound bombs to disperse people from the checkpoint'.[33] When the Israeli soldiers saw Jacir filming they confiscated her video recording and detained her at gunpoint for three hours. Israeli checkpoints in the Occupied Palestinian Territories are not solely, or even primarily, intended to function as part of the apparatus of surveillance or security, but are instead designed to produce uncertainty and humiliation and thus minimize, not regulate Palestinian movement (Handel

2011: 268–71). It is through this transformation of space that the colonization of the West Bank is facilitated. Road closures, the establishment of militarized checkpoints, arbitrary, temporary detention of those travelling and the random revocation of travel permits have effectively not only fragmented the Occupied Palestinian Territories into a territorial patchwork of unconnected, sealed spaces but also disconnected the Occupied Palestinian Territories from the Israeli labour market and disrupted local businesses by denying Palestinians access to their places of work, farm land and market places, thus crushing the Palestinian economy (Weizman 2012: 146, 156).[34] Furthermore, Hammond makes the point that by disrupting access to higher education (Birzeit University) the Surda checkpoint contributes to the Israeli policy of encouraging the 'transfer' of indigenous Palestinians from the area (2007: 264).[35] In a similar manner Jacir's *Entry Denied (a concert in Jerusalem)*, addresses the immobility of Palestinians through their exile (2003b). *Entry Denied* is a film of a musical performance by three Austrian nationals in an empty theatre in Vienna. Having been originally invited to perform at the 2003 Jerusalem Festival by the Austrian Embassy and the United Nations Development Programme, one of the three musicians, Marwan Abado was, at the last minute, detained by the Israeli authorities at Tel Aviv airport before his visa was revoked and he was sent back to Vienna (Kholeif 2013: 18).[36] Although in possession of Austrian citizenship, a valid visa and an official invitation, Abado was denied entry to his country of origin, presumably precisely because it was his country of origin.

In a very different way Muhammad Ali's series of drawings *Endless Days* (2015a) through its images of individuals stuck in rubbish bins or jars also conveys the inescapable immobility of those subject to an unequal recognition of their human rights as a result of conflict.[37] Young men hang suspended from their rucksacks, lie crushed by rocks or stand balanced on precarious platforms leaning forward trying to move while held back by restraints of some form, while others stand immobile with both feet sticking out of one trouser leg. During the present war in Syria the options for leaving were limited; people waited for safe passage, for visas, for an opportunity to leave besieged areas; people waited, hoping things would get better.

Article 25. (1) Everyone has the right to a standard of living adequate for the health and well-being of himself and of his family, including food, clothing, housing and medical care and necessary social services, and the right to security in the event of unemployment, sickness, disability, widowhood, old age or other lack of livelihood in circumstances beyond his control.

Muhammad Ali's drawings and video work also depict an otherizing that is not that of the neoliberal otherizing of migrants as a threat to Western democracy and lifestyle, but an otherizing that happens to people and communities in situations of extreme violence and stress, a breakdown of human relations. His series of drawings *Post-Thousand and One Nights* (2015b) features deformed, parasitical, insect-like creatures who swarm together, steal, cheat, deceive, assault and hate each other: a visual metaphor for the desperate, dehumanizing situation of those living through a conflict of particular horror.[38] Similarly, *Neither Human, Nor Stone* (2014) is an allegorical representation of the collapse of society.[39] Here Muhammad Ali bears witness not only to the collapse of individuals on the streets of Damascus but also to the collapse of society manifested by the fact that although others see the distress of those who have fallen they do nothing and continue on. This collapse of society, the intolerable physical, emotional and mental strain people endure is generally elided and ignored in narratives of migration in the global north beyond an almost casual 'aestheticization of misery' and the scopic border spectacle that frames migration as an 'unmanageable crisis' (Demos 2013: xvii).[40] We choose not to see what has forced people to move, instead we speculate on what potential disorder migrants may bring to our lives. Despite the prevalence of a transnational globalized economy and free-market capitalism, for many the freedom such an economic system brings is restricted to the free movement of goods, not people. Nation states are militarizing their borders and restricting the movement of people in an attempt to maintain the privileged position of particular, and exclusive, political and economic communities (Demos 2013: 109). Such a position suggests that the Muhammad Ali's depiction of the collapse of society should not simply be read as a consequence of war in a particular country, but it could perhaps more pertinently describe the violence of Fortress Europe's border regime and its refusal to provide support and refuge to those who need it.

In the mediatized border spectacle that underpins the articulation of the intertwined ontology and sovereignty of Fortress Europe, it is the body of the migrant, which is 'inscribed in the order of power' (Mbembe 2003: 12, 14). As Mbembe has argued, sovereignty is the capacity to define who matters and who does not; who is disposable and who is not; it is embodied as a power over mortality (27, 11–12). Embedded in the exercise of sovereignty by Fortress Europe is an ongoing racism that permits the exercise of Foucauldian biopower and ultimately works to create 'the condition for the acceptability of putting to death' (Mbembe 2003: 17). Against the dominant media narratives that frame migration in terms of states of 'exception, emergency and a fictionalized notion of the enemy', the *Liquid Traces – The Left-to-Die Boat Case* (2014) project led by Charles Heller and Lorenzo Pezzani is an example of a militant investigation into the power asymmetries and necropolitics behind Europe's transformation of the Mediterranean into a zone of exclusion and a space of death for the disposable, those consigned to unfreedom (Mbembe 2003: 16–17, 34, 39). This project documents the deaths of sixty-three migrants on a boat off the Libyan coast in 2011, not simply to bear witness to their deaths but to make visible the violence perpetuated by, and inherent in, the securitization of the European border regimes.[41]

The 'left-to-die' vessel left Libya early in the morning of 27 March 2011 with seventy-two migrants on board, heading for Lampadusa. Approximately fifteen to eighteen hours later, running out of fuel, the migrants placed a distress call by satellite phone, and the position and distress status of the vessel was signalled to all boats in the area by the International Maritime Rescue Coordination Centre (MRCC); NATO HQ Allied Command was also informed. During this time period, as a result of the enforcement of a NATO arms embargo off the coast of Libya starting 23 March 2011, the Libyan coast was under an exceptional degree of surveillance and monitoring which certainly would also have allowed NATO to monitor the boat in distress. Yet, following the distress signal the vessel drifted unaided until 10 April when it ran aground on the coast near Tripoli. During this time, the vessel was approached by a military ship, but no assistance was offered; two military helicopters also flew over the boat, and one dropped biscuits and water.[42] In a manifestation of the disobedient gaze, the project deliberately repurposed the various sensing technologies, instruments and methodologies of state surveillance and control usually employed to police migration in order to make visible the violence of the border regime and those subject to it. In so doing, the data from these surveillance technologies has not only recognized 'that each act of escape is an act of political struggle, where subjects do not need to be legitimized by sovereign powers "to claim and perform (citizenship) rights, protection and movement"', but it also constitutes a digital archive of the violence perpetuated against migrants (Mazzara 2019: 13). The fundamental motivation behind this project is to hold to account those responsible for 'a crime that should not be mistaken for an accident'.[43] As such the data has not only been presented in numerous art exhibitions but has also been submitted as evidence of responsibility for the crime of non-assistance in legal proceedings in France, Belgium, Spain and Italy.[44]

How can those read as an existential threat, consigned to the 'bare life' (Demos 2013: xix), a form of death-in-life in 'globalization's shadows'

(Mbembe 2003: 21) be politically represented?[45] How can the state of exception in which they are confined be made visible and challenged? How can the necropolitics that underpins the inequalities arising from neoliberal capitalism be made visible? How can the ethnographic gaze, the patronizing 'compassionate heart', the 'otherizing' hostility towards migrants be avoided in representation, and replaced with recognition of both shared humanity and an acknowledgement of the injustice of extant inequality? Can there exist a 'reciprocal extraterritoriality' that decentres national identities and the dichotomies of us/them inherent in narratives of migration (Demos 2013: xix)? Art as a form of past-talk can raise provocative and necessary questions about the disparity in the value of a human life, im/mobility and justice. It also gives voice to the experiences and narratives of migrants in a way that history doesn't.[46] The artists discussed here challenge us to recognize that sentimental displays of empathy with refugees, or proclamations of solidarity with their plight, are insufficient; that they are used as too-easy moralizing gestures.[47] Instead they defy us to desist in conspiring in the inequality of the distribution of human rights; they emphasize the need to understand the struggle of migrants as 'the price humanity is paying for the global economy' and instead demand the universal applicability of human rights (Zizek 2016: 101, 110). They draw attention to the hypocritical irony that for the global north migrants have a greater visibility, and are accorded more compassion, in death than life.[48]

Although Gatrell argues that writing refugees themselves into historical accounts strongly reduces the risk of essentializing notions of 'the refugee' through an examination and location of the refugee experience in broader webs of meaning, we are not so sure. As Dening, citing Marcuse, argues, in an important way the reification of experience into an authoritative historical account is a 'transformation of lived experience into things' and that in turn leads to a silencing: a forgetting (2007: 103). Dening counters such an exclusion by advocating historying: a moral act; an unclosed action of making histories that refuses closure, reification and the transformation of lived experience into a single authoritative narrative; a process by which pasts are transformed into words, images or performances. Dening wonders whether to be truly compassionate his stories should in fact be poems. We think maybe he is right, and that neither history nor historying can fight the reification, otherization and objectification of the stories of migrants. We think that at the present time the praxis and politics of institutionalized historicization processes (including historying) do not provide a productive resource or practical intervention into securing the human rights of migrants. In contrast, artists have far more successfully mobilized the image of the migrant in their past-talk as an oppositional force against, and a critique of, the unequal political and economic implications of globalization. Maybe Marcuse was right, and in the end it is only art that effectively fights reification; and the only way to effect the necessary compassion to secure the human rights of everyone is through an unhistorying (Dening 2007: 103).

8

Historical Evitability

The Return of the Philosophy of History

Aviezer Tucker

We live in interesting times, not least for philosophers of history and historiography.[1] The wings of the owl of Minerva are flapping again. Philosophers of history may emphatically understand Augustine upon hearing of the sack of Rome by the Visigoths. Now that history is back, so should the philosophies of history and historiography. I show here that philosophers of history and historiography have a unique set of intellectual perspectives and tools to analyse, dissect and understand the current crisis.

I have devoted most of my philosophical efforts over the last quarter century to the epistemology of our knowledge of the past. I started with the trivial observation that knowledge of the past is not empirical since the past is imperceptible through our senses, nor is historiography fiction because it is neither arbitrary nor reducible to power or interests because of the many agreements about history between very different historians who had different identities and interests. I concluded that knowledge of the past is inferential and probabilistic. Past events and processes transmit information signals to the present. Historians distinguish signal from noise in present evidence and then use that information to infer its origins, the past, sometimes with the help of information theories. That inference is probabilistic. Since we cannot have apodictic *a priori* or empirical knowledge of the past, we aspire for high enough probability in context. I have used this framework to reanalyse and reinterpret classical problems in the philosophies of historiography and history, concluding that historical truth means sufficiently probable propositions about the past in a context of inquiry. Historiographic explanations are justified by the information signals historical events and causal processes sent to the present. Anachronism is the inability to distinguish information preserving signal from noise. Historiographic revisionism is giving precedence to wishful thinking and political values over the cognitive values that underlie the inference of probable pasts from its information preserving receivers in the present (Tucker 2004; 2006: 299–317; 2008: 1–16; 2010: 64–84; 2012: 274–97; 2014: 232–59). Now, I want to use this theoretical framework to re-examine topics in the philosophies of history and historiography that were raised mostly though not exclusively during the second-third of the previous century facing the consecutive crises of advanced economies in the 1930s, the collapse of democracies, the rise of two particularly virulent types of totalitarianisms, the self-destruction of Europe and the Cold War. The totalitarian power that survived and won the Second World War expressed allegiance to a robust philosophy of history, Marxism, thereby pushing philosophers of history to the forefront of the Cold War of ideas. Contested questions included most notably: Is history inevitable? What is the significance of the individual, or 'hero', in history? Is history cyclical, progressive, regressive or directionless? Does history repeat itself, or merely rhymes? Can we learn from history and what is the role of historiography in this process? These questions were abandoned rather than resolved by the later 1960s. Even before communism and its ideology imploded at the end of the 1980s, East European Marxism became a stolid dogma that did not pose a challenge in the battle of ideas. Western Marxism did not emphasize the historical as distinct of critical Marx. At the same time within the philosophies of history and historiography, questions about history rather than its representation received the abusive moniker of 'speculative' in the sense of baseless, without proof. It was also called 'substantial' and contrasted with 'analytical'. By whatever name, it was abandoned because it became associated with the discredited philosophies of history associated with Hegel, Marx, Spengler and Toynbee and so on, or with eschatological religion.

Meanwhile, some of the mid-century topics in the philosophy of human history reappeared mutandis mutatis in the philosophy of natural history, especially the philosophy of evolutionary biology. The treatment of these questions or their cognates in the philosophy of biology demonstrates that it is possible to approach these problems without resorting to the synthetic *a priori* realm. Instead of conceiving the philosophies of science and historiography as distinct meta-disciplines above and beyond science and historiography, they can be continuous with them and with each other, in accordance with the Quinean view of philosophy. Philosophers of science first sought to analyse scientific and philosophical concepts like historical inevitability and necessity, contingency and overdetermination, and then applied them to the best scientific accounts of natural and evolutionary history. I propose that the same approach can be applied to the philosophy of historiography: We can analyse and clarify the concepts and then apply them to historiography and history, even contemporary ones.

Before proceeding to offer an analysis of historical inevitability, the role of the individual in history, the structure and direction of history, and repetition and lessons of history, in light of contemporary philosophy of science and current politics, I want to outline the alternative views. In Table 8.1, I distinguish four attitudes to these questions. It would be a stretch to call them *philosophies of history*. Rather they are ideological reactions to questions in the philosophy of history. Unlike totalitarianism, liberalism and progressivism, contemporary populism does not really have an ideology because it is anti-intellectual, eschewing any attempt to come up with a consistent world view, rather than express passions. It does have an attitude though, so it would be a summary of its attitudes to questions in philosophy of history.

Totalitarian philosophies of history considered it inevitable because they considered large impersonal forces such as race and class to be the determining forces of history, or at least what they considered the biological and economic essences of history. When totalitarian ideologies began to promote personality cults of revolutionary leaders, they generated an inner contradiction: If history is inevitable, why should Lenin, Stalin or Hitler matter? The ideological response

Table 8.1 Four Ideologies as Philosophies of History

	Totalitarian	Liberal	Progressive	Populist
Historical Inevitability/ Evitability	Inevitable	Evitable	Inevitable	Too many syllables
The Individual in History	Insignificant, in relation to large impersonal forces	Individualist	Insignificant, except in the vanguard of large impersonal forces	Individualist
Direction of History	Regressive and then progressive	Conditionally Progressive	Absolute progressive	Regressive
Historical Repetition Vs. Uniqueness	Repetitive	Unique	Unique	Repetitive
Can We Learn from History	No, except for tactical lessons	Yes	No	No

was to resort to the logical part-whole fallacy, the identification of the properties of a whole with those of its parts. The totalitarian leaders ceased being individuals and became identified with the class, national or historical whole: History = the people = the class or race = the party = the cadres = the leader Tucker (2015: 95ff, chapter 7). The totalitarian concept of history was cyclical. History repeats itself in periodic cycles of class or racial conflicts. The aim of totalitarian utopias was to transcend cyclical history by putting a stop to it and to generate classless or racially pure societies: a future utopia that was also a return to primeval naturalness when hunter-gatherers had no private property or when noble savages fought each other without the encumbrances of morality. Since history is inevitable, nothing is to be learned from it. If the historical process can be likened to a pregnancy, we can at most 'shorten the birth pangs', as Marx put it, when the revolutionary avant-garde draws tactical lessons from historical experience and the defeated capitalist class recognizes the inevitable and surrenders.

Liberals, like Karl Popper and Isaiah Berlin, countered the mid-century Marxists by arguing that history is contingent and evitable (Berlin 1955; Popper 1957). Liberals emphasize that minor events and individuals may have major historical consequences; human decisions and free choices affect the course of history. From the perspective of liberal values, it is possible to perceive several types of historical progress over different time frames: economic progress over the last millennia; cultural and scientific progress since the Renaissance; and political progress since the Glorious, American and French Revolutions, if not since Magna Carta. Liberals conceive progress as conditional on particular historical contexts and circumstances. Therefore, liberal social sciences study modernity, democratization, economic development and their interconnections in an attempt to discover their historical preconditions, the preconditions for liberal progress. Liberal social engineering tries to replicate these conditions or stimulating causes, to nudge history in the liberal direction, since decisions have historical consequences and there is no progressive inevitability. History need not repeat itself; 'some people believe that history repeats itself, others read the *Economist*', as the advertisement for the liberal weekly magazine went. Though history is not cyclical or repetitive, it is conditional; therefore, liberals believed that much could be learned from it, especially from the conditions that gave rise to past mistakes and wrong turns. This learning process affected especially the construction of liberal institutions. The founders of the United States studied the self-destruction of the Roman Republic as they set to build a new Republic on better institutional foundations. At the end of the Second World War, liberal policymakers in the West set out to construct a political, social and global order that would institutionally prevent repetitions of the catastrophic mistakes of the first-half of the twentieth century, especially the policy mistakes that led to the transmutation of a financial crisis generated by few banks into a global calamity, and the political errors that allowed totalitarian political parties to take over states and start wars. Wiser decisions and better institutions in the 1930s could have pre-empted the globalization of the crisis and the rise of totalitarianism. These institutional reforms created the basis for the world order that is under attack now.

Progressivist belief in an inevitable historical progress dates back to the nineteenth century, but took off following the end of the Cold War. As President Obama put it, quoting Martin Luther King (who was not the first to use the expression), 'The arc of the moral universe is long, but it bends toward justice.' Philosophers like Peter Railton formulated this approach as a version of *moral realism*: history as the story of the survival of morally fit societies (Railton 1986: 163-207). Moral progress, over the long term, is inevitable despite acknowledged historical backsliding, twists and turns because less moral societies collapse under the weight of their own injustices. The teleological arc of history does *not* usually repeat itself, as it bends towards justice. Progressive individuals can join the great march to justice, but they do not have to. The march will continue without them. Accordingly, studying history and the philosophy of history are redundant at best. They may be regressive in offering alternatives to the modernizing agenda of constructing a progressive world of technological progress, managed prosperity and egalitarianism founded on empathy. At most, history may offer some exemplary inspiring stories about progressive and scientific heroes who incarnated the spirit of progress that can be taught with little context to children. The progressive agenda privileged solving historical problems through the technocratic mastery of marketing (the most popular major in American colleges), computer science, engineering and above all management. Managers should not be bound by history. To be innovative and competitive, they cannot stick to what worked in the past. Since history progresses rapidly, they should not be deterred from trying things that failed in the past, especially since managers have no idea what happened in the past, and do not need to know it because it will not repeat itself. The prices of housing and financial assets will continue to rise, since they have been rising recently. Why consider the Tulip bubble except to amuse ourselves with arcane historical anecdotes? The contingency that civilization might have to fall back on its historical lessons when the managerial engine of economic progress fails and jumps off the progressive track did not appear realistic. The economic track jump of 2007-9 and the political track jump of 2016–17 taken together mark 'Santayana's revenge', the return of history to haunt the progressivists who denied it.

From the perspective of philosophy of history, contemporary populism takes the progressivist ignoring of history to an extreme. It is not just ignorant of the mistakes of the past that it unwittingly attempts to repeat, but it lacks *any* historical orientation in time, any historical consciousness at all beyond a vaguely reactionary, mostly inarticulate, sense that history has been regressive lately; but that a strong leader may halt the decline and make us young again.

Contemporary Cyclical Historical Inevitability

If we recall any history at all, a sense of nauseous noxiousness spreads in our body politic as we witness contemporary politics. A sense of helplessness fits a belief in historical inevitability, as a sense of historical déjà vu fits a cyclical concept of history of the past two centuries.[2]

Historical inevitability and economic determinism are back in vogue for the first time since the 1930s. Confronted with the rise of anti-liberal and anti-intellectual mass movements that appeal to base irrational passions, members of the educated and sometimes privileged-thinking classes have deemed themselves powerless as they have watched recession, slow growth, frozen social mobility and rising inequality undermine social comity and trust, and then spread out over borders to undermine, weaken and deconstruct the post-war liberal world order. A wave of irrational political passions has propelled vulgar and vile populist politicians that bear resemblance – rhyme but not repeat – some of the odious characters who came to power in Europe after the previous Great Depression. They explain the apparent divide between open and closed societies, between norms of embracing toleration, innovation, plurality and diversity and those that would arrest change to restore an imaginary past to shelter fragile, insecure identities by the difference between a GDP growth of 2 and 4 per cent per annum averaged over a decade. The case for economically determined, historically cyclical inevitability as an explanation of the past ten years would run something like this.

As Marx foresaw, capitalism is a wonderful force for innovation, economic growth and globalization of prosperity through trade. Since the end of the Cold War, the global economy underwent what Richard Baldwin called *the great convergence* and consequently experienced the largest reduction in poverty in world history (Baldwin 2016). The gap between the global rich and poor has contracted to levels not seen since the eighteenth century, when greater global equality resulted from universal poverty.

Unfortunately, though global capitalism is so wonderful, it has a near fatal flaw. It is given to unpredictable and inevitable financial crises and recessions. When capital managers make different mistakes at different times, markets compensate and remain at an overall equilibrium. But when, sooner or later, herd-like, they all over-extend credit to form a bubble at the same time, the global economy keels over. Technocratic and political elites cannot prevent misallocations of credit or effectively reverse them once it becomes apparent that they have happened. Instead, elites react to severe economic downturns by attempting to preserve their own social and economic status leading them to block social mobility because in a close-to-zero-sum game upward mobility for some necessitates downward mobility for others. In short, when the pie stops growing, the elites 'rig' the rules of the socio-economic game, as Donald Trump and Robert Reich agree.

Consequently, the elite becomes increasingly concentrated, closed, distrusted and alienated from those below it in the social hierarchy. This short-term elite strategy *inevitably* leads to the long-term self-destruction of the elite as a class, because it generates a backlash from groups whose mobility is blocked or pushed downwards. The 'revolt of the masses' pushes back through the political extremes of the Right and Left. The Right tends to represent the lower middle classes who scapegoat those even weaker and more unfortunate than themselves, especially dynamic ethnic group that prefer spicy foods and garlic; the Left tends to target its aggression upwards against the elites. The centre cannot hold.

Prolonged recessions undermine personal, professional and vocational security and identity. Consequently, they awaken from their evolutionary slumber parts of the psyche that were adaptive when our simian ancestors lived in small tribes and were subjected to extreme forms of natural selection. Sensing existential threat, people look to a tribe for protection, scapegoats to blame for their troubles and other tribes to attack, to increase their share of the limited resources, by excluding some members of the inn group and stealing from outgroups. In the complex yet threatening modern world where there are no tribes and no natural selective extinction, atavistic emotions short-circuit weak reason to construct shadowy reflections of primeval dramas and replay them. Passions direct us to search for a pathological chieftain who lacks empathy and loves risk, a psychopath or a narcissist, to best lead the struggle for survival. In the modern global interlinked and interdependent world, instead of encouraging and facilitating trade and migration to stimulate the global economy and generate growth that can shorten and moderate the severity of recessions, instinctively people limit them to rely on their own flints and scrapers and conquer the neighbouring waterhole. When personal identity is linked to the market value of one's labour and that market generates little demand and even less sense of personal value, people look for alternative identities. When being human, a reflection of the image of God, is too universal or unconvincing in post-religious societies, constructed tribes: races, nations, classes and ethnicities create the illusion of filling in the void (Fidelis 2017: 60–7). Xenophobia and scapegoating are in this respect like sea or car sickness. We did not evolve to adapt to shake on unstable ground. Some people's mental mechanisms misinterpret the effects of rough seas or bumps on the road on their inner ears as 'being poisoned'. The atavistic mechanism then is to vomit. This mechanism was extremely well adapted to protecting our bodies in the context of eating things that may be poisonous. But vomiting in cars today is not helpful.

Once these archaic demons awake, it is difficult to lay them back to rest, even when the economy is well on its way to recovery. This turns an economic crisis into a catastrophe. A vicious cycle of economic decline, breakdown of trade and geographical mobility, economic and political hostilities, and isolation takes over and spreads. Historically, this downward economic and political spiral resulted in wars such as the two world wars. Wars finally open meritocratic channels for upward mobility; being well connected may help soldiers survive wars but not win them. Members of the old elites go to war and die, and others lose their property; the elite is decimated, and so war creates space for increased social equality. After the war, economic reconstruction eventually creates prosperity, trade and migration, a virtuous cycle of increasing prosperity and social and economic openness, until the next inevitably unexpected financial recession – and so on and on. Arguably the world economy has been reiterating such cycles in different contexts at least since the crisis that resulted in the French Revolution. Marx's mistake was to impose an eschatological-messianic Judeo-Christian economic narrative on cyclical, economically determined, history. There is no historical equivalent of nirvana, no escape from the historical cycle of destruction and rebirth. That was a communist illusion. Central planning only made things worse because it consistently misallocated capital and blocked innovation, thus generating sustained decline interspersed with low growth generated by selling natural resources to advanced capitalist economies.

This inevitable cycle of this ideal eternal history (to borrow Vico's term) is independent of human volition. Nobody wills it, yet no one can stop or escape it. Economic risk cannot be managed and controlled indefinitely. During recessions, individual members of the elite concentrate wealth and power and use it to block upper mobility despite the long-term self-destructiveness of this strategy to the elite as a class. Since behind the thin veneer of rationality and civilization people are irrational overgrown simians, when subjected to economic pressure passions like fear bypass their rationality, such as it is, and react as though they were under selective evolutionary pressure and turn tribal, xenophobic, authoritarian and, given the context of the modern global economy, self-destructive. Passions trump rationality; De Maistre gets his last laugh at the ideals of the Enlightenment and popular sovereignty; modern democracy commenced with Robespierre and now resulted and concludes with Trump. History repeats itself first as a tragedy, then as a comedy, and finally as a reality show.

Historical Evitability

A critical examination of historical inevitability, whether or not humanity is imprisoned in cyclical history of its own making like mice in a treadmill, running forward only to stay put, requires a clarification of the conceptual distinction between *historical necessity* and *historical contingency*. I have argued that this distinction is founded on the sensitivity of historical events to initial conditions.[3] Necessary processes are insensitive to initial conditions, for example, because they are overdetermined. Once Caesar entered the forum on the Ides of March, given the number of assassins, his assassination was overdetermined. Large processes like the Industrial Revolution likewise had multiple overdetermining causes that made them necessary. Many innovators and entrepreneurs worked on similar projects to overdetermine the Industrial Revolution. Other large historical processes were not overdetermined but were necessary because they were linear. When large causes cause commensurably large effects the effects are not sensitive to small variations. For example, once the Soviet Union and the United States joined the Second World War on the side of the British Empire, the Axis powers could not have won the war because of the overwhelming balance of power aligned against them. Even if many small things were different, the Axis powers would have still lost the war. Irrespective of the results of this or that battle, the war was lost. Similarly, once it became obvious in 2008 that there was a massive financial crisis, it was too late to pre-empt it by regulation. Only equally large fiscal or monetary actions could have mitigated it. Some historical failures of social engineering resulted from misunderstanding of how linear some large processes are, insensitive to intervention. For example, the attempts to turn Poland into a socialist and atheistic nation, Iraq into a liberal democracy and Russia into a society governed by the rule of law were doomed to failure because of the linear effects of entrenched cultures that could not be changed even by occupation and massive international aid.

At the opposite end of the scale there are non-linear processes. The most non-linear systems are chaotic in which processes would have turned entirely different had initial conditions been slightly and imperceptibly different, like the proverbial 'butterfly effect' when the flapping of butterfly wings in Brazil cause a tornado in Texas, or in politics, 'for want of a nail, the kingdom fell'. History, as a system, is not chaotic, except when described in a metaphoric flourish. Had it been chaotic it would have been entirely incomprehensive and unpredictable. A tribesman in the Amazon would have shot an arrow and consequently Democrats would have won the elections in Texas. History did however obviously have non-linear junctures when small changes had huge effects. For example, when individual decisions affected societies and states and were not overdetermined. The 'no Hitler, no Holocaust' equation conveys the idea that Hitler's personal decision to unleash the Holocaust was not overdetermined, not by any other Nazi leader or anything else, yet caused the deaths of nearly six million people and altered the history of Eastern Europe and the Middle East (Tucker 2016: 76–88). Colonel Heinz Brandt probably pushed a suitcase he did not know contained a bomb on 20 April 1944, thus pre-empting the assassination of Hitler and a military coup d'état that would have likely been successful in ending the war earlier, before Russia occupied East Europe. Since totalitarian dictatorships invest so much power in a supreme leader, that leader's tiny personal peculiarities can shape history more contingently than the decisions of democratic leaders that must take into considerations many pressure groups and interests that do not change from leader to leader but overdetermine some policies, as the balance of power between these groups. For this reason, it is difficult to change the status quo in many controversial issues in liberal democracies. There are opposite assignments of contingency and necessity to elections and legal verdicts in liberal-democratic and authoritarian states. The results of elections and the decisions of courts are far more contingent in liberal democracies where elections are decided by voters who can change their minds and trials are decided on the contingencies of the evidence. In authoritarian states the results of elections and trials are decided in advance. As the subjects of states without the rule of law know, trials end with convictions, otherwise the procuracy would not have initiated the legal proceedings.

Any event may be described as contingent if its description is sufficiently information rich, detailed. Proponents of counterfactual theories of causation responded to the challenges of overdetermination and pre-emption that undermine their theories by bringing causes that do not satisfy counterfactual conditions as counterexamples, by proposing that information rich, 'fine-gained' or 'fragile' descriptions of effects that at the very least specify their temporal and special location can avoid causal overdetermination and pre-emption (Lewis 1986; 2004: 75–106, pp. 85–8; Paul 2000: 223–34; Coady 2004: 325–40; Maar 2016: 349–69). 'Alternations' in pre-empting causes should affect fragile effects, while alterations in pre-empted causes would not. Some descriptions of historical events may be made fragile and contingent by reduction to lower, more information rich, ontological levels. But it is difficult to perform such reductions to fragility without loss of information from the higher ontological level. For example, had one of Caesar's assassins gotten squeamish, Caesar's corpse would have had only twenty-two, rather than twenty-three, wounds. The fragility of the effect would be achieved by describing Caesar's corpse as in an autopsy report, on a physiological lower ontological level to the supervening political level of the event, which dominates historiography, the conceptualization of Caesar's death as a political event, the assassination of a dictator by the Republican elite that led to the unintended end of Republican Rome, civil war and the establishment of the empire for half a millennium. Such a reduction would add irrelevant information because historians care little for the exact locality, time and place, of Caesar's assassination, whether he was assassinated in the Senate, Forum or bathhouse, or on the Ides of March or the Ides of April by twenty-three, thirty or ten assassins. The defining political characteristics of the historical event would not have been affected by such alternations. Similarly, if the description of the Battle of Waterloo is information rich and includes the exact sequence of military moves with the exact number of dead and wounded that it had, rather than as Napoleon's and the French Empire's ultimate defeat, then obviously it was contingent on its exact causes rather than overdetermined and necessary. To the extent that the Battle of Waterloo was the ultimate 'Defeat of Napoleon's Empire', it was necessary because of the gap between the military power of the decimated French military following the Russian debacle and the might of its enemies. Whether historians choose a fragile, informative or robust and supervenient, description of the same event depends on historiographic rather than historical contexts, what historians and their intended audience find significant, important, interesting or pragmatically useful. For example, most readers of history are interested in the Battle of Waterloo for its ending of Napoleon's reign and Empire and ushering in the age of European Restoration from 1815 to 1848, just as most historians are interested in the assassination of Caesar as the last failed attempt to restore the

Roman Republic. By contrast, military historiography may be interested in the tactics of the battle, whereas the Waterloo Tourist Board may be more interested in the exact fragile and contingent details of the battle. The question of historical contingency then is closely linked with value-laden judgements of significance. Unsurprisingly, the value-laden choice of fragile or robust descriptions of events resembles similar value-laden judgements in the philosophy of historiographic causation, of which conditions of events are considered its causes (Conkin 1974: 1–20; Hammond 1977: 103–28; Hart and Honoré 1985; Martin 1989: 53–84). Such value-laden judgements are necessary, yet are not arbitrary or relative to the perspectives of historians. The criteria of judgement of significance enjoy broad consensus within a context of inquiry, and can be made explicit and defended. Historians of Rome can agree that it does not matter how many stab wounds ended Caesar's life. While historians of Europe are not interested in the exact details of the Battle of Waterloo, military historians are interested in its tactics but not in every bullet or canon ball fired, while the Waterloo Tourist Board or historical archaeologists may be interested in each bullet. Each of these descriptions should be based on available evidence.

Philosophical debates about whether the past was contingent or necessary have been dominated in the last half-century by arguments about the history of life, whether it resulted more from the contingency of random variation or the necessity of natural selection. Stephen Jay Gould upheld contingency and path dependency, arguing that the diversity that preceded mass extinctions in the history of life proves that the history of life is the story of the survival of the luckiest more than the fittest and the history of life is then contingent. The opposite view finds necessity in the history of life, manifested in convergent variations, where irrespective of initial conditions, natural selection picked similar traits, such as the shapes of species that occupy similar ecological niches like marine reptiles and mammals, in species with different histories. Critics of convergent variations point out that all life shares common ancestries so even when natural selection affects similarities between remote species on the tree of life like mammals and reptiles, they still share common ancestry and path dependency manifested in shared DNA. This is even more true of human societies that are all path dependent on recent ancestral population in Africa and have almost identical genetic heritage. Sterelny concluded that it is not only too difficult to find out whether necessity or contingency fit best the history of life but also too difficult to decide on a methodology to decide between necessity and contingency (Sterelny 2007).

Trivially, if contingency is transitive like causation, if history had a single-contingent episode, all that followed must be contingent as well. Since over time, global history has become causally intertwined, even a single-contingent episode deep enough in the past would imply that much of history is contingent. Yet, as in the history of life, there may have been long periods of necessity, followed by rapid contingent episodes, or necessary processes in the sense of overdetermined or linear taking place alongside contingent processes. In a non-trivial sense, the evidence cannot decide how contingent or necessary the sum total of historical events and processes have been, how sensitive they were to their initial conditions, overdetermined or linear, or non-linear. The problem in evaluating general claims about the contingency or necessity of human history is for the most part the opposite of the problem in evaluating similar theses about natural history: the evidence that survived the ravages of time from the long history of life is insufficient for inferring the contingency or necessity of much of the history of life. There is too much complex evidence for considering all the complex overdetermining processes and non-linear causes and effects in human history. It is possible to examine particular historical episode through the evidence and infer fairly probable answers to the question of contingency or necessity. For example, the evidence for the destruction of the French army in Russia is that it was so devastated that it was no match to Napoleon's enemies. Irrespective of any of the other factors – Napoleon's genius, the quality of his soldiers and so on – Napoleon's defeat was overdetermined. By contrast, there is no evidence for multiple alternative causal chains that could have led to a French invasion of Russia irrespective of Napoleon's decision. There were no geopolitical constraints that would have forced any French leader to invade Russia, or major political forces in France that would have pressured any French leader to embark on a military adventure in Russia. But such studies are too few and non-representative of history to generalize from.

Sterelny suggested that 'historical trajectories are robust when they depend only on aggregate effects of interactions in populations' or when they are 'well-designed mechanisms', simple, isolated from perturbations, yet with redundancies. By contrast, 'contingency affects mostly, or most directly, the explicit targets of command-and-control decision-making. Politics is the engine of contingency'. The advance of command and control institutional and especially state structures has increased the fragility of history by concentrating power in few erratic hands (Sterelny 2016: 534–7. Cf. Inkpen and Turner 2012: 1–19). Politics, nevertheless, can limit the fragile contingencies Sterelny associates with it, through well-designed institutions for limiting contingencies. The fewer decisions can be made by one or few people, the less contingent and more linear and necessary they would tend to be. The institutions of liberal democracy were designed to reduce such contingency, in comparison with the institutions of authoritarian dictatorships and especially totalitarian autocracies.

Application

Having clarified the meaning of historical contingency versus necessity, we can apply it to our present civilizational predicament: there is no denying that the Great Recession of 2007–9 and the anaemic recovery in North America and Europe were *necessary* conditions for the current crisis of liberal democracy. But they were not *sufficient* conditions. The recession created political contingencies rather than necessities. Very small, even minute, differences in initial conditions could have led to entirely different political results. Understanding these historical contingencies is useful not just for avoiding the conclusion that periodic civilizational breakdown is our inevitable destiny but more importantly for designing institutions to better withstand the kind of self-destructive pressures that economic recessions generate.

The contingency of political results on electoral systems is manifest in the different outcomes of similar distributions of votes in different countries. A substantial minority of voters sufficed for deciding the US presidential election. An even smaller minority of votes gave absolute parliamentary majority to illiberal populists in Poland. The populist Austrian candidate for the presidency lost with an almost identical portion of votes to the one that allowed Trump to win. If the United States had an Austrian or French electoral system with two rounds, Trump and Clinton would have faced each other without alternative choices. If only most of the Green voters in Michigan, Wisconsin and Pennsylvania had voted in such a second round for what they would have considered the lesser evil, there would have been a different president today.

Though illiberal governments assumed power in Hungary and Poland before the Brexit vote in the summer of 2016, Brexit signalled that the crisis has reached the Western core. But Brexit did not have to happen. The British liberal institutions have been sufficiently robust and resilient to pre-empt a contingent result like Brexit. But they were undermined from above and within by Prime Minister David Cameron 'gambler's ruin'; he believed he had a sure thing, bet the farm on it and lost everything. Brexit has been entirely contingent on this decision since Cameron could have continued to tolerate a Eurosceptic wing of the Conservative Party and the loss of some votes to the Independence Party. The British tradition of government does not include plebiscites (though they were used a few times), for good reasons. Plebiscites oversimplify complex issues and appeal to the raw passions of the voters. The English who voted against the European Union had irreconcilable political agendas and different party affiliations. Some wanted a deregulated Singapore on the Northern Sea if they could only gain export markets; others wanted Little England without foreigners, nurses, plumbers and edible food. Still others would have voted for anything that would have upset the establishment. Any parliamentary vote that would not have oversimplified the issue into a 'yes' or 'no' choice without details would have fragmented the Brexit voter.

Another example for contingent decision-making that led to the current crisis is the European Union unconditional subsidy of Hungary's authoritarian illiberal regime. Since Hungary has no alternative source of income to external subsidies, as Russia or Saudi Arabia do, it has been dependent on the European Union. European leaders could have used the imbalance of political and economic power to isolate illiberalism once it emerged and pre-empt its spread elsewhere, rather than wait in vain for the plague to pass. American Isolationist disinterest in Europe, timidity and indecision under President Obama facilitated the emergence of illiberalism in the old continent until it spread to the land of progress.

Since the current crisis of liberal democracy was contingent, evitable, it is possible to consider what we can learn from the past decade to devise institutional reforms that may prevent remission and pre-empt another self-destructive reaction when the next economic cycle hits a recession, as it very likely will. But this is not a policy paper, so I will stop here with this general conclusion.

Learning from History

For philosophers of history, the most obvious contingency that contributed to the current crisis is the absence of any kind of historical learning process from past mistakes. For an historically educated person, experiencing contemporary politics resembles having to watch repeatedly a bad and disgusting horror movie that always ends bad. As Wynne McLaughlin put it, 'Maybe history wouldn't have to repeat itself if we listened once in awhile.' If people learn only from their personal historical experience, every two generations societies would repeat the same forgotten mistakes.

'Those who cannot remember the past are condemned to repeat it', George Santayana famously wrote in 1905 (Santayana 1905). Santayana sought to articulate an Aristotelian *via media* virtue of remembering history, between historical amnesia and life in historical trauma. He warned against becoming prisoners of traumatic historical experiences, reliving them obsessively by repetitively reacting to new experiences as if they were the old traumatic ones. Continuous adaptation is the price of historical and personal longevity. To adapt Santayana's insight to the contemporary predicament, not every tyrant with bad heir is a new Hitler, not every agreement with a dictator is a re-enactment of appeasement, and not every international intervention is a new 'Iraq'. On the other hand, Santayana thought that historical progress and personal maturity result from learning from experience: When individuals or nations remember their mistakes, they do not repeat them. When we consider what we could have done better in the past, we do things better in the future. When historical experience is not retained, the results are permanent political and personal infancy. We make then the kind of mistakes children do, because they have little experience to instruct them. It is no coincidence that much of current populist politics appears infantile. Santayana recommended balancing the retention of the lessons of history with a plasticity of reaction to new situations, an Aristotelian virtuous *via media* between childish forgetfulness and debilitating traumatic obsession.

Democratic philosophers at least since Thomas Jefferson and John Stuart Mill have warned that democracy can thrive only when voters are educated, possess historical virtue in Santayana's sense. An educated citizenship is the 'infrastructure' of democracy. Scolding populists for being historically ignorant when they are in the grip of fear, anxiety and personal insecurity is useless or even counterproductive, when formal education is misused for blocking social mobility, accusing somebody of historical ignorance or economic illiteracy is interpreted as the condescending assertion of class superiority that begets resentment. Ignorance needs to be pre-empted before it becomes a badge of honour.

Today's populism advocates an amalgam of policies that failed in the past two centuries, leading to two world wars and the deepening of the economic depression of the 1930s: blocking international trade routes and breaking production chains through barriers and tariffs, scapegoating refugees, entrepreneurial and risk-taking economic migrants, and ethnic and religious minorities for economic difficulties. This kind of populism was not supposed to happen anymore. During the twentieth century, humanity subjected itself to a painful learning process by trying ideologies from the totalitarian extremes of the Right and Left. The extreme Right led to the catastrophe of the Second World War. The extreme Left collapsed with the Soviet Bloc in 1989. At the end of the Cold War, Francis Fukuyama argued that humanity had learned the lessons from its history, and, by elimination, of all the ideologies, only liberal democracy was left standing at the philosophical end of history (Fukuyama 1992). A minor assumption in Fukuyama's reasoning was that after societies make historical mistakes, they learn from history, retain the lessons and pass them on. Fukuyama, though, did not examine at any length the possibility that societies might not retain knowledge and lessons from failed historical experiments, and so unwittingly repeat versions of them. Societies devoid of historical consciousness are condemned to 'Sisyphean politics', following the ancient Greek (and Camus's existentialist) myth about King Sisyphus who spends eternity rolling a huge boulder up a mountain. When he reaches the top of the mountain, the boulder rolls down, and Sisyphus must roll it up the mountain yet again. Without historical memory and consciousness, history becomes Sisyphean, as societies retry the same failed ideologies and policies that lead to disaster, again and again, in endless cycles.

Much of the resistance to populism in continental Europe today benefits from lingering memories of previous experiments with populist and nationalist politics before and during the Second World War. A comparison of the demographics of the supporters of Trump, Brexit and France's Le Pen is instructive: they all appeal to the uneducated and the rural as opposed to urban, educated and professional voters. Yet there is a huge gap in the support for xenophobic nationalism among old people. Older French voters who remember Petain, Laval and the Nazi occupation, or lived sufficiently close to those events to receive the recent memories of others, are the least nationalist voters in France. What should happen when this generation passes away?

One of the weirder manifestations of contemporary irrationality, fear and distrust of expertise is the movement of parents who endanger their children by preventing their inoculation against diseases that in the past killed millions. If few children are not inoculated, it does not matter because when the vast majority are inoculated, nobody can infect them. But it should come as no surprise that when a sufficient number of children are not inoculated, diseases that we thought had been eradicated return. Knowledge of history, especially of its worst mistakes, is intellectual inoculation against the pathologies of Sisyphean politics, the eternal return of the same failed politics each two generations.

If the purpose of education is exclusively vocational and there are few 'jobs' in 'history', and even fewer in philosophy of history, it is irrational to spend time and resources, especially public ones, on teaching history or its philosophy. Donald Trump himself has said so: he is 'not interested' in the past. The majority of young people should study only specialized vocational skills for the new economy. But populist policies and xenophobic international conflicts are not exactly cheap; they are much costlier than historical education, like treating diseases is much more expensive than universal inoculation. The experience of 2016–17 should serve as a 'Sputnik' moment for education in history and the social sciences, as the Soviet launching of Sputnik forced the United States to re-examine American education in STEM subjects and foreign languages. Civil mass education must include history, not history of past glories but histories of human folly that should not be repeated: the fall of the Greek polis and the Roman Republic, the French Revolution and its demise, the rise of nationalism and the wars of the twentieth century, the Great Depression and the rise of fascism, the Second World War and the Holocaust, the histories of totalitarianism, racism and colonialism and so on. Studying history pre-empts temporal provincialism. Historical consciousness demonstrates that we are more than cogs in hyper-specialized Fordist labour machines that go haywire if ejected out of the machine. But most importantly, it should prevent educated people from unwittingly reliving the worse parts of history.

Philosophy of History

Unlike earlier outbreaks of xenophobia and populism, at least for now, there are no significant intellectual inspirations, legitimizations or fellow travellers, like Heidegger, Gentile and Merleau-Ponty. Contemporary populism is more anti-intellectual than 'anti-anything else', so philosophers of history like other intellectuals are not wanted in the movement. At least in the United States, the smart money bets that the populist episode will pass, and here learning from history is important because intellectuals who know history know how it unfolded for some intellectuals who discredited themselves and their thought by associating with destructive and immoral ideologies.

Yet, populism's approach to history and historiography, unsophisticated and unreflective though it is, can still teach a few lessons for the philosophy of historiography. Populism's idea of truth is emotivist. Truth is what populists feel strongly about. Historiography would be then a narrative representation of strong emotions, wishful thinking. For example, if a populist really dislikes Hilary Clinton, then she must be running a paedophile ring from a pizza shop in Washington. If a person feels helpless and afraid, there must be a conspiracy involving alien lizards, Masons and Jewish financiers behind it all. If a populist is full with narcissistic insecure megalomania, then an event they speak in must be the largest ever, their wealth must be the biggest ever, and they must be the greatest, again and again. The criterion for historical narrative truth then is that it feels good, feels correct, in accordance with one's identity and emotional expression. History has no independent existence from the historiographic narrative about it and the narrative is not about the past, but about the identity and emotions of those who author it; it is indistinguishable from fiction. Sounds familiar?

Philosophies of historiography that do not distinguish historiography from fiction and reduce historical truth to power relations, the post-structuralists who follow Hayden White and the postmodernists who denied historical truth outside the text, can now observe how their epistemology works in political practice. They had no influence on populism and their politics are usually to the far left of it, but the epistemological similarity is striking. Epistemologies of our knowledge of the past that appeared progressive are actually consistent with populist emotivist politics of truth. The inability (or unwillingness) to distinguish fiction from reality has been the hallmark not just of contemporary authoritarian and populist politics but also of 'reality shows' and wrestling matches, carefully scripted situations that are presented as authentic and spontaneous human interactions. Reality shows and the World Wrestling Federation are the cultural and institutional contexts from which what may be called current American postmodernist populism has emerged. Voters may have believed on some level that they would become a part of a reality show where excitement and drama follow in quick succession, all problems have easy solutions, and political or historical truth is whatever the viewers feel strongly about. If the contest between historiographic narratives is decided on the basis of identities and strong emotions, the fragile and narcissistic identities of the populists who are convinced they are victims of elites, foreigners and experts are bound to be the loudest. If passions decide the historiographic narratives, fear, hate, blaming scapegoats and avoiding responsibility will compete unfairly with compassion, empathy and care. The best antidotes to the historiography of identities and passions are then reason, evidence and probable inference. Historiographic reason, probable inference from information preserving evidence in the present, does not mutate according to personal identities or passions. The historiographic substructure of probable inferences of the past is not affected by the narrative superstructure built on it. Living in a true historical world rather than in lies requires making the epistemic distinction between probable historiography founded on information preserving aspects of the present, and improbable fake and fictional versions of the past founded on strong passions. This is the project I dedicated the bulk of my research to, in my philosophy of historiography (cf. note 2). Over time, one hopes, the truth will prevail.

Part Three

(Re)drawing the Boundaries of Philosophy of History

History and Philosophy of History (HPH)
A Call for Cooperation
Herman Paul

Introduction

In a recent article, the philosopher Jutta Schickore laments what she perceives as a widening gap between philosophers of science, on the one hand, and historians of science, on the other. Although historians and philosophers of science sometimes work together in programmes labelled 'HPS' (history and philosophy of science), their cooperation is increasingly frustrated, or so Schickore believes, by historians of science. Under influence of a 'cultural turn' in the humanities and social sciences, these historians are exchanging their traditional subject matter – scientific concepts and theories in their historical development – for a much broader variety of themes, varying from laboratory practices and cultures of note-taking to scientific masculinities and geographies of science. In Schickore's words,

> Today, historians of science are interested in the usage in education and circulation of diagrams; the streets, shops, back alleys, and gardens, the merchants, gardeners, barber-surgeons, midwives, engineers, and alchemists of Elizabethan London who set the stage for the Scientific Revolution; or the role of commerce for scientific exchanges in the early modern period. Such interests are of course legitimate and important for history of science, but these orientations make it harder for philosophers to find relevant 'test cases' [for their philosophical projects]. (Schickore 2011: 465–6)

What kind of implications, one might wonder, does the cultural turn among historians of science have for the cooperation institutionalized as HPS? Will HPS come to an end, with historians and philosophers drifting away from each other?

Does HPS need to be reinvented, for instance as 'integrated HPS' (Arabatzis and Schickore 2012; Scholl and Räz 2016; Stadler 2017)? Or can philosophers do without historians of science, for instance by writing their own histories of scientific theories (Schickore 2018: 196)?

To a considerable extent, Schickore's observations about historians moving away from traditional philosophical themes also apply to historians of historiography. In a not-too-distant past, historical and philosophical reflection on historical studies used to go hand in hand. The Commission of the History of Historiography, for instance, was founded in 1980 under auspices of the International Committee of Historical Sciences to shed historical light on the theoretical and methodological quarrels that divided historians at the time (Erdmann 2005: 278–98).[1] Likewise, history and philosophy of history were close to inseparable in what Western European historians called *Historik* (historics) or *theoretische geschiedenis* (theoretical history) (Otto 1998). Such cooperation is no longer self-evident, though. Recent work in the history of historiography tends to focus on cultural–historical themes like the gendered aspects of historians' work (Schnicke 2015; Porciani 2009; Smith 1998), the habits and routines of historians working in archives (Müller 2019; Trüper 2014; Saxer 2013; Wimmer 2012) or the commemorative practices in which historians engage (Paul 2017; Creyghton 2016; Tollebeek 2015). This reveals not only an interest in other themes than explanation, narrative or representation but also a methodological orientation on other fields than philosophy. Jo Tollebeek (2008), most notably, calls for an 'anthropology of modern historical scholarship', characterized by thick description instead of conceptual analysis. (Arguably, historians of historiography are not alone responsible for this growing distance: philosophers of history also contribute their share. When in 2007 the *Journal of the Philosophy of History* was founded with the aim of fostering dialogue between philosophers of history and analytical philosophers of language, historians of historiography were not mentioned at all [Ankersmit et al. 2007].) This lends some urgency to the question as to how historians and philosophers of history relate to each other: Will they continue to drift apart?

In this chapter, I will argue that a parting of their ways is detrimental to the project of understanding historical studies, that is, understanding what historians do when they study the past. Such a project requires historical sensitivity (which historians of historiography can bring to the table) and conceptual clarity (which philosophers of history are able to offer). Arguing in favour of historical-philosophical cooperation is not the same, though, as trying to revitalize *Historik* or *theoretische geschiedenis*. While these genres focused near exclusively on historians' concepts, ideas and ideologies, the approach defended in this chapter is much broader: it wants to do justice to the entire variety of practices, discourses, materialities and emotions that make up historical studies. I will therefore propose a new term and argue in favour of 'HPH' – a historical equivalent of HPS called 'history and philosophy of history'. Obviously, I do so in full awareness of the problems that have surrounded HPS, including especially the false expectations raised by that label. So I will start with some brief comments on HPS – what it is and what it is not. Subsequently, I will present four arguments in favour of HPH. Finally, I will respond to some questions that my proposal might provoke, suggesting among other things that HPH is not something to be built from scratch but a form of cooperation that is already among us, whether we call it by that name or not.

HPS

What is HPS? When Ronald Giere (1973) described the history and philosophy of science as a 'marriage of convenience' rather than an intimate love relationship, he introduced a metaphor with which historians and philosophers of science have been playing ever since (McMullin 1976; Burian 1977; Krüger 1979; Domski and Dickson 2010: 1–3).[2] Surely, there were signs of attraction, perhaps even love, between historians and philosophers of science in the 1960s. By the 1970s, conferences, book series and educational programmes, all carrying HPS in their titles or names, suggested that flirting and dating had turned into a serious relationship (Schickore 2011; Gooday 2006). Both partners seemed convinced that understanding science required combination, perhaps even integration, of conceptual and empirical perspectives. Yet the question nagged: Did the partners really love each other or was their 'marriage for the sake of reason' mainly grounded in a negative desire to leave the parental home? Sharing a flat named HPS, said Giere (1973: 283), 'may be better than living with one's parents, history and philosophy respectively. ... But does it have the passionate involvement and deep communication that one was led to expect?'

Analysing 'the marriage, relationship prospects, and level of intimacy' of HPS in the 1960s and 1970s, Schickore (2011: 455) observes that especially philosophers in the 1970s engaged in intensive 'marriage counselling'. Ironically, however, their diagnoses and advices were so divergent as to call the entire marriage metaphor into question. Historians and philosophers engaged in HPS were too diverse in terms of their agendas, projects and expectations to fit the image of a romantic couple. In Schickore's grimmer imagery, the HPS arena rather 'was one of several battlefields' (2011: 455). On top of that, the marriage metaphor obscured that HPS not only enabled philosophers and historians to meet each other. From the very beginning, there was also science itself – which led Lorenz Krüger (1979: 112) to propose a marriage à trois – as well as 'sociology of scientific knowledge' and 'science and technology studies', nephews who maintained difficult relationships with HPS (Riesch 2014).

In retrospective, the marriage metaphor seems to have done HPS little good. It was too romantic an image, if only because it raised expectations ('a union of souls', marital fidelity) that were quite inappropriate for what was, after all, nothing but a cautious attempt at interdisciplinary exchange and cooperation. Would it have been more appropriate to characterize HPS as a 'trading zone' or 'contact zone'? Surely these terms, borrowed from Peter Galison (1997, 2010), are more to the point. They emphasize contact, communication and exchange across disciplinary divides without imposing an ideal, romantic or otherwise, of how such exchange ought to look like. At the same time, 'trading zone' and 'contact zone' are rather general terms: they don't convey that historians and philosophers of science engage in joint activities with the specific purpose of learning from each other 'how science works' (Giere 2012: 61).

Let me therefore propose an alternative label, freely borrowed from philosophers in the Gadamerian tradition. I would like to think of HPS as a hermeneutic space: a realm where scholars encounter, try out, appropriate, reject or otherwise engage with ideas, concepts, methodologies and practices from outside of their own fields (Figal 2010). As the adjective 'hermeneutic' conveys, the purpose of this exchange is not to reach common ground or to institutionalize cooperation but to facilitate learning processes that hopefully yield new ideas and fresh approaches. As with workshop sessions and conference panels, or spontaneous chats with colleagues at the coffee machine, the outcome of such exchanges can never be predicted. However, within these limitations, conditions favourable to mutual learning can be created. If historians and philosophers of science spend time together – trying to understand each other's questions, listening to each other's arguments, opening themselves up to unfamiliar idioms or practices, analysing case studies from a variety of conceptual perspectives, trying to translate historians' ideas into philosophical language and vice versa, subjecting grand claims to critical scrutiny and testing conceptual distinctions against empirical examples – there is a fair chance that their understanding of 'how science works' will be deepened. So, by calling HPS a hermeneutic space, I seek to draw attention not to institutionalized modes of transdisciplinary cooperation but to what I regard as the heart of the matter: patient exchanges between historians and philosophers of science who believe that, in some way or another, they can learn from each other. As Scott Weingart (2015: 202) helpfully puts it, 'The question should not be whether history of science and philosophy of science can be fully integrated, but to what extent each can contribute to the other, and whether interesting results can come of studies pulling ideas and methodologies from both.'

Why HPH? (Part 1)

To what extent would a historiographical equivalent of HPS so conceived of be desirable? What would be the benefits of philosophers of history, historical theorists, historians of historiography and historians of historical culture engaging in history and philosophy of history (HPH)? Three or perhaps even four arguments in favour of such exchange can be given. There is, in the first place, a broadly felt (though never uncontested) need to naturalize philosophy of history. Just as philosophy of science in the wake of Thomas S. Kuhn and W. V. O. Quine has gradually exchanged the normative question as to how science *should* look like for the empirical question how science *actually* looks like (Zammito 2004), philosophy of history is often believed to benefit from taking a naturalizing approach to the study of history (Bevir and Paul 2012). Concretely, this means that interpretations, explanations, inferences, narratives and so on should not primarily be studied *conceptually*, in order to identify the ideal features of a historical interpretation, explanation, inference or narrative, but *empirically*, with an eye to uncovering what kinds of interpretations, explanations, inferences and narratives historians (and others) actually produce or consume.

One of the most outspoken advocates of such a naturalized philosophy of history is Raymond Martin, whose 1989 book *The Past within Us* was one long plea for an 'empirical approach to philosophy of history'. Observing that philosophers of history had been 'primarily concerned with what is possible in principle, rather than with what is actual or with what is possible in fact' (1989: 5), Martin urged his colleagues to redirect their attention to 'an examination of facts, the most central of which are the ways historians argue that one interpretation is better than its competitors' (1989: 6). Accompanying articles in *History and Theory* illustrated the kind of research that Martin had in mind: detailed analysis of how historians evaluate the merits of competing historical interpretations and measure 'progress' in their fields of study (Martin 1997, 1998).

In paying close attention to historians' work, Martin followed a model laid out by William Dray (1964: 41–58) and Alan Donagan (1969, 1970), well before 'naturalizing' became a household term among philosophers of science. Martin's example, in turn, has been taken up by Chris Lorenz and Martin Bunzl, among others.[3] Both argue that philosophers of history have the task of elucidating historians' practice by analysing how this practice actually looks like. If historians turn out to spend much energy debating the relative plausibility of their historical accounts, philosophers of history have to make sure they can account for such debates, which Lorenz (1994) and Bunzl (1997: 3, 14, 23, 107) believe that only some philosophical approaches are capable of doing. So here we have a first raison d'être for HPH: philosophy of history should be able to offer insight into real-existing historical studies.

Closely related is a second motive behind both HPS and HPH: a desire to subject philosophical claims about scientific (historical) practice to empirical scrutiny. As illustrated by Larry and Rachel Laudan's so-called VPI project on scientific change,[4] empirical testing of philosophical theories is an enterprise fraught with difficulty, if only because the data selected to this end are always theory-laden (McAllister 2018; Dumouchel 1991; cf. Donovan, Laudan and Laudan 1992). Yet despite the project's flaws, the basic intuition behind it was correct, or so I would argue. Philosophers of science cannot make empirical claims about scientific practice without offering empirical support for these claims. So, if they assert, as Thomas Kuhn once did, that 'new assumptions are introduced, and initially accepted, chiefly by scientists who are either young or new to the field' (Kuhn 2012: 90, 151–2, as paraphrased in Laudan et al. 1986: 186), they have the burden of proof to demonstrate that there is an actual correlation between scientists' willingness to accept new theories and their degree of academic socialization. Likewise, if philosophers of history argue that historians 'seldom explicitly formulate general causal theories' (Dray 1989: 56), generally 'agree on theories and evidence' (Tucker 2004: 142), 'in seeking to explain their own discipline, do not characteristically use historiography to do it' (Gorman 2008: 9), and typically strive 'to achieve the "history narrator as nobody" effect' (Jenkins 2003: 11), they put forward empirical claims that, as such, must be able to stand up to empirical testing.

Bunzl and Lorenz engage in such theory testing when they subject some of Arthur Danto's and Frank Ankersmit's work to empirical scrutiny. In response to Danto's assumption that all historians write narratives, Bunzl (1997: 32–3) points out that narrative modes of representation are not equally important in all historical genres: cross-cultural and cross-temporal studies like Natalie Zemon Davis 1978 study of male–female festive role inversions in cultures across the globe badly fit Danto's model. Likewise, Lorenz takes issue with Ankersmit's thesis that historical representations can only be evaluated on aesthetic grounds. Judging by, for instance, the German *Historikerstreit*, historians evaluate competing accounts of the past on epistemic grounds, too (Lorenz 1994: 314). Although it is questionable to what extent this falsifies Ankersmit's thesis, the case does raise important questions. How representative, for instance, is the *Historikerstreit* for historians' debating conventions? Is it true, as Ankersmit suggests, that historians debate epistemic issues only at statement level? And in case the answers to these questions vary across the spectrum of historical studies, is it true that philosophers of history often draw their examples from specific types of historical studies (Ankersmit 2001: 262), which implies – given the heterogeneity of historical practice – that their empirical claims tend to have local rather than universal validity (Bunzl 1997: 23)? These are issues of the sort that HPH is well positioned to examine.

On top of that, HPH offers historians conceptual tools for reflection on their own practice.[5] Varying on Laudan's argument that philosophers' conceptual distinctions may help historians develop more finely textured understandings of the history of science (Laudan 1989: 10), one might argue that historians' understanding of the 'causes' of A, the 'intentions' of B or the 'influences' of C might benefit from explicit reflection on what the concepts of 'causality', 'intention' and 'influence' entail. In a classic article on concepts of causation in historical studies on the origins of the Second World War, William Dray illustrated this point by showing that A. J. P. Taylor and his critics, including especially Hugh Trevor-Roper, spilled much ink debating whether Adolf Hitler 'intended the war', but never specified what they understood 'intended' and 'the war' to mean – thereby leaving it 'extraordinary obscure exactly what [was] being debated' (Dray 1978: 155). Likewise, Dray pointed out that the controversy evoked by Taylor's thesis about Hitler's foreign policy being not unusual for European government leaders in the 1930s might have been much more productive if Taylor and his critics had tried to clarify their 'standards of normality' and the implicit comparisons on which these standards were based (Dray 1978: 162). By identifying shared assumptions behind disagreements and by classifying different ways in which historians used terms like 'cause' and 'intention', Dray thus offered philosophical assistance to historians debating the merits of Taylor's work, in the hope of helping them avoid talking at cross purposes.[6]

Why HPH? (Part 2)

The three arguments in favour of HPH that I have offered so far are obviously related, not merely because the project of increasing the level of conceptual reflectivity among historians (no. 3) will surely fail without proper attention to historians' actual work (no. 1) but also because they are all inspired by HPS. Indeed, all authors cited so far are interested in the 'scientific' aspirations of academic historical studies and, consequently, try to analyse historians' work analogous to how philosophers of science scrutinize science. Yet there is no reason why HPH should focus exclusively on what I have elsewhere called historians' 'epistemic relations' with their pasts – that is, on engagements with the past that aim for epistemic goods like knowledge and understanding. If philosophers of history want to understand historical studies (concern no. 1), test philosophical theories (no. 2) or help historians reflect on what they are doing (no. 3), among the first things they should realize is that historians always maintain *multiple* relations with their subject matter, including aesthetic, moral and political ones (Paul 2015a, b).[7] These aesthetic, moral and political dimensions of historical studies, in turn, can be subjected to similar analysis as the epistemic aspect on which the authors mentioned so far have focused their attention. Indeed, they *should* be studied with similar vigour if philosophers of history have the ambition of understanding historical studies as they actually exist.

This is to say that philosophers of history, in addition to continuing work on classic epistemic themes, might want to subject aesthetic, moral and political aspects of historical studies to more rigorous philosophical study than these subjects have received so far. For although the so-called narrativist turn in philosophy of history, half a century ago, has produced important insights into the aesthetic, moral and political aspects of historical *writing*, the question as to how this writing emerges out of historical *studies* – historians' habits of reading, note-taking, thinking, corresponding, collaborating, teaching, supervising and reviewing (not to mention writing grant applications) – has hardly been addressed so far. Consequently, when it comes to aesthetics, morality and politics, studies in philosophy of history – perhaps with the exception of Frank Ankersmit's *Sublime Historical Experience* (2015) – usually have little to say about these themes except insofar as they show up in historical writing. To the best of my knowledge, a philosophy of historians' research ethics has not yet been developed. A philosophy of 'feelings rules' in historical studies – it is allowed to weep over the execution of the Dutch grand pensionary Johan van Oldenbarnevelt, as a Dutch historian reportedly did in his lecture course on seventeenth-century history (Van der Meiden 1982)? – does not yet exist. And why does philosophy of history persist in studying historical studies through the prism of individual historians, while collaboration in various forms is increasingly becoming the standard in our age of grand-scale research projects?

From this it follows that the 'cultural turn' that philosophers of science committed to HPS perceive as a threat to the project of confronting philosophical theories with historical evidence may actually turn out not to be a threat at all (Pinnick and Gale 2000; Schickore 2011: 465–6).[8] While it is true that the cultural turn has inspired historians of science to explore themes that are rather far removed from philosophy of science's traditional subject matter – think of recent work on geographies of science (Livingstone 2003; Nayler 2005), moral economies (Daston 1995), scientific personae (Daston and Sibum 2003) and scientists' emotions (Dror 2006; White 2009) – philosophers of science might take this as an invitation to reflect philosophically on these still understudied aspects of science.[9] Likewise, philosophers of history might benefit from a cultural turn in the history of historiography. Although studies on historians' working manners, social codes, commemorative practices and gendered self-images examine aspects of historical studies quite different from the interpretations, explanations, inferences and narratives that have dominated philosophy of history in the past half a century, precisely for this reason they might serve as welcome provocations. Philosophers of history might want to explore whether and how these themes fit their theories of historical studies – and what needs to be done in case they fit badly.

Arguably, historical research can even put new items on the philosophical agenda. Recent historical studies on historians' virtues and vices, for instance – the kind of work in which I am currently involved – raises questions that philosophers of history do not yet know how to answer: What roles do virtues in the sense of personal dispositions or character traits play in the acquisition of historical knowledge? To what extent can historians' evaluative standards – Noël Carroll's (1990) 'truth-tracking criteria' or Mark Bevir's (1999) 'criteria of comparison' – be formulated in terms of virtues (Nievergelt 2018)? How can historical studies be demarcated from other genres if their standards of virtue largely mirror the moral codes and social expectations of their culture? Do only individuals possess virtue or can groups or institutions also be bearers of virtue? If virtues are deeply ingrained habits, then to what extent can 'historian' still be considered a role-identity, distinct from other role-identities like 'citizen', 'spouse' and 'parent'? Or on a more conceptual level: How do virtues relate to skills, qualities and competencies? Are these different words for the same type of dispositions or are there substantial differences between, say, virtues and skills?[10] These are all questions that emerge out of historical research and are still awaiting philosophical treatment.

This brings us to a fourth and final argument in favour of HPH. In the hermeneutic space of HPH, philosophers of history can familiarize themselves with the history of historical studies, not merely to acquire data for theory testing but also to explore understudied aspects of historical studies. Keeping current with historiographical literature can help them avoid relying on stock examples of what historians do. Likewise, cooperation with historians of historical studies can provide them with fresh insight into the intricacies of historical studies. For philosophers of history, then, HPH may serve as a space of innovation: a space in which new ideas sometimes emerge.

Four Questions

At this point, I can imagine readers to raise a couple of questions. Although few readers will be against cooperation as such, they might want to hear more about the aims and limits of such cooperation, perhaps especially at a time when talk of 'interdisciplinarity' runs a risk of becoming so clichéd as to lose any distinct meaning (Brown and Schubert 2007; Jacobs 2013: 1–3). I can imagine, therefore, that readers raise at least four questions: (1) If HPH aims to understand 'historical studies', does this phrase refer exclusively to *academic* historical studies? (2) Why should only historians and philosophers be invited to the table? (3) If 'understanding' historical studies is the aim, then who defines what understanding is? After all, depending on their theoretical leanings, historians and philosophers may well have different ideas of what understanding implies. (4) Is HPH something to be built from scratch? Or is it already among us, in one form or another? I will respond to these questions in turn.

(1) Is it necessary for HPH to limit itself to *academic* historical studies such as practised in history departments or in other parts of the humanities?[11] I have argued on other occasions that a focus on 'relations with the past' not only has the advantage of broadening philosophy of history's traditional epistemic scope but also can cover more than only academic historical studies. All human beings, after all, in one way or another, maintain relations with the past (Paul 2015a). So if the second 'H' in HPH can encompass people's relations with the past, cannot HPH also encompass scholarship on nostalgia as a mode of dealing with loss (Becker 2018), historicization of racism in the American Black History Month

(Van de Mierop 2016) or the 'practical past' in Hayden White's (2014) sense of the word?

Although, *in principle*, such a broad understanding of the second 'H' in HPH can only be applauded, it might be *strategically* more beneficial to start with what most historians and philosophers of history have in common: an interest in academic historical studies. Given that philosophers of history are still largely unfamiliar with the cultural–historical prisms through which historians have begun to examine historical studies, shared explorations of how academics read, think, teach, write and tweet about the past may already yield a lot of new insight. Also, even though an expansion of philosophy of history beyond 'philosophy of historiography' would be very welcome, this would not necessarily be a move from which historians of historiography can profit, given that they increasingly cooperate with historians of science and historians of the humanities more than with historians of historical culture. So if the analogy with HPS assigns priority to historians and philosophers reflecting together on what professional historical studies are, it does so on pragmatic, strategic grounds – not because it would be less pertinent to study how non-academics relate to their pasts.

(2) Something similar applies to the second question: If the challenge is to deepen our understanding of historical studies, then why are history and philosophy the only disciplines that are invited to the table? Given that HPH is largely modelled after the example of HPS, it would not be far-fetched to think that HPH might include historical equivalents of sociologists examining laboratory cultures or anthropologists studying the working habits of high energy physicists.[12] Such an 'anthropology of historians' even seems to be in the making, judging by recent work by Van Troi Tan and Patrick-Michel Noël (2018). This is exciting, if only because anthropological fieldwork might teach historians and philosophers of history alike that academics writing books and debating historical interpretations are always situated subjects, busy grading student papers and preparing PowerPoints for their next class while having a Skype conversation with colleagues abroad about a potential collaborative grant application and writing a letter of recommendation for a recent graduate who tries to enter the academic job market.[13] Still, given that historians and philosophers of history have a more established tradition of analysing historical studies, they are likely to be most interested in contributing to the project called HPH.

(3) What exactly does 'understanding' historical studies mean? As Richard Mason (2003) and others have argued, different disciplines have different understandings of understanding. This has serious implications for any 'multi-'

or 'interdisciplinary' project that tries to build bridges between fields. If historians assume that understanding has been reached when empirical descriptions are as complete as possible, while philosophers believe that understanding requires extraction of universal truths from historical contingencies, then historians telling philosophers what the aim of their cooperation is, or vice versa, amounts to an act of disciplinary imperialism that almost certainly discourages further attempts at cooperation.

Fortunately, however, this hermeneutic situation of a conversation between people committed to different views on the aim of the conversation is not peculiar to discipline-transcending initiatives like HPH. Disagreement over the nature of understanding also exists within disciplines (De Regt 2017). As said, the Commission of the History of Historiography was founded in 1980 in response to historians who strongly disagreed about what historical understanding entailed – whether it would require patterns and regularities, as social science enthusiasts at the time believed, or take the form of stories, as narrative-oriented historians claimed (Erdmann 2005: 278–98). And as philosophers of history know well, even historians committed to storytelling might hold different views on what a story is or what kind of 'emplotment' is appropriate in historical writing (White 1973). This implies that divergence of views on what it means to understand historical studies should not be regarded as a special obstacle to HPH. Divergence on ultimate aims is a common feature of hermeneutic practices even within monodisciplinary contexts.

Therefore, if I argue that historians and philosophers of history can help each other deepen their understanding of historical studies, this does not imply that, at the end of the day, historians and philosophers should be able to issue a joint declaration on realized learning objectives. I already quoted Scott Weingart (2015: 202) as saying that cooperation is successful as soon as 'interesting results' come out of it, irrespective of whether all parties involved agree on what makes an interesting result. The hermeneutic space called HPH is not a laboratory designed for executing well-delineated research projects but an open space in which questions can be raised, ideas can be exchanged and hypotheses can be tried out. The only demand that this space makes upon participants is that they are, and remain, committed to dialogical virtues (curiosity, generosity, empathy, open-mindedness) without which no productive exchange can take place.

(4) Finally, one may wonder: Is HPH a project that has to be started from scratch or does it already exist, in one form or another? As suggested by the examples of Dray, Donagan, Martin, Bunzl, Lorenz and other scholars committed to bringing history and philosophy of history into conversation with each other,

quite a bit of work at the intersection of philosophy of history and the history of historical studies has already been done. Wherever historians or philosophers of history use philosophical concepts for understanding historical studies, test philosophical theories against historiographical evidence, hold up a philosophical mirror to 'working historians' or explore historiographical literature in the hope of developing new philosophical ideas, something like HPH takes place. Cross-fertilization between historical and philosophical perspectives is also the explicit aim of workshops of the kind organized by the International Commission for the History and Theory of Historiography (ICHTH).

Last but not least, not unlike HPS, HPH exists in educational settings, most notably in 'historical theory' or 'historiography' courses offered to majors or graduate students in history.[14] Given that history students do not usually have much philosophical baggage, not a few of these courses are so designed as to encourage students to test philosophies of history against evidence from their own historical practice. Instead of requiring students to engage in amateur philosophizing, this didactic format allows them to familiarize themselves with philosophical texts through confronting Carl G. Hempel, Arthur C. Danto or Hayden White with their own niche of historical studies.[15] For much the same reason, textbooks like Mark Day's *The Philosophy of History* (2008b) and my own *Key Issues in Historical Theory* (2015) abound with historiographical examples aimed to illustrate, or challenge, philosophical theories about how historians interpret, explain and narrate the past.

As these examples show, HPH is clearly not a project waiting to be realized. It is not an 'ground-breaking' line of research or a teaching paradigm that requires historians and philosophers of history to abandon their current working habits. HPH is already among us, whether we call it by that name or not.

Conclusion

History and philosophy of history (HPH) as advocated in this chapter seeks to enrich historical and philosophical studies of historical scholarship by cultivating a hermeneutic space in which historians and philosophers of history can learn from each other. The idea of this hermeneutic space is not to let historians and philosophers work on pre-defined problems or force them into the straitjacket of a common line of research. Instead, HPH encourages historians to try out philosophical concepts, while inviting philosophers of history to test their theories against historiographical evidence. More interestingly, perhaps, HPH allows philosophers to stumble upon new ideas – there is a wealth of cultural-historical approaches to historical studies that has not yet been subjected to philosophical scrutiny – while encouraging historians to use philosophical tools in reflecting on their own practice.

By invoking history and philosophy of science (HPS), not as a model for imitation but by way of instructive analogy, the HPH label suggests that historians and philosophers of history may interact as fruitfully as historians and philosophers of science sometimes manage to do. Just as the historians of science Lorraine Daston and Peter Galison (2007) make productive use of concepts borrowed from philosophers of science, while philosopher Guy Axtell (2016) in his turn tries to learn from Daston's and Galison's genealogies of scientific objectivity, so historians and philosophers of history may enrich each other's work.

Although this exchange is premised on the assumption that cross-fertilization between historical and philosophical insights is beneficial to understanding historical studies (academic historical studies in the first place), I have emphasized that historians and philosophers do not need to agree on what 'understanding' means to be able to profit from questions and concerns raised by scholars from other disciplinary backgrounds. Just as in real life, instructive exchanges between historians and philosophers can take place without participants agreeing on the aims of the conversation. The only thing that HPH asks from them is an unwavering commitment to dialogical virtues like curiosity, generosity, empathy and open-mindedness.

Like HPS, then, HPH is not a marriage or some other kind of love relationship: Ronald Giere's metaphor has to be rejected as inapt. HPH more resembles a meeting room with a large round table, soft chairs, a coffee machine and windows with outside views that can be opened to let in lots of fresh air. Initially, the round table conversation seems to benefit most from an invitation policy restricted to historians and philosophers of history. Given that they have an established tradition of studying historical studies, historians and philosophers seem currently best positioned to engage in HPH. Only time can tell whether sociologists and anthropologists interested in historical studies will at some point also be invited to the table.

Acknowledgements

Drafts of this chapter were presented to the Philosophy of History Seminar at the Institute of Historical Research in London (December 2017), at an ICHTH workshop, 'What Are Historians Doing: Practice and Pragmatics of History Writing', at Tallinn University (August 2018), and to the Philosophy of History Study Group at the University of Amsterdam (September 2018). It's my pleasure to thank Kalle Pihlainen, Marek Tamm and Rik Peters for their kind invitations and the audiences at all three occasions for their perceptive feedback. Also, I would like to thank the editor of this book, Jouni-Matti Kuukkanen, for his thoughtful engagement with the theme of this chapter in a lengthy video interview, recorded at the Center for Philosophical Studies of History at Oulu University (October 2019) and available on YouTube: https://t.co/CCiXLyfyQg. Funding was generously provided by the Netherlands Organization for Scientific Research (NWO).

10

The Paradigm Shift in the Contemporary Humanities and Social Sciences

Ewa Domańska

The present argument has been developed in the context of what I term the comparative theory of the humanities and social sciences. This theory examines the coming and going of research trends, approaches, perspectives and categories that result from and reflect the changes in today's world (Bachmann-Medick 2016). The ideas presented in this article do not concern the dominant trends in the humanities but are instead based on the work of those scholars who propose alternative, cutting-edge research perspectives such as Jane Bennett, Rosi Braidotti, Edoardo Viveiros de Castro, Dipesh Chakrabarty, Donna Haraway, Tim Ingold, Bruno Latour, Walter Mignolo, Anna Tsing, among others. I reflect on how the interpretative frameworks of the avant-garde trends in the humanities and social sciences which lead the way in heated debates, have shifted markedly in recent years. Since the late 1990s the humanities and social sciences have been going through major changes caused by declining poststructuralist influence and the end of postmodernism, symbolically marked by 9/11. It results in the emergence of a field of multidisciplinary knowledge that might be termed non- or post-anthropocentric and non- or post-Western humanities. It tries to describe, comprehend and 'digest' problems generated by global capitalism, migration, the ecological crisis, climate change, natural disasters, mass killings, terrorism and technological progress.

In the widely read *Times Literary Supplement*, Alison Gibbons published an article with the telling title 'Postmodernism Is Dead. What Comes Next?' (2017). Gibbons wrote:

> Critics – such as Christian Moraru, Josh Toth, Neil Brooks, Robin van den Akker and Timotheus Vermeulen – repeatedly point to the fall of the Berlin Wall in 1989, the new millennium, the 9/11 attacks, the so-called 'War on Terror'

and the wars in the Middle East, the financial crisis and the ensuing global revolutions. Taken together, these events signify the failure and unevenness of global capitalism as an enterprise, leading to an ensuing disillusionment with the project of neo-liberal postmodernity and the recent political splintering into extreme Left and extreme Right. The cumulative effect of these events – and the accompanying hyper-anxiety brought about by twenty-four hour news – has made the Western world feel like a more precarious and volatile place, in which we can no longer be nonchalant about our safety or our future. (Gibbons 2017)

The phenomena outlined in this quote that mark the end of postmodernism and signal a paradigm shift should be positioned in the context of the crisis of liberal democracy and left-wing movements, as well as the concomitant 'conservative turn'. This situation has led to the polarization of world views, something that is also reflected in shifting research interests and approaches. These reconfigurations relate not only to the sociopolitical conditions outlined by Gibbons, which have impacted on the state of the humanities in a world of global capitalism, mass migration, terrorism and wars, but also to the ecological crisis, escalating natural disasters and biotechnological progress. Various changes resulting from the growing influence of the market economy are also affecting the academy (Lorenz 2012). It is noteworthy that the humanities in the United States (as well as Australia and Canada) are undergoing what Devon Mihesuah and Angela Wilson termed the 'indigenization of the academy' (Mihesuah and Wilson 2004). As a result, increasing numbers of people of indigenous (or, generally speaking, non-Western) backgrounds are becoming researchers, thus enriching scholarship with traditional ecological knowledge. They thus loosen the shackles of Eurocentric knowledge, particularly with respect to understandings of rationality, the scientific and subjecthood, and with respect to relations between nature and culture, interspecies relations and the place of human beings in the world.[1] This process is, in my view, of great significance to the humanities.[2]

In 2012 I did extensive research surveying the current condition of the humanities and social sciences. I investigated around 1,200 issues of 300 academic journals published between 2010 and 2012.[3] I came to the conclusion that we are going through a major paradigm shift marked by processes of ecologization and naturalization of the humanities. We are also witnessing attempts to build a holistic and inclusive system of knowledge (and alternative ways of knowing) that will combine humanities, social sciences and natural (life and Earth) sciences with indigenous knowledges (and indigenous ways of knowing). Since then, however, the situation has changed even further. Recently, the icon of contemporary humanities and social sciences Bruno Latour and the visionary anthropologist Eduardo Viveiros de Castro announced that we are witnessing not only a paradigm shift in various fields of knowledge but also a change of far greater scope and significance. According to Latour and Timothy M. Lenton, we are witnesses to 'a shift in worldview', meaning a major change in the 'distribution of traits affecting science as well as politics, morality, and the arts' (Latour and Lenton 2019: 661). As Viveiros de Castro argues, 'a cosmological paradigm shift' is taking place before our very eyes, leading to the emergence of a new world view. In this context, as Viveiros de Castro claims, it is not enough to accept ontological pluralism. Instead, he proposes the term 'ontological anarchism' to 'characterize the proper meta-mode of existence in the Anthropocene' (Viveiros de Castro 2019: 296, 298).

These are not new ideas, though. It is worth recalling that in the 1990s, Frithof Capra stated that we are witnessing a paradigmatic shift in the sciences, away from physics and towards the life sciences. For Capra, the new paradigm is holistic and ecological, and it is characterized by a number of turns: from rationality to intuition, from self-affirmation to integration, from domination to partnership, from competition to cooperation, from the notion of structure and its parts to the notion of the whole and process (Capra 1996: 5–13). This paradigm rests on systems theory with particular interest in the issue of self-organization, and it is tied in with the emergence of new forms of spirituality, supporting the perception of the world through the categories of 'the fundamental interconnectedness and interdependence of all phenomena and of embeddedness in the cosmos' (Capra, Steindl-Rest and Matus 1991: 70). Even though the ideas of Capra, similarly to those of Ilya Prigogine and Isabelle Stengers, are frequently grouped alongside what has become known as the intellectual New Age, and, as such, are viewed by many with scepticism, there has indeed been a definite shift from the constructivist and interpretive paradigm to the ecological paradigm, which is marked by criticism of anthropocentrism, Eurocentrism, secularism and scientism (science as a systematic study of the world based on Cartesian rationality, objectivism and neutrality).

The aim of this chapter is to outline the typical traits emerging from alternative perspectives that make clear the need, in light of the changes and bottom-up process mentioned earlier, to fundamentally rethink our understanding of life, human nature, the sacred and religion – thus following the postsecular turn. It is also necessary to rethink the relationship between the human and non-human, organic and nonorganic, while transcending typically anthropocentric Western thought with its reductive understanding of material as empty, dead and lacking in agency. My analysis of this process posits a 'paradigmatic shift', using the term to refer to the strategic position of a scholar who occupies the challenging, liminal space 'between and betwixt' the humanities and social sciences whose interpretative frameworks are shifting.

Richard Rorty has argued that the antirepresentationalist account, which renders irrelevant the distinction between explaining 'hard' phenomena and interpreting 'soft' ones, 'does not view knowledge as a matter of getting reality right, but rather as a matter of acquiring habits of action for coping with reality' (Rorty 1991: 1). In light of this, it could be argued that the objective of knowledge building is not (or not only) social and political change, as it was in the case of the emancipatory and insurrectional new humanities, but rather (or also) adaptation to changing conditions, triggering the imagination and future-oriented thinking in order to construct alternative future scenarios (beyond the catastrophic). What is therefore also important in this context is developing visions of research about the past that are capable of meeting this challenge, while also equipping such research with adequate approaches and analytical categories. While I do not propose reducing knowledge to its practical value, Rorty's pragmatist approach may be helpful today as the humanities confront a world that becomes increasingly difficult to handle. It is also worth considering that, as Deborah Bird Rose and Libby Robin have observed, in today's changing world the lack or incompleteness of knowledge is not so much an obstacle as a condition for participation in the living system of our planet and a necessary factor for survival (Bird Rose and Robin 2004).

New Approaches to Thinking About the Past in the Humanities and Social Sciences

The main challenge for today's historical research lies not so much in asking questions or proposing theories and methods of analysis which would spring from *current* trends in humanities, but in applying a future-oriented position and positioning the research itself in the context of the emerging paradigm of knowledge that is post-anthropocentric, post-Western, post-global (planetary/cosmic) and postsecular. In light of this, I would claim that as long as philosophers and theorists of history are interested in the problem of the status and nature of historical knowledge (and the status of history as a field of knowledge), in explaining, interpreting, representing and understanding the past, in status of facts, sources and evidences, causes and effects and so on, they would have a lot to do in the coming years, since all these basic factors are the subject of very lively discussion in the field of bio-, eco-, geo-, indigeno-, necro-, neuro-, phyto-, techno- and zoo-humanities while the philosophy and theory of history seems to be stuck in postmodernism and problems related to narrativism (postnarrativism) and social constructivism.

It will be a challenge for historical knowledge to remain focused on human self-knowledge, since the emergent paradigm is more interested in animals, plants, objects and the non-humans than in humans as such. This has something to do with the fact that in today's world, the understanding of humanity has undergone radical change. There is increasing criticism of the narcissistic human subject with its privileged position in the world, and increasing talk not so much of a human cultural or social community as of a community of species, of the collective of humans and non-humans and the relations between them and of issues of species identity. From the perspectives of these avant-garde tendencies, the concept of a global world is becoming increasingly reductive, while planetary identification backed by the ideas of transculturalism looks increasingly interesting (Spivak 2003; Chakrabarty 2018a; Elias and Moraru 2015; Keller 2018). Considerations of human subjects deprived of personhood (dehumanized prisoners of camps, the stateless, those enmeshed in extreme poverty), of those who have transcended humanity thanks to biotechnological progress (disabled persons given special abilities thanks to prostheses and transplants) and of the non-dead (the corpses and, in popular culture, zombies and vampires) have become particularly interesting. The non-human has become the paradigmatic figure of the contemporary and the guidepost to the future.

Among the ongoing changes, I would also include the strengthening of the connection and cooperation between the humanities and the life and earth sciences; the conventionalization of the paradigm frequently defined as interpretive and constructivist; and the appearance of various tendencies (often contradictory) associated with posthumanism (Wolfe 2010; Badmington 2000; Braidotti 2013), new materialism and new empiricism, combining the 'rejection of the text' with an advocacy for a 'return to things' and materiality (and to what is present and accessible 'here and now'). Scholars are exploring new aims and norms, hence renewed interest in such 'world-historical' problems as the eternal dilemmas of good and evil, truth, values and virtues, universals, human nature, relations between human and non-human, and the sacred. Additionally, they have resumed the search for the practical wisdom that could help to build a holistic knowledge; knowledge of – as Bruno Latour says – 'how to live together' (Latour 2005: 254, 259, 262; Latour 2009: 1), in conflicts – I would add.

A classical figure in French historiography, Marc Bloch predicted long ago that our civilization would turn its back on history (Bloch 1992: 5). To meet the challenges of the contemporary world (and the humanities that convey its problems), history becomes a sort of practical knowledge, that is, knowledge that, on the one hand, enables human being to adapt flexibly to changing conditions both cultural and natural and, on the other hand, inculcates in human beings an ethical instinct.[4] With efforts now underway to redefine humanity and the relations between human and the non-human, history understood as human self-knowledge becomes overridingly important, on the condition that it takes a critical view of the affirmation of humanity. We need history that encourages us to be human (with relations to various non-humans) without making it something egoistic. Such knowledge may well face the supremely important task and challenge of demonstrating the possibility of creating and reinforcing a feeling of 'shared humanity' and species solidarity; of showing what this depends on and how it has changed. This would be a matter of creating the kind of knowledge about the past that would be worthwhile for individuals and communities not only in terms of survival in critical situations but also in terms of putting ethical principles into action. History is also becoming more future friendly, that is, oriented towards creating knowledge about the past which has significant value for the future. In order to achieve it, there is a need for a 'revival of futurity' – to use Fredric Jameson's expression (Jameson 2010: 42–3) in reflections about the past. Indeed, as John Torpey in his book *Politics and the Past* (2003) argues, the worldwide idea of 'coming to terms with the past' (memory boom) has caused a fixation on the (traumatic) past. As a result, declining trust in alternative visions of the future has become evident (Torpey 2003: 1).

Taking up the previously mentioned challenge requires new theories and methods. The humanities need a new metalanguage, which cannot be created without rehabilitating the concepts that exist within tradition, on the one hand, and generating new ones, on the other. We should bear in mind the essentially banal truism that new concepts and theories are needed when the *empiria* (the phenomena appearing in the reality around us) exceed the capacity of the existing concepts and theories to comprehend them. In the current situation of paradigm shift, the development of theory cannot anticipate the emergence of new facts.

What Constitutes a Paradigm Today?

Before continuing the present argument, I would like to clarify my use of the term 'paradigm'. With its obvious echoes of Thomas Kuhn, the word cannot be used without reservations, if only because Kuhn's theory of scientific revolutions is based upon a fairly stereotypical conception of science and the relations between the humanities and the natural sciences. The concept of paradigm, and Kuhn's theory as a whole, needs to be problematized and historicized. Indeed, in response to the criticism his book provoked, Kuhn himself considered replacing paradigm with a disciplinary matrix. I propose understanding a paradigm as a research model (Gk. *paradeigma,* model, pattern) or, following Kuhn, as a disciplinary matrix, a set of theories and concepts that define the interpretative framework for research conducted in a given place and at a given time by researchers who share ontological, epistemological, aesthetic and ethical assumptions about their work (Kuhn 2012: 181; see also Agamben 2009). I am aware that the variety of research trends and approaches constituting the contemporary humanities and social sciences cannot be subsumed under homogeneous paradigms even though some of those trends and approaches converge in a number of ways. My discussion of the struggle of two paradigms – the interpretivist-constructivist and the posthumanist (and/or ecological) – is an attempt to present a simplified model of the changes and shifts which have occurred in the humanities and social sciences in the past decades.

While I am sceptical of Kuhn's structuralist approach, I nevertheless find his take on paradigms as diverse worlds inspiring, likewise the fact that he approaches paradigmatic preferences in terms of categories of conversion rather than choice. In light of current debates over various ontologies, as well as the relations between science and religion, it is worth recalling Kuhn's opinion that revolutions change world views, and it is for this reason that they demand (or stimulate) conversions. As he argued in *The Structure of Scientific Revolutions,* 'What were ducks in the scientist's world before the revolution are rabbits afterwards. ... The choice between competing ... paradigms proves to be a choice between incompatible modes of community life' (Kuhn 2012: 111–12, 94). As I returned to this well-known book recently, I started to consider what exactly are these (various) worlds (cosmologies and paradigms) that researchers convert to? What kind of worlds would they actually like to inhabit?

I believe that Kuhn's idea of scientific revolutions cannot adequately describe the changes in the human and social sciences after the Second World War. I am convinced that they could be addressed more effectively through Imre Lakatos's methodology of scientific research programmes. In his essay 'Science and Pseudoscience', Lakatos argues, 'In a progressive research programme, theory leads to the discovery of hitherto unknown novel facts. In degenerating programmes, however, theories are fabricated only in order to accommodate known facts.' Accordingly, Lakatos adds, 'where theory lags behind the facts, we are dealing with miserable degenerating research programmes' (Lakatos 1978: 5–6). I argue that we can currently observe the degeneration of the research programme of constructivism (or some of its versions, like textual or interpretive constructivism), which has not yet fully given way to another programme. Consequently, we are suspended in a paradigmatic gap 'betwixt and between' a program that has not yet been overthrown and another program which is not yet visible. The reason for this frustrating situation is that the degenerating program has created an effective mechanism to solve the problem of 'anomalies' and constructed a broad buffer zone to prevent the destruction of its 'hard core'. (In case of history understood as a specific approach to the past developed in the Greco-Judeo-Christian tradition, it is anthropocentrism.) The development of theory today fails to anticipate the appearance of new facts. Theory seems to lack imagination and intuition; it is stagnant and, as Lakatos puts it, 'lags behind the facts', awkwardly trying to explain the facts identified by competing theories.

This process can also be observed in the humanities and social sciences, with their recent interest in animals, plants and things. However, quite often while they are treated as interesting research topics and examined by means of known theories, researchers hesitate to address the relationship between humans and non-humans in the context of the radical avant-garde of critical posthumanism, although it is the latter that anticipates the appearance of new facts (e.g. Rosi Braidotti, Donna Haraway, Tim Ingold, Bruno Latour, Cary Wolfe). Scholars are increasingly interested in 'disobedient subjects', which often require complementary approaches combining the human, social and natural sciences, such as environmental studies, animal studies, plant studies and so on. The theories used in the humanities and social sciences today struggle with the problem of incommensurability: the results of their research are 'incommensurable' with the changing reality and social expectations. That is to say, although scholars observe the ongoing changes, write about them and create new research areas, they lack adequate tools to conceptualize them. This lack constitutes a major problem in today's humanities and social sciences.

The Conventionalization of Interpretivist-Constructivist Approaches

The interpretivist-constructivist paradigm is not a homogeneous whole but a set of various research approaches and perspectives which have evolved in time and space. In the argument that follows, I will regard this paradigm as characteristic of the so-called new humanities, which includes a variety of interdisciplinary trends such as gender and queer studies, postcolonial studies, ethnic studies and disability studies (Fuery and Mansfield 1997; Miller and Spellmeyer 2008). The interpretivist-constructivist paradigm, which was stimulated to a significant degree by the work of a generation of leftist French intellectuals (and thus came to be known as French Theory), has played an interventionist, emancipatory and even insurrectionary role, actively participating in social change (Cusset 2008). During its domination of the humanities, scholarship became a form of political activism.[5] The characteristics of this paradigm include a pragmatic approach to research, its politicization, emphasis on the relations between knowledge and power, ideological engagement of the researcher who wants to participate in social change and the struggle for justice, unmasking the practices of power, belief in the social construction of social reality and focus on reclaiming the forgotten and/or excluded past. In terms of epistemology, the interpretivist-constructivist paradigm has promoted interdisciplinary approaches and epistemological relativism, the theory of the situational subject of knowledge (i.e. its subjectivity) and reflexivity and has emphasized the pertinency of interpretation rather than its truth.

A representative example of the interpretivist-constructivist paradigm is the following statement about qualitative sociological research:

> The civic-minded qualitative researcher ... attempts to identify the many persuasions, prejudices, injustices, and inequalities that prevail in a given historical period. ... The researcher always asks how the practices of qualitative research can be used to help create a free democratic society. ... The researcher-as-interpretive-*bricoleur* is always, already in the material world of values and empirical experience. This world is confronted and constituted through the lens that the scholar's paradigm or interpretive perspective provides. The world so conceived ratifies the individual's commitment to the paradigm or perspective in question. This paradigm is connected at a higher ethical level to the values and politics of an emancipatory, civic social science. (Denzin and Lincoln 2005: 375)

Consider also the following remark of Kathy Charmaz:

> Should knowledge transform practice and social processes? Yes. Can grounded theory studies contribute to a better world? Yes. Should such questions influence what we study and how we study? Yes. (Charmaz 2006: 185)

Theory and methodology in the new humanities are often taken to be merely instruments of political struggle or a political practice. Chela Sandoval's *Methodology of the Oppressed* (2000) constitutes a typical example (Sandoval 2000).

Its epigraph comes from Subcomandante Marcos, the legendary leader of the Mexican Zapatista Army of National Liberation (EZLN): 'We seek a world in which there is room for many worlds.' It is noteworthy that Sandoval is a professor of Chicano/a Studies at the University of California-Santa Barbara, and her book has a foreword by Angela Davis, a philosophy professor at the University of California-Santa Cruz and one of the premier black feminist activists in the United States. Sandoval's study presents the theory and methodology of the human sciences as a means to creating an oppositional consciousness in the groups that struggle against various forms of racial, social and gender oppression. By definition, it does not aspire either to objectivity in the positivist sense[6] or to the neutrality of the researcher, or to the search for truth as the goal of research. 'Methodology of the oppressed is what enables the enactment of the differential mode of oppositional social movement that I described in the example of U.S. third world feminism as interventionist praxis', Sandoval declares (Sandoval 2000: 82).

From Textualism to (New) Materialism

The changes in the world and in our everyday lives shift our attention to different research problems and provoke different questions. For example, biopolitics enter our lives in the form of biometrics and the questions of transplants or reproduction (Rose 2007). We witness the birth of genetically engineered children, the emergence of disabled persons who are superhumans (Oscar Pistorius, whose prosthetic legs enable him to run faster than able-bodied runners – Triviño 2013; Marcellinia et al. 2012), the creation of animal hybrids and mutated life forms (e.g. Eduardo Kac and his fluorescent rabbit or 'Edunia', a flower which contains the artist's DNA) (Kac 2000, 2007), not to mention extending the concept of mass murder and holocaust to animals and plants (animal holocaust; ecocide – nature extermination) (Patterson 2002; Broswimmer 2002). However, a shift is coming not only from above (changes in the world) but also from the bottom up, meaning that individual experiences (and knowledge that comes from these experiences) plays an important role in the current paradigm shift. Experiences generate different values and required a change in views and beliefs. Interpretivism with its focus on text and narrative has attempted to address all these problems but has done so inadequately (according to current expectations). Hence today's interest in ontology, the empirical, matter. Hence also the absence or occasional presence in the avant-garde scholarship I am reading today of concepts like discourse, text or narrative.

The limitations of the interpretivist-constructivist paradigm are evident in relation to the process that the sociologist of science Andrew Pickering described as the 'posthumanist displacement of our interpretative frameworks' (Pickering 1999: 561). One manifestation of this process is the emergence of the posthumanities.[7] The posthumanities can be defined as a set of tendencies and research trends related to the intellectual movement and ethical stance known as posthumanism. They construct a knowledge that critiques and/or rejects humans' central position in the world, hence their preference for non- or anti-anthropocentric approaches. In a sense, the posthumanities can be thought of as nonanthropocentric humanities, although this definition is too paradoxical to be embraced without reservations.[8] The primary research interests of the posthumanities include the boundaries of species identity, relations between the human and the non-human (the human's relations with technology, the environment, animals, things) and questions of biopower, biopolitics and biotechnology. The point is not to exclude the human from scholarship but to approach critically the view of the human as the master and centre of the universe (Domańska 2018a).

In a sense, this paradigm shift marks a return to the evolutionary understanding of scholarship as adjusting to the changing reality and a resumption of the debates about whether scholarship (the human and social sciences) has any survival value for the human species and for life in general (Domańska 2010a). This shift is interesting and important because it adopts new points of reference and new goals for the building of knowledge. One of its reference points is life itself or *zoe*, often considered in negative terms. Human and social scientists are urged to take into account the physics of entropy (the second law of thermodynamics), which states that every isolated system will eventually reach an equilibrium, and hence, that every system has a limited lifespan (Rifkin 1980; Weisman 2007). Accordingly, we have to consider the real possibility of human extinction: a realization that ought to change our attitude to nature, the environment and non-human subjects.

In the introduction to the important book *New Materialisms: Ontology, Agency and Politics* (2010), Diana Coole and Samantha Frost write:

> The dominant constructivist orientation to social analysis is inadequate for thinking about matter, materiality, and politics in ways that do justice to the contemporary context of biopolitics and global political economy. While we recognize that radical constructivism has contributed considerable insight into the workings of power over recent years, we are also aware that an allergy to 'the real' that is characteristic of its more linguistic or discursive forms ... has had

the consequence if dissuading critical inquirers from the more empirical kinds of investigation that material processes and structures require. (Coole and Frost 2010: 6; see also Barad 2007)

New Materialisms manifests a departure from the traditional (Cartesian) concept of matter as passive and lifeless. Characterized by focus on technological progress and humans' growing dependence on things, validation of indigenous cultures' view of the relations between humans and things, and reliance on quantum physics, new materialism proposes a thorough rethinking of the concepts of matter, vitalism and animism in the completely new context of today's world. Matter and things become active, unpredictable forms of constant becoming with non-intentional agency (Knappett and Malafouris 2008; Bennett 2010; Lury, Kember and Fraser 2006; Harvey 2006).

Entanglement, Flat Alternatives and the Idea of Symmetry

Working within the framework of the interpretivist-constructivist paradigm, Sandoval observes that oppression is being 'democratized' as a result of changes in the concept of power since the end of the twentieth century. The vertical concept of power (the pyramidal model), where power spreads from the top to the bottom, that is, from the autocratic ruler to the lowest strata, has been replaced by the horizontal model, where the position of the subject of power can be described in terms of a network of factors such as race, class, gender or age. The 'flat' or horizontal character of power does not mean, however, that subjects have better access to power, since other forms of oppression are at work. Such concepts as bottom, subordinated, top and elevated have given way to concepts drawn from the methodologies of oppositional movements, such as margin and centre, boundary, hybridity, diaspora and location (Sandoval 2000: 73–4).

Sandoval's ideas are indicative of the major reconfigurations in the theory of the humanities and social sciences that manifest themselves in the broader shift of research perspective from the vertical to the horizontal. Generally speaking, the vertical model of knowledge is being replaced by the horizontal model as what are known as flat alternatives and/or relational approaches grow in importance. Indeed, it is legitimate to say that contemporary humanities and social sciences are all about relations and interconnectedness. Among the many factors stimulating this shift are the influences of both ecological thinking, which endorses an ontology of connectivity between humans and non-humans, and humans and the environment, and, secondly, of science and technology studies, which examines the relations between humans and things and quantum physics (Hörl and Burton 2017), with both sharing the conviction that all things are connected. However, as Raymond Pierotti and Daniel Wildcat indicate, 'it is not simply a homily and a romanticized *cliché*, but instead is a realization that no single organism can exist without the web of other life forms that surround it and make its existence possible' (Pierotti and Wildcat 2000: 1336; Hart 2010). The pyramidal metaphor of viewing reality has given way to the metaphor of horizontal relations, a web, net, network but also associations, assemblages, collectives, companions and symbiotic communities, various kinships and entanglements. Examples of such 'flat ontologies' are Bruno Latour's actor-network theory, Manuel DeLanda's assemblage theory, and Ian Hodder's project of relational archaeology (Holbraad and Pedersen 2017; Escobar 2007; DeLanda 2006; Hodder 2012). They share a critical approach to traditional social constructivism, whose idea of society as socially constructed establishes a certain social determinism (sociocentrism) focused on human subjects (Delanty 1997). Many scholars agree with Latour, who argues that 'society is constructed, but not socially constructed', that is, society is not constructed exclusively by humans but emerges as a result of human–non-human interactions (Latour 1999: 198, 209). In this context the idea of hierarchy is being replaced with that of symmetry.

The idea of symmetry has become so widespread in the human and social sciences that avant-garde archaeologists, following in Latour's footsteps, have formulated the project of 'symmetrical archaeology'. The phrase echoes the French subtitle of Latour's well-known book *We Have Never Been Modern*, 'An Essay on Symmetrical Anthropology' (*Nous n'avons jamais été modernes. Essai d'anthropologie symétrique*, 1991). Following the definition of one of the leading figures in this strand of thought, Christopher L. Witmore, symmetrical archaeology is based on the principle that 'humans and non-humans should not be regarded as ontologically distinct, as detached and separated entities, *a priori*. ... Any *radical* separation, opposition and contradiction between people and the material world with which they live is regarded as the outcome of a specifically modern way of distributing entities and segmenting the world' (Witmore 2007: 546).

In his *In Defense of Things* (2010), Norwegian archaeologist Bjørnar Olsen presents an egalitarian approach and a more symmetrical view of reality. He assumes that things, and material culture in general, are beings that coexist with other beings like humans, animals or plants. They all have material properties and share the world they inhabit (Olsen 2010). Symmetry in this context does not mean that all these beings are equal or the same; they are seen as different and diversified forms of being, but the differences among them should not be framed as ontological dualisms or negations. Rather, they are nonoppositional, relative differences that foster collaboration, transmission and exchange.[9]

Conclusion

Pinpointing mutual influences of the trends, approaches and perspectives is difficult because all of these fields are, I believe, indicators not only of an emergent new paradigm but also of the emergence of a new world view. It is evident in avant-garde approaches and trends that are in and of themselves non- or post-anthropocentric (hence the nonanthropocentric humanities). These approaches (all those prefixed with bio-, eco-, geo-, necro-, neuro-, zoo-humanities) construct a holistic vision that combines the humanities and natural sciences while drawing on ecological thought and values together with a whole assemblage of various, often mutually contradictory approaches that are known as the non- or post-anthropocentric humanities, the posthumanities, environmental humanities and/or biohumanities. Furthermore, it is often noted that such approaches are post-European (in the sense of a critique of the imperialist West as Europe is no longer the centre of knowledge production), posthuman (conceptions of the human are shifting in light of the potential diversification of the species with the emergence of biological or technological forms of *homo*), postsecular (given the return of spirituality, religious eclecticism and noninstitutional religious practices), postgender (with a shift away from gender identifications) and postwhite (the white race is no longer the ruling race).

The future of the humanities and social sciences is inseparably connected with reflection on the future of the Earth, the human species, transspeciation and of life itself. Thus, knowledge about the past becomes more a future-oriented knowledge that facilitates adaptation and is relevant insofar as it supports the continuation of life of various species (in both social and biological context).[10] As such, it also becomes part of the planetary (or even cosmic) project where emerging knowledge opens the way for the humanities and social sciences to think about the multispecies world of future communities.

In this context, what we need to do today is what Rorty advocated in one of his essays: Instead of worrying if particular beliefs are justified, we must ask whether we have enough imagination to propose interesting ideas that would provide an alternative to the prevailing beliefs (Rorty 1999: 34, 221) or research instruments and interpretative categories whose efficacy would be measured not by how accurately they describe, explain or represent the object but by how successful they are in causing change. We must ask ourselves such questions as the following: What kind of change is the aim of our actions? What kind of future is worth our efforts? Are we going to fight for survival at all costs or, as environmental scientists predict, undergo a radical transformation that will lead us to understand our role in the cosmic drama of creating a not-only-human community?

To support the aforementioned predictions, I want to quote the sociologists Egon G. Guba and Yvonna S. Lincoln, who argue that

> we may also be entering an age of greater spirituality within research efforts. The emphasis on inquiry that reflects ecological values, on inquiry that respects communal forms of living that are not Western, on inquiry involving intense reflexivity regarding how our inquiries are shaped by our own historical and gendered locations, and on inquiry into 'human flourishing' … may yet reintegrate the sacred with the secular in ways that promote freedom and self-determination. (Guba and Lincoln 2005: 212)

The debates discussed earlier render insufficient the traditional definition of history as 'the study of people in time' (Marc Bloch). History must change if it wants to defend its position among other disciplines that study the past and build knowledge about the past which is relevant to the future. What we seek in the past is determined by what troubles the present, and today we are seeking the human, or humanity, even in its non-human form. Accordingly, the role of history as human self-knowledge has gained crucial importance but the challenge now is to adopt a critical view of the affirmation of humanity.[11] As the study of change and continuity, history demonstrates what it means to be human, not only in the cultural sense but also as a species (Chakrabarty 2015). It is particularly noticeable in such disciplines as (new) environmental history, animal history, biohistory and neurohistory (deep history), which emphasize the mutually complementary character of research into biological, geological and sociocultural identity as well as the natural and cultural heritage, while simultaneously warning against biological determinism and historicizing previous connections between history and biology. History is becoming the study of both the human and non-human condition, as well as ways of remaining human (in the context of the diversification of the human species and the emergence of new species, including some created by humans).

It might prove to be the case that the current sociopolitical situation will inspire or even force researchers to focus on the particularities of their local conditions, thus adapting their discussions on the modes and objectives of knowledge production to local needs. While I am interested in ecohumanities and nonanthropocentric approaches to research on the past, I have not stopped reading the 'postmodernists', although I do now read them differently because I locate them in different interpretative frameworks. Thus, for example, I use the deconstructive approach to history (Kleinberg 2017) as a platform (or springboard) that helps us 'reinvent the future', or rather, enables a 'revival of futurity' for thinking about the past. For me, deconstruction (and Jacques Derrida's work in general) is an affirmative exercise that allows us to think about social values as methods of historical inquiry (although not by using deconstruction as a method, which would go against Derrida's intention) that are oriented towards the future and permit us to build alternative visions of a community-to-come (*l'avenir*).[12] For these reasons, instead of reading Derrida's *Of Grammatology*, I focus on his books on friendship, forgiveness and hospitality.[13]

I would like to conclude this chapter by emphasizing the need for a practical (and pragmatic) turn, of the kind that Hayden White proposed in the realm of historical theory, while Veronica Tozzi also developed a pragmatic approach to the theory of history and historical writing (Tozzi 2012). In light of the arguments presented in this article, I would like to refer to Rick Vogel who proposed a re-reading of Kuhn's original works to advance a practice-based understanding of paradigms. Instead of emphasizing the act of 'believing in' the paradigm, Vogel highlighted the 'doing of' it. While I am supportive of Vogel's endeavour, especially with his remark that teaching does not 'encourage critical thinking about the paradigm but train[s] students in its essential practices' (Vogel 2012: 37) my goal would be to develop the practice-based understanding of paradigms even further.

For many years already, I have been preaching that historians will not be able to advance theory and participate in theoretical discussions that are taking place in (and changing) contemporary humanities and social sciences if we continue to merely teach young adepts of the historical craft how to apply historical theories without encouraging them to develop their own analytical tools and small-range theories based on case study analyses. For me at least, reality is always more interesting (and richer) than theory. What I propose, then, is developing the ability to construct repeatable research procedures that are an outcome of the empirical material under investigation and a source of analytical frameworks, concepts and procedures that can subsequently be employed by other researchers. Inspired by sociological grounded theory, I have since 2006, in collaboration with my master's and doctoral students, been conducting a project focused on 'practical methodology'.[14] It is a response to the changes affecting contemporary humanities – a field in dire need of a new metalanguage, new theories and new approaches.

I am also promoting the idea of potential history, proposed by the Israeli scholar and artist Ariella Azoulay in the context of investigations into the Israeli-Palestinian conflict (Azoulay 2013). Azoulay's project is relevant for reflecting on conflicts elsewhere and might even offer a means for working through conflicts as such. Research conducted within the framework of potential history explores unrealized potential in the past in an attempt to reveal the conditions that must be created to allow people to adapt to one another and coexist (Appiah 2010: 110ff, 181). Such research also stresses the investigation of successful initiatives which have contributed to and continue to contribute to the construction of economic, social and cultural endeavours that link various nations and ethnic and/or religious groups. In this context, history, which explores 'the past as the storehouse of human possibility' – to use Susan Buck-Morss's phrase (Buck-Morss, Bojarska 2014), becomes a kind of laboratory for revealing the conditions of coexistence and cohabitation in the world.

In this sense, potential history is part of the shift in focus evident in the humanities and social sciences today away from research on conflicts and towards research on collaboration, coexistence, conviviality, critical hope, good neighbourly relations, friendship and social trust. It is no longer conflict (war and conquest) but (and perhaps above all) cooperation and a form of coexistence based on the cooperation of various ethnic, cultural and religious groups (without of course denying existing problems) that has become the driving force of the historical process. This is not a matter of privileging naive ideas of reconciliation and consensus but of considering how historical knowledge depicting the conditions of the coexistence of people, nations, communities and social groups in the past can assist in building knowledge of conviviality (Illich 1973) and/or coexistence in conflicts that has a prefigurative potential.

Translated by Magdalena Zapędowska and Paul Vickers

Acknowledgements

This chapter contains elaborated, revised and updated ideas presented in the texts: 'Die paradigmatische Lücke (*paradigmatic gap*) in den heutigen

Geistes- und Sozialwissenschaften', trans. by Michael G. Esch. *Historie. Jahrbuch des Zentrums für Historische Forschung Berlin der Polnischen Akademie der Wissenschaften*, no. 4, 2010/2011: 34–54 and 'Archaeological Theory: Paradigm Shift', in: *Encyclopedia of Global Archaeology*, ed. by Claire Smith. New York: Springer 2014: 375–9.

Funding

The translation of this article was enabled by financial support from the Department of History, Adam Mickiewicz University in Poznan, Poland.

11

More-Than-Human History

Philosophy of History at the Time of the Anthropocene

Marek Tamm and Zoltán Boldizsár Simon

Philosophy of History and the New Human Condition

The twenty-first century has brought about a sense of rapid global and planetary changes. Discussions of novel kinds of ecological and technological transformations have been around since the immediate post-war years, but in the last two decades they have become core issues of public debate. Today, there is a growing awareness about human-induced climate change and biodiversity loss radically transforming the Earth system, about new biotechnologies, transhumanism and artificial intelligence research promising previously unforeseen changes that point beyond the human condition, and about the potential new dimensions all this adds to the already manifold ways in which inequalities pervade the sociopolitical sphere. At a time when immense changes seem to accelerate in various domains of life (Rosa 2013), when those domains exhibit multiple temporalities (Jordheim 2014), when we witness the metamorphosis of the world in which 'what was unthinkable yesterday is real and possible today' (Beck 2016: xii), when change in some domains depart from a processual scheme of modern historical thinking and take the shape of 'unprecedented change' by bringing about a disconnection between visions of the future and past conditions (Simon 2019a), when 'the future ceases to be made of the same matter as the past' and 'becomes radically *other*, not-ours' (Danowski and Viveiros de Castro 2016: 26), one may ask: Where is the philosophy of history to make sense of this new human condition and the experience of momentous transformations?

For it seems to be nowhere, at least not as a respectable and legitimate form of knowledge production. Despite the fact that making sense of the world of human affairs as changing over time has been a task associated with the philosophy of history in Western modernity, and despite the fact the world is experienced today as being on the verge of changes more tectonic than ever, there is hardly any philosophy of history around to comprehend these experiences historically. As common knowledge has it, philosophy of history has been transformed into a philosophy of historiography in the last more than half century. Whereas philosophies of history of the late Enlightenment and the nineteenth century sketched long-term scenarios of human development gesturing towards ultimate meanings, a disillusionment with such grand schemes in post-Second World War societies gave way to philosophies of history which typically put forward analyses and explanations of the business of professional historiography.

The transformation of philosophy of history is fairly well known, and we do not wish to analyse here the way in which it took place. It seems more important to raise awareness of one of its most crucial consequences: the altered nature of the relationship between such philosophy of history and historical studies. Throughout Western modernity, both philosophy of history and the freshly professionalized historiography operated as first-order disciplines. Their relationship was based on the existence of mutually recognized ties, on the one hand, and a rivalry in saying meaningful things about change in human affairs, on the other. They developed competing methods and argued with each other over the question of what constitutes reliable historical knowledge. In doing so, however, they were jointly debating change over time in the human world as a shared concern external to both, and jointly fulfilled the function of societal self-understanding as 'historical'. But post-Second World War philosophy of history transformed into a second-order discipline studying the first-order discipline of history, which remained engaged in studying and debating the changing world of human affairs. From the viewpoint of historiography, this philosophy of history appeared as the uninvited *Besserwisser* which claims to know better the dealings and nature of historical studies than it claims to know itself. The rivalry between historical studies and philosophy of history has been reduced into a rivalry about saying meaningful things about the self-understanding of the former. They ceased to debate a shared concern external to both; they were debating instead – with not much enthusiasm from the side of historiography – a concern internal to one of the parties involved. Accordingly, their functions parted ways. Historical studies stuck with the role of providing societal self-understanding as 'historical', while philosophy of history became the (oftentimes bad) conscience of historiography's disciplinary self-understanding.

Phrased in the simplest way, philosophy of history and professional historiography were talking about the same thing – historical change – in the modern period and stopped doing so with the transformation of the former into a philosophy of historiography in the postwar period. The consequences of the changed relation have been devastating to both. Post-Second World War philosophy of history – maybe with a very few although spectacular exceptions – has been relegated into one of the dustiest and most abandoned corners of academic work, without being able to integrate into institutional structures. At the same time, since the two no longer talks about the same thing, historical studies is struggling with maintaining its wider societal relevance and thereby with fulfilling its function to provide societal self-understanding as 'historical'. Neither of them seems to benefit from this constellation.

In this chapter, we intend to rewire this relationship while arguing for two interrelated theses: (1) *philosophy of history has to broaden its scope and embrace a new concept of history*; and (2) *it has to be a new philosophy of history as a new knowledge formation designed to address the most pressing concerns of our own times which escape the confines of studying the human world*. The first thesis implies the necessity of reconnecting of philosophy of history with historical studies in coming to terms with the emerging new notion of history. The function of societal self-understanding as 'historical' can be fulfilled only insofar as the two are able to discuss jointly the concerns of the changing world and only insofar as they reinforce each other in that. The second thesis responds to the challenge implied in recent ecological and technological prospects. Whereas modern historical knowledge emerged as one of the human sciences designed to understand the simultaneously constituted human being as a subject of study (Foucault 2002), recent ecological and technological discussions extend beyond such confines in addressing the concerns of a more-than-human world – of animals, plants, machines, artificial intelligence, Earth system changes – and their relation to the human world. To be able to make sense of concerns for the more-than-human, historical knowledge as we know it might as well have to transform beyond recognition.

As to the first thesis, the new century already witnessed a growing dissatisfaction with the narrow scope of philosophy of history understood as a philosophy of historiography. Eelco Runia (2006, see also Runia 2014; Runia and Tamm 2019) was among the firsts to take a firm stand against the reduction and the 'ban on speculation'. By that time, François Hartog (2015, in the French original 2003) has already opened new vistas by venturing into an exploration of 'regimes of historicity', that is, into the ways in which past, present and future relate to each other in experiences of time. Aleida Assmann (2013) shortly joined to such investigations, while Berber Bevernage (2012) suggested that a philosophy of such historicity that extends its scope over non-academic temporalities and relations to the past may replace both old-style philosophies of history and post-war philosophies of historiography. Finally, even in venues originally devoted to a sceptical take on history it became possible to argue for a philosophy of history understood as the philosophy of historical change in the shape of a 'quasi-substantive philosophy of history' (Simon 2016).

Needless to say, none of this entails a straightforward revival of modern philosophy of history as sketches of grand schemes of human development and ideas of a meaningful historical process. Novel concerns are not to be conceived of as new versions of an old end point of humanity's quest of self-understanding, although there is a tendency to interpret the latest ecological and technological thoughts in such framework. The respective examples may be, first, Clive Hamilton (2017: 76–87) arguing for seeing the Anthropocene as the latest unifying grand narrative of humanity, and second, the story told by Yuval Noah Harari (2017) about technological developments leading to humans becoming gods as the latest stage of their development. This, we think, is not the shape that a reliable philosophy of history may take today. It is rather the shape that historical thinking took in the nineteenth century. Unlike such efforts, a philosophy of history engaged in the exploration of historicities and configurations of change over time would rather be occupied with conceptualizing novel *types* of change as 'historical' and novel kinds of configurations of past, present and future, in conversation with historical studies invested in exploring what exactly changes and how.

These remarks already coincide with the second thesis concerning the necessity of a renewed philosophy of history to extend its scope beyond the confines of the human world and possibly beyond the confines of historical knowledge as we know it. Many other disciplines are much ahead in this respect. A large part of the humanities and social sciences are already on their way to explore a more-than-human world, including historical studies. The aforementioned growing interest in questions of historical time and historicity in the theoretical field coincides with the broadening of the scope, scale and the time horizon in historical studies, as is most apparent in the rise of deep history, evolutionary history and planetary history, or in the agenda of *The History Manifesto* (Guldi and Armitage 2014).

It was in a milieu of 'transtemporal history' (Armitage 2012) that historical studies found its way to the transdisciplinary debate on the Anthropocene

(Tamm 2018). The notion of the Anthropocene originally emerged within Earth system science as a proposed epoch signalled by human activity transforming the Earth system (Zalasiewicz et al. 2019). It nevertheless has quickly become a contested concept by acquiring sociocultural and political meanings, due to the intervention of humanities and social scientific scholarship (Lorimer 2017; Ellis 2018; Lewis and Maslin 2018). Since a co-authored piece of Libby Robin and Will Steffen (2007) on the necessity of history for the Anthropocene, the more impactful discussion-opener piece of Dipesh Chakrabarty (2009), and the article of Julia Adeney Thomas (2014) in the leading journal of academic history writing, historical approaches to the Anthropocene and the more-than-human world are on a rapid rise. In negotiating the relation between change in the natural world on a geological scale and change in the human world, they significantly contribute to turning the Anthropocene into a wider cultural predicament.

Yet the theoretical underpinnings of the potentially new historical condition underlying this wider Anthropocene predicament and the extent to which historical understanding as we know it is (un)able to cope with the novel predicament are yet to be explored (Simon 2020; Tamm and Olivier 2019). In our view, these questions constitute a part of a new agenda of a renewed philosophy of history. The overall agenda must of course be much wider and the Anthropocene predicament must be understood broadly enough. Its scope should encompass not only the entangled human and natural world as it appears in the transdisciplinary Anthropocene debate but also – among others – all the freshly emerging and oftentimes intersecting approaches of critical posthumanism, environmental humanities, multispecies approaches in anthropology and archaeology, and debates on biotechnology, human enhancement, transhumanism and artificial intelligence.

Although the immense sociopolitical transformations entailed by newer concerns for the more-than-human world of planetary scope are also part of the larger agenda, we wish to retain our focus in mapping the ongoing rearrangement of knowledge. This is largely due to the fact that recent changes in the ecological and technological domains have not yet triggered a deep structural transformation of world politics, still framed by negotiating nation states and international organizations. Migration due to anthropogenic changes in the Earth system, issues of climate and environmental justice, the potential colonization of Mars, the potential overtake of the labour market by artificial intelligence technologies, the perils of military AI, or the inequalities arising out of enhancement technologies available to the rich are of course serious political challenges. All these are widely addressed questions in climate and technological discussions, but they have not yet altered the political domain to the extent that there would be a new historicity or temporality to investigate for a philosophy of history.

Yet this does not mean that discourses on the Anthropocene, on a more-than-human world or on technological futures, do not have their implied 'politics' as humanities and social scientific scholarship conventionally understand it. They do. Isabelle Stengers (2015), for instance, has good reasons to fear that catastrophism about climate may result in securing the life of the rich but not of the poor in a coming barbarism. Besides, all the talk about changes that are 'anthropogenic' has its own 'politics' (Sayre 2012), and biotechnologies may entail a new kind of biopolitics of life and new ways of engineering vitality (Rose 2007). But again, these questions reflect long-established concerns of humanities scholarship and none of them seem to indicate a new configuration of political change or a new political temporality.

All in all, when assessing the role of a redefined philosophy of history in the Anthropocene engaged in mapping the historicity and the underlying temporality of a more-than-human world, we understand such world as one that includes all forms of the more-than-human, from the natural and biological to the mechanical and digital. Accordingly, on the coming pages we will argue for a more-than-human history by surveying fresh perspectives across disciplines. Although certain approaches – such as critical posthumanism (Braidotti and Hlavajova 2018; Braidotti 2019) or the technology-conscious approach of Dolly Jørgensen (2014; Jørgensen, Jørgensen and Pritchard 2013) to environmental history – blend ecological and technological non-humans, we find it useful to analytically distinguish between two major forms of concerns that extend beyond the confines of studying the human world: the more-than-human as it typically appears in ecology-inspired thinking and the better-than-human as it usually features in technological discussions.

In light of these considerations, on the coming pages we argue for a new notion history and a new agenda for philosophy of history. To avoid misunderstandings, we do not argue for or share all individual theoretical positions we introduce; what we argue for is a new notion of history that brings together the issues that new approaches to the more-than-human world debate. In outlining the new understanding of history appropriate for the time of the Anthropocene, we focus on its three main aspects. First, we begin by outlining the challenge of investigating a more-than-human world which will entail a *multispecies history*. Then we turn themes more familiar in philosophy of history: the relation between the question of scale and historical time. In doing so, second, we make the case for *a multiscalar notion of history* that entangles timescales; and third, we argue for a *non-continuous history* that departs from linear, processual and developmental configurations of historical time.

For a New Notion of History

The impact of the Anthropocene on human understanding is multiple and only partially graspable. In many respects, the Anthropocene has opened a new situation for humanity, 'a new human condition' (Bonneuil and Fressoz 2016). Most fundamentally the dawning of the Anthropocene blurs and even scrambles some crucial categories by which humans have made sense of the world and their lives. More specifically, 'it puts in crisis the lines between culture and nature, fact and value, and between the human and the geological or meteorological' (Clark 2015: 9). We contend that each discipline in the present economy of knowledge must reappraise its boundaries and assumptions in the Anthropocene's shadow (Farrier 2019: 3). In the context of history, the Anthropocene requires us to overcome many deeply rooted conceptual divisions: natural history versus human history, written history versus deep history, national/global history versus planetary history and so on. But more profoundly, the Anthropocene compels us to work out a new notion of history that radically decentres humans and positions our actions in the multispecies entanglements and in the configuration of multiple times. In other words, the Anthropocene forces a radical shift in how we understand our past relationship to the more-than-human world. Bruno Latour (2017b: 48) has succinctly captured the main lesson of the Anthropocene: 'It gives another definition of time, it redescribes what it is to stand in space, and it reshuffles what it means to be entangled within animated agencies.'

Multispecies History

The difficulty to be faced right away in trying to explore a more-than-human world is that the concept of history as we know it refers implicitly to 'human history'. History deals only with humans, while the rest of the non-human world belongs to the province of an entirely distinct 'natural history'. One could argue more specifically that it was only after nature acquired its own history that the modern notion of history became possible (Hamilton 2017: 7). This distinction between human and natural history goes back to the eighteenth century, to the famous *Sattelzeit* defined by Reinhart Koselleck, and it was formulated most memorably in the philosophy of Hegel. History is for Hegel the universal process of the realization of the spirit, and nature has no role to play in this process: 'We do not see the universal emerge in nature, which means that the universality of nature has no history' (Hegel 1970, vol. 3: 18). While history is a realm in which creative and self-reflective human agents make progressive change, nature encompasses ceaseless movement without forward motion, change without alteration (Kolb 2008, 2011). The verdict of Hegel that 'nature has no history' became the cornerstone of nineteenth-century historical research and this tradition is well summarized by Marc Bloch in his *Historian's Craft*: 'Long ago, indeed, our great forbears, such as Michelet or Fustel de Coulanges, taught us to recognize that the object of history is, by nature, man. [...] The good historian is like the giant of the fairy tale. He knows that wherever he catches the scent of human flesh, there his quarry lies' (Bloch 1953: 25–6). Until recently, historians have acted mainly as the giants of the fairy tale, turning their noses only to where they could smell the human.

Dipesh Chakrabarty was one of the first to argue that the Anthropocene has challenged 'the assumption that our past, present, and future are connected by a certain continuity of human experience' (Chakrabarty 2009: 197). He contends that in the situation where humans have become geological agents, 'the distinction between human and natural histories [...] has begun to collapse' and that the consequences of this 'make sense only if we think of humans as a form of life and look on human history as part of the history of life on this planet' (Chakrabarty 2009: 207, 213). This 'Great Ontological Collapse' (LeCain 2016: 16) has revealed more clearly than ever the anthropocentric character of history (Domańska 2010a). It has challenged the deeply rooted illusion of humans as the sole actors on the stage of history. Bruno Latour (2018: 43) describes eloquently the new situation: 'Today, the decor, the wings, the background, the whole building have come on stage and are competing with the actors for the principal role. This changes all the scripts, suggests other endings. Humans are no longer the only actors, even though they still see themselves entrusted with a role that is much too important for them.' In the light of this new situation, it is increasingly important to ask what history would look like if seen not from the human but from the non-human perspective. This question was first formulated by advocates of animal history who are no longer interested to study only the human–animal relations in the past but also the history 'from the animal's point of view' (Baratay 2012). Indeed, what would happen to the notion of history if considered from the non-human or from the interspecies perspective? To what extent would this approach problematize the epistemological foundations of historical research? And, in the first place, it is possible at all to adopt a non-human perspective to history?

Widely known is the thought experiment by Thomas Nagel (1974) concerning the question 'What is it like to be a bat?' Nagel concluded that such knowing is unattainable to humans, because we cannot grasp how the bat experiences the world. However, in one of the footnotes to his article, Nagel admits that his conclusion is about experience not knowledge, and that a partial understanding of a bat's perspective may still be possible:

> It may be easier than I suppose to transcend inter-species barriers with the aid of the imagination. [...] My point, however, is not that we cannot *know* what it is like to be a bat. I am not raising that epistemological problem. My point is rather that even to form a *conception* of what it is like to be a bat (and a fortiori to know what it is like to be a bat) one must take up the bat's point of view. If one can take it up roughly, or partially, then one's conception will also be rough or partial. Or so it seems in our present state of understanding. (Nagel 1974: 442, fn 8)

To understand, even if only partially, the animal perspective is one of the main aims of today's animal history. One of the leaders in the field, Erica Fudge, admits in her recent article titled 'What Was It Like to Be a Cow' (2017) that, in fact, the starting position of human and animal historians is not fundamentally different, as both try to understand how historical subjects have experienced changes over time. At the same time, Fudge does not claim that the new purpose of historical writing should be to replace the human perspective with an animal one. Instead, she calls for a multiple perspective:

> I no longer only want to know (or to try to know) what the experience of an animal was, although I do still hold that as a desire – impossible as it will be to fulfil. I also want to know (or to try to know) what the animals' experience of being with humans might have been, what the animals' experience of being with other animals was, and what the humans' experience of being with animals was. (Fudge 2017: 272)

Probably one of the most original and ambitious animal historians nowadays is Éric Baratay, who believes that it is high time to move forward from the usual 'human history of the animals' (*histoire humaine des animaux*) and to exchange the human perspective for the animal's perspective. Baratay has shown new avenues for animal history in several studies, but one of his most innovative books is *Biographies of Animals* (2017). It attempts to study the life experience of about a dozen of animals in nineteenth and twentieth century on the basis of diverse written evidence, research done by ethologists and the imagination of the author. The main aim of Baratay is to restore the historical individuality of animals, to show that it is possible to write the history of a specific animal instead of a specific species. Baratay explains that he tries to 'place himself on the animal's side in order to pass on what this animal at some moment, during a certain period of time, or through his life, has experienced and felt' (Baratay 2017: 21–2). On the pages of the book we get acquainted with a giraffe from Egypt, presented as a gift to the French king in 1826, with a British war horse called Warrior who became famous in the First World War, with the bull Islero who was killed at the Linares bullfighting arena in 1947, or with a Chimpanzee called Consul who was able to learn most of the human behaviours and won much attention in late nineteenth-century Manchester. Baratay's approach is made original by putting the emphasis on the reconstruction of how animals themselves understood and experienced the humans. He does not fear to write in the first person and to experiment with various typographic techniques to convey what, for example, the bull Islero might have experienced in the last minutes of his life on 28 August 1947 (Baratay 2017: 107–20).

But the new notion of history means more than a simple integration of the animal perspective into our understanding of the past; it forces us to rethink the very idea of history along multispecies lines. Ewa Domańska (2018a: 337) has called recently for a 'multispecies knowledge of the past' based on the fundamental recognition that human life is closely entangled with other forms of life. Such an approach is inspired by multispecies ethnography as proposed by Eben Kirksey and Stefan Helmreich (2010, cf. Ogden, Hall and Tanita 2013). The multispecies ethnography 'centers on how a multitude of organisms' livelihoods shape and are shaped by political, economic, and cultural forces' (Kirksey and Helmreich 2010: 545) and on the question of the extent to which the recognition of other species are integral and not subsidiary to what it means to be human. We have seen recently also attempts to build a multispecies archaeology which encourages the archaeologists to 'dig deeper into considerations of life; into a wider ecology of interactions with plants, fungi, microbes, and even the fundamental building blocks of life, DNA' (Pilaar Birch 2018: 2, cf. Hamilakis and Overton 2013). The main questions posed by multispecies archaeology – namely 'What can we learn about the past without humans as the focus of the question? What can we learn if we frame ourselves as one actor among others in the long march of time? […] How might situating humans within a wider ecology serve to extend or alter our knowledge of the past?' (Hamilakis and Overton 2013: 2–3) – remain most relevant also in the context of history.

The milestones for a multispecies history have been laid out in the last few years (Domańska 2018b; O'Gorman 2017; Onaga 2013; Tsing 2015) with the aim to see humans within temporally and spatially dynamic 'webs of interspecies dependence' (Tsing 2012: 144). Domańska (2018b: 120) argues that multispecies history should seek '"innovative forms of agency" that go beyond human agency, finding them also in non-human factors – so, in animals, plants, objects, microorganisms (as well as in sound and light)'. In other words, the notion of history from a multispecies perspective should include all agencies of human and other-than-human species, whether they are animals, plants, fungi, bacteria or viruses. One classic example of an early approach to multispecies history is John McNeill's *Mosquito Empires* (2010), demonstrating how the conquest and colonization of the Greater Caribbean depended not so much on the military capabilities of the parties involved but on their ability to cope with mosquito-borne viruses such as yellow fever and malaria. Multispecies history challenges also the traditional understanding of historical sources, extending our attentiveness to the traces left by various non-human organisms. Anna Tsing convincingly argues that

> there is no reason not to spread our attention to the tracks and traces of nonhumans, as these contribute to our common landscapes [...]. Whether or not other organisms 'tell stories', they contribute to the overlapping tracks and traces that we grasp as history. History, then, is the record of many trajectories of world making, human and not human. (Tsing 2015: 168)

The multispecies notion of history does not only offer a new knowledge of the past but also undermines most of the epistemological certainties in contemporary historical research. According to Domańska (2017: 271), it requires 'a different way of knowing the past from the one offered by historical epistemology with its specific understanding of time, space, change, rationality, and causality'. And, we may add, explicating the epistemology of a multispecies history in order to better navigate among the aforementioned knowledge-claims and their feasibility or unfeasibility requires the renewed philosophy of history we advocate.

Multiscalar History

Bruno Latour has described compellingly in his book *We Have Never Been Modern* how the modern delusion of the clear difference between nature and culture took shape and how from this distinction the very notion of linear 'historical time' was born with its sharp distinction between the past and the future. Latour (1993: 71) writes:

> The asymmetry between nature and culture becomes an asymmetry between past and future. [...] Modernization consists in continually exiting from an obscure age that mingled the needs of society with scientific truth, in order to enter into a new age that will finally distinguish clearly what belongs to atemporal nature and what comes humans.

The Anthropocene challenges this conventional understanding of historical time and invites us to think beyond our usual anthropocentric scales (Tamm and Olivier 2019). The problem is, however, that none of the traditional historical timescales can account for what it means to be an agent or a force on a planetary scale (Jordheim 2019: 45). According to Chakrabarty (2018b: 6; 2019: 220), any historical understanding at the time of the Anthropocene has to combine human and planetary time in a single, multiscalar framework. In the end, this may result in a novel way to situate ourselves in time. As Paul Warde, Libby Robin and Sverker Sörlin (2019: 166) put it, 'Perhaps [the Anthropocene] also holds out the promise of a new understanding of time itself and the roles of humans in it.'

The historian's time horizon seems indeed surprisingly limited from the perspective of the Anthropocene. Historically, both in the geological and biological sense, historians are interested in a curiously short time period. Already Walter Benjamin (2007: 263) pointed out that the history of *Homo sapiens* does not occupy more than two seconds in the 24-hour period of the history of organic life. John L. Brooke reminded of this recently when he imagined the five million years of human evolutionary time as a 24-hour period. Then the entire 300,000 years of modern humanity would comprise about an hour and a half, the 60,000 years since modern humans left Africa comprise about seventeen minutes, and the 12,000 years since the end of the Pleistocene and its aftershocks comprise slightly more than four minutes. But against a similar 24-hour clock of the geological time of evolving earth systems since 4.6 billion years ago, these epochs are even more minutiae: about six seconds since the emergence of modern humanity, one second since the first successful departure from Africa, and a few nanoseconds since the end of the ice ages (Brooke 2014: 114).

We need a much longer temporal view of our past as E. O. Wilson acknowledged a couple of decades ago; we need a 'deep history' that would 'combine genetic and cultural changes that created humanity over hundreds of thousands of years' (Wilson 1996: X). Wilson's call has been recently picked up by Daniel Lord Smail, who, together with scholars from various fields, has been committed to develop the principles of 'deep history', aiming nothing less than to propose 'a new architecture for human history' (Shryock and Smail 2011: XII). According to Smail (2008), the notion of history should not rest on the invention of writing but should encompass the entire development of the human species, stretching millions of years into the past. This means, of course, that historical research must be based on close cooperation with disciplines like anthropology, archaeology, genetics, neurophysiology and evolutionary biology. 'Histories can be written from every type of trace, from the memoir to the bone fragment and the blood type', Shryock and Smail (2011: 13) contend.

The initiative of deep history is close to the project of evolutionary history, proposed a few years ago by Edmund Russell (2011). Evolutionary history focuses on how human and non-human populations have coevolved or continually changed in response to each other. Besides, it also aims to show also how humans have fundamentally shaped the evolution of a variety of species, embedding organisms in social, economic and technological contexts (Russell 2011: 2). The project of big history (Christian 2004, 2018; Spier 2015) runs parallel to these initiatives inasmuch as it offers an interpretation of history on the largest possible scale, with human history seen within the history of the universe.

Taken together, all these endeavours clearly point towards a need for a new notion of time in history, to look at ourselves 'in the mirror of deep time' (Grinspoon 2016: X). To a certain extent, they also fit what the Anthropocene has taught us, namely, that time and historicity are not specifically human: 'We may not build our interaction with nature by claiming a monopoly on the short term any more than we may hive off the long-term onto a world beyond the human without agency or "thought"' (Sawyer 2015: 12). It is no longer sufficient to see ourselves only in terms of human development; 'we must have a broader perspective, a geological perspective, one that prompts the idea of deep time' (Wood 2019: 6).

But there is also an extent to which deep, evolutionary and big histories resonate less with the Anthropocene predicament. For the new notion of historical time is not only about expanding our temporal horizon deep into the past. It is more about a pluralistic understanding of temporality that is open to its multiple rhythms, events and trajectories over different scales. This was already the original message of the initial engagement of Chakrabarty (2009) with the Anthropocene, to situate human history with the geological timescale in a meaningful way, and this is what drives his recent efforts to find a way to translate ideas that work on the scale of Earth history to the language of the history of the human world (Chakrabarty 2018b). Or, as Rosanne Kennedy and Maria Nugent (2016: 65–6) assert, the Anthropocene 'pushes the question of scalarity [...] away from the horizontal plane registered by cultural and human flows across borders to the vertical scales of geology, earth and deep time'. We should be able to move between multiple temporal scales, even to 'play with the scales', to follow the conceptual metaphor of Jacques Revel (1996). It is important to 'shuttle between scales, explaining how small-scale phenomena (like a factory adopting a steam engine) generated large-scale phenomena (particulate emissions, acid rain, climate change) via multiple, recursive, aleatory acts' (Otter et al. 2018: 595; cf. Fitz-Henry 2017), just as well as it is important to explore how such large-scale phenomena shape actions on smaller scales.

Non-continuous History

Mutiscalarity is nevertheless not the last issue to consider in relation to historical time. If we venture into deep time with an attentiveness towards multiple timescales and rhythms, then we also need to be mindful of alternatives to historical continuity. The greatest shortcoming of big, deep and evolutionary history approaches is precisely that they habitually align with a notion of history inherited from Western modernity in telling an overarching story of development informed by a deep temporal continuity. Although multiscalarity to a large extent does way with the idea that we can tell a single unfolding story of practically everything since the birth of the universe, it is still prone to result in simply retaining the developmental temporality and continuity in change in all its entangled timescales. If we think that the Anthropocene predicament challenges the conventional understanding of historical time, this must also mean a challenge to continuity.

This is where recent work in philosophy of history may already come handy. For the linear notion of historical time that Latour thinks is challenged by the Anthropocene is of ill repute in the humanities and the social sciences since quite some time. It is another question that we still seem to lack feasible alternatives to it. But twenty-first-century philosophy of history has already ventured into exploring the possibility of non-developmental historical time and the question of non-continuous change. Runia (2014) even argued that the most pertinent question to come to terms with in philosophy of history today is the one concerning discontinuity over time, without giving in to the urge to cover its traces by historical works (which is precisely what big and evolutionary histories do today). Besides, long before Runia, Foucault has already devoted both his archaeological (2002) and genealogical approaches (1984) to the endeavour of conceptualizing alternatives to the developmental historicity of Western modernity.

It is of course true that neither Foucault nor Runia has much to say about anthropogenic changes in a more-than-human world. It is equally true that discontinuity (which belongs to the same order as continuity, being each other counterparts) may not be the perfect term to describe the radical transformations entailed by the Anthropocene predicament. But their general concerns for historical disruptions may find resonance with concerns about anthropogenic changes in the natural world which are perceived today as abrupt transformations with unforeseeable consequences. What brings them to the same platform is their shared objection to hypothesize linearity and continuity in the human and the more-than-human worlds respectively. Accordingly, what we argue for is a broad notion of non-continuous history that potentially covers all kinds of non-continuity, including but not reduced to discontinuous, abrupt, disconnective, disruptive transformations.

As an example in the more-than-human world, think of the notion of 'planetary boundaries' that intends to define a safe operating space for humanity through identifying 'key Earth System processes associated with dangerous thresholds, the crossing of which could push the planet out of the desired Holocene state', while such thresholds 'are defined as non-linear transitions in the functioning of coupled human-environmental systems' (Rockström et al. 2009). Transgressing planetary boundaries to a large extent threatens with transitions in Earth system conditions that are considered to be 'catastrophic' and 'deleterious' to human societies. Such changes, needless to say, can hardly be reconciled with the deep continuity of historical time as we know it throughout Western modernity.

The same non-continuity applies to runaway changes in the technological domain. To begin with, singularitarians expect an event to happen in the near future called 'technological singularity' (or sometimes simply 'singularity'), that is, the most profound alteration of the human condition and practically everything we know through surpassing general human capacities by technological means (Eden et al. 2012). Such non-continuous transformations may be brought about through superintelligence scenarios (Bostrom 2014) or as the result of human enhancement and transhumanist aspirations (Savulescu and Bostrom 2009; Ranish and Sorgner 2014; Fuller and Lipinska 2014). For our present purposes, the latter matters more not only because 'singularitarianism may be the best known public face of transhumanism' (Thweatt-Bates 2012: 51) as is well exemplified by the fact of a transhumanist candidate running a presidential campaign in the United States in 2016, but also because the aim of technologically engineering beings whose capacities escape the realm of human limitations connects to the multispecies history aspect discussed earlier.

Theories of species companionship typically consider technological beings part of their entanglements, making claims that 'as a nature cultural compound, a dog – not unlike other products of techno science – is a radical other' (Braidotti 2013: 69). On closer inspection, however, things do not look that simple, plain and unambiguous. Enhanced humans and subjects of transhumanist aspirations do not resonate well with the way in which 'the humanities are extending their debates about identity, alterity and exclusion to encompass nonhuman entities' (Domańska 2010a: 124). For the technological non-human of transhumanism and enhancement debates is not simply one among the many in a more-than-human world of species equality. It is not a subject that needs to be emancipated but a subject remarkably exceptional: it is better-than-human being (Simon 2019b) in the sense that it outperforms human capacities. The ultimate aim of transhumanism is not simply to act on the Enlightenment ideal of human perfectibility as transhumanism itself oftentimes claims but to transcend the biological limitations of being human. In the most primordial sense, such technological beings – just as well as enhanced humans – may be part of a multispecies assemblage. But their exceptionality does not really fit together with the anti-exceptionalist and egalitarian sensitivity of theories of multispecies companionship.

Both ecological and technological non-humans compel us to rethink the human and its interspecies relations, but the ways in which they respectively do so differ and may even entail contradictions and aporias within the larger picture. For now, it seems to us that whereas ecological approaches to a more-than-human world much more forcefully display the multispecies aspect of the new notion of history, technological approaches to the better-than-human more clearly manifest the non-continuity aspect, while the relation between the two is yet to be explored. What is certain is that the agenda 'to apply technology to overcome limits imposed by our biological and genetic heritage' (More 2013: 4) escapes the logic of mere improvement and points beyond the ideal of perfectibility. By escaping biological limits, human enhancement and transhumanist scenarios leave behind the realm of continuous evolutionary transformations and entail radical changes that can no longer be associated with a 'human' condition. At its most extreme, such changes align with singularity scenarios that represent a leap into the complete unknown and unfathomable future (to our human minds). Inasmuch as such abrupt changes revolve around events that trigger wholesale transformations, they defy the continuity of processual historical time and represent an 'evental temporality' (Simon 2019a: 101–3).

Although paying attention to such evental eruptions, we believe, is a key feature of non-continuous history, we do not of course wish to argue that from now on nothing can be conceived of in terms of any versions of continuity. Cumulative, progressive, developmental and processual temporalities may still dominate the ways we conceive of both certain human and natural phenomena. What a non-continuous history entails is a new dimension of large-scale wholesale transformations that became thinkable due to the entanglement of the human and the natural worlds and the unprecedented technological capacities. In similar ways, multispecies history and multiscalar history do not put a definite end to historiographies of the human world but open up a potentially new historical knowledge unconceivable within the confines of an exclusively human-focused modern notion of history.

For a New Philosophy of History

At the time of the Anthropocene and rapid technological changes we need a new notion of history on which a new agenda for philosophy of history can be built. In turn, the first phase of this new agenda consists of the very work of theorizing the new notion of history. The two endeavours presuppose and reinforce each other: the notion of history we need includes all forms of life (multispecies history), extends deep in the past and supports the interaction and integration of multiple time scales (multiscalar history), and takes seriously the role of transformative events and disruptions on a deep timescale (non-continuous history); at the same time, the new philosophy of history has to come to terms with an extremely broad set of interrelated questions inherent in the new notion of history. Our task is neither to provide answers right away nor to outline all potential questions one may ask within the new agenda. What we can do here in place of a conclusion is to offer a few intriguing themes deriving from the challenges we touched upon in this chapter, themes that most certainly gesture towards the possibility of the new philosophy of history.

The themes are typically a mixture of refocused older debates and adventures into unexplored territories. To begin with, one can think of the necessity to readdress epistemological questions and to redefine the limits of historical knowledge. To study a more-than-human world, we need to come to terms with the extent to which historical knowledge must or must not be grounded in human experience. We need to assess whether the claims to study animals' experiences – quite strong claims such as that of Baratay's we introduced earlier – are amount to an epistemologically feasible enterprise. In doing so, we need to develop answers to the question whether anthropocentrism is inescapable and the human remains exceptional in one sense or another: Is the 'multispecies knowledge of the past' of Domańska (2018a: 337) possible or will it necessarily remain what we may call 'a human knowledge of a multispecies past'? But this question is focused primarily on animals and the ecological other. Taking into consideration the prospect of technologically enhanced beings makes the picture far more complex with the assumed exceptionality of the technological other. Not to mention that confines of human experience are exceeded also in terms of larger-than-human lifetime natural phenomena that may not be a subject of primary experience even if such phenomena are now intertwined with human activity. And, of course, the main question is whether these interrelated themes and concerns are reconcilable with and supplement each other or, to one extent or another, are rather built on contradictory premises.

Tackling these issues, as we argued in the introductory section, brings philosophy of history and historical studies to a joint platform in studying a world whose new 'historical' character they jointly explore. The same applies to the potentially new themes that philosophy of history in the Anthropocene must grapple with. Inasmuch the scope is broadened to encompass the more-than-human world and inasmuch as the limits of historical knowledge are redefined, the new philosophy of history – just as well as historical studies and the new notion of history – interferes with the domain formerly associated with the natural and life sciences. Yet this does not mean a simple intrusion. It rather points towards an emerging transdisciplinary knowledge regime in which all former knowledge formations may transform beyond recognition. It may be that a novel role and function of the new concept of history and the new philosophy of history needs to be theorized within such a knowledge regime. But it may equally be that, in the long run, the main agenda of a new philosophy of history turns out to author the transition into a knowledge economy without a notion of history, either old or new.

12

In Defence of a Humanistically Oriented Historiography

The Nature/Culture Distinction at the Time of the Anthropocene

Giuseppina D'Oro

Introduction

This chapter examines a recent challenge to the idea of a humanistically oriented historiography.[1] I refer to this recent challenge as 'the new challenge', in order to distinguish it from a better-known criticism of the autonomy of historical explanations that was articulated by Hempel in the 1940s and 1950s: a criticism which I will refer to as 'the old challenge'. In speaking of a new challenge, I do not refer to a school of thought whose members explicitly identify with a set of tenets or share a common manifesto. I refer rather to a cluster of claims that share a certain family resemblance, one that is sufficiently robust to justify seeing them as emerging from a similar set of metaphilosophical assumptions. Proponents of the new challenge (Chakrabarty 2009; Bonneuil and Fressoz 2016; Latour 2017a) argue that the advent of the Anthropocene, a geological period in which humankind has become a significant geological force capable of initiating environmental changes, spells the end of the distinction between the historical and the natural past. According to the new challenge, narratives of historical development should go well beyond the relatively recent human past (with which historical narratives have been traditionally concerned) and view human history in the context of a deeper, longer-term geological history. Advocates of the new challenge argue that the distinction between the historical and the natural past (a distinction that was pivotal to the defence of a humanistically oriented historiography against the old challenge) relies on questionable anthropocentric assumptions that treat human beings as if they were not basically or essentially *natural* beings. They condemn the distinction between the historical and the natural past as an unacceptable dichotomy committed to a form of human exceptionalism which pits the human being against the rest of nature.

There is a soft and a hard version of the new challenge. The soft version claims that traditional histories, the history of the Egyptian and the Roman civilization, for example, and long-term geological histories, should criss-cross. For if these two histories are kept in complete isolation from one another, then it is very difficult to expose human activity as a crucial factor in climate change. It is only when these different histories are entangled that it is possible to see, for example, that 'James Watt's design of the steam engine in 1784' coincides with the 'beginning of growing global concentrations of carbon dioxide and methane' in the air trapped in polar ice (Crutzen 2002: 23), or that the cooling of the climate known as 'the little ice age' followed the drastic fall in the indigenous population after Columbus's 'discovery' of America (Lewis and Maslin 2015: 175–6). This kind of criss-crossing is not new. But whereas traditional histories tended to mention the way in which nature impinges upon civilization (they discussed, for example, the ways in which droughts impacted upon Pharaohs's abilities to rule effectively in ancient Egypt), Anthropocene narratives change the direction of fit: they expose the influence that civilization has on nature rather than nature on civilization. The soft version of the new challenge does not deny that longer term, 'deep' geological histories and the history of civilizations are different kinds of histories, with different methods, suited to answer different kinds of questions: an argument against the compartmentalization of knowledge is not the same as an argument against disciplinary boundaries. The hard version, however, is a different kettle of fish and considerably more radical than its soft counterpart. It argues not merely against the compartmentalization of knowledge which prevents the historian of ancient civilization from knowing anything about the findings of geologists but also against the very idea of disciplinary boundaries which was invoked to defend the possibility of a humanistically oriented historiography against the old Hempelian challenge. While the old challenge sought to reduce historical explanations to scientific ones, the new challenge, in its most radical form, undermines the disciplinary boundaries between science and history by denying that the concept of historical agency is sui generis. By replacing the sui generis category of 'historical agent' with an undifferentiated concept that includes microbes, characters in novels and military commanders alike, the most radical form of the new challenge does away with the distinction between rational and causal explanations that demarcated the domain of history (traditionally understood) from that of science. I take Dipesh Chakrabarty, Christophe Bonneuil and Jean-Baptiste Fressoz to be articulating, *for the most part*, a soft version of the challenge, calling for entanglement, and Bruno Latour as articulating the more radical version, calling for abolition. The dividing line between these two versions of the challenge, however, is not always clear cut, and the distinction between the two is more like one that ought, in principle, to be made than one that is actually drawn in practice. It is the abolitionist view that I am mostly concerned with in this chapter, a view from which those who call for entanglement do not always sufficiently distance themselves.[2]

This chapter has two goals. First it defends a humanistically oriented historiography against the charge that it is inextricable from an unacceptable form of human exceptionalism. *Humanistically oriented* historiography, I argue, is not the same as *human* history. The subject matter of a humanistically oriented historiography is not humans, understood as a biological species, and the time of humans on planet earth, but the norms which govern any beings whose conduct can be explained as responding to certain normative demands rather than as conforming to natural laws. The new challenge to the possibility of a humanistically oriented historiography conflates the idea of the historical past with that of the human past. The historical past is *not* the human past; it is the past understood in a way that is different from the way in which it is approached by, say, the palaeontologist or the geologist. And because what defines the historical past is how it is explained, the historical past is not an insignificantly brief temporal segment of the geological past (the time of the humans, or the time when written records began) because it is not a segment of time at all but a different way of approaching and understanding what happened in the past. It is the conflation of the historical with the human past that gives rise to the objection that traditional histories are premised upon a form of human exceptionalism. Second, this chapter resists the weakening of the notion of historical agency that inevitably follows from denying the distinction between the historical and the natural past. It argues that if there were no distinction between the historical and the natural past, no disciplinary boundaries between history and science and no distinction between historical and other kinds of agents, then the anticipation of the future would become a mere spectator's sport analogous to the activity of predicting the weather.

To be clear, the goal of this chapter is not to take issue with geologists who claim that in years to come the rocks will bear traces of a sudden acceleration in climate changes caused by human activity, changes comparable to those which occurred in the transition from the Cretaceous to the Tertiary, when it is widely believed that the impact of a meteor led to the disappearance of the dinosaurs (Bonneuil and Fressoz 2016: 13). This chapter takes issue not with climate scientists but with those philosophers of history and science who claim that the appropriate response to the findings of the science of climate change is to undo the nature-culture distinction. In defending the distinction between the natural and the historical past this chapter seeks to make room (philosophically speaking) for the possibility that the future climate of the planet may be shaped by responding to environmentally friendly norms, rather than merely forecast as the inevitable consequence of climate changes which humans have set in motion *qua forces of nature*. This chapter does not deny that by deforesting land and burning fossil fuels humans have initiated or causally contributed to global warming. What it argues is that it is only *qua historical agents* that they can look to the future as something that they can *shape* by changing the norms to which they responded in the past rather than as something that they merely *facilitate* by playing a role analogous to that of yeast in the chemical process of fermentation.

The Old Challenge

Before the so-called narrativist turn much analytic philosophy of history was preoccupied with the task of specifying the nature of the methodologies at work in the sciences.[3] The question which dominated the debate was whether historical explanations of past events are covert retrodictions which share the same logical structure as scientific predictions of future events or whether, on the other hand, they have a completely different logical form. Hempel (1942) argued that the nomological model of explanation, according to which to explain something is to subsume the explanandum under a general law, can be employed either to predict the future or to retrodict the past. The fact that historians are typically concerned with the past rather than the future does not entail that historical explanations are different in kind from scientific explanations if we accept that historical explanations of past events have the same logical form as scientific predictions of future ones. The historian's focus on the past and the scientist's focus on the future, for Hempel, merely obscures the fact that scientific and historical explanations share the same (nomological) form and that historical explanations at best differ from scientific ones only in degree, in so far as the generalizations used by historians invoke probabilistic laws which cannot be falsified by a single counter-instance.[4]

W. H. Dray (1957, 1963)[5] responded to Hempel's argument for methodological unity in the sciences. He conceded that the distinction between the past and the present cannot be mobilized to defend the methodological autonomy of history but denied that the past, as understood, for example, by a cultural anthropologist or medieval historian, is the same past as that which is investigated by big bang physicists: historians do not retrodict Caesar's crossing of the Rubicon in the way in which astronomers retrodict the explosion of a star that occurred millions of years ago. While historians are concerned with the past, they are not concerned with the *natural* past. But what is this non-natural past with which historians are concerned? It is the study of the norms which govern the conduct of certain beings who are taken to be distinctive kinds of agents, that is, *historical* agents. These beings are taken to be *historical* agents neither because they live in the past rather than the present nor because they are human rather than non-human but because they are responsive to norms. The contrast that is relevant to a defence of the autonomy of history against the old challenge is not the distinction between the past and the present. It is the distinction between nature and culture. This distinction is not a distinction between humans and other 'lesser' beings because it is not an empirical taxonomy such as the one that, for example, is invoked to distinguish human mammals from other mammals as, for example, chimpanzees; it is a methodological distinction between the presuppositions informing forms of inquiry which serve different explanatory needs. For the sake of predicting the future and retrodicting the past physicists assume that nature is uniform, that the laws of nature are the same in the Victorian and Edwardian period and that water will freeze at 0°C under the reign of King Edward VII as well as that of Queen Victoria. For the sake of understanding historical agents, by contrast, historians assume that the norms by which historical agents lead their lives may differ from their own. From the point of view of the physicist 'nature has no history'. This is not because natural beings are unaffected by the passage of time (fruits first ripen and then rot) nor because nature never changes (the earth was a very different place millions of years ago than it is now) but because the scientific investigation of nature operates under the assumption of the uniformity of its underlying laws.[6] By contrast, the historical investigation of the past operates on the assumption that agents are responsive to norms, and that these norms are not historically invariant. For example, historians explain why in plague-stricken Britain people rubbed live chickens on their wounds by invoking the epistemic norms prevalent at the time. What makes this explanation *historical* is not that it applies to human beings who lived in the past but that it explains human beings as responding to the state of medical knowledge at that time, much as the behaviour of a driver who stops at a red traffic light is explained by invoking traffic regulations rather than by identifying natural laws. If the Slitheen, the Time Lords, the Daleks and the Silurians had not been alien fictional creatures in the TV series *Dr Who*, but ancient civilizations predating the Egyptians and the Mesopotamians, they would be appropriate subject matter for history even if they did not belong to the biological species 'human'. The question that one should ask to establish whether certain life forms can be studied historically is not 'Are they mammals?' or 'Are they higher mammals?' or 'Are they human?' but 'Are they civilized?' And if they are, then they will need to be understood in different ways from the rocks and the waves, not because they have a supernatural 'inside' over and above a natural/observable 'outside' that the rocks and waves do not have but because to the extent that they live by self-given rules which they take to be binding, their behaviour cannot be explained as that of the sunflower which turns towards the sun, or the moon which orbits round its planet. Such is the nature of norms: unlike natural laws they can be disobeyed, but they will cast light on the behaviour of those who follow them in such a way as to show, for example, that the individual rubbing a live chicken on his wounds is not plain mad.

The distinction between nature and culture which was invoked to defend the methodological autonomy of history in the middle of the last century did not capture the divide between the human and the non-human. Nature and culture are distinct explicanda that are known through the presuppositions and methods of science and history respectively. Even if both history and science look at the past, they never really look at it in the same way. The big bang could never be explained historically, just as the significance of Caesar's crossing of the Rubicon could not be grasped through the methods of science. But this is not because Caesar has an unobservable supernatural inside which eludes the third-person perspective of science but because the significance of Caesar's crossing of the Rubicon can be understood only against the background of Republican Law, not by reference to the laws of nature. Caesar's crossing of the Rubicon was an act of disobedience that is understood historically when it is understood in the way in which one explains the action of the driver who disregards a traffic regulation, that is, as a failure to abide by the norms of conduct dictated by Republican Law, rather than as a counterexample to a natural law. The defence of a humanistically oriented historiography against the old challenge conceived of the historical past neither as a segment of time that lags behind the present and grows bigger as each day goes by (the metaphysical view that time is a growing block) nor as the all-too-human past of kings and queens, of Queen Elizabeth rather than the queen bee (the view that what is meant by historical time is the time of the humans on planet earth). The defence of the autonomy of historical explanations against the claim for methodological unity was premised on the assumption that history and natural science have different investigative goals and are governed by different presuppositions, presuppositions that are reflected by the adoption of different forms of inference. Since the defence of a humanistically oriented historiography against the old challenge assumed that nature is the correlative of a particular form of (scientific/nomological) inference and culture is the correlative of a different form of (historical) inference, it entailed that a change in the form of inference also entails a change of subject matter. The reason why the (historical) significance of Caesar's crossing of the Rubicon would elude an empirical scientist seeking to retrodict it through the application of inductive tools is that the application of the methods of natural science turns everything that it tries to explain into a natural event, just as King Midas turns everything he touches into gold.[7] Scientists directing their methods to the study of biological humans do not write history; they change the subject matter because the past can be understood historically only when it is investigated by the methods of history. And the other way around too: if historians tried to explain the big bang in the way in which they seek to render intelligible the actions of past agents, they would not be writing science but rather mythological accounts of the past. The distinction between the historical and the natural past that was invoked to defend the possibility of a humanistically oriented historiography against the argument for methodological unity in the sciences, therefore, is not the same as the distinction between the human and the non-human past. Nor does the defining characteristic of the historical past lie in the fact that it is no longer present. Rather, what is no longer present constitutes the historical past in so far as it is looked at through the lens of beings who, as Heidegger would say, have an understanding of Being. Historians tracing the rise and fall of civilizations are not palaeontologists seeking to date the extinction of biological species through the study of their fossilized remains. While palaeontologists look at the fossilized remains of dinosaurs as providing evidence for the existence and evolution of a now-extinct animal species, the mummified remains of ancient Egyptians are of interest to humanistically oriented historians *not* in so far as they provide evidence to document the existence and evolution of a now-extinct ethnic group but insofar as they symbolize the belief that the preservation of the body is required for the soul to find an appropriate home in the afterlife. The defence of the idea of a historical past against the old challenge was therefore based not on an arbitrary divide between human and non-human animals but on the assumption that to understand the past *historically* is to approach it as a *space of reasons*[8] in which the action of historical agents are understood as abiding by (as well as contesting) norms.

There is much more that could be said about the defence of humanistic understanding against the old challenge. While in the early and mid-twentieth century the debate for and against methodological unity was conducted primarily on the terrain of philosophy of history and social science, these issues were also the object of extensive discussions in the philosophy of mind and action[9] where it was perhaps much clearer that the defence of the irreducibility of action explanation to event explanations did not hinge upon defending a dichotomy between humans and other beings but on the nature of the inferences that are adopted in different contexts of inquiry. Davidson, for example, argued that the mental has a normative dimension that finds no echo in scientific explanations (Davidson 1963); many others have argued that the explanation of action is sui generis because it has an irreducibly teleological dimension (Malcom 1968; von Wright 1971; Tanney 1995; Sehon 2005). The current debate concerning the role of history at the time of the Anthropocene about whether historical narratives should shift their focus from the relatively recent human past to a deeper past of the human species in order to expose the interdependence of human life on other species (and nature at large) seems to forget that the old defence of the irreducibility of humanistic explanations to naturalistic ones in its various forms was an argument against scientism that did not hinge upon a commitment to an ontological divide between the human and the non-human. It is arguably a new form of naturalism which is making a comeback, in a different and subtler form, in the new challenge.

The New Challenge

The distinction between nature and culture which informed the defence of a humanistically oriented historiography against the old challenge has come under attack on the basis of reflections about what it means to live in the Anthropocene: a new geological epoch characterized by cataclysmic human-induced climate changes which could potentially lead to the extinction of human life on earth. Stratigraphic proof for the end of the Holocene and the beginning of the Anthropocene is still outstanding, and there is no consensus among geologists as to the identifiable beginning of this new epoch, some dating its onset to the time of the first nuclear explosion in 1945 (Zalasiewciz et al. 2015), some to the year 1784, the date of the invention of the steam engine as a symbol of the beginning of the Industrial Revolution (Crutzen 2002: 23), and others dating its onset further back to 1610, when a drastic fall in the indigenous population following Columbus's 'discovery' of America led to a decline in atmospheric CO_2 and the cooling of the climate known as the 'little ice age' (Lewis and Maslin 2015). While there is no clear consensus as to whether the Anthropocene has succeeded the Holocene and if so, what its precise start date is, the Anthropocene has increasingly been described as that slice of geological time in which humans have become causal forces so powerful as to be able not only to selectively intervene in nature but also to radically alter its course. Whether or not the Anthropocene will be given scientific recognition as a separate geological era is ultimately a matter for geologists to determine. What we are concerned here is not the scientific claim that the Anthropocene is a new slice of geological time, in which traces of human activities are being carved into the earth's strata, but rather the philosophical claim that we should cast aside the distinction between the historical and the natural past either as philosophically dubious or as an obsolete categorial distinction that no longer serves our present needs. Since we stand on the threshold of an environmental catastrophe, so the argument goes, humans should see themselves in the context of a longer term, geological history of planet earth, one in which the history of kings and queens unfolds in the batting of a geological eyelid. During what, from a geological perspective, is an infinitesimally short period of time, human beings fought revolutions, waged wars and plotted against each other. During this period of time those same human beings enslaved members of their own species with a different skin colour, devised class systems which exploited large sections of humanity for the benefit of a selected few and created myths to provide ideological support for racial segregation and class exploitation. This is the focus of traditional histories: the domain of human affairs or the time of the human species on earth and their internal quarrels and conflicts. Historical narratives at this momentous time, where humanity is on the cusp of self-destruction, should focus on a different kind of time, a time long before any of the written records that professional historians study, to uncover the 'deep history' of humankind (Chakrabarty 2009: 212). Anthropocene-inspired criticisms of the idea of a distinctively historical past therefore tend to highlight the brevity and comparative insignificance of human time – a time during which humans became the predominant species: a species whose skills in mastering the natural environment eventually led them to fancying themselves as being other-than-nature.

As well as urging historians to shift their attention away from historical to geological time, proponents of the new challenge seek to undermine what they see as the unacceptable dichotomy between the subjects of traditional history (human agents) and the object (nature), a dichotomy that they see as integral to the distinction between the natural and the historical past. The realization that human activity is responsible for global warming and the ensuing 'natural' catastrophes undermines the distinction between the traditional agents of history (humans) and the immutable backdrop against which their deeds take place (nature). As Chakrabarty puts it, climate scientists, in positing 'that the human being has become something much larger than the simple biological agent than he or she has always been …', are 'unwittingly destroying the artificial but time-honoured distinction between natural and human history' (Chakrabarty 2009: 206). In traditional histories nature is portrayed as an unchanging 'silent and passive backdrop' (Chakrabarty 2009: 203), against which human history unfolds; it only makes sporadic appearances in historical narratives when it either facilitates or somehow hinders human endeavours. The weather, for example, is mentioned in Second World War histories because on 7 December 1941 the clear skies made the Japanese attack on the American base in Pearl Harbour easier or, in histories of the Great War, because persistent rain weakened the structural integrity of the trenches on the western front. But in traditional histories nature is generally portrayed as a constant backdrop against which human affairs unfold. It is seen as the 'other' of history: whereas civilizations change, the seasons alternate in an eternal recurrence of the same natural cycle, indifferent to human turmoil and unaffected by it. This view of nature as the other of history, an external and static backdrop indifferent and impregnable to human action, is shattered by the discovery that human activity is the catalyst for global warming, that deforestation and the industrialization of farming play a role in the process of climate change that is not different in kind from the one that, for example, microbes play in the development of diseases. The science of climate change shows that just as the balance of nature would remain inexplicable without taking into account the 'actions' of living organisms, so the disruptions to the natural cycles that have for so long been taken for granted could not be explained without the agency of humans. The Anthropocene brings the realization that human agency is the catalyst of climate change, that humans are geological forces of nature (Latour 2017a: 92 ff.) just as Pasteur demonstrated that sugar could not be transformed into alcohol without the presence of yeast. The dividing line between a dead or de-animated nature that can be explained by appealing to physics and chemistry alone and history, to be understood, on the other hand, teleologically, as the achievement of the goals of human agents, is shattered by the twin realization that just as the balance of nature could not be accounted for without taking into consideration the actions of living organisms, so the disruption to this balance cannot be accounted for without taking into account the actions of humans. The onset of the Anthropocene therefore challenges not only the distinction between human agents as the subject of history and a dead/deanimated nature to be understood mechanistically rather than teleologically; it also challenges the distinction between the agents that feature in traditional histories and other kinds of agents: microbes, yeast and so on.

As the distinctions between history and nature, between historical and other kind of agents comes under attack, so does the view that there are different modes of understanding that correspond to the (allegedly) distinctive explananda of the *Naturwissenschaften* and the *Geisteswissenschaften*. Bruno Latour claims that the way one understands the working of General Kutuzof's mind in Tolstoy's *War and Peace* is not significantly different from the way one understands how the Corticotropin releasing factor works. The reason why one might find it easier to grasp the psychology of the general in Tolstoy's novel than a scientific text describing the function of the factor releasing Corticotropin is simply due to lack of familiarity with the scientific context (Latour 2017a: 49 ff.).[10]

The distinction between nature and culture also becomes the target of gentle mockery as the question 'Don't the historical beings who feature as main characters in traditional histories have a natural environment as well as a culture?' is teasingly posed. Sloterdijk, for example, asks whether Dasein does not have a habitat as well as a 'world' in the Heideggerian sense (a language, a culture a history). 'When you say that the Dasein is thrown into the world, into what it is actually thrown? What is the composition of the air it breathes there? How is the temperature controlled?'[11] The nature-culture distinction presupposed by the notion of a distinctively historical past leads not only to an unacceptable dichotomy between humans and the rest of nature; it also treats historical agents as if they were ethereal creatures who do not need to eat, breathe and perform any physiological functions, or so the argument goes. These objections are closely interlinked: if there are no distinctive *historical* agents, then there is no significant difference between culture and habitats and no distinctive methods for studying them are required as a result.

The new challenge questions the methodological distinction between different modes of understanding as based on an unacceptable ontological distinction between humans and the rest of nature. Once the ontological distinction between subject and object in its various manifestations (historical time vs geological time, historical subjects vs the object [nature]; historical agents vs other non-historical agents, humans vs other lesser beings) is rejected, so too are the methodological distinctions that underpin the study of nature and culture, the *Naturwissenschaften* and the *Geisteswissenschaften*. From the perspective of the new challenge, the nature-culture distinction which emerged in the twentieth century and which was invoked to defend the idea of a distinctively *historical* past[12] is at best humanity's ultimate delusion of grandeur and at worst a self-destructive ideology invoked by the human species to justify the exploitation of nature, just as the idea of the free market functioned as the ideology through which the emerging bourgeoisie sanctioned the exploitation of the working classes. Bonneuil and Fressoz, for example, advocate going 'beyond the great separation' of nature and culture, of 'the natural sciences with their non-human objects' and the 'a-natural' humanities and social sciences, the former postulating 'physical continuity between human and other entities', the latter 'defined by a metaphysical discontinuity between humans and everything else' (Bonneuil and Fressoz 2016: 32). The Anthropocene, they argue, once it is recognized 'as the reunion of human (historical) time and Earth (geological) time, between human agency and non-human agency, gives the lie to this – temporal, ontological, epistemological and institutional – great divide between nature and society' (Bonneuil and Fressoz 2016: 32). The *temporal* divide between human and geological time, the *ontological* divide between humans and the rest of nature, the epistemological/*methodological* divide between the humanities and science all stand or fall together, the result of the same unacceptable dualist metaphilosophical standpoint.[13]

The Same Boring Old Conceptual Distinctions?

Does the nature-culture distinction that is presupposed by the defence of a humanistically oriented historiography either rest on or entail an ontological distinction between humans and the rest of nature? To see why the considerations raised by the new challenge fundamentally misconstrue the assumptions on which the idea of a distinctively historical past rests one needs to understand what kind of distinction the nature-culture distinction is. As intimated earlier, nature and culture are the explicanda of two different modes of inquiry with distinctive methods and investigative goals.[14] The nature-culture distinction captures a joint or juncture in the way reality is conceptualized in different areas of inquiry; it does not 'cut reality at the joints'. It is not a Cartesian[15] (real or metaphysical) distinction entailing that historical subjects/agents could exist without a physical body, that there could be culture without nature, a 'World' (in the Heideggerian sense)[16] without a habitat, in the way in which Descartes argued that the concept of mind, being really distinct from that of the body, could exist apart from the body. Defending the nature-culture distinction does not, for example, entail denying that the Egyptians and the Mesopotamians ate and breathed, or that their bodies aged and eventually decayed. What it entails, rather, is that it is not with their physiological functions that the Egyptologist (*qua* humanistically oriented historiographer) is concerned. Collingwood (1993 [1946]), whose philosophy of history loomed large behind Dray's defence of the autonomy of historical explanation against Hempel's claim for methodological unity in the sciences, put the point as follows:

> A great many things which deeply concern human beings are not, and never have been, traditionally included in the subject-matter of history. People are born, eat and breathe and sleep, and beget children and become ill and recover again, and die; and these things interest them, most of them at any rate, far more than art and science, industry and politics and war. Yet none of these things have been traditionally regarded as possessing historical interest. Most of them have given rise to institutions like dining and marrying and the various rituals that surround birth and death, sickness and recovery; and of these rituals and institutions people write histories; but the history of dining is not the history of eating, and the history of death-rituals is not the history of death. (Collingwood 1999: 46)

Collingwood's point is not that it is not possible to write natural histories. Nor is he advocating a linguistic reform and arguing that the term 'history' should be reserved to denote histories of a certain kind, those which have been concerned with rituals rather than physiological facts. But while we may continue to speak as we wish, we should be wary of the bewitchment that words can exercise on our intelligence[17] and assume that because we use one and the same word, 'history', there is no difference between the subject matter of the Egyptologist, or of the historian of ancient Rome, and that of the palaeontologist. Nor does it follow from the fact that the humanistically oriented historiographer and the natural scientist have different interests that there exist different kinds of beings, material and immaterial beings, *res cogitans* and *res extensa*, that correspond to their different subject matters.

At times it is philosophers, more than ordinary people, who tend to be under the spell of words. The Gladstone Pottery museum in Stoke-on-Trent[18] traces the history of the toilet from the humble chamber pot to the modern flushing toilet.

Museum visitors are not normally surprised to find that the chamber pots and toilets on display contain no human excrement. If they are not surprised, this is because, echoing Collingwood, they tacitly acknowledge that the *history* of toilet rituals is not the same as the *history* of a physiological function. They do not infer from the fact that no human excrement is contained in the chamber pots and toilets on display, that the beings who used them were angel-like creatures who never needed to relieve themselves. Yet it is precisely this sort of inference that gives rise to the glib question 'Does Dasein not have a habitat? Does it not breathe? What kind of temperatures can it withstand?' Defending the irreducibility of the *Geisteswissenschaften* to the *Naturwissenschaften* is not tantamount to assuming an ontological separation between humans and the rest of nature; it is rather to make the point that the concept 'historical agent' is sui generis and irreducible to that of 'natural agent' and to advance an argument for the existence of disciplinary boundaries that reflect the different concerns and investigative goals of science and the humanities. The new challenge gets the direction of fit between ontology and epistemology upside down: the argument against methodological unity in the sciences was premised on the metaphilosophical assumption that there is a reciprocal relation between method and subject matter, that nature is the *explanandum* of science, just as culture is the *explanandum* of history; it was *not* premised on the assumption that the methods of the *Geisteswissenschaften* and the *Naturwissenschaften* are different because mind and nature are metaphysical entities which can be known 'as they are' independently of the investigative goals of history and natural science. Defending the nature-culture distinction and the possibility of a humanistically oriented historiography does not mean providing an argument for metaphysical dualism,[19] or being committed to it by default. It is to argue, rather, for the disunity of science, for the claim that science and history ask different kinds of questions and therefore that, just as the questions asked by scientists are not answered by the methods of history, so the questions asked by historians are not answered by adopting the methods of science.

Yet, quite often, when one mentions the old debate for and against methodological unity in the sciences one is met with a yawn: *how boring, how old hat, you are stuck in the 1950s! Since then much work has been done to show that there are different models of causal explanation that do not invoke generalizations, such as, for example, counterfactual accounts of causation. Since the argument for the unity of science as articulated by Hempel was based on a nomological account of causal explanation, defending the inapplicability of this nomological model to a humanistically oriented historiography is tantamount to fighting a strawman.* The nomological model of explanation, so the objection goes, has long been superseded, and the debate between those who defended it and those who attacked it is stale. But whatever one might think about the nomological model of causal explanation (it is not my intention to take sides on whether causation should be understood in terms of regularities or counterfactuals), adopting a counterfactual rather than a nomological account of causal explanation does *not* undermine the distinction between the space of reasons and that of causes, the very distinction which was at stake in the old debate for and against methodological unity. Those who argued against methodological unity in the sciences did so on the grounds that the actions of historical agents must be understood in an intensional context, if they are to be understood *historically* at all. To illustrate, suppose that a tourist from a distant galaxy with no knowledge of the Catholic faith arrived on earth when the cardinals are gathered in Conclave. One day the tourist notices crowds in St Peter's square cheering and wonders why, since she noticed no such cries of jubilation the previous day. Yet the weather was the same, the air temperature similar and the merchants selling silk scarves were positioned in exactly the same spots. She consults video footage of the previous days and notices one difference: the colour of the smoke. On the day in which the crowds cheered, unlike the previous days, the smoke was white, not black. Having spotted this difference the tourist concludes that the crowds cheered *because* the smoke was white and that, had the smoke been black, they would not have cheered. She has provided a counterfactual causal explanation for the cheering of the crowds. Now, even if one were to concede that the intergalactic tourist could isolate the white smoke as the relevant counterfactual (why not the fact that, on the day the crowd cheered, the silk scarves on the merchants' stands were a different colour, or the bored kids screaming their heads off were positioned in a sunny rather than a shady spot of St Peter's square?), this counterfactual does not explain, in a particular sense of 'explain', why the crowds cheered. For the crowds did not cheer on account of the white smoke. They cheered because the cardinals gathered in Conclave elected a new leader of the Catholic Church.[20] Even if the tourist succeeded in providing an explanation for the crowds' cheering that would enable to predict similar behaviour in the future,[21] this kind of explanation still singularly fails to capture the symbolic significance of the white smoke; it does not explain the cheering of the crowds in the way in which the tourist would like the event to be explained if she were a historian.[22] If the intergalactic tourist were a historian she would ask what the white smoke meant to the crowd, what is its symbolic significance, just as the Roman historian is interested not merely in the fact that in 49 BC some men with shields and horses waded across a stream (which later historical narratives glorified by calling it a river) but in what the crossing of that stream by a provincial governor meant to a Roman senator. The historical context of explanation is an intensional context in which the reaction of the crowds to the white smoke is understood against the background of the Catholic faith, just as Caesar's crossing of the Rubicon is understood in the context of Roman Law. A counterfactual explanation that limits itself to an extensional context, to the occurrence of white smoke emanating from a chimney, for example, but ignores the intensional context (the significance of the white smoke for the Catholic faith) may at best be able to predict or retrodict the behaviour of the crowds, but it would fail to explain it in the way that would satisfy the curiosity of the intergalactic tourist if the tourist were after a particular kind of *historical* explanation. Understanding the past historically, as Winch puts it, is a reflective or conceptual task:

> Historical explanation is not the application of generalizations and theories to particular instances: it is the tracing of internal relations. It is like applying one's knowledge of a language in order to understand a conversation rather than like applying one's knowledge of the laws of mechanics to understand the workings of a watch. (Winch 1990 [1958]: 133)

Winch contrasts historical explanations to generalizing/nomological ones; but his claim that we understand an event *historically* in the way in which we understand a language stands, whether or not one believes the (nomological) model of explanation to be an outdated model. Winch's point is that just as someone who has mastered the English language knows (by entailment) that if something is a washing machine then it is an electrical appliance, so if you are a Roman (or a Roman historian) and you know Roman Law then you know (by entailment) that crossing the Rubicon with an army signifies challenging Republican Law. Just as the concept of washing machine analytically entails that of electrical appliance, so Roman Law entails that certain acts are punishable transgressions. To understand Caesar's crossing of the Rubicon as a challenge to Roman Law is to subsume human agency under a certain kind of explanation, one that is rather different from that used to explain human agents *qua* catalysts for climate change, that is, as beings that play a role in global warming analogous to that which yeast plays in the process of fermentation. For while scientists have discovered empirically that a certain kind of human action (deforestation and the burning of fossil fuels) causes global warming, historians understand the magnitude of Caesar's wading across a small stream because they know the 'grammar' of Roman Law.

The defence of a humanistically oriented historiography against the old challenge rests on the consideration that in order to understand an event historically one must go beyond a purely extensional context of explanation. This consideration is not rendered obsolete by the claim that since counterfactual causal explanations need not invoke covering laws, the argument against methodological unity articulated by Dray, Winch and others was directed at a straw man. Counterfactual causal explanations, just like nomological ones, miss the significance of the white smoke and of the crossing of the Rubicon if they do not consider how things appear or look like for that being who (as Heidegger says) has 'an understanding of Being'. A history of how humankind sleepwalked into global warming along the lines of Christopher Clarks *The Sleepwalkers: How Europe Went to War in 1914* (Clarks 2012), cannot simply be a history of the consequences that deforestation, the industrialization of farming and the burning of fossil fuels have on the earth's climate because only agents who can rethink who they are and reconceptualize their relationship to their habitat could possibly be awoken from their environmental slumber. The facts of climate science can be understood as a wake-up call to alter the way one lives only if one presupposes precisely what advocates of the new challenge at times appear to be to denying, that is, that there is a distinctive kind of (historical) agent that is the correlative of a distinctive kind of (historical) explanation, one, to say it with Heidegger again, who has an understanding of Being.

The argument for the possibility of a humanistically oriented historiography was not an argument in support of some sort of ontological or metaphysical dualism but an argument in support of the existence of disciplinary boundaries between science and history, one motivated by the consideration that historians and scientists have different concerns. Since interdisciplinarity is the buzz word of the day, and an argument for the existence of disciplinary boundaries could easily be misconstrued as an attack on the very idea of interdisciplinarity, it is important to take some time to explain that defending the idea of disciplinary boundaries does not mean belittling the importance of cooperation among disciplines. Consider, for example, the relationship between crime detection and forensic science. Detectives enlist the help of forensic scientists to establish the location and time of a crime scene. By learning that the grit under the victim's fingernails originates from a remote area of the country that was inaccessible to the prime suspect at the time of the crime, a detective will then be able to rule out the suspect from their investigation. The detective's goal is not to know the chemical composition of the grit; it is to solve the murder mystery, but she would not be able to infer that the prime suspect could not have been present at the crime scene without the assistance of the forensic scientist. Architects choose cladding materials with fire-retardant properties or glass panels which prevent homes from losing heat. But it is not their job to know what chemical composition the cladding panels must have in order to be fire-retardant or what scientific properties the glass must have to prevent the heat from escaping. Cooperation of this kind, between say, the detective and the forensic archaeologist (or the architect and the chemist), does not require denying that mutually supportive spheres have different goals. So understood, interdisciplinarity requires acknowledging the distinctive goals of, say, the detective and the forensic archaeologist, the architect and the chemist; in fact, interdisciplinarity makes no sense except against the background of disciplinary boundaries. The goals of those who argue that, in response to the Anthropocene, we should develop new 'environmental humanities' (Bonneuil and Fressoz 2016: 288) can be achieved by putting the knowledge that is generated in biology, chemistry and physics at the service of architects, town planners, garbage disposal firms, just as the police can avail itself of the assistance of forensic science. Chakrabarty is absolutely right in saying that 'the crisis of climate change calls on academics to rise above their disciplinary boundaries because it is a crisis of many dimensions' (Chakrabarty 2009: 215). But rising above disciplinary boundaries is not the same as undoing them. There is no need to dissolve the historical past into the geological past or to undo the nature-culture distinction in order to change human habitats and foster environmentally friendly ways of living. What is required is joining the dots between, for example, chemistry and architecture so that the knowledge gained in one sphere can be mobilized to achieve the goals of another, just as forensic science has become a tool in crime detection. To acknowledge the existence of disciplinary boundaries and to understand interdisciplinarity as the interlocking of different spheres with distinctive methods is not synonymous with being an enemy of interdisciplinarity. Nor does understanding interdisciplinarity as the interlocking of distinctive spheres with their own distinctive goals and methods entail a commitment to the view that science can fix it all, that there is a purely technological solution to the problems of climate change.[23] The defence of the possibility of a humanistically oriented historiography, one must remember, is premised precisely on the assumption that scientism, understood as the view that science has the answer to all questions, precludes the possibility that the past could be understood as a response to self-given norms and thus that the future could be shaped through political agency just as the historical past was. Undoing the nature-culture distinction is not the key to solving the climate crisis[24] because it is only in so far as one acknowledges the idea of historical agency that one can also make room for the possibility that the future may be shaped by the adoption of environmentally friendly norms rather than simply anticipated, in the way in which one expects rain after consulting the weather forecast.

Before drawing to a close I should make clear (again) that defending a humanistically oriented historiography is not the same as defending an anthropocentric historiography that excludes in principle the possibility of ascribing historical agency to non-human animals. The concept of 'human' and that of 'historical agent' are as distant as the concept of 'human' and that of 'Dasein'. Lizards or aliens from a distant galaxy can be historical agents if they have what Heidegger calls 'an understanding of Being'. Some animals – dolphins, elephants, higher primates – may have historical agency. This chapter is not concerned with determining who does or does not have historical agency, but with the more general point that the history of those beings (human or not) who do have a culture cannot be the same as the history of those beings (human or not) who do not have it: if there are beings who have a culture, then they have to be understood in a different way from beings who do not have it, as distinctive kinds of agents, and this is what distinguishes a humanistically oriented (which is not the same as *human*) history from other kinds of history. It is clearly possible to write animal histories,[25] but the question still remains as to what kind of history one should write about animals. The objection that the nature-culture distinction rests on a form of human exceptionalism conflates the distinction between different types of inferences or explanations with the distinction between two kinds of beings: human and non-human. A defence of a humanistically oriented historiography is therefore not an argument for speciesism; it is rather an argument against a new and subtler form of naturalism that seeks to deny the existence of methodological differences between forms of inquiry by undoing the distinction between nature and culture.

Conclusion

There is something politically progressive about the literature on the Anthropocene and resulting reflections on what entering this new geological epoch may entail for the writing of historical narratives. It may be no coincidence that the analogy of 'the house on fire' recently used by Greta Thunberg[26] to describe the need for urgent action against climate change is to be found, and perhaps originates, in Latour's *Facing Gaia*.[27] Those who contrast human time with geological time philosophize in response to the challenges of our times. These reflections on the nature of time, whether it should be subdivided into the Holocene and the Anthropocene, rather than, say, the Elizabethan, Victorian and Edwardian eras, are not the musings of philosophers living in an ivory tower. In comparison to these reflections the debates concerning the nature of time which rage in contemporary analytic metaphysics between endurantists and perdurantists,[28] on whether or not time is a fourth dimension such that – if only we had the right means of transport – we could travel through it like Dr Who, may seem like indulgent scholastic disputes whose participants are no better than Nero, playing the lyre as the world is burning. But while there is no denying that we should be shocked by the Anthropocene, undoing the nature-culture distinction is not the right response to its onset since humans, *understood not as a biological species of featherless bipeds but precisely as interpreting and self-interpreting beings*, are the only ones who may be able to respond to the climate crisis. As Jeff Malpass said in a conversation at a recent conference on the role of the philosophy of history, 'The birds and the bees are not going to save us.'[29] There is no contradiction in describing humans (*qua* biological beings) as the cause of climate change and humans (*qua* historical agents) as the potential solution to it. It is just that, when human actions are explained causally, their behaviour is explained as if it were like that of the sunflower which turns towards the sun, rather than like that of Roman legionaries obeying the commands of their centurion. We often switch seamlessly from one explanation to the other. When, for example, I reprimand my daughter for not picking the wet towels off the bathroom floor, I treat her as capable of responding to the norms of common living. When, on the other hand, I tell my partner 'Don't bother to reprimand our (lovely) teenager for banging the door: it is not her; it is her hormones', I treat my daughter as a force of nature. No parent of a teenage daughter needed to wait for the onset of the Anthropocene to learn that humans are forces of nature. What the Anthropocene has taught us is the extent to which these causal powers extend, *not* the fact that we have them.

The recent challenge to a humanistically oriented historiography hypostatizes the methodological distinction between different forms of explanation and, as a result, erroneously identifies their respective explicanda with the ontological distinction between biological humans and the rest of nature. In seeking to combat human exceptionalism by rejecting the disciplinary boundaries between the human and the natural sciences it undermines the possibility of historical agency. In so doing, it inadvertently threatens to make the historical future as inevitable as the natural past. What appears to be a politically progressive argument motivated by the noble intention of curbing disrespect for the rest of nature (a clearly laudable goal) comes dangerously close to endorsing a fatalistic outlook that forecloses the possibility of taking affirmative action against climate change. This is what is ultimately at stake in defending the nature-culture distinction and why protecting it is important. It is not *qua* natural but *qua* historical beings that we can act to halt or to reverse what we started, to avoid the environmental catastrophe that climate science warns us about. The role of the philosophy of history is not to encourage a form of fatalism born out of the abolition of the nature-culture distinction rather than, say, out of belief in divine providence, or a commitment to old fashioned reductive naturalism, but rather to appeal to our historical nature to bring about those changes which it is still possible to bring about.

Notes

Chapter 1

1. I thank my co-writers in this book for their fruitful suggestions regarding this introduction. I am also grateful for their unwavering support during the entire editorial process.
2. See Kleinberg, Scott and Wilder's attempt to show why and how theory is unavoidable and useful in historiography in their 'Theory Revolt', http://theoryrevolt.com/.
3. Pihlainen (2017) is perhaps the most determined application of Whitean thinking in contemporary theory of history.
4. Frank Ankersmit in private correspondence.
5. All pages numbers in this chapter refer to this book unless otherwise mentioned.

Chapter 3

1. For an overview of the main tenets of empiricism (and rationalism), see Markie (2017).
2. The situation would not be in fact this simple, as Sellars has argued about the 'myth of the given'. See Sellars's essay (1956) 'Empiricism and the Philosophy of Mind'. Sellars argues that recognizing that something is green, for example, requires an ability to detect characteristics of the objects that are green and distinguish them from other objects, including other objects of colour. Therefore, recognizing that something is green seems to entail that one already has the concept of 'green' and other colour concepts. Sellars thinks that there is no such observational immediacy that works in isolation from language and concepts and that could serve as a foundational epistemic building block for other knowing.
3. And there may be other reasons too, such as Sellars's point that any *knowledge* claim is a claim, including the most simple and basic observation, in a pre-conceptualized logical space of reasons. For example Sellars (1956: 298–300).
4. If someone remarks that the situation is no different in other sciences, or in the sciences, because often data needs interpretation or because evidence may have been collected prior to analysis, I take this to mean that knowledge in all sciences

is inferential and mediate. Still there are differences regarding the availability of the research object, which could be used to verify or corroborate assumptions. In many natural sciences, the research object is assumed to be accessible, invariable and uniform, while in historiography the past is normally perceived to be totally beyond access. To repeat, the point here is conceptual: to highlight the inferential and mediate nature of historiographical knowledge irrespective of the situation in other sciences.

5   We could imagine that historiographical knowledge is reduced via causal links to the original witness statements of historical phenomena. However, this causal link over generations would be a mediated chain backwards and not knowing in the sense of immediacy or evidence. Further, this would limit the scope of historiographical knowledge. Consider that no one can have witnessed, even in principle, the historical phenomenon of the Second World War.

6   But see Goering (2013); Piercey (2017).

7   Cf. what Sellars writes: 'No philosopher who has attacked the philosophical idea of givenness or, to use the Hegelian term, immediacy, has intended to deny that there is a difference between *inferring* that is the case, and, for example, *seeing* it to be the case' (1956: 253).

8   https://www.merriam-webster.com/dictionary/inference, accessed June 26 2020.

9   See Kleinberg, Scott and Wilder's *Theses on Theory and History*; accessible online at https://theoryrevolt.com/

10 The original title of the book in Finnish is *Kapina tehtailla. Kuusankoski 1918*. This book was awarded the most prestigious prize for non-fiction literature in Finland in 2018: the Finlandia prize.

11 See Kuukkanen (2015: 161–6).

12 Naturally, semantics can be understood more widely as a systematic study of linguistic meaning covering also the issues of communication and understanding, for example. However, in analytic philosophy semantical question deal typically with the questions of word-world relationship.

13 This sample of statements comes from the book *Revolt at Factories. Kuusankoski 1918*, written by Seppo Aalto. The book is written in Finnish, and the sentences are translations to the best of my ability. However, although it is important that they reflect the kind of language that historians use, their exact wording in English is not crucial, only their type.

14 But this assessment itself is frame-dependent. While it is commonly accepted that the civil war begun on 27 January, the reasons for this practice can be studied in more detail considering, what it means to begin a war (what counts as the 'beginning of the war') and what happened on that date and around that time. The war is understood to have begun on 27 January, because the red guards had lifted a red lantern in the tower of the workers community hall in Helsinki and then ceased

the control of the premises of the senate, the railway station and police stations in Helsinki. However, there was unrest and armed conflict earlier throughout January 2018.
15 A perceptive reader might note here that this creates a regress. One claim stems from another, which stems yet from another, and so on. Where does it end? And if it does not end, is this any form of justification? Naturally, this is a typical foundationalist critique of coherentism. Here I also provide a typical reply from the coherentist point of view: justification is a holistic affair and it is not individual beliefs that are justified, but the whole system in which each belief has a certain functional role. Coherentist justification is a matter of degree and a system can be clearly more or less justified. For example, see Bonjour (1985).
16 Naturally, remembering the context, that the temperance movement against alcohol was deeply embedded in the working-class movement, this episode becomes more understandable. I thank Kari Väyrynen for this reminder.
17 It is possible to criticize this kind of claim for the failure to distinguish a description and a moral valuation more clearly. It is true that Aalto does not explicate the set of moral beliefs from which this claim is in part inferred, although the beliefs can be assumed to be commonly understood and shared. The main sticking point here is whether the reasoning leading to this statement is either implicitly or explicitly traceable and acceptable.
18 This relates to the problem of testimony: whose testimony can be considered reliable. The point here is that, if a historian is considered to be reliable, some claims in a text can be taken on trust (due to the proven skill and expertise).

Chapter 4

1 Quoted in Zammito (2004: 47).
2 Dillmann (1891). He was followed in his account of the Leibnizian concept of representation by several others, such as Cassirer, Heimsoeth, Schmalenbach and, above all, by Paul Köhler. See Köhler (1913: 162). For a synthesis of most that was written on Leibniz on the turn of the century see the most useful study by Mahnke (1925).
3 See for this distinction between 'strong' and 'weak' individuals my 'History as the Science of the Individual' (2013: 396–426).
4 I'm undaunted by the protest that true statements are always formulated in a certain language and that what true statement S_1 states in language L_1 about some fact F may therefore conflict with what true statement S_2 states in language L_2 about F. In that case I shall say that F can stand for both F_1 (what S_1 is true of) and F_2 (that S_2

is true of) and that the truth of S_1 does not exclude the truth of S_2. Compatibility of S_1 and S_2 has then been restored again. If incompatibility stubbornly persists, we do well to distrust L_1 and L_2 and look for an alternative language L_a capable of explaining and removing the incompatibility of S_1 and S_2.

5 'Das Universum, das die Monaden vorstellen, ist die Allheit und der Inbegriff der räumlich-zeitlichen Erscheinungen: aber eben diese Erscheinungen selbst bieten in ihrer Ordnung in ihr durchgängiger gesetzlichen Verknüpfung dem Denken einen Inhalt and Grundbestand dar, wie er ein gediegener und sicherer nicht gefordert werden kann. Hier findet der Gedanke seinen Halt und sein objective Bestimmtheit [...]. Es ist lediglich eine Selbsttäuschung, wenn irgend eine Metaphysik glaubt noch hinter dieses Phänomen zurück gehen zu können. Auf die Frage warum überhaupt eine Vielheit und ein Wandel von Vorstellungsinhalten statttfindet, hat daher die Leibnizsche Philosophie allerdings kein Antwort mehr.' E. Cassirer, Einleitung, in Leibniz (1966: 97).

6 To put it in the terminology I used before: each of the two paintings presents us with a different aspect of the landscape, and where the aspect is part of the landscape. When entering a dark chamber with a torchlight, the aspects of the furniture illuminated by the torch-light are aspects of the furniture (and not of the torchlight).

7 'Operative Schriften erfüllen eine doppelte Aufgabe: Sie dienen als ein Medium und zugleich als ein Werkzeug geistiger Arbeit. Metaphorisch gesprochen: Mit ihnen werden Sprachen als eine Technik eingesetzt. Es ist also diesen Doppelfunktion, zu repräsentieren un zugleich mit dem, was repräsentiert wird auch zu operieren, worin die intellektuelle Wirkungskracht der Kalküle wurzelt. Was sie zu eine 'symbolische Maschine', zu einem mechanischen 'Intelligenzverstärker' macht, ist, dass die Regeln der symbolischen Operation keinen Bezug nehmen auf das, was die Symbole jeweils bedeuten.' Krämer (1997: 115, 116). I'd like to thank Jaap den Hollander for having made me aware of Krämer's publications.

8 Leibniz (1976: 639). Leibniz formulated his principle already in his *Discourse on Metaphysics* of 1684: 'As for the simplicity of the ways of God, this is shown especially in the means which he uses, whereas the variety, opulence, and abundance appears in regard to the ends and the results.' Leibniz (1976: 306).

9 'Car comme un moindre mal est une espèce de bien, de même un moindre bien est une espèce de mal, s'il fait obstacle à un bien plus grand; et il y aurait quelquechose à corriger dans les actions de Dieu, s'il n'y avoit moyen de mieux faire. Et comme dans les mathématiques, quand il n'y a point de maximum ni de minimum, *rien enfin de distingué, tout se fait également; ou quand ce la ne se peut, il ne se fait rien du tout*; on peut même dire en matière de parfaite sagesse, qui n'est pas moins réglée

que les mathématiques, que s'il n'y avait pas le meilleur (*optimum*) parmi tous les mondes possibles, Dieu n'en aurait produit aucun' (my italics). Leibniz (1969: 108).

Chapter 5

1 See Kleinberg (2017: 1–4). Much of what follows is a distilled version of the argument presented fully in the book.
2 I place a bar across the "is" both striking it out and indicating an obstruction that restricts all access.
3 I break slightly with Derrida because I see this as applicable to all 'histories' be they written or oral whereas Derrida draws a distinction between 'written' and 'oral' communication here. This is because I see the making present of the past via transmission as a form of 'writing' and thus different from what Derrida describes as 'oral communication'. See Saussy (2016).
4 In Derrida the passage reads: 'One can expose only that which at a certain moment can become *present*, manifest, that which can be shown, presented as something present, a being-present in its truth, in the truth of a present or the presence of the present. For if *différance* is (and I also cross out the "is") what makes possible the presentation of the being-present, it is never presented as such. It is never offered to the present.' Derrida (1972a: 6).
5 Derrida (1995: 108; 1998: 67).

Chapter 6

1 Another meaning that was once widely given to the term 'popular history' is '[historical] scholarship that concerns itself with the affairs of ordinary people' (Strauss 1991: 130; see also Beik 1993 and Strauss 1993). This meaning brushed aside the thought that there might be a historiography *by* 'ordinary people'.
2 The published volumes of the Canadian censuses of 1956 and earlier are available in digital form via the Map and Data Library, Robarts Library, University of Toronto, https://mdl.library.utoronto.ca/collections/numeric-data/census-canada/historical.
3 Saskatchewan's location, shape and topography are indicated at 'Saskatchewan' (2019), https://en.wikipedia.org/wiki/Saskatchewan.
4 Drawing from earlier US models, in the 1870s the Canadian government established a framework for surveying the arable land in Western Canada and for granting homesteads to settlers (the eventual result was the largest single survey of arable land ever carried out on the planet) (Friesen 1984: 181–4; Widdis 1992:

254–67). The survey was carried out using imperial measurements, but in the 1970s Canada mostly converted to metric, and so distances are now almost always stated in kilometres. I here use miles when referring to what was set up in the past and kilometres when I am mainly thinking of the present. A kilometre is about 5/8 of a mile.

5 Still, there are indications that First Nations people sometimes passed through the RM as itinerants (Rosenberg, N., ed. 1980: 77), and that some were hired to help bring in the harvest before mechanization transformed the harvesting process (Haimovitch 2014). Possibly they would have camped out during visits to the RM; even as late as the 1960s, sometimes First Nations people would do so on public land or on unused private land.

6 The photograph, as well as the label 'Edenbridge', was visible on Google Earth in 2016, but as of 2 June 2019 both had disappeared. Janette I. Stuart has provided the more recent photograph reproduced here. The coordinates of the synagogue are Lat. 53° 3′35.86″N, Long. 104°20′37.89″W. Its cemetery is 270 metres to the west among the woods.

7 I thank Robin and Mark Miazga for making me aware of this remarkable book.

8 In May 1922 sixty-seven pupils were attending the school. Only the James G. Piper family was not of Ukrainian or Polish descent (Gronlid 1991: 525). This is indicative of the heavily 'ethnic' settlement pattern in the area. A surviving Edenbridge School class roll from January 1922 lists forty-seven pupils, most of them from Jewish families but with a smattering of other names (Rosenberg, N., ed. 1980: 36–7).

9 In 2016, Saskatchewan's census count was 1,098,352 (Saskatchewan 2019), only 19 per cent higher than it had been eighty years previously.

10 Initially, most of the Norwegians arrived from the United States, to which they had previously emigrated, usually gravitating to the northern US Great Plains. By the early twentieth century some of them were attracted by the prospect of better and cheaper land in Canada (Hall 2007: 91).

11 On Canadian government immigration advertising, see Detre (2004) and Hall (2007).

12 Apparently, Louis Vickar's brother Samuel wrote to the Canadian Department of the Interior in Ottawa, stating that 'we are Jews who keep Saturday as our day of rest' and asking whether they would be welcome in Canada. As reported by Samuel, after six weeks the reply came back that there was freedom of religion in Canada and that everybody was welcome. Samuel tells a different story than his brother did about how the group learned about free land in Canada. Samuel reports that he learned of it from an article in the American Yiddish newspaper *Der Amerikaner* by a man named Miller, who extolled the health benefits of the farming life and pointed out that good land was still available in Western Canada (Vickar 1966, Part II, February, p. 6).

13 Here I rely on a 'Homestead Settlements Map' (Willow Creek 1980) which was produced as a souvenir for Saskatchewan's seventy-fifth anniversary. The map aspires to indicate the first settler on every homesteaded quarter-section in the RM. My thanks to Vicki Baptist, RM Administrator, for making me aware of this and other resources.

14 Fox has investigated the settlement pattern in the RM of Willow Creek, No. 458, particularly in the four townships in which Jewish immigrants settled (Fox 1979: 79–85). There was a heavy concentration of Jewish settlers along Grid Road 681, attributable to the fact they were among the earliest settlers here and were thus able to choose homesteads along the road with the best access to the rail point. As Orthodox Jews, they also had a strong incentive to be within walking distance of the synagogue.

15 This was an important task. By 1914, almost half the people living in the three Prairie Provinces had been born in another country, and non-anglophones made up 40 per cent of the population (Friesen 1984: 244). In Maryville and Edenbridge these figures were significantly higher. Moreover, young children born in Canada of non-anglophone parents, on homesteads that were relatively isolated, obviously needed to go to school to transition from their heritage language to English.

16 The 1991 and 1996 Willow Creek census figures were supplied to me by Michelle Giese, Reference Librarian, Saskatchewan Legislative Library, Regina.

17 Three photographs by Larry Easton show the care that went into renovating the synagogue's interior (Hryniuk and Korvemaker 2014: 118–19). It may be doubted whether the working synagogue ever looked so good.

18 On 3 July, 2019, Vicki Baptist (Baptist 2019) reported to me that RM records show two parcels of land in the vicinity of Holy Ascension held in the name of 'The Shewchenko Ukrainian National Home Association' (1 acre) and of 'The Ukrainian Greek Orthodox Church of St. [sic] Ascension' (3.24 acres). In 1963 the joint executive board of these two non-profit entities consisted of Peter Handzuk, George Nikoluk and Andrew Kozak (Gronlid 1991: 17), none of whom, in 2019, could be traced.

19 On the Maryville and Edenbridge Schools, see Gronlid (1991: 219–21, 525–36, 565–8). Some additional information on Edenbridge School can be found in Rosenberg, N., ed. (1980: 23–38).

20 The Regina [SK] Public Library holds an extensive collection of local histories from the region, and has a search function (at https://catalogue.sasklibraries.ca) that accesses province-wide resources as well as its own collection. See also Maier (1990).

21 *Edenbridge, The memory lives on … . A History* was itself preceded by other writings on Edenbridge, including Samuel Vickar's account (Vickar, S. 1966); a vivid memoir in Yiddish by an immigrant who made his way from Byelorussia to

Edenbridge after four years working in London, Michael Usiskin (Usiskin 1983 [1945]); an opinionated memoir by Abe L. Plotkin, rich in details about Edenbridge life and Saskatchewan politics (Plotkin 1960); and other, shorter writings, such as a geographically inaccurate newspaper article written in 1942 by a journalist, later to be an eminent Canadian novelist, Gabrielle Roy (Roy 1982 [1978]), which noted tension in the colony between the Lithuanian founders and other residents with working-class connections.

22 The present chapter is dedicated to the memory of Robert and Lil (Vickar) Gitlin (Figure 8), and of Dr Philip H. Gordon. Robert Gitlin was the butcher in the town of X, whose face I encountered with a shock of recognition in *Our Courageous Pioneers* (Gronlid 1991: 272). I met Phillip Gordon (1942–2018) in passing while he was a medical student at the University of Saskatchewan. These were two of many people with connections, unknown to me at the time, back to Maryville and Edenbridge.

Chapter 7

1 Explaining the political urgency of his project, Agamben argued that 'the refugee should be considered for what it is, namely, nothing less than a limit-concept that at once brings a radical crisis to the principles of the Nation-State and clears the way for a renewal of categories that can no longer be delayed' (1996: 162).
2 Nonetheless, the observation is correct. As Agamben stated, 'There is no autonomous space in the political order of the Nation-State for something like the pure human in itself', (1996: 161). His thinking here was indebted to Arendt (1973: 267–302).
3 The contemporary situation of refugees, migrants and displaced people, for example, calls into question the limits of abstract terms like 'the people', 'sovereign nation' and 'citizen rights'. This issue is also identified by Étienne Balibar (2004: 33). For an extended discussion of the same, see Staples (2012).
4 Following Mazzara, we favour the use of the terms 'migrant' and 'migration' wherever possible in our discussion because they encompass a range of different migratory circumstances (including voluntary and forced movement) while also acknowledging the shared right of free movement for everyone regardless of the motivations behind each decision to move (Mazzara 2019: 3). Where we employ the term 'refugee', we do so because we are referring to instances where it has been used within given classificatory and discursive contexts.
5 We take the term 'refugeeness' from Peter Nyers, who uses it because it 'highlights the very political process of becoming refugee'. Refugees, he argues, should be seen as subjects of the classification scheme of refugeeness. See Nyers (2006: xiii, xv).

6 By 'imagination' here White meant political imagination, something that was akin to Althusser's use of the term 'ideology'. Indeed, he referred specifically to Althusser's description of the process of 'interpellation' by which political regimes transformed individuals into subjects by inducing in them an identity or subjectivity that was submissive.
7 This setting aside of the principles of asylum happened across Europe in 2015–16. It culminated in the EU-Turkey Agreement on Refugees in 2016, which sought to confine Syrian refugees in Turkey and out of Greece and other EU states.
8 Recent examples from key meta-history journals illustrate the point: *History and Theory* published an issue on 'Historians and Ethics' in 2004; *Rethinking History* produced themed issues on 'Politics and History' in 2009 and 'Historical Justice' in 2014. Also, the International Network for Theory of History's second conference, in Ouro Preto, Brazil in August 2016, was on 'The Practical Past: On the Advantages and Disadvantages of History for Life'.
9 For a detailed discussion of how deconstructionist approaches simultaneously set academic agendas and provoked an intellectual backlash, both of which peaked in the mid-1990s, see Kleinberg (2017).
10 Again, we are indebted to Kalle Pihlainen's argument that despite a 'broad and vocally expressed desire to move on' from questions around language and representation, it is far too early to cease thinking about poststructuralism and the politics of historical representation. Pihlainen (2017: xiii).
11 We note here that Marfleet did not explain at any length how or why an ahistorical perspective on these refugee crises was necessarily problematic.
12 For example, they might focus on these issues in relation to subjects such as slavery, colonial partitions, dislocations caused by the world wars, the situation of displaced persons in post-war Germany or the chaotic effects of different genocides and ethnic cleansings.
13 A representative and by no means comprehensive list would include works such as Loescher and Scanlan (1986); Kushner and Knox (1999); Marrus (2002); Mandel (2003); Zamindar (2007); Chatty (2011); Gatrell (2013). We also note here a special issue of the *Journal of Refugee Studies*, 25, no. 3 (2012), that examined how 'the refugee' as a category of person developed in different post-war settings, and a double issue of *Patterns of Prejudice* on 'Refugees Then and Now: Memory, History and Politics in the Long Twentieth Century', 52, no. 2–3 (2018).
14 The phrase is from Shahid Amin, 'Writing Alternative Histories: A View from South Asia' (unpublished paper).
15 Since 1979 Sudan had been faced with the arrival of refugees from Uganda, an influx that rose to emergency proportions in 1982.
16 https://www.unhcr.org/uk/archives-and-records.html, accessed 5 April 2019.

17 Discussions with Muhammad Ali about his work were pivotal in our reconception of migration as a problem of im/mobility and a denial of basic human rights including the freedom of movement, https://www.mhd-ali.com/, accessed 12 June 2019. We are very grateful for the time Muhammad Ali gave in discussing his work with us. While undertaking research for this article we also became aware of Jacir's invocation of the concept of (im)mobility and her use of it in her artist statement 'Where We Come From: (Im)Mobility', What's Up 15 (2003), n.p. cited in Demos (2013: 273).
18 *Universal Declaration of Human Rights,* http://www.un.org/en/universal-declaration-human-rights/, accessed 15 March 2019, henceforth referred to as the *Declaration*.
19 For the idea of the 'strong passport', see Spivak (1988: 273). For smooth and striated space, see Deleuze and Guattari (1987). See also http://www.protevi.com/john/DG/PDF/ATP14.pdf, accessed 13 March 2019; Demos (2013: xiv).
20 The fact that many migrants originate in areas of former European colonial occupation and areas where Europeans subverted existing property arrangements, dominated and controlled the extraction of raw resources, and themselves migrated en masse to is conveniently elided in the media representation of migration. Victoria Burgher's work *Don't Let Them Drown* (2015) draws attention to the central role that European colonialism plays in current migration through her rewording of Ambalavaner Sivanandan's aphorism on postcolonial migration, from 'we are here because you were there' to 'they are here because we were there' – see the catalogue from the exhibition *Sink without Trace: Exhibition on Migrant Deaths at Sea*, curated by Federica Mazzara and Maya Ramsey at P21, London (13 June–13 July), 10.
21 Sheikh (2015). It is Volume 2 of *The Erasure Trilogy*. See also Sheikh and Weizman (2015), which provides a narrative essay in response to *Desert Bloom*.
22 Sunna (2014). A selection of his work was shown in Sunna (2018–2019). See also *Koncessionsrenskötsel* (2014), http://anderssunna.com/2014-2/; *States* (2017), http://anderssunna.com/2017-2/#!prettyPhoto[1]/http://anderssunna.com/wp-content/uploads/2017/09/states-2-1280x781.jpg, accessed 15 July 2019.
23 *Struggle #1 with Anders Sunna,* https://www.youtube.com/watch?v=owKXQGztVx0, accessed 15 March 2019. He states that in 1986 the government forced his family away using police patrols, forbade their reindeer marks and built a 30-kilometre fence to prevent the reindeer migrating back to their original pastures. He adds that his family received more than 300 police notifications for guerrilla reindeer herding. Although most of the instances of Sámi forced relocation occurred in the first half of the twentieth century there have been more recent instances: two of the most well known are the removal of land use rights from the Sámi village of Girjas in 1993 (which was successfully challenged in 2016) and the movement of the city

of Kiruna onto Sámi reindeer pastures as a result of mining causing the collapse of the original city. See Orange (2016); Crouch (2016); Michael (2018).

24 The mining, hydroelectric and forestry industries are the main reasons for appropriating or curtailing Sámi reindeer pastures. For more on the history and legislation of Sámi reindeer herding in Sweden, see https://www.laits.utexas.edu/sami/diehtu/siida/herding/herding-sw.htm, accessed 15 March 2019 and Carstens (13002016: 75–116).

25 Asad (2007: 59 citing Tuck 1999). For overwhelming evidence of a societal acquiescence in and antipathy to the deaths of hundreds of thousands of migrants one only needs to consider that despite the evidence in daily newspapers about these deaths, they are rarely a subject of conversation nor of action by individuals or governments https://www.theguardian.com/world/2019/jun/09/mediterranean-sea-of-blood-migrant-refugee-rescue-boats-un-unhcr, accessed 15 March 2019. In November 2017, EU migration commissioner, Dimitri Avramopoulos, noted that 'we are all conscious of the appalling and degrading conditions in which some migrants are held in Libya' and yet since then EU member states have spent millions of euros developing the Libyan Coast Guard's ability to intercept migrant boats, return migrants to the degrading and brutal conditions in Libyan detention centres and thus prevent them from reaching Europe, https://www.hrw.org/news/2019/01/21/libya-nightmarish-detention-migrants-asylum-seekers; see also https://www.irishtimes.com/news/world/africa/deaths-pile-up-in-libyan-detention-centre-leaked-un-report-shows-1.3937256; https://www.independent.co.uk/news/world/middle-east/libya-airstrike-tripoli-migrant-centre-refugees-detention-death-toll-a8985431.html, accessed 31 July 2019.

26 https://assets.publishing.service.gov.uk/government/uploads/system/uploads/attachment_data/file/631643/deprivation-nullity-Chapter-55.pdf, accessed 15 March 2019.

27 The denial of a right of return to Palestinians who fled the conflict in 1948 in contravention of UN Resolution 194, article 11, contrasts with the Israeli Law of Return that grants non-Israeli Jews the right to immigrate to Israel and subsequently claim Israeli citizenship. Similarly, while the Law of Return also grants citizenship to the non-Jewish spouse of a non-Israeli Jew, amendments to the Israeli Citizenship and Entry Law have made Palestinian inhabitants of the Palestinian Occupied Territories (the West Bank and Gaza Strip) ineligible for the automatic granting of Israeli citizenship that usually follows marriage to an Israeli citizen https://en.wikipedia.org/wiki/Israeli_citizenship_law#Citizenship_by_marriage and https://en.wikipedia.org/wiki/Citizenship_and_Entry_into_Israel_Law, accessed 30 July 2019. This law also prevents the reunification of Palestinian families who live on different sides of the Green Line, see Zureik (2016: 124). Although Palestinian present absentees (but not Palestinian refugees) were granted Israeli citizenship

in 1952 they were prevented from returning to their homes and land which were then subsequently expropriated by the state under various Absentees' Property Laws and the Transfer of Property Law (1950). There are four distinct groups of internally displaced Palestinians living in Israel: those displaced as a result of the 1948 conflict; those displaced post-1948 as a result of internal transfer, house demolition and land appropriation; those displaced as a result of the 1967 conflict; and those displaced since 1967 especially in East Jerusalem as a result of the revocation of residency rights, land expropriation and so on. For these definitions and a greater discussion of present absentees see the introduction by Masalha in Masalha (2005; 2012: 229–33). The ongoing destruction of the villages of the Negev Bedouin documented by Fazal Sheikh and discussed earlier is in part facilitated by the fact that Israel classifies the Bedouin (and their descendants) as internally displaced peoples and, as a consequence, their villages are 'unrecognized'. A similar inequality is present in the de facto citizenship restrictions imposed on Palestinians living in East Jerusalem. Following Israeli occupation of East Jerusalem in 1967 and its annexation under full Israeli sovereignty, Palestinians of East Jerusalem should technically be able to apply for Israeli citizenship, but in practice they are instead offered the special status of 'permanent residency' thereby denying them citizenship of the state in which they live. Khamaisi (2011: 335–52, 338–9).

28 For examples from Jacir (2001–3), see Jacir, Rollig and Rückert (2004: 50–9). For further examples and images from her installation see Binder and Haupt (2003).

29 He was also sentenced to twenty-five years in prison. The revocation of his citizenship will leave Zayoud stateless, and it is therefore a violation of international human rights law. Up to 2600 Bedouin Israeli citizens were also stripped of their Israeli citizenship after a registration error – see https://www.jpost.com/Israel-News/Government-strips-2600-Beduin-of-citizenship-due-to-registration-error-503664, accessed 30 July 2019.

30 In Norton and Donnelly (2016: 192–216), we consider the decision by the United States to revoke the US citizenship of Palestinian-American Rasmea Odeh.

31 For interviews with Begum, and the Home Secretary's decision to block her return and revoke her nationality see https://www.theguardian.com/uk-news/2019/feb/17/shamima-begum-who-fled-uk-to-join-isis-has-given-birth-say-family, accessed 15 March 2019. It should be noted that Begum acknowledged the oppression and corruption of the regime and stated that because of this it deserved to be defeated.

32 https://www.ibraaz.org/publications/42, accessed 11 June 2019.

33 Cited in Saljooghi (2009: 23–9, 28); reference is given as Emily Jacir (2003) www.daratalfunun.org; Sacco (2009: 19, 35, 128–33), provides an account of the effects that roadblocks, checkpoints and a separate road infrastructure system for Israeli settlers had on Palestinian residents in the Gaza Strip before Israel withdrew. B'Tselem The Israeli Information Centre for Human Rights in the Occupied

Territories records the routine harassment that arbitrary Israeli roadblocks, checkpoints and the closure of military-installed village gates cause for Palestinians see https://www.btselem.org/freedom_of_movement/20190520_military_blocks_access_roads_to_four_villages, accessed 12 June 2019. See also the Human Rights Watch report on restrictions to the freedom of movement of Palestinians and arbitrary detention https://www.hrw.org/world-report/2019/country-chapters/israel/palestine accessed 12 June 2019. See the OCHA (United Nations Office for the Coordination of Humanitarian Affairs) factsheet on Movement and access in the West Bank (2017), https://www.ochaopt.org/content/west-bank-movement-and-access-west-bank, accessed 12 June 2019.

34 All of Weizman chapter 5 is useful on the forensic architecture of checkpoints. For more on the sociocultural and economic effects of the Israeli restriction of Palestinian movement see B'Tselem, https://www.btselem.org/topic/freedom_of_movement, accessed 12 June 2019.

35 See also Hass (2019). See also the OCHA fact sheet on Palestinians at risk of forcible transfer https://www.ochaopt.org/content/west-bank-palestinians-risk-forcible-transfer, accessed 12 June 2019.

36 The work was part of Jacir's exhibition at the Whitechapel Gallery, London 2015–16, https://www.whitechapelgallery.org/exhibitions/emily-jacir-europa/, accessed 12 June 2019.

37 Ali (2015a). A selection of drawings from this series were shown in *The Moderna Exhibition 2018. With the Future Behind Us,* 20 October 2018 to 6 January 2019.

38 See https://www.mhd-ali.com/pro-1-2012-15-from-the-diary-of-a-r, accessed 12 June 2019. There are also instances of compassion in these images, occasions where the figures feed others from their body. His work *366 Days of 2012* similarly features fantastical drawings of disturbing and disturbed figures inspired by his encounters with Syrians in 2012. These grotesque creatures are reminiscent of the mythical creatures of medieval travel books that depict an 'other' people so different from ourselves that they have only one large foot, a single eye, a face in their chest, multiple limbs or wings.

39 Ali (2014). This video was shown in *The Moderna Exhibition 2018. With the Future Behind Us,* 20 October 2018–6 January 2019.

40 Mazzara (2019: 1–2), notes that the term 'scopic regime' appears in an essay by Jay (1988: 3–23).

41 Information about the project, including an eighteen-minute long video is available on their webpage, https://forensic-architecture.org/investigation/the-left-to-die-boat. The video has been shown at a number of art exhibitions, the most recent being the *Sink without Trace* exhibition, http://p21.gallery/exhibitions/exhibition-sink-without-trace/, see also https://www.sinkwithouttrace.com/, accessed 3 July 2019.

42 According to witness testimony fishing vessels were also signalled by those on the boat, but they offered no assistance.

43 Catalogue from the exhibition *Sink without Trace: Exhibition on Migrant Deaths at Sea*, curated by Federica Mazzara and Maya Ramsey, 12. The quote is from a discussion of photographer Max Hirzel whose work also featured in the exhibition.
44 https://forensic-architecture.org/investigation/the-left-to-die-boat, accessed 3 July 2019.
45 Mbembe (2003: 40) describes the creation of death-worlds, forms of social existence where people are subjected to conditions of life conferring on them the status of the living dead.
46 For example, a number of the artists exhibiting their work in the exhibition *Sink without Trace* themselves are migrants or work with migrants to establish archives, make films and run workshops that document and promote the migrant voice. See for example Dagmawi Yimer, Art Refuge UK, Aida Silverstri, Shorsh Saleh, Mariwan Jalal, catalogue from the exhibition *Sink without Trace* 38, 32, 30, 28, 14.
47 Of course, as Max Hirzel points out art can also function as a sentimental display of compassion that absolves us from responsibility and action to rectify the unequal distribution of human rights. See his comments on the lack of contextualization and audience reactions to Christoph Büchel *Barca Nostra* in Bromwich (2019). He notes that the boat functions as a 'monument to European compassion' in a broader narrative that treats the deaths of migrants in the Mediterranean as some kind of natural disaster rather than a consequence of the formation of a European militarized judicial regime that imagines the Mediterranean as a zone of exception that creates 'the condition for the acceptability of putting to death'; see also Mbembe (2003: 17) citing Foucault Il faut défendre la société, 228. Hirzel's work *Migrant Bodies* is featured in the *Sink without Trace* exhibition at the P21 Gallery https://www.sinkwithouttrace.com/, accessed 3 July 2019, see also https://maxhirzel.photoshelter.com/index/G00004NTbJ8ILraE, accessed 15 July 2019.
48 Dagmawi Yimer, *Asmat.Nomi per tutte le vittime in mare [Names in Memory of All Victims at Sea]* names the 368 Eritreans who died at sea when the boat they were travelling on sank on 3 October 2013. In so doing, Yimer not only works 'to defy the attention and patience of the public, in order to bring back the numbers of the tragedy to the reality of names', but also forcefully notes that 'we are more visible dead than alive'; see catalogue from the exhibition *Sink without Trace*, 38–9. It is particularly ironic that those migrants who survive crossing the Mediterranean are criminalized, detained or deported, whereas those who die during the attempt are embraced, however temporarily, as possible citizens – see the comment of Italian prime minister Enrico Letta in 2013 that 'the hundreds who lost their lives off Lampedusa yesterday are Italian citizens as of today'. Rygiel (2016: 545–60, 550).

Chapter 8

1 This chapter draws partly on Tucker (2018: 25–35; 2016).
2 For an overview, see Saval (2017). Saval notes that globalization benefitted extensively mostly six Asian countries, but fails to name them so the reader misses that they comprise the majority of humanity. For a more academic and nuanced approaches see Rodrick's work, especially *Populism and the Economics of Globalization:* https://drodrik.scholar.harvard.edu/publications/populism-and-economics-globalization.

   James (2009). Even the world view of Steven Bannon, such as it is, seems to have been inspired by a cyclical philosophy of history: Strauss and Howe (1997).
3 Tucker (2004: 220–39). I followed Yemima. Ben-Menahem (1997: 99–107).

Chapter 9

1 In 1995, the commission was renamed as the International Commission for the History and Theory of Historiography.
2 On Giere's choice of metaphor, see also Giere (2012: 59 n. 1).
3 Those others include Mark Day, whose analysis of historians' standards of evaluation such as expressed in book reviews appears in Day (2008a: 21–4).
4 'VPI' refers to Virginia Polytechnic Institute, where Larry and Rachel Laudan, among others, carried out the 'Testing Theories of Scientific Change' project described in Laudan et al. (1986).
5 That is, for professional self-reflection of the kind illustrated by Gershoy (1963).
6 On Dray's insistence that philosophers of history should reflect on what historians actually do, see also Rubinoff (1991).
7 The metaphor of relations with the past is borrowed from Day (2008a).
8 On the 'cultural turn' in the history of science, see Clark (2015).
9 As happens, for instance, in Kochan (2013).
10 I offer some tentative reflection on these issues in Paul (2011, 2012).
11 For those 'other parts of the humanities', see the interesting explorations in Kelley and Rose (2018).
12 Classic studies are, of course, Latour and Woolgar (1979); Knorr-Cetina (1981); Traweek (1988).
13 Although feminist philosophy of science has long insisted on the real-life situatedness of the knowing subject, feminist philosophy of history is still *in statu nascendi*. See only Honkani (2005).
14 On the perceived educational promises of HPS, see Matthews (1994).

15 In my experience at Leiden University, where I teach a research master's course on historical theory, this format greatly helps turning students' initial scepticism about philosophical reflection ('Why do we have to read this stuff?') into creative energy ('Let's see whether these guys understand what we are doing!').

Chapter 10

1 It should be stressed that many researchers involved in discussions on this subject are reluctant to accept indigenous knowledges and epistemologies and Western science and scholarship as radically different. What is deemed more significant is acceptance of 'a plural conception of knowledge to allow for different ways of knowing' (Meijl 2019: 155).
2 It is quite surprising that when progressive representatives of the young generation of history theorists write of the future of the theory and philosophy of history, they seem to completely overlook trends that, in my view, are fundamentally transforming contemporary humanities. For example, when Berber Bevernage, Broos Delanote, Anton Froeyman, Kenan Van De Mieroo mention 'the paradigm shift' they mean 'a dialogue between philosophers of history and the non-academic engagements with the past'. The intuition is obviously correct, and it goes along with current discussions on participatory research, public history, but, as the authors notice themselves, this is only a change of focus that will not produce a radically new philosophy of history (Bevernage et al. 2014: 148; see also Susen 2015). An exception is Zoltán Boldizsár Simon, who includes the theory of history in his discussion of the Anthropocene and climate change (Simon 2019a).
3 Both my own research and also an N-gram analysis suggests that there was a significant shift around 1996–8 where there was a decline in the frequency of the usage of key terms related to the interpretative paradigm (such as postmodernism, deconstruction, poststructuralism) and a rise in the frequency of terms characteristic of the emerging paradigm (such as biopolitics and forensics) (Domańska 2013).
4 This is one of the reasons why Hayden White's idea of 'practical past' becomes of special interest of scholars (White 2014; see also Polyakov 2012).
5 Paraphrasing Louis Althusser, we may argue that academic debates have become a locus of a class, race, gender and, perhaps even, species struggle in theory. I am referring to Althusser's statement that 'philosophy represents the class struggle in theory'. Althusser goes on to argue that philosophy

is situated somewhere in the vicinity of ideologies, as a kind of theoretical laboratory in which the fundamentally political problem of ideological hegemony – that is, of the constitution of the dominant ideology – is experimentally put to test, in the abstract. The work accomplished by the most abstract philosophers does not remain a dead letter: what philosophy has received from the class struggle as a demand, it gives back to it in the form of systems of thought which then work on the ideologies in order to transform and unify them (Althusser 2006: 287).

6 These approaches do not reject objectivism as such but only its specific version that incorporates cognitive transcendence and adopts the 'divine point of view'. For example, Donna Haraway views the question of objectivity, closely related to the situated subject and situated knowledge, as a primary problem of feminist epistemology, while Sandra Harding has formulated the concept of 'strong objectivity'. There is extensive literature on the subject (Haraway 1988; Harding 1993). In different philosophical frames, an idea of subjectivity is explored by Frank Ankersmit (Ankersmit 2004; see also Førland 2017).

7 See Cary Wolfe, 'Introduction to "PostHumanities"', https://www.upress.umn.edu/book-division/series/posthumanities. Wolfe started the interdisciplinary 'PostHumanities' series, which has included the books such as Michel Serres, *The Parasite* (2007), Donna Haraway, *When Species Meet* (2007), David Willis, *Dorsality. Thinking Back through Technology and Politics* (2008), Roberto Esposito, *Bios: Biopolitics and Philosophy* (2008); Nicole Shukin, *Animal Capital: Rendering Life in Biopolitical Times*, 2009; John Protevi, *Political Affect: Connecting the Social and the Somatic* (2009).

8 Ideas of a nonanthropocentric paradigm appeared as early as the 1990s (Emmenegger and Tschentscher 1994).

9 In his *Reassembling the Social*, Latour ultimately rejects the principle of symmetry. He realized that his theory was misread as pertaining to a symmetrical study of subjects and objects, humans and non-humans. As Latour argues emphatically,

> There exists no relation whatsoever between 'the material' and 'the social world', because it is this very division which is a complete artifact. ... ANT [actor-network theory – ED] is not, I repeat is not, the establishment of some absurd 'symmetry between humans and non-humans'. To be symmetric, for us, simply means *not* to impose *a priori* some spurious *asymmetry* among human intentional action and a material world of causal relations. There are divisions one should never try to bypass, to go beyond, to try to overcome dialectically. They should be rather ignored and left to their own devices, like a once formidable castle now in ruins.

In a footnote, he adds, 'The last thing I wanted was to give nature and society a new lease on life through "symmetry"' (Latour 2005: 75–6).

10 I avoid the term 'survival' here, since I am aware that – as Zygmunt Bauman claims – survival is a 'social construct' that marks its ambiguity and political bias (Bauman 1992). Besides, my aim is not simply to affirm life (I believe that the right to death and to be dead could in future prove to be as important as the right to life) but rather to sustain the forces and processes generating and driving movement, change and transformations.

11 As R. G. Collingwood famously argued, 'History is "for" human self-knowledge. It is generally thought to be of importance to man that he should know himself. … Knowing yourself means knowing, first, what it is to be a man. … The value of history, then, is that it teaches us what man has done and thus what man is' (Collingwood 1994: 10).

12 'Derrida: "In general, I try to distinguish between what one calls the future and 'l'avenir'. The future is that which – tomorrow, later, next century – will be. There's a future that is predictable, programmed, scheduled, foreseeable. But there is a future, l'avenir (to come), which refers to someone who comes whose arrival is totally unexpected. For me, that is the real future. That which is totally unpredictable. The Other who comes without my being able to anticipate their arrival. So if there is a real future beyond the other known future, it's l'avenir in that it's the coming of the Other when I am completely unable to foresee their arrival"' (Dick and Kofman 2005: 53).

13 I refer to Derrida's *The Animal That Therefore I Am* (2008), *The Gift of Death* (2007), *History of the Lie* (in: *Futures: of Jacques Derrida*, 2001), *Politics of Friendship* (1997, 2005), *On Cosmopolitanism and Forgiveness* (2001), *The Work of Mourning* (2001) and *Of Hospitality* (2000).

14 I present an outline of this practical methodology in the article 'Problematizing Comparative Historical Studies' (Domańska 2010b: 79–81) and in the book chapter 'Metodologia praktyczna' [Practical Methodology] (Domańska 2012: 161–83). Of course, I am not suggesting that all historians ought to be interested in constructing theories but that degree programmes in history should prepare and encourage students to do so.

Chapter 12

1 I am very grateful to the audiences at the conference on the Role of the Philosophy of History in Oulu 2017 and at the INTH in Stockholm 2018 for their comments and to Marek Tamm whose paper 'More-Than-Human History: The Role of Philosophy of History at the Time of Anthropocene' first presented in Oulu 2017

(and published in this collection) first prompted me to embark on a defence of a humanistically oriented historiography.
2   For a discussion of the distinction between the entanglement of different kinds of history versus the absorption of one kind of history into another see Simon (2020). In this collection Tamm and Simon speak of 'the entangled human and natural world as it appears in the transdisciplinary Anthropocene debate', but it is unclear whether the new philosophy of history which they advocate rests on the traditional notion of cooperation between different disciplines or whether it calls for a disruption of old distinctions that is closer to Latour's 'abolitionist' stance.
3   For an account of how narrativism turned away from the methodological debates concerning the logical structure of historical explanation in analytic philosophy of history, see Kuukkanen (2015).
4   Hempel originally argued that nomological explanations are deductive explanations in which the explanandum is strictly entailed by a universal law and the antecedent conditions. He later conceded that covering laws in history are at best probabilistic laws and that in historical explanations the explanandum is only probabilistically entailed by the general laws and the antecedent conditions from which it is deduced, thereby allowing for a distinction in degree (but still not in kind) between the human and the natural sciences.
5   Dray was part of an anti-causalist consensus which governed the philosophy of action in mid-century and which was motivated by the view that rationalizations are irreducible to causal explanations. On this See D'Oro and Sandis (2013).
6   The claim that science operates under the presupposition of the uniformity of nature is not invalidated by the observation that in the Anthropocene the alternating of the seasons is disrupted by irregular and unprecedented weather patterns. For such unprecedented changes were in fact predicted by climate scientists.
7   For this claim, see D'Oro (2018).
8   This expression was coined by Sellars (1963) although I am using it here in a slightly different way.
9   For a recent collection of essays linking the debates in the philosophy of action and history, see Schumann (2019) and his introduction to this book.
10 Of course, a humanistically oriented historiographer would retort that since what is needed in the context of humanistic explanations is familiarity with the space of reasons, lack of familiarity with the scientific context is irrelevant to the task at hand: what is at stake precisely is what kind of context one should invoke when explaining General Kutuzof and the Corticotropin releasing factor.
11 Sloterdijk, quoted in Latour (2017a: 123).
12 Contrary to what critics of the nature-culture distinction argue, the defence of the methodological autonomy of the *Geisteswissenschaften* as one finds it in

Windelband (2015 [1894]), Collingwood (1993 [1946]) and Oakeshott (1962, 1975, 1983) does not rest on the identification of the subject matter of traditional histories with a particular kind of biological being, but with the identification of a distinctive methodology matching certain distinctive concerns. I have discussed the defence of the notion of the historical past in the tradition of British Idealism in D'Oro (2015).

13 This objection, as we shall see later, rests on a hypostatization of the methodological differences between explanatory practices that is not needed to defend the claim that the *Geisteswissenschaften* and the *Naturwissenschaften* have distinctive and irreducible explicanda.

14 I have explored the reciprocal relation holding between method and subject matter in idealist philosophy of histories in D'Oro (2015). For an account of this in Oakeshott, see Kaldis (2012).

15 Descartes (2008 [1641]), Meditation 6. On the real distinction, see Murdoch (2009).

16 For Heidegger's discussion of the world, see Heidegger (1962 [1927]: §43).

17 'Philosophy is a battle against the bewitchment of our intelligence by language' Wittgenstein (1963: §109).

18 https://www.stokesentinel.co.uk/news/history/insight-toilets-longtons-gladstone-pottery-1987920.

19 For an account of how to disconnect a methodological claim for the disunity of science from a metaphysical claim for ontological dualism, see D'Oro, Giladi and Papazoglou (2019).

20 For a discussion of the role of the intensional context of explanation in historical narratives see Ahlskog and D'Oro (forthcoming).

21 One could legitimately entertain serious doubts as to whether this is possible.

22 Quine's account of 'radical translation' (1960: chapter 2), exemplifies this purely extensional model explanation.

23 On the dangers of purely technological solutions, see Helena Paul and Rupert Read (2019).

24 For a recent defence of the nature/culture distinction, see Malm (2019).

25 On animal histories, see Domańska (2017).

26 https://www.theguardian.com/environment/2019/jan/25/our-house-is-on-fire-greta-thunberg16-urges-leaders-to-act-on-climate.

27 I do not know whether it is a coincidence or an explicit reference to Latour's work.

28 For a critique of the discussions concerning the nature of time in contemporary analytic metaphysics, see Tallis (2017). On the debate between endurantists and perdurantists, see Hales and Johnson (2003).

29 Conversation with Jeff Malpas at the INTH conference in Stockholm, August 2018.

Works Cited

Aalto, S. (2018), *Kapina Tehtailla. Kuusankoski 1918*, Helsinki: Siltala.

Agamben, G. (1996), 'Beyond Human Rights', C. Casarino (trans.), in P. Virno and M. Hardt (eds), *Radical Thought in Italy: A Potential Politics*, 159–65, Minneapolis: University of Minnesota Press.

Agamben, G. (2009), 'What Is a Paradigm', in L. D'Isanto and K. Attell (trans.), *The Signature of All Things: On Method*, 9–32, New York: Zone Books.

Ahlskog, J. and G. D'Oro (forthcoming), 'Against Narrativism: The Historical Past and Why It Can Be Known', *Collingwood and British Idealism Studies*.

Ali, M. (2014), *Neither Human, Nor Stone*, video. https://www.mhd-ali.com/videos, accessed 13 March 2019.

Ali, M. (2015a), *Endless Days*, ink on paper. https://www.mhd-ali.com/copy-of-dra-2-2009-self-violence-1, accessed 13 March 2019.

Ali, M. (2015b), *Post-Thousand and One Nights*, ink on paper.

Althusser, L. (2006), 'Philosophy and Marxism', in *Philosophy of the Encounter: Later Writings, 1978–1987*, 251–89, London: Verso.

Anderson, B. (1983), *Imagined Communities: Reflections on the Origin and Spread of Nationalism*, London: Verso.

Ankersmit, F. R. (1983), *Narrative Logic: A Semantic Analysis of the Historian's Language*, The Hague, Boston and London: Martinus Nijhoff Publishers.

Ankersmit, F. R. (1995), 'Historicism: An Attempt at a Synthesis', *History and Theory*, 34: 143–61.

Ankersmit, F. R. (2001), *Historical Representation*, Stanford: Stanford University Press.

Ankersmit, F. R. (2004), 'In Praise of Subjectivity', in D. Carr, Th. R. Flynn and R. A. Makkreel (eds), *The Ethics of History*, 3–27, Evanston, IL: Northwestern University Press.

Ankersmit, F. R. (2005), *Sublime Historical Experience*, Stanford: Stanford University Press.

Ankersmit, F. R. (2012), *Meaning, Truth and Reference in Historical Representation*, Ithaca and London: Cornell University Press.

Ankersmit, F. R. (2013), 'History as the Science of the Individual', *Journal of the Philosophy of History*, 7 : 396–426.

Ankersmit, F. R. (2018), 'Reply to My Critics', *Journal of the Philosophy of History*, 12: 470–90.

Ankersmit, F. R., M. Bevir, P. A. Roth, A. Tucker and A. Wylie (2007), 'The Philosophy of History: An Agenda', *Journal of the Philosophy of History*, 1: 1–9.

Appiah, K. A. (2010), *Cosmopolitanism: Ethics in a World of Strangers*, New York and London: W. W. Norton.

Arabatzis, T. and J. Schickore (2012), 'Ways of Integrating History and Philosophy of Science', *Perspectives on Science*, 20: 395–408.

Arendt, H. (1973), 'The Decline of the Nation-State and the End of the Rights of Man', in *The Origins of Totalitarianism*, 267–302, Orlando, FL: Harcourt Brace & Company.

Arendt, H. (2017), *The Origins of Totalitarianism* [1951], London: Penguin Classics.

Armitage, D. (2012), 'What's the Big Idea? Intellectual History and the Longue Durée', *History of European Ideas*, 38 (4): 493–507.

Asad, T. (2007), *On Suicide Bombing*, New York: Colombia University Press.

Assmann, A. (2013), *Ist die Zeit aus den Fugen? Aufstieg und Fall des Zeitregimes der Moderne*, Munich: Hanser.

Austin, J. L. (1962), *Sense and Sensibilia*, London: Oxford University Press.

Austin, J. L. (1975), *How to Do Things with Words*, Cambridge, MA: Harvard University Press.

Axtell, G. (2016), *Objectivity*, Cambridge: Polity Press.

Azoulay, A. (2013), 'Potential History: Thinking Through Violence', *Critical Inquiry*, 39 (3): 548–74.

Bachmann-Medick, D. (2016), *Cultural Turns: New Orientations in the Study of Culture*, trans. A. Blauhut, Berlin and Boston: Walter De Gruyter GmbH.

Badmington, N., ed. (2000), *Posthumanism*, Basingstoke: Palgrave.

Baldwin, R. (2016), *The Great Convergence: Information Technology and the New Globalization*, Cambridge, MA: Harvard University Press.

Balibar, E. (2004), *We, the People of Europe? Reflections on Transnational Citizenship*, trans. James Swenson, Princeton, NJ: Princeton University Press.

Baptist, V. (2019), Personal Communication (email), July 3.

Barad, K. (2007), *Meeting the Universe Halfway: Quantum Physics and the Entanglement of Matter and Meaning*, Durham: Duke University Press.

Baratay, É. (2012), *Le point de vue animal. Une autre version de l'histoire*, Paris: Seuil.

Baratay, É. (2017), *Biographies animales*, Paris: Seuil.

Bauman, Z. (1992), 'Survival as a Social Construct', *Theory Culture Society*, 9 (1): 1–36.

Bauman, Z. (2002), *Society Under Siege*, Cambridge: Polity Press.

Beck, U. (2016), *The Metamorphosis of the World*, Cambridge: Polity.

Becker, T. (2018), 'The Meanings of Nostalgia: Genealogy and Critique', *History and Theory*, 57 (2): 234–50.

Beik, W. (1993), 'The Dilemma of Popular History', *Past & Present*, 141 (November): 207–15.

Benjamin, W. (2007), 'Theses on the Philosophy of History', in H. Arendt (ed.) and H. Zohn (trans.), W. Benjamin, *Illuminations: Essays and Reflections*, 253–64, New York: Schocken Books.

Ben-Menahem, Y. (1997), 'Historical Contingency', *Ratio*, 10 (2): 99–107.

Bennett, J. (2010), *Vibrant Matter: A Political Ecology of Things*, Durham: Duke University Press.

Berlin, I. (1955), *Historical Inevitability*, Oxford: Oxford University Press.

Bevernage, B. (2012), 'From Philosophy of History to Philosophy of Historicities: Some Ideas on a Potential Future of Historical Theory', *Low Countries Historical Review*, 124 (7): 113–20.

Bevernage, B., B. Delanote, A. Froeyman and K. Van De Mieroo (2014), 'Introduction: The Future of the Theory and Philosophy of History', *Journal of the Philosophy of History*, 8 (2): 141–8.

Bevir, M. (1999), *The Logic of the History of Ideas*, Cambridge: Cambridge University Press.

Bevir, M. and H. Paul (2012), 'Naturalized Epistemology and/as Historicism: A Brief Introduction', *Journal of the Philosophy of History*, 6 (3): 299–303.

Binder, P. and H. Gerhard (2003), 'Emily Jacir: Where We Come From', *Nafas Art Magazine*, October, https://universes.art/nafas/articles/2003/emily-jacir-where-we-come-from/, accessed 13 March 2018.

Bird, R. D. and L. Robin (2004), 'The Ecological Humanities in Action: An Invitation', *Australian Humanities Review*, 31–2, available online: http://www.australianhumanitiesreview.org/archive/Issue-April-2004/rose.html (accessed 20 July 2019).

Bloch, M. (1953), *The Historian's Craft*, trans. P. Putman, New York: Vintage Books. Reprinted in 1992.

BonJour, L. (1985), *The Structure of Empirical Knowledge*, Cambridge, MA: Harvard University Press.

Bonneuil, C. and J.-B. Fressoz (2016), *The Shock of The Anthropocene: The Earth, History and Us*, trans. D. Fernbach, London: Verso.

Bos, J. (2018), 'Ankersmit's Dutch Writings and Their Audience', *Journal of the Philosophy of History*, 12: 450–72.

Bostrom, N. (2014), *Superintelligence: Paths, Dangers, Strategies*, Oxford: Oxford University Press.

Bradley, F. H. (1874), *The Presuppositions of Critical History*, Oxford: James Parker.

Braidotti, R. (2013), *The Posthuman*, Cambridge: Polity Press.

Braidotti, R. (2019), *Posthuman Knowledge*, Cambridge: Polity Press.

Braidotti, R. and H. Maria (eds) (2018), *Posthuman Glossary*, London: Bloomsbury.

Brandom, R. (1998), *Making It Explicit: Reasoning, Representing & Discursive Commitment*, Cambridge, MA: Harvard University Press.

Braudel, F. (1972) [1949], *The Mediterranean and the Mediterranean World in the Age of Philip II*, vol. I, trans. S. Reynolds, London: Collins.

Bromwich, K. '"We Should Be Ashamed": Bearing Witness to Migrant Deaths at Sea', *The Guardian*, 8 June 2019, https://www.theguardian.com/artanddesign/2019/jun/08/migrant-deaths-at-sea-exhibiton-sink-without-trace, accessed 3 July 2019.

Brooke, J. L. (2014), *Climate Change and the Course of Global History: A Rough Journey*, Cambridge: Cambridge University Press.

Broswimmer, F. J. (2002), *Ecocide. A Short History of the Mass Extinction of Species*, London: Pluto Press.

Brown, T. and A. Schubert (2007), 'The Growth of Research on Inter- and Multidisciplinarity in Science and Social Science Papers, 1975–2006', *Scientometrics*, 73: 345–51.

Buck-Morss, S. and K. Bojarska (2014), 'Solidarność w historii – ludzie i idee. Susan Buck-Morss w rozmowie z Katarzyną Bojarską' [Comm(o)nism of the Idea – Solidarity in the Face of History. Susan Buck-Morss in Conversation with Katarzyna Bojarska], trans. K. Bojarska. *Teksty Drugie/Second Texts*, 5: 200–211.

Bunzl, M. (1997), *Real History: Reflections on Historical Practice*, London: Routledge.

Burckhardt, J. (1890), *Civilisation of the Renaissance in Italy*, trans. S. G. C. Middlemore, New York: G. Allen & Unwin.

Burgher, V. (2015), *Don't Let Them Drown*, http://www.victoriaburgher.com/lsvkrav99l1bike84gnfwcf9yxgvrd, accessed 18 May 2020.

Burian, R. M. (1977), 'More than a Marriage of Convenience: On the Inextricability of History and Philosophy of Science', *Philosophy of Science*, 44: 1–42.

Burns, R. (1786), 'To a Louse, On Seeing One on a Lady's Bonnet at Church' [poem], various sources.

Butalia, U. (1998), *The Other Side of Silence: Voices from the Partition of India*, Delhi: Viking Penguin.

Butalia, U. (2001), 'An Archive with a Difference: Partition Letters', in S. Kaul (ed.), *The Partitions of Memory: The Afterlife of the Division of India*, 208–41, Bloomington: Indiana University Press.

Canada [Government of] (1902), *Fourth Census of Canada 1901, Vol. 1*: Population, Ottawa: Department of Agriculture, https://mdl.library.utoronto.ca/collections/numeric-data/census-canada/historical (this also links to the historical censuses below).

Canada [Government of] (1912), *Fifth Census of Canada, 1911*, Vol. I, Ottawa: Department of Commerce.

Canada [Government of] (1936), *Seventh Census of Canada 1931*, Vol. I: Summary, Ottawa: Department of Trade and Commerce.

Canada [Government of] (1949), *Census of the Prairie Provinces 1946*, Vol. I, Ottawa: Department of Trade and Commerce.

Canada [Government of] (1953), *Ninth Census of Canada, 1951*, Vol. 1: Population, Ottawa: Dominion Bureau of Statistics.

Canada [Government of] (2016), *Statistics Canada*, Census Profile, 2016 Census, https://www12.statcan.gc.ca/census-recensement/2016/dp-pd/prof/index.cfm?Lang=E.

Capra, F. (1996), *The Web of Life: A New Scientific Understanding of Living Systems*, New York: Anchor Books.

Capra, F., D. Steindl-Rest and T. Matus (1991), *Belonging to the Universe: Explorations on the Frontiers of Science and Spirituality*, San Francisco: Harper San Francisco (part III: 'The Current Shift of Paradigms').

Carroll, N. (1990), 'Interpretation, History, and Narrative', *The Monist*, 73 (2): 134–66.

Carstens, M. (2016), 'Sami Land Rights: The Anaya Report and the Nordic Sami Convention', *Journal on Ethnopolitics and Minority Issues in Europe*, 15 (1): 75–116. https://www.ecmi.de/fileadmin/downloads/publications/JEMIE/2016/Carstens.pdf, accessed 15 March 2019.

Chakrabarty, D. (2009), 'The Climate of History: Four Theses', *Critical Inquiry*, 35 (2): 197–222.

Chakrabarty, D. (2015), 'Decentering the Human? Or WhatRemains of Gaia', in *The Human Condition in the Anthropocene*. The Tanner Lectures in Human Values delivered at Yale University, 18–19 February, 165–88, available online: https://tannerlectures.utah.edu/Chakrabarty%20manuscript.pdf, accessed 23 July 2019.

Chakrabarty, D. (2018a), 'Planetary Crises and the Difficulty of Being Modern', *Millennium: Journal of International Studies*, 46 (3): 259–82.

Chakrabaty, D. (2018b), 'Anthropocene Time', *History and Theory*, 57 (1): 5–32.

Chakrabarty, D. (2019), *The Crises of Civilization: Exploring Global and Planetary Histories*, New Delhi: Oxford University Press.

Chatty, D. (2011), *Displacement and Dispossession in the Modern Middle East*, Cambridge: Cambridge University Press.

Charmaz, K. (2006), *Constructing Grounded Theory: A Practical Guide Through Qualitative Analysis*, London and Thousand Oaks, CA: Sage Publications

Christian, D. (2004), *Maps of Time: An Introduction to Big History*, Berkeley and Los Angeles: University of California Press.

Christian, D. (2018), *Origin Story: A Big History of Everything*, New York: Little, Brown and Company.

Clark, C. (2012), *The Sleepwalkers: How Europe Went to War in 1914*, London: Penguin Books.

Clark, J. F. M. (2015), 'Intellectual History and History of Science', in R. Whatmore and B. Young (eds), *A Companion to Intellectual History*, 155–69, Chichester: Wiley-Blackwell.

Clark, T. (2015), *Ecocriticism on the Edge: The Anthropocene as a Threshold Concept*, London: Bloomsbury Academic.

Coady, D. (2004), 'Preempting Preemption', in J. Collins, N. Hall and L. A. Paul (eds), *Causation and Counterfactuals*, 325–40, Cambridge, MA: The MIT Press.

Collingwood, R. G. (1939), *Autobiography*, Oxford: Clarendon Press.

Collingwood, R. G. (1940), *An Essay on Metaphysics*, Oxford: Clarendon Press.

Collingwood, R. G. (1946), *The Idea of History*, Oxford: Clarendon Press.

Collingwood, R. G. (1993) [1946], *The Idea of History, Revised edition, with Lectures 1926–1928*, ed. J. van der Dussen, Oxford: Oxford University Press.

Collingwood, R. G. (1999), *The Principles of History*, eds W. H. Dray and J. van der Dussen, Oxford: Oxford University Press.

Conkin, P. K. (1974), 'Causation Revisited', *History and Theory*, 13 (1): 1–20.

Coole, D. and S. Frost, eds (2010), *New Materialisms: Ontology, Agency, and Politics*, Durham and London: Duke University Press.

Cowling, M. (1971), *The Impact of Labour 1920-1924: The Beginning of Modern British Politics*, Cambridge: Cambridge University Press.

Creyghton, C. (2016), 'La survivance de Michelet: historiographie et politique en France depuis 1870', PhD thesis, University of Amsterdam.

Critchley, S. and R. Kearney (2001), 'Preface', in J. Derrida, *On Cosmopolitanism and Forgiveness*, trans. M. Dooley and M. Hughes, vii–xii, London: Routledge.

Crouch, D. (2016), 'Sweden's Indigenous Sami People Win Rights Battle Against State', *The Guardian*, 3 February, https://www.theguardian.com/world/2016/feb/03/sweden-indigenous-sami-people-win-rights-battle-against-state.

Crutzen, P. J. (2002), 'Geology of Mankind', *Nature*, 415: 23.

Cusset, F. (2008), *French Theory: How Foucault, Derrida, Deleuze, & Co. Transformed the Intellectual Life of the United States*, trans. J. Fort, J. Berganza and M. Jones, Minneapolis: University of Minnesota Press.

Danowski, D. and E. Viveiros de Castro (2016), *The Ends of the World*, Cambridge: Polity.

Danto, A. C. (1965), *Analytical Philosophy of History*, Cambridge: Cambridge University Press.

Danto, A. C. (1967), 'Letter Responding to Hexter's Review', *The New York Review of Books*, 18 May 1967, 41–2.

Danto, A. C. (1983), *The Transfiguration of the Commonplace: A Philosophy of Art*, Cambridge, MA: Harvard University Press.

Daston, L. (1995), 'The Moral Economy of Science', *Osiris*, 10 (1): 2–24.

Daston, L. and H. O. Sibum (2003), 'Introduction: Scientific Personae and Their Histories', *Science in Context*, 16 (1–2): 1–8.

Daston, L. and P. Galison (2007), *Objectivity*, New York: Zone Books.

Davidson, D. (1963), 'Actions, Reasons and Causes', *Journal of Philosophy*, 60 (23): 685–700.

Davidson, D. (1963), 'Actions, Reasons and Causes', Reprinted in A. R. White (ed.), *The Philosophy of Action*, 79–94, London: Oxford University Press, 1968, .

Davis, N. Z. (1978), 'Women on Top: Symbolic Sexual Inversion and Political Disorder in Early Modern Europe', in B. A. Babcock (ed.), *The Reversible World: Symbolic Inversion in Art and Society*, 147–90, Ithaca, NY: Cornell University Press.

Day, M. (2008a), 'Our Relations with the Past', *Philosophia*, 36: 417–27.

Day, M. (2008b), *The Philosophy of History: An Introduction*, London: Continuum.

'Declaration on European Identity', Copenhagen, 14 December 1973, Bulletin of the European Community, no. 12, Luxembourg. Available at https://www.cvce.eu/obj/declaration_on_european_identity_copenhagen_14_december_1973-en-02798dc9-9c69-4b7d-b2c9-f03a8db7da32.html (accessed 25 March 2019).

DeLanda, M. (2006), *A New Philosophy of Society: Assemblage Theory and Social Complexity*, London: Continuum.

Delanty, G. (1997), *Social Science: Beyond Constructivism and Realism*, Buckingham: University of Minnesota Press.

Deleuze, G. and F. Guattari (1987), *A Thousand Plateaus, Capitalism and Schizophrenia*, Minneapolis: University of Minneapolis Press.

Demos, T. J. (2013), *The Migrant Image: The Art and Politics of Documentary During Global Crisis*, Durham and London: Duke University Press.

Dening, G. (2007), 'Performing Cross-Culturally', in Keith Jenkins, Sue Morgan and Alun Munslow (eds), *Manifestos for History*, London: Routledge.

Denzin, N. K. and Y. S. Lincoln, eds (2005), 'Part III: Strategies of Inquiry', in *The Sage Handbook of Qualitative Research*, 3rd ed., 375–640, Thousand Oaks: Sage Publications.

De Regt, H. W. (2017), *Understanding Scientific Understanding*, Oxford: Oxford University Press.

Derrida, J. (1967a), *L'Écriture et la Différence*, Paris: Éditions de Seuil.

Derrida, J. (1967b), *De la Grammatologie*, Paris: Les Editions de Minuit.

Derrida, J. (1972a), 'Différance', in *Marges de la philosophie*, Paris: Les editions de minuit.

Derrida, J. (1972b), *Positions*, Paris: Les Éditions de Minuit.

Derrida, J. (1972c), 'Signature Événement Contexte', in *Marges de la philosophie*, Paris: Les editions de minuit.

Derrida, J. (1978), *Writing and Difference*, trans. Alan Bass, Chicago: University of Chicago Press.

Derrida, J. (1982), *Margins of Philosophy*, trans. Alan Bass, Chicago: University of Chicago Press.

Derrida, J. (1988), *Limited, Inc.*, 'Signature Event Context', trans. S. Weber and J. Mehlman, Evanston: Northwestern University Press, 1988.

Derrida, J. (1995), *Mal d'archive*, Paris: Galilée.

Derrida, J. (1997), *Of Grammatology*, trans. G. C. Spivak, Baltimore: Johns Hopkins University Press.

Derrida, J. (1998), *Archive Fever*, trans. E. Prenowitz, Chicago: University of Chicago Press.

Derrida, J. (2002a), 'Derelictions of the Right to Justice (But What Are the '*Sans-Papiers*' Lacking?)' 133–44, in E. Rottenberg (trans. and ed.), *Negotiations: Interventions and Interviews, 1971–2001*, Stanford: Stanford University Press.

Derrida, J. (2002b), *Positions*, 2nd edn, trans. A. Bass, New York: Continuum.

Derrida, J. (2006), *Specters of Marx*, trans. P. Kamuf, New York: Routledge.

Descartes, R. ([1641] 2008), *Meditations on First Philosophy*, Oxford: Oxford University Press.

Detre, L. A. (2004), 'Immigration Advertising and the Canadian Government's Policy for Prairie Development, 1896 to 1918', PhD diss., The University of Maine, Orono.

DeVries, W. (2005), *Wilfrid Sellars*, London: Routledge.

Dick, K. and A. Z. Kofman, eds (2005), *Derrida: Screenplay and Essays on the Film*, Manchester: Manchester University Press.

Dickens, C. (1995), *A Christmas Carol and Other Stories*, New York: Modern Library.

Dillmann, E. (1891), *Eine neue Darstellung der Leibnizschen Monadenlehre auf Grund der Quellen*, Leipzig: Perthes.

Domańska, E. (2010a), 'Beyond Anthropocentrism in Historical Studies', *Historein*, 10: 118–30.

Domańska, E. (2010b), 'Problematizing Comparative Historical Studies', *Taiwan Journal of East Asian Studies*, 7 (1): 71–85.

Domańska, E. (2012), 'Metodologia praktyczna' [Practical Methodology], in E. Domańska, *Historia egzystencjalna. Krytyczne studium narratywizmu i humanistyki zaangażowanej* [Existential History: Critical Approach to Narrativism and Emancipatory Humanities], 161–83, Warszawa: PWN.

Domańska, E. (2013), 'Wiedza o przeszłości – perspektywy na przyszłość' [Knowledge of the Past: Future Perspectives], *Kwartalnik Historyczny*, CXX (2): 221–74.

Domańska, E. (2017), 'Animal History', *History and Theory*, 56 (2): 267–87.

Domańska , E. (2018a), 'Posthumanist History', in Marek Tamm and Peter Burke (eds), *Debating New Approaches to History*, 327–38, London: Bloomsbury.

Domańska, E. (2018b), 'The Eco-ecumene and Multispecies History: The Case of Abandoned Protestant Cemeteries in Poland', in Suzanne E. Pilaar Birch (ed.), *Multispecies Archaeology*, 118–32, London and New York: Routledge.

Domski, M. and M. Dickson (2010), 'Introduction: Discourse on a New Method, or a Manifesto for a Synthetic Approach to History and Philosophy of Science', in M. Domski and M. Dickson (eds), *Discourse on a New Method: Reinvigorating the Marriage of History and Philosophy of Science*, 1–20, Chicago: Open Court.

Donagan, A. (1969), 'Alternative Historical Explanations and Their Verification', *The Monist*, 53 (1): 58–89.

Donagan, A. (1970), 'Can Philosophers Learn from Historians?' in H. E. Kiefer and M. K. Munitz (eds), *Mind, Science, and History*, 234–50, Albany, NY: State University of New York Press.

Donovan, A., L. Laudan and R. Laudan (1992), 'Introduction to the Johns Hopkins Edition', in A. Donovan, L. Laudan and R. Laudan (eds), *Scrutinizing Science: Empirical Studies of Scientific Change*, 2nd edn, xi–xxiv, Baltimore, MD: Johns Hopkins University Press.

D'Oro, G. (2015), 'History and Idealism: Collingwood and Oakeshott', in J. Malpas and H. H. Gander (eds), *The Routledge Companion to Hermeneutics*, 191–204, London and New York: Routledge.

D'Oro, G. (2018), 'The Touch of King Midas: Collingwood on Why Actions Are Not Events', *Philosophical Explorations*, 21 (1): 1–10.

D'Oro, G. and C. Sandis (2013), 'From Anticausalism to Causalism and Back', in G. D'Oro and C. Sandis (eds), *Reasons Causes: Causalism and Anticausalism in the Philosophy of Action*, 7–48, Basingstoke: Plagrave Macmillan.

D'Oro, G., P. Giladi and A. Papazoglou (2019), 'Non-Reductivism and the Metaphilosophy of Mind', *Inquiry*, 62 (5): 477–503 in Non-Reductivism and the Metaphilosophy of Mind, special issue guest edited by G. D'Oro, P. Giladi and A. Papazoglou.
Dray, W. H. (1957), *Laws and Explanation in History*, Oxford: Clarendon Press.
Dray, W. H. (1963), 'The Historical Explanation of Actions Reconsidered', in S. Hook (ed.), *Philosophy and History*, New York: New York University Press.
Dray, W. H. (1964), *Philosophy of History*, Englewood Cliffs, NJ: Prentice-Hall.
Dray, W. H., ed. (1966), *Philosophical Analysis and History*, New York: Harper & Row.
Dray, W. H. (1978), 'Concepts of Causation in A. J. P. Taylor's Account of the Origins of the Second World War', *History and Theory*, 17 (2): 149–74.
Dray, W. H. (1989), *On History and Philosophy of History*, Leiden: E. J. Brill.
Dror, O. E. (2006), 'Fear and Loathing in the Laboratory and Clinic', in F. B. Alberti (ed.), *Medicine, Emotion and Disease, 1700–1950*, 125–43, Basingstoke: Palgrave Macmillan.
Droysen, J. G. (1893), *Outlines of the Principles of History*, trans. E. Benjamin Andrews, Boston: Ginn and CO.
Droysen, J. G. (1957), *Historik: Vorlesungen über enzyklopädie und methodologie der geschichte*, ed. Rudolph Hübner, Munich: R. Oldenbourg.
Dumouchel, P. (1991), 'Scrutinizing Science Scrutinized', *Inquiry*, 34 (4): 457–73.
Eden, A. H., J. H. Moor, J. H. Søraker and E. Steinhart, eds (2012), *Singularity Hypotheses: A Scientific and Philosophical Assessment*, Berlin and Heidelberg: Springer.
Elias, A. J. and C. Moraru (2015), *The Planetary Turn: Relationality and Geoaesthetics in the Twenty-First Century*, Evanston, IL: Northwestern University Press.
Elie, J. (2014), 'Histories of Refugee and Forced Migration Studies', in E. Fiddian-Qasmiyeh, G. Loescher, K. Long and N. Sigona (eds), *The Oxford Handbook of Refugee and Forced Migration Studies*, 23–35, Oxford: Oxford University Press.
Ellis, E. C. (2018), *Anthropocene: A Very Short Introduction*, Oxford: Oxford University Press.
Elton, G. R. (1991), *Return to Essentials: Some Reflections on the Present State of Historical Study*, Cambridge: Cambridge University Press.
Emmenegger, S. and A. Tschentscher, eds (1994), 'Taking Nature's Rights Seriously: The Long Way to Biocentrism in Environmental Law', theme issue, *Georgetown International Environmental Law Review*, 6 (3): 545–742.
The Encyclopedia of Saskatchewan [abbreviated as EncSK] (2005), Regina SK: University of Regina, Canadian Plains Research Center, https://esask.uregina.ca/.
Erdmann, K. D. (2005), *Toward a Global Community of Historians: The International Historical Congresses and the International Committee of Historical Sciences, 1898–2000*, trans. A. Nothnagle, 278–98, New York: Berghahn.

Escobar, A. (2007), 'The "Ontological Turn" in Social Theory', *Transactions of the Institute of British Geographies*, 32 (1): 106–11.
Evans, R. J. (1997), *In Defence of History*, London: Granta.
Farrier, D. (2019), *Anthropocene Poetics: Deep Time, Sacrifice Zones, and Extinction*, Minneapolis, London: University of Minnesota Press.
Fazal, S. (2015), *Desert Bloom*, Göttingen: Steidl.
Fiddian-Qasmiyeh, E., G. Loescher, K. Long and N. Sigona, eds (2014), *The Oxford Handbook of Refugee and Forced Migration Studies*, Oxford: Oxford University Press.
Fidelis, M. (2017), 'Right-Wing Populism and the New Morality: A Historical Reflection', *Aspen Review Central Europe*, (2): 60–7.
Figal, G. (2010), *Objectivity: The Hermeneutical and Philosophy*, trans. T. D. George, Albany, NY: State University of New York Press.
Figes, O. (2014), *Revolutionary Russia 1891–1991*, London: Pelican.
Fitz-Henry, E. (2017), 'Multiple Temporalities and the Nonhuman Other', *Environmental Humanities*, 9 (1): 1–17.
Førland, T. G., ed. (2017), *Values, Objectivity, and Explanation in Historiography*, New York and London: Routledge.
Foucault, M. (1984), 'Nietzsche, Genealogy, History', in P. Rabinow (ed.) and D. F. Bouchard and S. Simon (trans.), *The Foucault Reader*, 76–100, New York: Pantheon Books.
Foucault, M. (2002), *The Order of Things: An Archaeology of the Human Sciences*, London and New York: Routledge.
Fox, M. (1979), 'Jewish Agricultural Colonies in Saskatchewan with Special Reference to the Colonies of Sonnenfeld and Edenbridge', MA diss., The Faculty of Graduate Studies and Research, University of Regina.
Friesen, G. (1984), *The Canadian Prairies: A History*, Toronto: Toronto University Press.
Friesen, G. (2019 [2006]), 'History of Settlement in the Canadian Prairies', in *The Canadian Encyclopedia*. Historica Canada. Article published 7 February 2006; Last Edited 23 December 2019. https://www.thecanadianencyclopedia.ca/en/article/prairie-west
Fudge, E. (2017), 'What Was It Like to Be a Cow? History and Animal Studies', in L. Kalof (ed.), *The Oxford Handbook of Animal Studies*, 258–78, Oxford: Oxford University Press.
Fuery, P. and N. Mansfield, eds (1997), *Cultural Studies and the New Humanities: Concepts and Controversies*, Melbourne: Oxford University Press.
Fukuyama, F. (1992), *The End of History and the Last Man*, New York: Avon Books.
Fuller, S. and V. Lipinska (2014), *The Proactionary Imperative: A Foundation for Transhumanism*, Basingstoke: Palgrave Macmillan.
Galison, P. (1997), *Image and Logic: A Material Culture of Microphysics*, Chicago: University of Chicago Press.
Galison, P. (2010), 'Trading with the Enemy', in M. E. Gorman (ed.), *Trading Zones and Interactional Expertise: Creating New Kinds of Collaboration*, 25–52, Cambridge, MA: MIT Press.

Gallie, W. B. (1952), *Peirce and Pragmatism*, Harmondsworth: Penguin.
Gallie, W. B. (1964), *Philosophy and the Historical Understanding*, London: Chatto & Windus.
Gardiner, P. (1952), *The Nature of Historical Explanation*, London: Oxford University Press.
Gardiner, P. (1959), 'Recent Views Concerning Historical Knowledge and Explanation: Introduction', in P. Gardiner (ed.), *Theories of History*, New York: The Free Press, 265–74.
Gardiner, P. (1981), *The Philosophy of History*, Oxford: Oxford University Press.
Gatrell, P. (2007), 'Population Displacement in the Baltic Region in the Twentieth Century: From 'Refugee Studies' to Refugee History', *Journal of Baltic Studies*, 38 (1): 43–60.
Gatrell, P. (2013), *The Making of the Modern Refugee*, Oxford: Oxford University Press.
Geach, P. and M. Black, eds (1966), *Translations from the Philosophical Writings of Gottlob Frege*, Oxford: Basil Blackwell.
'Geography of Canada' (2019), https://en.wikipedia.org/wiki/Geography_of_Canada.
Gershoy, L. (1963), 'Some Problems of a Working Historian', in S. Hook (ed.), *Philosophy and History: A Symposium*, 59–75, New York: New York University Press.
Gettier, E. L. (1963), 'Is Justified True Belief Knowledge?' *Analysis*, 23: 121–3.
Gibbons, A. (2017), 'Postmodernism Is Dead. What Comes Next?' *TLS online* (The Times Literary Supplement), 12 June 12, available online: https://www.the-tls.co.uk/articles/public/postmodernism-dead-comes-next/ (accessed 20 August 2019).
Giere, R. N. (1973), 'History and Philosophy of Science: Intimate Relationship or Marriage of Convenience?', *British Journal for the Philosophy of Science*, 24 (3): 282–97.
Giere, R. N. (2012), 'History and Philosophy of Science: Thirty-Five Years Later', in S. Mauskopf and T. Schmaltz (eds), *Integrating History and Philosophy of Science: Problems and Prospects*, 59–65, Dordrecht: Springer.
Goering, T. (2013), 'Concepts, History and the Game of Giving and Asking for Reasons: A Defense of Conceptual History', *Journal of the Philosophy of History*, 7 (3): 426–52.
Goldstein, L. J. (1976), *Historical Knowing*, Austin and London: University of Texas Press.
Gooday, G. (2006), 'History and Philosophy of Science at Leeds', *Notes and Records of the Royal Society*, 60 (2): 183–92.
Gordon, P. H., Dr. (2018), Personal Communication (e-mail), February 20.
Gorman, J. L. (2008), *Historical Judgement: The Limits of Historiographical Choice*, Montréal: McGill-Queen's University Press.
Greenblatt, S. (1991), 'Resonance and Wonder', in I. Karp and S. D. Lavine (eds), *Exhibiting Cultures: The Poetics and Politics of Museum Display*, 42–56, Washington, DC: Smithsonian Institution Press.
Grinspoon, D. (2016), *Earth in Human Hands: Shaping Our Planet's Future*, New York and Boston: Grand Central Publishing.

Gronlid and District Historical Society [Gronlid] (1991), *Our Courageous Pioneers*, Melfort SK: Phillips.

Guba, E. G. and Y. S. Lincoln (2005), 'Paradigmatic Controversies, Contradictions, and Emerging Confluences', in N. K. Denzin and Y. S. Lincoln (eds), *The Sage Handbook of Qualitative Research*, 191–216, Thousand Oaks: Sage.

Guldi, J. and D. Armitage (2014), *The History Manifesto*, Cambridge: Cambridge University Press.

Haimovitch, M. (2014), 'A Journey to Saskatchewan's Jewish Past', *The Jerusalem Post*, December 21.

Hales, S. D. and T. A. Johnson (2003), 'Endurantism, Perdurantism and Special Relativity', *The Philosophical Quarterly*, 53 (213): 524–39.

Hall, D. (2007), 'Clifford Sifton's Vision of the Prairie West', in R. D. Francis and C. Kitzan (eds), *The Prairie West as Promised Land*, Calgary, AB: University of Calgary Press, 77–100.

Hamilakis, Y. and N. J. Overton (2013), 'A Multi-Species Archaeology', *Archaeological Dialogues*, 20 (2): 159–73.

Hamilton, C. (2017), *Defiant Earth: The Fate of Humans in the Anthropocene*, Cambridge: Polity Press.

Hammond, M. (1977), 'Weighing Causes in Historical Explanation', *Theoria*, 43 (2): 103–28.

Hammond, K. (2007), 'Palestinian Universities and the Israeli Occupation', *Policy Futures in Education*, 5 (2): 264–70.

Handel, A. (2011), 'Exclusionary Surveillance and Spatial Uncertainty in the Occupied Palestinian Territories', in E. Zureik, D. Lyon and Y. Abu-Laban (eds), *Surveillance and Control in Israel/Palestine: Population Territory, and Power*, 268–71, London: Routledge.

Harari, Y. N. (2017), *Homo Deus: A Brief History of Tomorrow*, New York: Harper.

Haraway, D. (1988), 'Situated Knowledges: The Science Question in Feminism and the Privilege of Partial Perspective', *Feminist Studies*, 14 (3): 575–99.

Harding, S. (1993), 'Rethinking Standpoint Epistemology: What Is "Strong Objectivity"?', in L. Alcoff and E. Potter (eds), *Feminist Epistemologies*, 49–82, New York and London: Routledge.

Harrell-Bond, B. E. (1986), *Imposing Aid: Emergency Assistance to Refugees*, Oxford: Oxford University Press.

Hart, H. L. A. and T. Honoré (1985), *Causation in the Law*, 2nd edn, Oxford: Claredon Press.

Hart, M. A. (2010), 'Indigenous Worldviews, Knowledge, and Research: The Development of an Indigenous Research Paradigm', *Journal of Indigenous Voices in Social Research*, 1 (1): 1–16.

Hartog, F. (2015), *Regimes of Historicity: Presentism and Experiences of Time*, trans. S. Brown, New York: Columbia University Press.

Harvey, G. (2006), *Animism: Respecting the Living World*, New York: Columbia University Press.

Hass, A. (2019), 'Transfer of Palestinians in Word and Deed', *Haaretz*, 12 June, https://www.haaretz.com/opinion/.premium-transfer-of-palestinians-in-word-and-deed-1.5465292, accessed 12 June 2019.

Hegel, G. W. H. (1970), *Hegel's Philosophy of Nature*, ed. and trans. M. J. Petry, 3 vols, London: Allen & Unwin.

Heidegger, M. ([1927] 1962), *Being and Time*, New York: Harper & Row.

Heith, A. (2015), 'Enacting Colonised Space: Katarina Pirak Sikku and Anders Sunna', *Nordisk Museologi*, 2: 69–83.

Heller, C. and L. Pezzani (2014), *Liquid Traces - The Left-to-Die-Boat Case*, https://forensic-architecture.org/investigation/the-left-to-die-boat, accessed 18 May 2020.

Hempel, C. G. (1942), 'The Function of General Laws in History', *The Journal of Philosophy*, 39 (2): 35–48.

Hexter, J. H. (1967a), 'The One That Got Away', *The New York Review of Books*, 9 February 1967, 24–8.

Hexter, J. H. (1967b), 'Reply to Morton White', *The New York Review of Books*, 23 March 1967, 29–31.

Hexter, J. H. (1968), 'The Rhetoric of History', in his *Doing History*, 15–76, London: George Allen & Unwin, 1971.

Hodder, I. (2012), *Entangled: An Archaeology of the Relationships Between Humans and Things*, Chichester, West Sussex and Malden, MA: Wiley-Blackwell.

Holbraad, M. and M. A. Pedersen (2017), *The Ontological Turn: An Anthropological Exposition*, Cambridge: Cambridge University Press.

Honkani, K. (2005), '"It Is Historically Constituted": Historicism in Feminist Constructivist Arguments', *European Journal of Women's Studies*, 12: 281–95.

Hörl, E. and J. Burton, eds (2017), *General Ecology: The New Ecological Paradigm*, London and New York: Bloomsbury Academic.

Hryniuk, M. and F. Korvemaker, photography by L. Easton [Hrynium et al.] (2014), *Legacy of Worship: Sacred Places in Rural Saskatchewan*, Regina: Coteau Books.

Huizinga, J. (1920), 'Het Historisch Museum', *Die gids: nieuwe vaderlandsche letteroefeningen*, 84 (1): 251–62.

Hume, D. (1739), *A Treatise of Human Nature*, Selby-Bigge edn, Oxford: Clarendon Press, 1888.

Illich, I. (1973), *Tools for Conviviality*, New York: Harper & Row.

Inkpen, R. and D. Turner (2012), 'The Topography of Historical Contingency', *Journal of the Philosophy of History*, 6 (1): 1–19.

Jacir, E. (2001–2003), *Where We Come from* installation.

Jacir, E. (2003a), *Crossing Surda (a record of going to and from work)* video.

Jacir, E. (2003b), *ENTRY DENIED (A Concert in Jerusalem)* installation.

Jacir, E., S. Rollig and G. Rückert, eds (2004), *Emily Jacir: Belongings. Arbeiten/Works 1998-2003*, Wein: Folio Verlag.

Jacobs, J. A. (2013), *In Defense of Disciplines: Interdisciplinarity and Specialization in the Research University*, Chicago: University of Chicago Press.

James, H. (2009), *The Creation and Destruction of Value: The Globalization Cycle*, Cambridge: Harvard University Press.

Jameson, F. (2010), *Utopia as Method or the Uses of the Future*, in M. D. Gordin, H. Tilley and G. Prakash (eds), *Utopia/Dystopia: Conditions of Historical Possibility*, 21–44, Princeton, NJ: Princeton University Press.

Jay, M. (1988), 'Scopic Regimes of Modernity', in H. Foster (ed.), *Vision and Visuality*, 3-29, Seattle: Bay Press.

Jenkins, K. (2003), *Refiguring History: New Thoughts on an Old Discipline*, London: Routledge.

Joad, C. E. M. (1944), *Philosophy*, London: The English Universities Press.

Jordheim, H. (2014), 'Introduction: Multiple Times and the Work of Synchronization', *History and Theory*, 53 (4): 498–518.

Jordheim, H. (2019), 'Return to Chronology', in M. Tamm and L. Olivier (eds), *Rethinking Historical Time: New Approaches to Presentism*, 43–56, London: Bloomsbury.

Jørgensen, D. (2014), 'Not by Human Hands: Five Technological Tenets for Environmental History', *Environment and History*, 20 (4): 479–89.

Jørgensen, D., F. A. Jørgensen and S. B. Pritchard, eds (2013), *New Natures: Joining Environmental History with Science and Technology Studies*, Pittsburgh: University of Pittsburgh Press.

Kac, E. (2000), 'GFP Bunny', in P. T. Dobrila and A. Kostic (eds), *Eduardo Kac: Telepresence, Biotelematics, and Transgenic Art*, 101–31, Maribor, Slovenia: Kibla.

Kac, E., ed. (2007), *Signs of Life: Bio Art and Beyond*, Cambridge, MA: MIT Press.

Kaldis, B. (2012), 'Worlds of Experience: Science', in E. Podoksik (ed.), *The Cambridge Companion to Oakeshott*, 64–85, Cambridge: Cambridge University Press.

Keller, C. (2018), *Political Theology of the Earth: Our Planetary Emergency and the Struggle for a New Public*, New York: Columbia University Press.

Kelley, M. J. and A. Rose, eds (2018), *Theories of History: History Read Across the Humanities*, London: Bloomsbury. .

Kennedy, R. and M. Nugent (2016), 'Scales of Memory: Reflections on an Emerging Concept', *Australian Humanities Review*, 59: 61–76.

Khamaisi, R. (2011), 'Territorial Dispossession and Population Control of the Palestinians', in E. Zureik, D. Lyon and Y. Abu-Laban (eds), *Surveillance and Control in Israel/Palestine: Population, Territory, and Power*, 335–53, London: Routledge.

Kholeif, O. (2013), 'Europa: Performance, Narration and Reconstitution', in E. Jacir and O. Kholeif (eds), *Emily Jacir: Europa*, 14–21, Munich: Prestel.

Kirksey, S. E. and S. Helmreich (2010), 'The Emergence of Multispecies Ethnography', *Cultural Anthropology*, 25 (4): 545–76.

Kleinberg, E. (2017), *Haunting History: For a Deconstructive Approach to the Past*, Stanford: Stanford University Press.

Kleinberg, E., J. W. Scott and G. Wilder (2018), *Theses on Theory and History*, Wild on Collective CCL, May 2018. https://theoryrevolt.com/.

Knorr-Cetina, K. D. (1981), *The Manufacture of Knowledge: An Essay on the Constructivist and Contextual Nature of Science*, Oxford: Pergamon Press.

Kochan, J. (2013), 'Subjectivity and Emotion in Scientific Research', *Studies in History and Philosophy of Science*, 44: 354–62.

Kofman, S. (1983), *Comment s'en sortir?*, Paris: Editions Galilée.

Köhler, P. (1913), *Der Begriff der Repräsentation bei Leibniz*, Bern: Verlag von A. Franke.

Kolb, D. (2008), 'Darwin Rocks Hegel: Does Nature Have a History?' *Bulletin of the Hegel Society of Great Britain* 29 (1–2): 97–117.

Kolb, D. (2011), 'Outside and In: Hegel on Natural History', *Poligrafi*, 16 (61–62): 27–42

Koselleck, R. (2002), 'On the Need for Theory in the Discipline of History', in T. S. Presner, K. Behnke and J. Welge (trans.), *The Practice of Conceptual History: Timing History, Spacing Concepts*, Foreword by Hayden White, 1–24, Stanford: Stanford University Press.

Kovch-Baran, A. M. and Ukrainian Catholic Council of Saskatchewan [Kovch-Baran] (1977), *Ukraïns'ki Katolyts'ki Tserkvy Saskachevanu = Ukrainian Catholic Churches of Saskatchewan*, translation into English by K. T. Pastershank, Saskatoon: Ukrainian Catholic Council of Saskatchewan.

Krämer, S. (1997), 'Kalküle als Repräsentation. Zur Genese des operativen Symbolismus in der Neuzeit', in H. J. Rheinberger, M. Hagner and B. Wahring-Schmidt (eds), *Räume des Wissens: Repräsentation, Codierung*, Spur, Berlin: De Gruyter.

Krüger, L. (1979), 'History and Philosophy of Science: A Marriage for the Sake of Reason', in *Abstracts*: 6th International Congress of Logic, Methodology, and Philosophy of Science: Hannover, 22–29 August 1979: Section 6, 108–12, s.l.: s.n.

Kuhn, T. S. (2012), *The Structure of Scientific Revolutions*, 2nd edn, Chicago: University of Chicago Press.

Kushner, T. and K. Knox (1999), *Refugees in an Age of Genocide: Global, National and Local Perspectives During the Twentieth Century*, London: Frank Cass.

Kuukkanen, J.-M. (2015), *Postnarrativist Philosophy of Historiography*, Basingstoke: Palgrave Macmillan.

Lakatos, I. (1971), 'History of Science and Its Rational Reconstructions', in R. S. Cohen and M. C. Wartofsky (eds), *PSA 1970; Boston Studies in the Philosophy and History of Science*, Vol. 8, 91–136. Dordrecht: Springer.

Lakatos, I. (1978), 'Introduction: Science and Pseudoscience', in J. Worrall and G. Currie (eds), *The Methodology of the Scientific Research Programmes*, Philosophical Papers, vol. 1, 1–7, Cambridge: Cambridge University Press.

Latour, B. (1993), *We Have Never Been Modern*, trans. C. Porter, Cambridge, MA: Harvard University Press.

Latour, B. (1999), *Pandora's Hope: Essays on the Reality of Science Studies*, Cambridge, MA and London: Harvard University Press.

Latour, B. (2005), *Reassembling the Social: An Introduction to Actor-Network-Theory*, Oxford: Oxford University Press.

Latour, B. (2009), 'Perspectivism: "Type" or "Bomb"', *Anthropology Today*, 25 (2): 1–2.

Latour, B. (2017a), *Facing Gaia: Eight Lectures on the New Climate Regime*, Cambridge: Polity Press.

Latour, B. (2017b), 'Anthropology at the Time of the Anthropocene: A Personal View of What Is to Be Studied', in M. Brightman and J. Lewis (eds), *The Anthropology of Sustainability: Beyond Development and Progress*, 35–49, New York: Palgrave Macmillan.

Latour, B. (2018), *Down to Earth: Politics in the New Climatic Regime*, trans. C. Porter, Cambridge: Polity Press.

Latour, B. and S. Woolgar (1979), *Laboratory Life: The Social Construction of Scientific Facts*, London: Sage.

Latour, B. and T. M. Lenton (2019), 'Extending the Domain of Freedom, or Why Gaia Is So Hard to Understand', *Critical Inquiry*, 45 (3): 659–80.

Laudan, L. (1989), 'Thoughts on HPS: Twenty Years Later', *Studies in the History and Philosophy of Science*, 20 (1): 9–13.

Laudan, L., A. Donovan, R. Laudan, P. Barker, H. Brown, J. Leplin, P. Thagard and S. Wykstra (1986), 'Scientific Change: Philosophical Models and Historical Research', *Synthese*, 69: 141–223.

Lears, J. (2010), *Rebirth of a Nation: The Making of Modern America, 1877–1920*, New York: Harper Perennial.

LeCain, T. (2016), 'Heralding a New Humanism: The Radical Implications of Chakrabarty's "Four Theses"', in 'Whose Anthropocene? Revisiting Dipesh Chakrabarty's "Four Theses"', R. Emmett and T. Lekan (eds), *RCC Perspectives: Transformations in Environment and Society*, 2: 15–20.

Leibniz, G. W. (1966), *Hauptschriften zur Grundlegung der Philosophie. Band II*, Hamburg: Felix Meiner Verlag.

Leibniz, G. W. (1969), *Essai de Théodicée. Sur la Bonté de Dieu, la liberté de l'Homme et l'Orgine du Mal. Chronologie et introduction par J. Brunschwig*, Paris: Flammarion.

Leibniz, G. W. (1976), *Philosophical Papers and Letters: A Selection Translated and Edited, with an Introduction by L. E. Loemker*, Dordrecht and Boston: Reidl Publishing Company.

Lewis, D. (1986), *Philosophical Papers*, vol. II, New York: Oxford University Press.

Lewis, D. (2004), 'Causation as Influence', in J. Collins, E. Hall and L. Paul (eds), *Causation and Counterfactuals*, 75–106, Cambridge, MA: MIT Press.

Lewis, S. L. and M. A. Maslin (2015), 'Defining the Anthropocene', *Nature*, 519 (7542): 175–6.

Lewis, S. L. and M. A. Maslin (2018), *The Human Planet: How We Created the Anthropocene*, London: Penguin.

Livingstone, D. N. (2003), *Putting Science in Its Place: Geographies of Scientific Knowledge*, Chicago: University of Chicago Press.

Loescher, G. and J. A. Scanlan (1986), *Calculated Kindness: Refugees and America's Half-Open Door, 1945 to the Present*, New York: Free Press.
Lorenz, C. (1994), 'Historical Knowledge and Historical Reality: A Plea for "Internal Realism"', *History and Theory*, 33 (3): 297–327.
Lorenz, C. (2012), 'If You're So Smart, Why Are You Under Surveillance? Universities, Neoliberalism, and New Public Management', *Critical Inquiry*, 38 (3): 599–629.
Lorimer, J. (2017), 'The Anthropo-scene: A Guide for the Perplexed', *Social Studies of Science*, 47 (1): 117–42.
Lury, C., S. Kember and M. Fraser, eds (2006), *Inventive Life: Approaches to the New Vitalism*, London: Sage.
Maar, A. (2016), 'Applying D. K. Lewis's Counterfactual Theory of Causation to the Philosophy of Historiography', *Journal of the Philosophy of History*, 10 (3): 349–69.
Mahnke, D. (1925), *Leibnizens Synthese von Universalmathematik und Individualmetaphysik*, Halle: Friedrich Frommann Verlag.
Maier, S. (1990), *Saskatchewan Local History Directory: A Locality Guide to Community and Church Histories in the Prairie History Room*, Regina, SK: Regina Public Library.
Malcom, N. (1968), 'The Conceivability of Mechanism', *Philosophical Review*, 77 (1): 45–72.
Malm, A. (2019), 'Against Hybridism: Why We Need to Distinguish Between Nature and Society, Now More than Ever', *Historical Materialism*, 27 (2): 156–87.
Mandel, M. S. (2003), *In the Aftermath of Genocide: Armenians and Jews in Twentieth-Century France*, Durham, NC: Duke University Press.
Mantu, S. (2018), '"Terrorist" Citizens and the Human Right to Nationality', *Journal of Contemporary European Studies*, 26 (1): 28–41.
Marcellinia, A., S. Fereza, D. Issanchoua, E. De Léséleuca and M. McNamee (2012), 'Challenging Human and Sporting Boundaries: The Case of Oscar Pistorius', *Performance Enhancement & Health*, 1 (1): 3–9.
Marfleet, P. (2007), 'Refugees and History: Why We Must Address the Past', *Refugee Survey Quarterly*, 26 (3): 136–48.
Markie, P. (2017). 'Rationalism vs. Empiricism,' *The Stanford Encyclopedia of Philosophy* (Fall 2017 Edition), E. N. Zalta (ed.), https://plato.stanford.edu/archives/fall2017/entries/rationalism-empiricism/.
Marrus, M. (2002), *The Unwanted: European Refugees in the Twentieth Century*, Philadelphia: Temple University Press.
Martin, R. (1989), *The Past Within Us: An Empirical Approach to Philosophy of History*, Princeton: Princeton University Press.
Martin, R. (1997), 'The Essential Difference Between History and Science', *History and Theory*, 36 (1): 1–14.
Martin, R. (1998), 'Progress in Historical Studies', *History and Theory*, 37 (1): 14–39.
Masalha, N., ed. (2005), *Catastrophe Remembered: Palestine, Israel and the Internal Refugees*, London: Zed Books.

Masalha, N. (2012), *The Palestine Nakba: Decolonising History, Narrating the Subaltern, Reclaiming Memory*, 229–33, London: Zed Books, https://en.wikipedia.org/wiki/Present_absentee, accessed 30 July 2019.

Mason, R. (2003), *Understanding Understanding*, Albany, NY: State University of New York Press.

Matthews, M. R. (1994), *Science Teaching: The Role of History and Philosophy of Science*, New York: Routledge.

Mazzara, F. (2019), *Reframing Migration: Lampedusa, Border Spectacle and Aesthetics of Subversion*, Oxford: Peter Lang.

Mbembe, A. (2003), 'Necropolitics', *Public Culture*, 15 (1): 11–40.

McAllister, J. W. (2018), 'Using History as Evidence in Philosophy of Science: A Methodological Critique', *Journal of the Philosophy of History*, 12 (2): 239–58.

McMullin, E. (1976), 'History and Philosophy of Science: A Marriage of Convenience?' in R. S. Cohen, C. Hooker, A. C. Michalos and J. Van Evra (eds), PSA *1974: Proceedings of the 1974 Biannual Meeting Philosophy of Science Association*, 585–601, Dordrecht: D. Reidel.

McNeill, J. R. (2010), *Mosquito Empires: Ecology and War in the Greater Caribbean, 1620–1914*, New York: Cambridge University Press.

Meijl, T. van (2019), 'Doing Indigenous Epistemology: Internal Debates About Inside Knowledge in Māori Society', *Current Anthropology*, 60 (2): 155–73.

Meyerhoff, H., ed. (1959), *The Philosophy of History in Our Time: An Anthology*, New York: Doubleday.

Michael, C. (2018), '"Will I Have Existed?" The Unprecedented Plan to Move an Arctic City', *The Guardian*, 2 December, https://www.theguardian.com/cities/2018/dec/02/kiruna-swedish-arctic-town-had-to-move-reindeer-herders-in-the-way, accessed 15 March 2019.

Michaelian, K. (2017), 'Episodic Imagination and Episodic Memory: What's the Difference?' https://junkyardofthemind.com/blog/2017/4/2/jbyv7ktlim6k466y0zh2bvfd1iw85i. Posted 5 April 2017. Accessed 8 April 2018.

Michelet, J. (1869), 'Preface to the History of France (1869)', in F. Kimmich, L. Gossman (trans.) and E. K. Kaplan (eds), Michelet, *On History*, L. Gossman, Cambridge: Open Book Publishers, 2013, 139–61, http://doi.org/10.11647/OBP.0036.

Mihesuah, D. A. and A. C. Wilson, eds (2004), *Indigenizing the Academy: Transforming Scholarship and Empowering Communities*, Lincoln: University of Nebraska Press.

Miller, R. E. and K. Spellmeyer, eds (2008), *The New Humanities Reader*, 3rd edn, Boston & New York: Houghton MIfflin.

Mink, L. O. (1987), *Historical Understanding*, eds B. Fay, E. O. Golob and R. T. Vann, Ithaca: Cornell University Press.

More, M. (2013), 'The Philosophy of Transhumanism', in M. More and N. Vita-More (eds), *The Transhumanist Reader*, 3–17, Malden, MA: Wiley-Blackwell.

Müller, P. (2019), *Geschichte machen: Historisches Forschen und die Politik der Archive*, Göttingen: Wallstein.

Murdoch, D. (2009), 'Descartes: The Real Distinction', in R. Le Poidevin, P. Simons, A McGonical and R. P. Cameron (eds), *The Routledge Companion to Metaphysics*, 68–77, Abingdon: Routledge.

Nagel, T. (1974), 'What Is It Like to Be a Bat?', *The Philosophical Review*, 83 (4): 435–50.

Nayler, S. (2005), 'Introduction: Historical Geographies of Science: Places, Contexts, Cartographies', *British Journal for the History of Science*, 38 (1): 1–12.

Nievergelt, O. (2018), 'Die Idee geschichtswissenschaftlicher Objektivität: Eine tugendepistemologische Erkundung', PhD thesis, ETH Zürich.

Norton, C. and M. Donnelly (2016), 'Thinking the Past Politically: Palestine, Power and Pedagogy', *Rethinking History*, 20 (2): 192–216.

Novick, P. (1988), *That Noble Dream: The 'Objectivity Question' and the American Historical Profession*, Cambridge: Cambridge University Press.

Nyers, P. (2006), *Rethinking Refugees: Beyond States of Emergency*, Abingdon: Routledge.

Oakeshott, M. (1933), *Experience and Its Modes*, Cambridge: Cambridge University Press.

Oakeshott, M. ([1962] 1991), 'The Activity of Being a Historian', in his *Rationalism in Politics and Other Essays*, 151–84, London and New York: Liberty Fund. Originally London: Methuen, 1962.

Oakeshott, M. (1975), *On Human Conduct*, Oxford: Oxford University Press.

Oakeshott, M. ([1983] 1999), 'Three Essays on History', in his *On History and Other Essays*, 1–129, Indianapolis: Liberty Fund. Originally Oxford: Blackwell, 1983.

O'Gorman, E. (2017), 'Imagined Ecologies: A More-Than-Human History of Malaria in the Murrumbidgee Irrigation Area, New South Wales, Australia, 1919–45', *Environmental History*, 22 (3): 486–514.

Ogden, L., B. Hall and K. Tanita (2013), 'Animals, Plants, People, and Things: A Review of Multispecies Ethnography', *Environment and Society*, 4 (1): 5–24.

Olsen, B. (2010), *In Defense of Things: Archaeology and the Ontology of Objects*, Lanham, MD: AltaMira Press.

Onaga, L. A. (2013), 'Bombyx and Bugs in Meiji Japan: Toward a Multispecies History?', *The Scholar & Feminist Online*, 3 (11). Available online: http://sfonline.barnard.edu/life-un-ltd-feminism-bioscience-race/bombyx-and-bugs-in-meiji-japan-toward-a-multispecies-history/ (accessed 7 May 2019).

Orange, R., 'Swedish Reindeer Herders win Historic Land Use Case', *The Telegraph*, 3 February 2016, https://www.telegraph.co.uk/news/worldnews/europe/sweden/12139166/Swedish-reindeer-herders-win-historic-land-use-case.html.

Otter, C., A. Bashford, J. L. Brooke, F. A. Jonsson and J. M. Kelly (2018), 'Roundtable: The Anthropocene in British History', *Journal of British Studies*, 57 (3): 568–96.

Otto, A. (1998), *Het ruisen van de tijd: over de theoretische geschiedenis van Jan Romein*, Amsterdam: Stichting Beheer IISG.

Patterson, C. (2002), *Eternal Treblinka: Our Treatment of Animals and the Holocaust*, London: Lantern Books.

Paul, L. A. (2000), 'Aspect Causation', *Journal of Philosophy*, 97 (4): 223–34.

Paul, H. (2011), 'Performing History: How Historical Scholarship Is Shaped by Epistemic Virtues', *History and Theory*, 50 (1): 1–19.

Paul, H. (2012), 'Weak Historicism: On Hierarchies of Intellectual Virtues and Goods', *Journal of the Philosophy of History*, 6 (3): 369–88.

Paul, H. (2015a), 'Relations to the Past: A Research Agenda for Historical Theorists', *Rethinking History*, 19 (3): 450–8.

Paul, H. (2015b), *Key Issues in Historical Theory*, New York: Routledge.

Paul, H. (2017), 'Weber, Wöhler, and Waitz: Virtue Language in Late Nineteenth-Century Physics, Chemistry, and History', in J. van Dongen and H. Paul (eds), *Epistemic Virtues in the Sciences and the Humanities*, 91–107, Cham: Springer.

Paul, H. and R. Read (2019), 'Geoengineering as a Response to the Climate Crisis: Right Road or Disastrous Diversion?', in J. Forster (ed.), *Facing Up to Climate Reality: Honesty, Disaster and Hope*, 109–30, London: Green House.

Pérez Triviño, J. L. (2013), 'Cyborgsportpersons: Between Disability and Enhancement', *Physical Culture and Sport: Studies and Research*, 57: 12–21.

Pickering, A. (1999), 'The Mangle of Practice: Agency and Emergence in the Sociology of Science', *The American Journal of Sociology*, 99 (3): 559–89.

Piercey, R. (2017), 'Narcissim or Facts? A Pragmatist Approach to the Philosophy of History', *Journal of the Philosophy of History*, 11 (2): 149–69.

Pierotti, R. and D. Wildcat (2000), 'Traditional Ecological Knowledge: The Third Alternative (Commentary)', *Ecological Applications*, 10 (5): 1333–40.

Pihlainen, K. (2017), *The Work of History: Constructivism and a Politics of the Past*, Abingdon: Routledge.

Pilaar, Birch, S. E. (2018), 'Introduction', in S. E. Pilaar Birch (ed.), *Multispecies Archaeology*, 1–7, London and New York: Routledge.

Pinnick, C. and G. Gale (2000), 'Philosophy of Science and History of Science: A Troubling Interaction', *Journal for General Philosophy of Science*, 31: 109–25.

Plotkin, A. L. (1960), *Struggle for Justice: The Autobiography of Abe. L. Plotkin*, New York: Exposition.

Plutarch (1960a), 'Life of Lysander', in I. Scott-Kilvert (trans.), *The Rise and Fall of Athens: Nine Greek Lives by Plutarch*, 287–319, London: Penguin.

Plutarch (1960b), 'Life of Themistocles', in Ian Scott-Kilvert (trans.), *The Rise and Fall of Athens: Nine Greek Lives by Plutarch*, 77–109, London: Penguin.

Polyakov, M. (2012), 'Practice Theories: The Latest Turn in Historiography?' *Journal of the Philosophy of History*, 6 (2): 218–35.

Pompa, L. (1975), *Vico: A Study of the 'New Science'*, Cambridge: Cambridge University Press.

Popper, K. R. (1957), *The Poverty of Historicism*, London: Routledge.

Porciani, I. (2009), 'Janus-Faced Clio: Gender in the Historical Profession in Europe', in C. Salvaterra and B. Waaldijk (eds), *Paths to Gender: European Historical Perspectives on Women and Men*, 11–30, Pisa: Pisa University Press.

Quine, W. V. O. (1951), 'Two Dogmas of Empiricism', reprinted in his *From A Logical Point of View*, 20–46, 2nd edn, New York: Harper and Row, 1961.
Quine, W. V. O. (1960), *Word and Object*, Cambridge, MA: The MIT Press.
Quine, W. V. (1971), *From a Logical Point of View: Logical-Philosophical Essays*, Cambridge, MA: Harvard University Press.
Railton, P. (1986), 'Moral Realism', *The Philosophical Review*, 95 (2): 163–207.
Ranisch, R. and S. L. Sorgner, eds (2014), *Post- and Transhumanism: An Introduction*, Frankfurt am Main et al.: Peter Lang.
Ranke, L. (1981), *The Secret of World History: Selected Writings on the Art and Science of History*, ed. R. Wines, New York: Fordham University Press.
Ranke, L. (2011), *The Theory and Practice of History*, ed. G. G. Iggers and trans. W. A. Iggers, London: Routledge.
Revel, J., ed. (1996), *Jeux d'échelles. La micro-analyse à l'éxpérience*, Paris: Gallimard and Seuil.
Ridgedale, Everything Changes but the Memories: Including Districts of Henderson, Old Ridgedale, Preston, Riverstone [Ridgedale] (1992), Ridgedale, SK: Ridgedale History Book Committee.
Riesch, H. (2014), 'Philosophy, History and Sociology of Science: Interdisciplinary Relations and Complex Social Identities', *Studies in History and Philosophy of Science*, 48: 30–7.
Robin, L. and W. Steffen (2007), 'History for the Anthropocene', *History Compass*, 5 (5): 1694–719.
Rockström, J., W. Steffen, K. Noone, Å. Persson, F. S. I. Chapin, E. Lambin, T. M. Lenton, M. Scheffer, C. Folke, H. J. Schellnhuber, B. Nykvist, C. A. de Wit, T. Hughes, S. van der Leeuw, H. Rodhe, S. Sörlin, P. K. Snyder, R. Costanza, U. Svedin, M. Falkenmark, L. Karlberg, R. W. Corell, V. J. Fabry, J. Hansen, B. Walker, D. Liverman, K. Richardson, P. Crutzen and J. Foley (2009), 'Planetary Boundaries: Exploring the Safe Operating Space for Humanity', *Ecology and Society*, 14 (2): art. 32.
Rifkin, J. (1980), *Entropy: A New World View*, New York: Viking Press.
Rorty, R. (1980), *Philosophy and the Mirror of Nature*, Oxford: Blackwell.
Rorty, R. (1989), *Contingency, Irony and Solidarity*, Cambridge: Cambridge University Press.
Rorty, R. (1991), *Objectivity, Relativism, and Truth*, Cambridge: Cambridge University Press.
Rorty, R. (1999), *Philosophy and Social Hope*, New York: Penguin Books.
Rosa, H. (2013), *Social Acceleration: A New Theory of Modernity*, trans. J. Trejo-Mathys, New York: Columbia University Press.
Rose, N. (2007), *The Politics of Life Itself: Biomedicine, Power, and Subjectivity in the Twenty-First Century*, Princeton and Oxford: Princeton University Press.
Rosenberg, N., ed. (1980), *Edenbridge, The Memory Lives On..... A History*, research material provided by N. Vickar, Melfort SK: Phillips.

Rosenberg, L. (1993 [1939]), *Canada's Jews: A Social and Economic Study of Jews in Canada in the 1930s*, ed. M. Weinfeld, Foreword by S. M. Lipset, Montreal, Kingston: McGill-Queen's University Press.

Roy, G. (1982 [1978]), *The Fragile Lights of Earth, Articles and Memories, 1942–1970*, trans. A. Brown, Toronto: McClelland and Stewart.

Rubinoff, L. (1991), 'Introduction: W. H. Dray and the Critique of Historical Thinking', in W. J. van der Dussen and L. Rubinoff (eds), *Objectivity, Method and Point of View: Essays in the Philosophy of History*, 1–11, Leiden: E. J. Brill.

Runia, E. (2006), 'Presence', *History and Theory*, 45 (1): 1–29.

Runia, E. (2014), *Moved by the Past*, New York: Columbia University Press.

Runia, E. and M. Tamm (2019), 'The Past Is Not a Foreign Country: A Conversation', *Rethinking History*, 23 (3): 403–33.

Russell, E. (2011), *Evolutionary History: Uniting History and Biology to Understand Life on Earth*, Cambridge: Cambridge University Press.

Rygiel, K. (2016), 'Dying to Live: Migrant Deaths and Citizenship Politics Along European Borders: Transgressions, Disruptions, and Mobilizations', *Citizenship Studies*, 20 (5): 545–60.

Sacco, J. (2009), *Footnotes in Gaza*, London: Jonathan Cape.

Saljooghi, A. (2009), 'From Palestine to Texas: Moving along with Emily Jacir', *Spectator*, 29 (1): 23–9.

Sandoval, C. (2000), *Methodology of the Oppressed*, London and Minneapolis: University of Minnesota Press.

Santayana, G. (1905), *The Life of Reason: The Phases of Human Progress*, New York: Dover.

Sapolsky, R. M. (2014), 'The Spirit of the 1914 Christmas Truce', *Wall Street Journal*, 19 December 2014.

Saussy, H. (2016), *The Ethnography of Rhythm: Orality and Its Technologies*, New York: Fordham.

Saval, N. (2017), 'Globalisation: The Rise and Fall of an Idea That Swept the World', *The Guardian*, 14 July 2017.

Savulescu, J. and N. Bostrom, eds (2009), *Human Enhancement*, Oxford: Oxford University Press.

Sawyer, S. W. (2015), 'Time after Time: Narratives of the Longue Durée in the Anthropocene', *Transatlantica. Revue d'études américaines*, 1: 1–17, available on-line: http://transatlantica.revues.org/7344 (accessed 7 May 2019).

Saxer, D. (2013), *Die Schärfung des Quellenblicks: Forschungspraktiken in der Geschichtswissenschaft 1840–1914*, Munich: Oldenbourg.

Sayre, N. F. (2012), 'The Politics of the Anthropogenic', *Annual Review of Anthropology*, 41: 57–70.

Schickore, J. (2011), 'More Thoughts on HPS: Another 20 Years Later', *Perspectives on Science*, 19 (4): 453–81.

Schickore, J. (2018), 'Explication Work for Science and Philosophy', *Journal of the Philosophy of History*, 12 (2): 191–211.

Schnicke, F. (2015), *Die männliche Disziplin: Zur Vergeschlechtlichung der deutschen Geschichtswissenschaft 1780-1900*, Göttingen: Wallstein.

Scholl, R. and T. Räz (2016), 'Towards a Methodology for Integrated History and Philosophy of Science', in T. Sauer and R. Scholl (eds), *The Philosophy of Historical Case Studies*, 69-91, Cham: Springer.

Schumann, G. (2019), 'Introduction', in G. Schumann (ed.), *Explanation in Action Theory and Historiography: Causal and Teleological Approaches*, 1-42, New York: Routledge.

Scott, J. (2005), 'The Evidence of Experience', reprinted in *Practicing History*, ed. G. Speigel, New York: Routledge. Originally published in *Critical Inquiry* (Summer 1991).

Sehon, S. (2005), *Teleological Realism: Mind, Agency, and Explanation*, Cambridge, MA: Bradford Book/MIT Press.

Sellars, W. (1956), 'Empiricism and the Philosophy of Mind', *Minnesota Studies in the Philosophy of Science*, 1: 253-329. Reprinted as *Empiricism and the Philosophy of Mind*, Cambridge MA: Harvard University Press, 1997.

Sellars, W. (1963), 'Philosophy and the Scientific Image of Man', in R. Colodny (ed.), *Science, Perception and Reality*, 7-43, Pittsburgh, PA: University of Pittsburgh Press.

Sellars, W. (2007), *In the Space of Reasons: Selected Essays of Wilfrid Sellars*, eds K. Sharp and R. B. Brandom, Cambridge, MA: Harvard University Press.

Sheikh, F. (2015), *The Erasure Triology*, 3. vol. Memory Trace; Desert Bloom; Independence/Nakba, Göttingen: Steidl.

Sheikh, F. and E. Weizman (2015), *The Conflict Shoreline*, Göttingen: Steidl.

Shryock, A. and D. L. Smail, eds (2011), *Deep History: The Architecture of Past and Present*, Berkeley: University of California Press.

Simon, Z. B. (2016), 'We Are History: The Outlines of a Quasi-Substantive Philosophy of History', *Rethinking History*, 20 (2): 259-79.

Simon, Z. B. (2019a), *History in Times of Unprecedented Change: A Theory for the 21st Century*, London: Bloomsbury.

Simon, Z. B. (2019b), 'Two Cultures of the Posthuman Future', *History and Theory*, 58 (2): 171-84.

Simon, Z. B. (2020), 'The Limits of Anthropocene Narratives', *European Journal of Social Theory*, 23 (2): 184-99.

Skinner, Q. (1988), *Meaning and Context: Quentin Skinner and His Critics*, ed. and intro. James Tully, Princeton: Princeton University Press.

Smail, D. L. (2008), *On Deep History and the Brain*, Berkeley: University of California Press.

Smith, B. G. (1998), *The Gender of History: Men, Women, and Historical Practice*, Cambridge, MA: Harvard University Press.

Spier, F. (2015), *Big History and the Future of Humanity*, 2nd edn, Malden, MA, and Oxford: Blackwell.

Spivak, G. C. (1988), 'Can the Subaltern Speak?' in C. Nelson and L. Grossberg (eds), *Marxism and the Interpretation of Culture*, 271–317, Urbana and Chicago: University of Illinois Press.

Spivak, G. C. (2003), 'Planetarity', in her *Death of a Discipline*, 71–102, New York: Columbia University Press.

Stadler, F., ed. (2017), *Integrated History and Philosophy of Science: Problems, Perspectives, and Case Studies*, Cham: Springer.

Staples, K. (2012), *Retheorising Statelessness: A Background Theory of Membership in World Politics*, Edinburgh: Edinburgh University Press.

Stengers, I. (2015), *In Catastrophic Times: Resisting the Coming Barbarism*, Chicago, IL: Open Humanities Press.

Sterelny, K. (2007), *Dawkins vs. Gould: Survival of the Fittest*, 2nd edn, Cambridge: Icon Books.

Sterelny, K. (2016), 'Contingency and History', *Philosophy of Science*, 83 (4): 534–7.

Stern, F., ed. (1956), *The Varieties of History*, Cleveland: Meridian.

Strauss, G. (1991), 'The Dilemma of Popular History', *Past & Present*, 132 (August): 130–49.

Strauss, G. (1993), 'The Dilemma of Popular History: A Reply', *Past & Present*, 141 (November): 215–19.

Strauss, W. and N. Howe (1997), *The Fourth Turning: An American Prophecy – What the Cycles of History Tell Us About America's Next Rendezvous with Destiny*, New York: Broadway Books.

Sunna, A. (2014), *Area Infected*, http://anderssunna.com/, accessed 14 March 2019.

Sunna, A. (2017), *States*, http://anderssunna.com/2017-2/#!prettyPhoto[1]/http://anderssunna.com/wp-content/uploads/2017/09/states-2-1280x781.jpg, accessed 18 May 2020.

Sunna, A. (20 October 2018–6 January 2019), *The Moderna Exhibition 2018. With the Future Behind Us*, Stockholm: Moderna Museet.

Susen, S. (2015), *The Postmodern Turn in the Social Sciences*, Basingstoke: Palgrave Macmillan.

Swyripa, F. (2004), 'European Immigration, 1897–1929', in G. Hallowell (ed.), *Oxford Companion to Canadian History*, Don Mills, ON: Oxford University Press Canada.

Tallis, R. (2017), *Of Time and Lamentation: Reflection on Transience*, Newcastle upon Tyne: Agenda Publishing.

Tamm, M. (2018), 'Introduction: A Framework for Debating New Approaches to History', in M. Tamm and P. Burke (eds), *Debating New Approaches to History*, 1–19, London: Bloomsbury.

Tamm, M. and L. Olivier (2019), 'Introduction: Rethinking Historical Time', in M. Tamm and L. Olivier (eds), *Rethinking Historical Time: New Approaches to Presentism*, 1–20, London: Bloomsbury.

Tanney, J. (1995), 'Why Reasons May Not Be Causes', *Mind & Language*, 10 (1–2): 103–26.

Thomas, J. A. (2014), 'History and Biology in the Anthropocene: Problems of Scale, Problems of Value', *American Historical Review*, 119 (5): 1587–607.
Thompson, E. P. (1966), *The Making of the English Working Class*, New York: Vintage Books.
Thweatt-Bates, J. (2012), *Cyborg Selves: A Theological Anthropology of the Posthuman*, Farnham: Ashgate.
Toguo, B. (2012), *Purification*, London: Tate Modern, https://www.tate.org.uk/art/ar tworks/toguo-purification-t14012 (accessed 15 March 2019).
Tollebeek, J. (2008), *Fredericq & Zonen: een antropologie van de moderne geschiedwetenschap*, Amsterdam: Bert Bakker.
Tollebeek, J. (2015), 'Commemorative Practices in the Humanities Around 1900', *Advances in Historical Studies*, 4 (3): 216–31.
Torpey, J. C. (2003), 'Introduction. Politics and the Past', in J. C. Torpey (ed.), *Politics and the Past: On Repairing Historical Injustices*, 1–36, Lanham, MD: Rowman and Littlefield.
Tozzi, V. (2012), 'Pragmatist Contributions to a New Philosophy of History', *Pragmatism and Law*, 3 (1): 121–31.
Tran, V. T. and P. M. Noël (2018), 'For an Anthropology of Historians', *Ethnologies*, 40: 49–73.
Traweek, S. (1988), *Beamtimes and Lifetimes: The World of High Energy Physicists*, Cambridge, MA: Harvard University Press.
Trüper, H. (2014), *Topography of a Method: François Louis Ganshof and the Writing of History*, Tübingen: Mohr Siebeck.
Tsing, A. (2012), 'Unruly Edges: Mushrooms as Companion Species for Donna Haraway', *Environmental Humanities*, 1 (1): 141–54.
Tsing, A. L. (2015), *The Mushroom at the End of the World: On the Possibility of Life in Capitalist Ruins*, Oxford and Princeton: Princeton University Press.
Tuck, R. (1999), *The Rights of War and Peace: Political Thought and International Order from Grotius to Kant*, Oxford: Oxford University Press.
Tucker, A. (2004), *Our Knowledge of the Past: A Philosophy of Historiography*, Cambridge: Cambridge University Press.
Tucker, A. (2006), 'Temporal Provincialism: Anachronism, Retrospection and Evidence', *Scientia Poetica*, 10: 299–317
Tucker, A. (2008), 'Historiographic Revision and Revisionism: The Evidential Difference', in M. Kopecek (ed.), *Past in the Making: Recent History and Historical Revisionism*, Budapest: Central European University Press.
Tucker, A. (2009), 'Introduction', in *A Companion to the Philosophy of History and Historiography*, ed. A. Tucker, 1–7, Chichester: Wiley-Blackwell.
Tucker, A. (2010), 'Where Do We Go from Here: A Jubilee Report on History and Theory', *History and Theory*, theme issue no. 49 (4): 64–84.
Tucker, A. (2012), 'Sciences of Tokens and Types: The Difference Between History and the Social Sciences', in H. Kincaid (ed.), *The Oxford Handbook of Philosophy of the Social Sciences*, 274–97, Oxford: Oxford University Press.

Tucker, A. (2014), 'Historical Truth', in V. Hosle (ed.), *Forms of Truth and the Unity of Knowledge*, 232–59, South Bend, IN: Notre Dame University Press.

Tucker, A. (2015), *The Legacies of Totalitarianism: A Theoretical Perspective*, New York: Cambridge University Press.

Tucker, A. (2016), 'Condemned to Populism', *The American Interest*, 29 August 2016 (online).

Tucker, A. (2016), 'The Malthusian Holocaust: Review of Timothy Snyder, Black Earth: The Holocaust as History and Warning', *The American Interest*, 11 (5): 76–88.

Tucker, A. (2018), 'The New-Old Fatalism', *The American Interest*, 13 (3): 25–35.

Turner, F. J. (1920 [1893]), *The Frontier in American History*, New York: Henry Holt, 1920.

Universal Declaration of Human Rights, http://www.un.org/en/universal-declaration-human-rights/ (accessed 15 March 2019).

Usiskin, M. (1983 [1945]), *Uncle Mike's Edenbridge: Memoirs of a Jewish Pioneer Farmer*, trans. from the Yiddish [*Oksen en Motoren*] M. U. Basman, Winnipeg, MB: Peguis.

Van De Mierop, K. (2016), 'On the Advantage and Disadvantage of Black History Month for Life: The Creation of the Post-Racial Era', *History and Theory*, 55 (1): 3–24.

Van der Meiden, G. W. (1982), 'Tranen bij de vaderlandse geschiedenis', in D. E. H. de Boer (ed.), *Leidse facetten: tien studies over Leidse geschiedenis*, 129–32, Zwolle: Waanders.

Vickar, S. (1966), 'Zimbale to Edenbridge: The Autobiography of Samuel Vickar, a Pioneer Jewish Farmer in Canada', in L. Rosenberg (ed.), *Canadian Jewish Congress Congress Bulletin*, Montreal, Parts I to V, January–May.

Viveiros de Castro, E. (2019), 'On Models and Examples. Engineers and Bricoleurs in the Anthropocene', *Current Anthropology*, 60 (Supplement 20): S296–S308.

Vogel, R. (2012), 'Paradigms Revisited: Towards a Practice-Based Approach', *Review of Contemporary Philosophy*, 11: 34–41.

Vogl, J. (2016), *Het Financiële Regime*, Amsterdam: Boom Uitgevers.

Von Wright, G. H. (1971), *Explanation and Understanding*, Ithaca: Cornell University Press.

Wacquant, L. (2007), *Urban Outcasts: A Comparative Sociology of Advanced Marginality*, Cambridge: Polity Press.

Walsh, W. H. (1951), *An Introduction to Philosophy of History*, London: Hutchinson University Library.

Walsh, W. H. (1963), *Metaphysics*, London: Hutchinson.

Warde, P., L Robin and S. Sörlin (2018), *The Environment: A History of the Idea*, Baltimore: John Hopkins University Press.

Weingart, S. B. (2015), 'Finding the History and Philosophy of Science', *Erkenntnis*, 80: 201–13.

Weisman, A. (2007), *The World Without Us*, New York: Picador.

Weizman, E. (2012), *Hollow Land: Israel's Architecture of Occupation*, London: Verso.

White, H. (1973), *Metahistory: The Historical Imagination of the 19th Century Europe*, Baltimore: The John Hopkins University Press.
White, H. (2011), 'Modern Politics and the Historical Imaginary', in C. Bottici and B. Challand (eds), *The Politics of Imagination*, 162–77, Abingdon: Birkbeck Law Press.
White, H. (2014), *The Practical Past*, Evanston, IL: Northwestern University Press.
White, M. (1965), *Foundations of Historical Knowledge*, New York: Harper and Row.
White, M. G. letter, *New York Review of Books*, 23 March 1967, p. 28.
White, P. (2009), 'Darwin's Emotions: The Scientific Self and the Sentiment of Objectivity', *Isis*, 100: 811–26.
Widdis, R. W. (1992), 'Saskatchewan Bound: Migration to a New Canadian Frontier', *Great Plains Quarterly*, 12 (4): 254–68.
Wilford, G. (2017), 'Israel Has Stripped Citizenship from an Arab Israeli for the First Time Ever', *The Independent*, 6 August, https://www.independent.co.uk/news/world/middle-east/israel-revokes-citizenship-stripped-arab-israeli-alaa-raed-ahmad-zayoud-haifa-kibbutz-gan-shmuel-a7879771.html (accessed 30 July 2019).
Willow Creek, No. 458, RM of [Willow Creek] (1962), *Jubilee Year, 1912-1962*, Melfort SK: Melfort Journal.
Willow Creek, No. 458, RM of [Willow Creek] (1980), 'Homestead Settlements Rural Municipality of Willow Creek No. 458 W. of 2nd Meridian [Homestead Settlements Map]', drafted by W. Mikulsky; data obtained from Sask. Land Titles by T. Danyluk and O. Sturby; additional data gleaned from Manitoba Archives by G. Hanson, completed 12 August, Brooksby, SK: RM of Willow Creek No. 458.
Willow Creek, No. 458 [Willow Creek], RM of (2013), *Celebrating Our 100 Year Anniversary 1913-2013 History Booklet*, Brooksby, SK.
Wilson, E. O. (1996), *In Search of Nature*, Washington, DC: Island Press.
Wimmer, A. and N. Glick Schiller (2003), 'Methodological Nationalism, the Social Sciences, and the Study of Migration: An Essay in Historical Epistemology', *International Migration Review*, 37 (3): 576–610.
Wimmer, M. (2012), *Archivkörper: Eine Geschichte historischer Einbildungskraft*, Konstanz: Konstanz University Press.
Winch, P. ([1958] 1990), *The Idea of a Social Science and Its Relation to Philosophy*, 2nd edn, London: Routledge.
Windelband, W. ([1894] 2015), 'History and Natural Science', in S. Luft (ed.), *The Neo-Kantian Reader*, 287–98, London and New York: Routledge.
Witmore, Ch. (2007), 'Symmetrical Archaeology: Excerpts of a Manifesto', *World Archaeology*, 39 (4): 546–62.
Wittgenstein, L. (1963), *Philosophical Investigations*, Oxford: Blackwell.
Wittgenstein, L. (1972), *On Certainty*, ed. G. E. M. Anscombe and G. H. von Wright, trans. D. Paul and G. E. M. Anscombe, New York: Harper Torchbooks.
Wolfe, C. (2010), *What Is Posthumanism?*. Minneapolis: University of Minnesota Press.

Wood, D. (2019), *Deep Time, Dark Times: On Being Genealogically Human*, New York: Fordham University Press.

Zalasiewicz, J., C. N. Waters, M. Williams and C. P. Summerhayes, eds (2019), *The Anthropocene as a Geological Time Unit: A Guide to the Scientific Evidence and Current Debate*, Cambridge: Cambridge University Press.

Zalasiewciz, J., C. N. Waters, M. W., A. D. Barnosky, A. Cearreta, P. Crutzen, E. Ellis, M. A. Ellis, I. J. Fairchild, J. Grinevald, P. K. Haff, I. Hajdas, R. Leinfelder, J. McNeill, E. O. Odada, C. Poirier, D. Richter, W.Steffen, C. Summerhayes, J. P. M. Syvitski, D. Vidas, M.l Wagreich, S. L. Wing, A. P. Wolfe, A. Zhisheng, N. Oreskes (2015), 'When Did the Anthropocene Begin? A Mid Twentieth-Century Boundary Level Is Statisgraphically Optimal', *Quaternary International*, 383: 196–203.

Zamindar, V. F.-Y. (2007), *The Long Partition and the Making of Modern South Asia: Refugees, Boundaries and Histories*, New York: Columbia University Press.

Zammito, J. H. (2004), *A Nice Derangement of Epistemes: Post-Positivism in the Study of Science from Quine to Latour*, Chicago: University of Chicago Press.

Zizek, S. (2016), *Against the Double Blackmail: Refugees, Terror and Other Troubles with the Neighbours*, London: Allen Lane.

Zureik, E. (2016), *Israel's Colonial Project in Palestine: Brutal Pursuit*, London: Routledge.

Index

Note: Page numbers followed by "n" refer to notes.

Aalto, Seppo   55–63, 238 n.12
Abado, M.   138
Absentees' Property Laws   247 n.27
absolute presuppositions   31, 34
actor-network theory (ANT)   253 n.9
acute mental discomfort   34–5
affectivism   4
affectivity (feeling)   4–5, 13, 14, 101–25, 130
Agamben, G.   126, 244 n.2
Alberta   104, 110, 111, 117
Ali, M.   138–9, 245–6 n.17, 249 n.37–9
Althusser, L.   244–5 n.6, 252 n.5
American Historical Association   23
anachronism   143–4
analytical philosophy of history   2–3, 23–6, 144
Analytical Philosophy of History (Danto)   25
analytic–synthetic distinction   29, 67–8
Anderson, B.   103
animal history   17, 184, 189, 194, 205–7, 215, 222, 234
Ankersmit, F. R.   3, 8, 9, 11–13, 15, 55, 101, 170–2, 237 n.4, 253 n.6
Anthropocene   7, 18, 41, 182, 255 n.6
  nature/culture distinction   216–36
  philosophy of history, role of   17, 198–215
  transdisciplinary   201–2, 254 n.2
anthropocentrism   18, 182, 187, 215
  non-anthropocentrism   17
  post-anthropocentrism   4
anti-foundationalism   70
anti-realism   5
anti-Semitism   112
ANT, *see* actor-network theory
a priori   2, 11, 28, 66–71, 84, 132, 143, 144, 192

Archive Fever (Derrida)   98
Arendt, H.   244 n.2
Aristotle   70, 158
art   15, 26, 95, 137, 140–2, 249 n.41, 250 n.47
artificial intelligence   198, 200, 202
Asad, T.   247 n.25
assemblage theory   192
Assmann, A.   201
atomistic empiricism   10, 34, 41
Austin, J. L.   37, 55, 56
authenticity   102
Avramopoulos, D.   247 n.25
Azoulay, A.   196

Baldwin, R.   148
Balibar, É.   130, 244 n.3
Baratay, É   206–7, 215
Baumann, Z.   253 n.10
Becker, C.   23
Bedouin, N.   248 n.27
Benjamin, W.   209
Ben-Menahem, Y.   251 n.2
Berkeley, B.   52
Berlin, I.   23, 146
Beth Israel (synagogue)   107, 114, 118, 242 n.6, 243 n.17
better-than-human   203, 213
Bevernage, B.   201, 252 n.2
Bevir, M.   173
Binder, P.   248 n.28
Biographies of Animals (Baratay)   206–7
biohistory   147, 194
biohumanities   193
Bloch, M.   17, 185, 194, 205
Bonjour, L.   239 n.14
Bonneuil, C. B.   218, 227
borders   14, 47, 88, 104, 110, 127, 128, 130, 133–5, 139, 140, 148, 211

Bradley, F. H.   23
Brandom, R.   11, 50–3, 60
Brandt, H.   152
Brooke, J. L.   209
Büchel, C.   250 n.47
Buck-Morss, S.   196
Bunzl, M.   170, 176
Burckhardt, J.   101
Burgher, V.   246 n.20
Burns, R.   31
Butalia, U.   133

Cameron, D.   156
Canadian Great Plains   103–6
Canadian Northern Railway   110
Canadian Pacific Railway   110
Cape Colony (South Africa)   112
capitalism   17, 135, 148
   free-market   139
   global   149, 180, 181
   neo-liberal   141
   totalitarian   134
Capra, F.   182
Carr, D.   69
Carroll, N.   173
Carstens, M.   247 n.24
Cassirer, E.   74, 81, 239 n.3, 240 n.6
causal explanation   24–6, 69, 217, 229, 230, 232, 255 n.5
causality   9, 16, 171, 208
Chakrabarty, D.   202, 205, 209–11, 218, 225, 233
Charmaz, K.   188
Chatty, D.   245 n.13
Christmas Carol, A (Dickens)   91
Civilization of the Renaissance in Italy (Burckhardt)   101
Clark, J. F. M.   251 n.8
Clarks, C.   232
Clinton, H.   160
coherentism   64, 239 n.14
Collingwood, R. G.   3, 23–4, 26, 31, 69, 123, 228, 229, 254 n.11, 255 n.12
colonialism   134, 135, 160, 246 n.20
Commission of the History of Historiography   166, 176
conditional assertion   53
conservative historians   64–5
constructivism   187

radical   190
research programme, degeneration of   187
social   184, 192
contingency   15, 34, 37, 39, 41, 89, 144, 152, 155, 157
historical   151, 154, 156, 176
political   156
continuity principle   81
Coole, D.   190–1
counterfactual explanation   231, 232
counterfactual theories of causation   152–3
covering-law theory   27, 31, 32, 38
Cowling, M.   40
crisis globalization   133
criteria of comparison   173
critical historians   64–5
critical philosophy of history   2
Crossing Surda (a record of going to and from work)   137
Crouch, D.   246 n.23
cultural turn, in history of historiography   173

Danto, A.   3, 9, 10, 25–32, 34, 35, 39, 73, 75–6, 170, 171, 177
Daston, L.   178
Davie, George   35
Davis, N. Z.   171
Day, M.   177, 251 nn.3, 7
Declaration on European Identity   130
deconstruction   85–98, 195
deep history   24, 194, 201, 209, 210
deep time   210, 211
DeLanda, M.   192
Deleuze, G.   246 n.19
Demos, T. J.   246 nn.17, 19
Dening, G.   141–2
Department of the Interior   112
Der Amerikaner (newspaper)   242 n.12
Derrida, J.   88–90, 92, 93, 96–8, 128, 195, 241 nn.3, 4, 254 n.12
Descartes, R.   28, 35, 38, 51, 128, 256 n.15
descriptive/prescriptive dilemma   27, 29
Desert Bloom (Sheikh)   134
Dickens, C.   91
différance   96–7

Dillman, E.   70, 239 n.3
Dillmann, E.   239 n.3
Dilthey, W.   98
Domańska, E.   4, 7, 9, 10, 16, 17, 207, 208, 215, 256 n.25
Donagan, A.   170, 176
Donnelly, M.   7, 8, 14–15, 248 n.30
Don't Let Them Drown (Burgher)   246 n.20
D'Oro, G.   9, 10, 18, 255 nn.5, 7, 12, 256 n.14, 19, 20
Dray, W. H.   23–7, 38, 170, 171, 176, 220, 228, 232, 251 n.6, 255 n.5
Dr Who (TV series)   221, 235

Earth system   198, 200, 202, 209, 212
Easton, L.   243 n.17
economic determinism   15, 148
economy principle   12, 66, 81
Edenbridge Hebrew Colony   14, 109, 113, 115, 119, 242 n.6, 243 n.21
  naming of   116
Edenbridge School   109, 114, 115, 119, 242 n.8, 243 n.19
Edenbridge, The memory lives on … . A History   119, 122, 243 n.21
egalitarianism   147
elementary laws of logic   29
Elie, J.   131
Elton, G.   26
empirical discipline   63–4
empiricism   11, 30, 184
  atomistic   10, 34, 41
  in historiography, paradox of   47–9
  Humean   28–9
  logical   3, 24
  post-empiricism   5
empiricist model of explanation   27
encompassing the future   23–43
  Hempel *vs*. Dray   23–6
  Hexter's empathy with Morton White   29–33
  Historian's objections   26–9
  holistic meaning   33–5
  making the world   39–43
  narratives, analysis of   25–6
  shared imagining   35–8
Endless Days (Ali)   138
entanglement   18, 86, 88, 97, 191–3, 204, 213, 214, 218, 254 n.2

Entry Denied (a concert in Jerusalem)   138
environmental history   17, 194
environmental humanities   193, 202, 233
episodic remembering   42
epistemology   12, 45, 64, 143, 161, 188, 229
  analytic   46
  feminist   253 n.6
  historical   208
  naturalized   11, 66, 67
European Community   130
European Union   130, 157
EU-Turkey Agreement on Refugees   245 n.7
Evans, R. J.   26
evidence   42, 48
  and evident, etymological link between   49
evolutionary history   144, 201, 210, 211
explanation   9, 166, 169, 173, 234, 235
  causal   24–6, 69, 217, 229, 230, 232, 255 n.5
  counterfactual   231, 232
  empiricist model of   27
  historical   24, 27, 216, 217, 219, 222, 228, 231, 255 nn.3, 4
  historiographic   143
  humanistic   223, 255 n.10
  nomological model of   219, 229–30, 231, 255 n.4
  scientific   219, 223

Facing Gaia (Latour)   235
fact/value distinction   27, 29
falsificationism   66
Faust, J. G.   45
Figes, O.   65
First Nations (Canada)   105–6, 242 n.5
flat alternatives   191–3
Foucault, M.   212
Foundations of Historical Knowledge (White)   9, 25, 27, 30
Frege, G.   33, 37, 41, 71
French Theory   188
Fressoz, J.-B.   218, 227
'Freud and the Scene of Writing' (Derrida)   89–90
Freud, S.   91
Frost, S.   190–1

Fudge, E.   206
Fukuyama, F.   2, 158–9
'Function of General Laws in History, The' (Hempel)   2

Gadamer, H.-S.   3, 69, 168
Galison, P.   168, 178
Gallie, W. B.   3, 9, 25–6, 29, 30, 35–6
Gardiner, P.   23, 24
Gatrell, P.   128–9, 131–3, 141, 245 n.13
Gentile, C.   160
Gershoy, L.   251 n.5
Gibbons, A.   180–1
Giere, R. N.   167, 178, 251 n.2
Giladi, P.   256 n.19
Gitlin [family]
   Robert (Bob)   106
   Robert and Lil (Vickar)   122, 244 n.22
Glick Schiller, N.   129
Goering, T.   238 n.6
Goethe, J. W. von   44, 45
Goldstein, L. J.   28
Gombrich, E.   72
Goodman, N.   72
Google Earth™, 106, 109, 242 n.6
Gordon, P. H., Dr.   244 n.22
Gould, S. J.   154
Greenblatt, S.   103
Grice, P.   68
Guattari, F.   246 n.19
Guba, E. G.   194

Hales, S. D.   256 n.28
Hammond, K.   138
Handzuk, P.   243 n.18
Harari, Y. N.   201
Haraway, D.   253 n.6
Harding, S.   253 n.6
Harrell-Bond, B. E.   132
Hartog, F.   200–1
Hass, A.   249 n.35
hauntology   87–8
Haupt, G.   248 n.28
Hegel, G. W. F.   2, 23, 76, 144, 205
Heidegger, M.   160, 222, 226, 228, 232, 234, 256 n.16
Heller, C.   140
Helmreich, S.   207

Hempel, C. G.   2, 23–7, 29, 39, 42, 177, 216, 219, 220, 228, 229, 255 n.4
Herder, J. G. von   2
Hexter, J. H.   9, 27–9, 35
   empathy with Morton White   29–33
Hirzel, M.   249 n.43, 250 n.47
Historian's Craft (Bloch)   205
Historian's objections to encompassing the future   26–9
historical agency   217, 218, 234, 235
historical agents   18, 58, 217, 219, 220, 223, 226, 227, 229, 230, 232, 234, 235
historical consciousness   33, 42, 127, 131, 148, 159, 160
historical contingency   151, 154, 156
historical evitability   143–61
   application of   156–7
   learning from history   157–60
historical explanation   24, 27, 216, 217, 219, 222, 228, 231, 255 nn.3, 4
historical inevitability   15, 144, 145
   contemporary cyclical   148–51
historical knowledge   11, 18, 26, 32, 48, 68–70, 79, 80, 84, 88, 126, 127, 159, 173, 183, 184, 196, 199–201, 214, 215
historical necessity   151, 156
historical rationality   80–4
historical representation   11, 12, 66, 71–6, 79–81, 83, 84, 102, 171, 245 n.10
historical sensation   101
historical studies   16, 166, 167, 170–8, 199–202, 215
historical time   38, 130, 131, 201, 204, 209–12, 214, 222, 227
historicism   67, 85, 86, 98, 132
historicity   129, 200, 201, 203, 210, 212
historiographical knowledge   10, 11, 44–65, 238 nn.4, 5
   beginning of   44–7
   empirical discipline and   63–4
   empiricism in historiography, paradox of   47–9
   inferentiality in historiography   52–5
historiography   1, 14, 26, 44–65, 127, 129, 132, 153, 170, 177, 238 n.4, 241 n.1

claiming in   55–63, 65
empiricism in, paradox of   47–9
and feeling   101, 123–5, 172
French   185
history of   166, 173
humanistically oriented   9, 18, 216–36
inferentiality in   52–5, 58, 64
linguistic acts in   63
military   154
narrativism   2, 3
as performative practice   54
philosophy of   6–8, 10, 17, 44–6, 53, 143–5, 161, 175, 199–201
populism   160
professional   8, 13, 199, 200
rationality of   12, 13
and sciences, relation between   11–12, 144
as wholly reasoned knowledge   123
history, *see also individual entries*
animal   17, 184, 189, 194, 205–7, 215, 222, 234
biohistory   17, 194
deep   24, 194, 201, 209, 210
environmental   17, 194
evolutionary   144, 201, 210, 211
learning from   157–60
multiscalar   208–11, 214
multispecies   204–8, 213–15
neurohistory   17, 194
non-continuous   211–14
philosophy (*see* philosophy of history)
planetary   201, 204
posthumanist   7, 17, 186, 190
potential   196
rhetoric of   32
'History and Fiction as Modes of Comprehension' (Mink)   89
history and philosophy of history (HPH)   9, 15, 16
history and philosophy of science (HPS)   15, 16, 165–70, 172, 173, 175 177, 178, 251 n.14
History and Theory (Martin)   169
historying   141
History Manifesto, The (Guldi and Armitage)   201
Hitler, A.   171
Hodder, I.   192

holistic meaning   33–5
Holy Ascension Ukrainian Greek Orthodox Church   107, 114, 118, 243 n.18
homestead system   105–6, 110–15, 241 n.4, 242 n.13, 243 nn.14, 15
and Chinese   106
and Indians   105
Honkani, K.   251 n.13
Howe, N.   251 n.2
How to Do Things in Words (Austin)   55
HPH, *see* history and philosophy of history
HPS, *see* history and philosophy of science
Huizinga, J.   101
human action   24–5
human exceptionalism   18, 217, 218, 234, 235
human experience   18, 205, 215
human history *vs.* natural history   204–5
humanism   17
posthumanism   4, 16, 18, 184, 187, 190, 202, 203
transhumanism   212, 213
humanistically oriented historiography   216–36
new challenge   223–7
old challenge   219–23
old conceptual distinctions   227–34
humanistic explanation   223, 255 n.10
humanities   141, 158, 165, 174, 175, 201–4, 209, 211–13, 224, 227, 229, 251 n.2
biohumanities   193
environmental   193, 202, 233
new   183, 188
non-anthropocentric   180, 193
paradigm shift in contemporary   16–17, 180–96
post-anthropocentric   180, 193
posthumanities   190, 193
post-Western   180
shared   185
thinking about the past in   183–5
human/non-human   187, 190–2, 194, 221–3, 227, 253 n.9
human rights   126, 127, 134, 135, 137, 138, 141, 142, 245 n.17, 248 n.29, 250 n.47
Humean empiricism   28–9

ICHTH, *see* International Commission for the History and Theory of Historiography
idealism   23, 52, 255 n.12
Idea of History, The (Collingwood)   23, 123
immigrants, to Canada
   Jewish   106, 242 n.12, 243 n.14
   Norweign   114, 242 n.10
   Polish   242 n.8
   Ukrainian   242 n.8
immigration, to Canada   104, 105, 111–14, 242 n.11
   to Prairie Provinces   243 n.15
im/mobility (or mobility)   14, 126–42
Impact of Labour 1920–1924: The Beginning of Modern British Politics, The (Cowling)   40
Imposing Aid (Harrell-Bond)   132
In Defense of Things (Olsen)   192–3
indigenization of the academy   181
inequality   14, 133, 134, 136, 137, 141, 148, 198, 202, 248 n.27
inevitability   70, 72, 74, 97, 147, 156, 218, 219, 236
   cyclical historical   148–51
   historical   15, 144, 145, 148, 151
inference   10, 59, 173, 222, 223, 234
   definition of   49–52
   in historiography   64
   material   52–3, 60
   probable inferences of the past   143, 144, 161
   textual   61, 63
inferentialism   8, 10, 11, 49–53
inferentiality in historiography   52–5, 58
influence   171
intention   16, 171
International Commission for the History and Theory of Historiography (ICHTH)   177
International Committee of Historical Sciences   166
International Maritime Rescue Coordination Centre (MRCC)   140
interpretivist-constructivist paradigm   17, 187–9
Introduction (Walsh)   23

Israeli Citizenship and Entry Law   247 n.27
Israeli Law of Return   247 n.27

Jacir, E.   135–6, 138, 246 n.17, 248 nn.28, 33
James, H.   251 n.2
Jameson, F.   185
Jefferson, T.   158
Joad, C. E. M.   34–5
Johnson, T. A.   256 n.28
Jørgensen, D.   203
Journal of Refugee Studies   129
Journal of the Philosophy of History   166
justification   10, 44, 49, 58–62
   coherentist   239 n.14
   metaphysical   75

Kaldis, B.   256 n.14
Kant, I.   2, 23, 28, 38
Kelley, M. J.   251 n.11
Kennedy, R.   211
Key Issues in Historical Theory (Day)   177
King, M. L.   147
Kirksey, E.   207
Kleinberg, E.   7, 8, 11–13, 53–4, 101, 241 n.1, 245 n.9
Knorr-Cetina, K. D.   251 n.12
knowledge   9, 17, 27, 28, 30, 35, 36, 41, 77, 90, 123, 128, 161, 168, 181, 182, 189–91, 193, 202, 204, 207, 208
   ecological   180
   empirical   143
   historical   11, 18, 26, 32, 48, 68–70, 79, 80, 84, 88, 126, 127, 159, 173, 183, 184, 196, 199–201, 214, 215
   historiographic   10, 11, 44–65, 238 nn.4, 5
   holistic   184
   immediate   10, 48
   inferential   10, 237 n.4
   mediate   10, 48, 237 n.4
   multidisciplinary   180
   and power   188
   practical   185
   production   195, 198
   scientific   67–9
   self-knowledge   184, 185, 194, 254 n.11

transdisciplinary 215
Knox, K. 133, 245 n.13
Kochan, J. 251 n.9
Kofman, S. 93-4
Köhler, P. 70, 239 n.3
Koselleck, R. 86, 205
Kozak, A. 243 n.18
Krämer, S. 78, 240 n.8
Krüger, L. 168
Kuhn, T. S. 9, 11, 26, 29, 30, 33, 39, 66, 67, 169, 170, 185-6, 195
Kushner, T. 133, 245 n.13
Kutuzof, General 226, 255 n.10
Kuukkanen, J.-M. 8, 10, 11, 15, 179, 238 n.10, 255 n.3

Lakatos, I. 5, 16, 186-7
Latour, B. 182, 184, 192, 204, 205, 208-9, 211, 218, 226, 235, 251 n.12, 253 n.9, 255 nn.2, 11, 256 n.27
Laudan, L. 170, 171, 251 n.4
Laudan, R. 170, 171, 251 n.4
Laws and Explanation in History (Dray) 24
Lears, J. 101
legitimacy 102, 107, 130
Leibniz, G. W. 11, 12, 66, 71-84, 239 n.3, 240 nn.6, 9, 10
Lenton, T. M. 182
liberalism 145, 157
 crisis of 15
 post-liberalism 4
 Western 135
Lincoln, Y. S. 194
Liquid Traces – The Left-to-Die Boat Case 140
Lithuania 112, 113, 244 n.21
local history (in Western Canada) 243 n.20
Loescher, G. 245 n.13
logic 76-80
logical empiricism 3, 24
logical-positivism 66
London Convention of 1818, 110
Lorenz, C. 170, 171, 176
loss, and history 116-19, 122-3

McLaughlin, S. 157
McNeill, J. 208

Mahnke, D. 70, 239 n.3
Making of the English Working Class, The (Thompson) 12, 95
making the world 39-43
Malm, A. 256 n.24
Malpass, J. 235, 256 n.29
Mandelbaum, Maurice 3
Mandel, M. S. 245 n.13
Manitoba 104, 105, 110-12, 117
Marfleet, P. 129, 131, 133, 245 n.11
Markie, P. 237 n.1
marriage metaphor 167-8
Marrus, M. 245 n.13
Martin, R. 169-70, 176
Marxism 144
Marx, K. 2, 144, 146, 148, 150
Maryville 107-9, 115, 116, 118, 243 n.15
Maryville School 109, 114, 116, 119, 121, 243 n.19
Masalha, N. 248 n.27
Mason, R. 175-6
materialism (new materialism) 16, 184, 189-91
Matthews, M. R. 251 n.14
Mazzara, F. 244 n.4, 246 n.20, 249 nn.40, 43
Mbembe, A. 139, 250 nn.45, 47
meaning 36
Megill, A. 7, 8, 13-14
Melfort 110, 117, 119
Merleau-Ponty, M. 160
Metahistory: The Historical Imagination of the 19th Century Europe (White) 3
Metaphilosophy (journal) 29
metaphysics 72-80
methodological nationalism 14, 129, 130
methodology 140, 154, 168, 169, 188, 189, 191, 219, 255 n.12
 of the oppressed 189
 practical 196, 254 n.14
 of scientific research
 programmes 186
Methodology of the Oppressed (Sandoval) 188-9
Michael, C. 246 n.23
Michaelian, K. 42
Michelet, J. 101
migration 126-42

Mihesuah, D.   181
military historiography   154
Mill, J. S.   158
Mink, L.   3, 69
monuments (historical)   102, 123–4
moral realism   147
more-than-human-world   17, 198–215
Mosquito Empires (McNeill)   208
MRCC, *see* International Maritime Rescue Coordination Centre
multiscalar history   208–11, 214
multispecies history   204–8, 213–15

Nagel, T.   206
narrative   2, 3, 24, 25, 29, 32, 43, 64, 65, 88–90, 92, 94–7, 141, 150, 160, 166, 169, 170, 176, 189, 201
    analysis   25–6
    historical   12, 26, 27, 85, 87, 94, 96, 161, 216, 223–5, 234, 256 n.20
    historiographic   161
    sentences   25, 39–40
    theories   33–4
Narrative Logic: A Semantic Analysis of the Historian's Language (Ankersmit)   3
narrativism   2, 3, 7, 255 n.3
    post-narrativism   5, 17, 184
narrativist philosophy of historiography   2, 7, 54
narrativist turn, in philosophy of history   172, 219
nation state   14, 126, 129, 139, 202, 244 nn.1, 2
NATO   140
natural history *vs*. human history   204–5
naturalism   4, 11, 223, 234, 236
nature/culture distinction   18, 216–36
necropolitics   133, 140, 141
Neither Human, Nor Stone (Ali)   139
neuroscience   42
new human condition, philosophy of history and   198–204
new humanities   183, 188
New Materialism: Ontology, Agency and Politics (Coole and Frost)   190–1
New York Review of Books, The (Danto)   28
Nikoluk, G.   243 n.18

Noël, P.-M.   175
nomological model of explanation   219, 229–30, 231, 255 n.4
non-anthropocentric humanities   180, 193
non-continuous history   211–14
non-human   1, 7, 10, 16, 182, 184, 185, 187, 190–2, 194, 203–5, 208, 220–3, 227, 234, 253
    ecological   203
    technological   203, 213
Norton, C.   7, 8, 14–15, 248 n.30
Novick, P.   28
Nugent, M.   211
Nyers, P.   244 n.5

Oakeshott, M.   23, 255 n.12, 256 n.14
Obama, B   147, 157
Of Grammatology (Derrida)   195
Oldenbarnevelt, J. van   172–3
Olsen, B.   192–3
On Certainty (Goethe)   44
'On the Writing and Rewriting of History' (Mink)   88
ontological dualism   193, 256 n.19
ontological realism   11, 12, 86, 87, 90, 92, 95
Orange, R.   246 n.23
other-than-human species   208
Our Courageous Pioneers (Gronlid and District Historical Society)   109, 119, 121–4, 244 n.22
Our Knowledge of the Past (Tucker)   69
Oxford Handbook of Refugee and Forced Migration Studies, The   131

Papazhoglou, A.   256 n.19
paradigm   4, 8, 69–70, 128, 177, 252 n.3
    interpretivist-constructivist   9, 187–9
    nonanthropocentric   253 n.8
    paradigm shift   9, 16, 180–97, 252 n.2
    posthumanist   17, 186
    today   185–7
particularity, and generality   115–16, 124–5
past-talk   15, 127, 133, 141, 142
Past Within Us, The (Martin)   169
Paul, H.   5, 9, 15–16, 251 n.10, 256 n.29
Peregrin, J.   11, 50

Pezzani, L.   140
phaenomenal reality   73
Philosophical Analysis and History
   (Dray)   23
Philosophical Essay on Probabilities
   (Mink)   89
Philosophy and the Historical
   Understanding (Gallie)   25
Philosophy and the Mirror of Nature
   (Rorty)   51
philosophy of historiographic
   causation   152-4
philosophy of history   160-1, *see also*
   individual entries
   analytical   2-3, 23-6, 144
   Anthropocene   198-215
   boundaries of, (re)drawing   15-19
   critical   2
   ideology of   145
   new   214-15
   and new human condition   198-204
   priorist argument of   66-71
   quasi-substantive   201
   as reflective discipline   1, 2
   speculative   2, 23, 144
   substantial   2
Philosophy of History, The (Day)   177
Pickering, A.   190
Piercey, R.   238 n.6
Pierotti, R.   192
Pihlainen, K.   10, 237 n.3, 245 n.10
Piper, J. G.   242 n.8
planetary history   201, 204
Plato   37-8, 70
Plotkin, A. L.   243 n.21
Plutarch   33-4
politics   13-15
Politics and the Past (Torpey)   185
Popper, K. R.   23, 66, 67, 146
popular history   13-15, 102-3, 118-25,
   241 n.1
   and populist history   14, 124
populism   1, 8, 13-15, 19, 145, 148,
   158-61
post-anthropocentric humanities   180,
   193
posthumanism   4, 16, 18, 184, 187, 190,
   202, 203
posthumanist history   7, 17, 186, 190

posthumanities   180, 193
postmodernism   8, 17, 180-1, 184
'Postmodernism is Dead. What Comes
   Next?'   180-1
postmodern theory with historical
   intent   85-98
post-narrativism   5, 17, 184
Postnarrativist Philosophy of
   Historiography (Kuukkanen)   54
Post-Thousand and One Nights (Ali)   139
potential history   196
'praedicatum inest subjecto'
   principle   71-3
pragmatism   4, 6, 8, 11, 30-2, 36, 37, 53,
   66
pre-established harmony   73, 74
Presuppositions of Critical History, The
   (Bradley)   23
Prigogine, I.   182
priorist argument, of philosophy of
   history   66-71
progressivism   15, 145
Purification (Toguo)   133

quasi-substantive philosophy of
   history   201
Quine, W. V. O.   11, 30, 36, 47, 66-70,
   169, 256 n.22

racism   136, 139, 160
   historicization of   174
   institutional   134
radical constructivism   190
Railton, P.   147
Ramsey, M.   249 n.43
Ranke, L. von   23, 69, 101
rationalism   5, 237 n.1
rationality   12, 15, 151, 159, 181
   historical   80-4
   scientific   67
Read, R.   256 n.23
realism   8, 52
   moral   147
   ontological   11, 12, 86, 87, 90, 92, 95
   post-realism   5
realistic representation   86, 89, 97
Reassembling the Social (Latour)   253 n.9
reciprocal extraterritoriality   141
refugeeness   127, 128, 244 n.5

refugees 8, 14, 19, 126–34, 136, 137, 141, 158, 244 nn.1, 3–5, 245 nn.7, 11, 13, 15
relational archaeology 192
religion, social role of 114–16
representationalism 8, 50–2
representation, theory of 73
res cogitans 228
res extensa 228
Return to Essentials (Elton) 26
Reval, J. 211
Revolt at Factories (Kapina Tehtailla) (Aalto) 54–63, 238 n.12
Revolutionary Russia 1891–1991 (Figes) 65
rhetoric of history 32
Ricoeur, P. 69
RM, *see* Rural Municipality
Robin, L. 183, 202, 209
Role of Philosophy of History, The (conference, University of Oulu) 4
Rollig, S. 248 n.28
Roman Law 231
Rorty, J. 41
Rorty, R. 11, 41, 51, 66, 183, 193–4
Rose, A. 251 n.11
Rose, D. B. 183
Roy, G. 244 n.21
Rubinoff, L. 251 n.6
Rückert, G. 248 n.28
Runia, Eelco 101, 200, 211–12
Rural Municipality (RM) 13
Russell, E. 47, 210

Sacco, J. 248 n.33
Saint Helen's Catholic Church 108, 118
Saint Nicholas Ukrainian Catholic Church 108, 114
Saljooghi, A. 248 n.33
Sandis, C. 255 n.5
Sandoval, C. 188–9, 191
Santayana, G. 157–8
Sapolsky, R. M. 85
Saskatchewan 104, 110, 111, 113, 117, 119, 241 n.3, 242 nn.9, 13, 243 n.21
Saskatchewan Wildlife Federation 118
Saval, N. 250–1 n.2
Scanlan, J. A. 245 n.13

Schickore, J. 165, 166, 168
schools (rural), in Canada 118–19, 242 n.8, 243 n.15
Schumann, G. 255 n.9
science 25, 182
'Science and Pseudoscience' (Lakatos) 186
scientific explanation 219, 223
Second World War 47, 49, 113, 117, 144, 146, 151, 158–60, 171, 186, 199, 200, 225, 238 n.5
securitization 133, 140
Sellars, W. 11, 50, 52, 53, 59, 60, 237 nn.2, 3, 238 n.7, 255 n.8
semantics 11, 53, 70, 76–80, 238 n.11
shared imagining 35–8
Sheikh, F. 134, 246 n.21, 248 n.27
Shryock, A. 210
Sifton, Clifford 111
signs 78–80
Simon, Z. B. 4, 7, 9, 10, 16, 17, 252 n.2, 254 n.2
singularitarianism 212
singularity 212, 213
Sink Without Trace: Exhibition on Migrant Deaths at Sea (exhibition) 249 nn.41, 43, 250 nn.46, 48
Sisyphean politics 159
Sivanandan, A. 246 n.20
Skinner, Q. 55
Sleepwalkers: How Europe Went to War in 1914, The (Clarks) 232
Smail, D. L. 210
social constructivism 184, 192
social determinism 192
sociocentrism 192
sociological grounded theory 195
solidarity 41, 141, 185
Sörlin, S. 209
Specters of Marx (Derrida) 88
speculative philosophy of history 2, 23, 144
Spengler, O. 2, 144
Spivak, G. C. 246 n.19
Staples, K. Y. 244 n.3
Star City 110, 113, 116
Steffen, W. 202
Stengers, I. 182, 203
Sterelny 154, 155

Stoney Creek   110
Strauss, G.   251 n.2
Strawson, P. F.   68
Structure of Scientific Revolutions, The
    (Kuhn)   26, 186
Stuart, J. I.   242 n.6
Sublime Historical Experience
    (Ankersmit)   101, 172
substantive philosophy of history   2
Substanzbegriff und Funktionsbegriff
    (Cassirer)   81
sui generis   18, 217, 223, 229
Sunna, A.   134, 246 n.22
symmetrical archaeology   192
symmetry   191–3, 253 n.9

Tallis, R.   256 n.28
Tamm, M.   4, 7, 9, 10, 16, 17, 179, 254 n.2
Tan, V. T.   175
Taylor, A. J. P.   171
temporality   89, 198, 201, 203, 210, 211, 214
temporal provincialism   160
textual conclusion   61
textualism   189–91
things   24, 30, 41, 51, 72, 77, 83, 191–3
thinking about the past   183–5, 195
Thomas, J. A.   202
Thomson, E. P.   12, 95–6
366 Days of 2012 (Ali)   249 n.38
Thunberg, G.   234
Toguo, B.   133, 246 n.18
Tolstoy, L.   226
Torpey, J.   185
totalitarianism   15, 144–7, 160
Toynbee, A.   2, 144
Tozzi, V.   195
transculturalism   184
Transfer of Property Law   247 n.27
transhumanism   212, 213
transtemporal history   201–2
Traweek, S.   251 n.12
truth-tracking criteria   173
Tucker, A.   2, 7, 8, 12, 15, 69, 146, 250 n.1, 251 n.3
Turner, F. J.   110–11

UN, *see* United Nations
UNCHR   133

understanding   42, 174–8
    historical   25–7, 36, 43, 123, 176, 202, 209
    self-understanding   199–201
    temporal   8, 10, 42
United Church of Canada   106
United Nations (UN)   14, 133
    Resolution 194, article 11, 247 n.27
Universal Declaration of Human
    Rights   14
    Article 3, 134–5
    Article 9, 137–8
    Article 13, 133–4
    Article 14, 134–5
    Article 15, 135–7
    Article 25, 138–42
US Confederacy (monuments to)   87, 102
Usiskin, M.   243 n.21

Vickar (family)
    David   112
    Isaac (Ike)   106
    Louis   112, 242 n.12
    Samuel   112, 242 n.12, 243 n.21
Vico, G.   2, 39, 40
Vieta   78
Viveiros de Castro, E.   182

Wall Street Journal   85
Walsh, W. H.   3, 23, 24
War and Peace (Tolstoy)   226
Warde, P.   209
We Have Come a Long Way   123
We Have Never Been Modern
    (Latour)   192, 208–9
Weingart, S   169, 176
Western liberalism   135
'What Was It Like To Be a Cow'
    (Fudge)   206
Where We Come From (Jacir)   135–6
White, H.   3, 7, 39, 69, 127, 175, 177, 195, 252 n.4
    Hexter's empathy with   29–33
White, M.   3, 9, 25–8, 34–6, 39
Wildcat, D.   192
Willow Creek, RM of, No. 458, 13, 104–6, 109, 114–20, 124, 125
    popular histories of   119–25

population in   116–19, 243 n.16
Wilson, A.   181
Wilson, E. O.   209–10
Wimmer, A   129
Windelband, W.   255 n.12
Witmore, C. L.   192
Wittgenstein, L.   35, 44, 45, 53, 56, 256 n.17

xenophobia   150, 151, 159, 160

Yimer, D.   250 n.48

Zamindar, V. F.-Y.   245 n.13
Zammito, J. H.   239 n.1
Zureik, E.   247 n.27

www.ingramcontent.com/pod-product-compliance
Lightning Source LLC
Chambersburg PA
CBHW072124290426
44111CB00012B/1764